IT DIDN'T
HAPPEN HERE

BY SEYMOUR MARTIN LIPSET

Agrarian Socialism

Union Democracy (with Martin Trow and James S. Coleman)

Social Mobility in Industrial Society (with Reinhard Bendix)

Prejudice and Society (With Earl Raab)

Political Man: The Social Bases of Politics

The First New Nation: The United States in Historical and Comparative Perspective

Estudiantes universitarios y politica en el tercer mundo

Revolution and Counterrevolution

The Politics of Unreason: Right-Wing Extremism in America 1790–1970 (with Earl Raab)

Group Life in America

Rebellion in the University

Professors, Unions, and American Higher Education (with Everett C. Ladd)

Academics, Politics, and the 1972 Election (with Everett C. Ladd)

The Divided Academy: Professors and Politics (with Everett C. Ladd)

Education and Politics at Harvard (with David Riesman)

Dialogues on American Politics (with Irving Louis Horowitz)

The Confidence Gap: Business, Labor and Government in the Public Mind (with William Schneider)

Consensus and Conflict: Essays in Political Sociology

Continental Divide: Values and Institutions of the United States and Canada

Distinctive Cultures: Canada and the United States

The Power of Jewish Education

Jews and the New American Scene (with Earl Raab)

American Exceptionalism: A Double-Edged Sword

BY GARY MARKS

Unions in Politics: Britain, Germany, and the United States in the Nineteenth and Early Twentieth Centuries

The Crisis of Socialism in Europe (with Christiane Lemke)

Reexamining Democracy: Essays in Honor of Seymour Martin Lipset (with Larry Diamond)

Governance in the European Union (with Fritz Scharpf, Philippe Schmitter, and Wolfgang Streeck)

Continuity and Change in Contemporary Capitalism (with Herbert Kitschelt, Peter Lange, and John Stephens)

Multi-level Governance and European Integration (with Liesbet Hooghe)

IT DIDN'T
HAPPEN HERE

Why Socialism Failed in the United States

Seymour Martin Lipset and Gary Marks

W. W. Norton & Company

New York · London

For information about permission to reproduce selections from this book, write to
Permissions, W. W. Norton & Company, Inc., 500 Fifth Avenue, New York, NY 10110

The text of this book is composed in Berling with the display set in Maximus.
Composition by Thomas Ernst.
Manufacturing by Courier Companies, Inc.
Book design by Chris Welch.

Library of Congress Cataloging-in-Publication Data

Lipset, Seymour Martin.
It didn't happen here : why socialism failed in the United States /
by Seymour Martin Lipset and Gary Marks.
p.   cm.
Includes bibliographical references and index.
ISBN 0-393-04098-4
1. Socialism—United States—History. I. Marks, Gary Wolfe. II. Title.
HX83.L55   2000
335'.00973—dc21   00-021489

W. W. Norton & Company, Inc., 500 Fifth Avenue, New York, N.Y. 10110
www.wwnorton.com

W. W. Norton & Company, Ltd., 10 Coptic Street, London WC1A 1PU

1 2 3 4 5 6 7 8 9 0

CONTENTS

PREFACE

P arties calling themselves Socialist, Social Democratic, Labor, or Communist have been major forces in every democratic country in the world with the exception of the United States. From the time of Karl Marx and Friedrich Engels, those on the political left have tried to make sense of the failure of socialism in America and the conundrum that working-class consciousness was stronger in Europe than in the most developed capitalist industrial society of the world. As it became clear that American socialists were unable to establish a strong and durable party, socialists themselves came up with a long list of plausible explanations.

Academic scholars have also been deeply interested in this issue. Foremost among these are historians wishing to explore basic features of American political development by posing the question "Why is there no socialism in America?" The academic literature on this topic numbers in the hundreds of books and thousands of articles. In recent years, several historians have argued forcefully that the United States cannot be understood in isolation from other societies. As historians have lauded the potential for comparative history, so political scientists and sociologists have been urged to take the historical cure. This book reflects these currents.

9

Our goal is to explore the explanatory power of comparison—within the United States, across (and within) different national contexts, and over time—for a classic question of American historiography.

The challenge confronting such a project is not that there are too few plausible explanations, but that there are too many. Explanations of socialism's weakness in America are as numerous as socialists were few. Some writers attribute the weakness of socialism to the failures of socialist organizers and leaders. Another school ascribes socialism's bankruptcy to its incompatibility with America's core values, while still others cite the American Constitution as the decisive factor. And these only begin to touch upon a literature so abundant as to suggest that little new may be said on the issue.

It is the purpose of this book to examine the validity of the main lines of explanation that have been put forward in these literatures. In doing so, we hope to provide not only a political sociology of socialism's failure in the United States, but larger insights into American society and polity. Our project has been guided from the beginning by the conviction that however politicized the intellectual terrain, we could offer an explanation as plausible to a person whose sympathies lie on the right of the political spectrum as to one whose sympathies lie on the left.

In Chapter 1, we summarize explanations put forward by socialists and left intellectuals for the failure of socialists in America. Such explanations also engage the question of how the United States differs from other advanced industrial societies. As the reader may note, these are surprisingly positive evaluations and overlap considerably with the ideas of Alexis de Tocqueville, the intellectual father of "American exceptionalism." The following six chapters evaluate and refine what we consider to be the most compelling explanations for the failure of American socialists. We examine in depth the causal role of American political values and institutions, the split between American unions and the Socialist party, immigration and the fragmentation of the American working class, the strategic choices of socialists, and state repression. Our concluding chapter asks whether the absence of a socialist party continues to set the United States apart and examines some of the broader consequences of socialist failure for contemporary American society and public policy.

Throughout the book we refer, sometimes in considerable detail, to historical episodes in the life and times of the American Socialist party. But this book is definitely not intended to be a history of American socialism. Both the Socialist and Communist parties, as well as smaller, sectional radical movements, have been described at length by historians. Historical description is relevant here only to the extent that it helps us evaluate particular explanations. Hence we examine Franklin Delano Roosevelt's success in co-opting socialists to understand the flexibility of American political parties, and we detail relations between the Socialist party and the unions to substantiate the persistent failure to create a labor party.

We are acutely aware that the question we pose—why did socialists fail in the United States—may never be ultimately resolved. Obviously, our own effort reflects our intellectual limitations, and perhaps our unconscious biases. But there is an objective reason for believing this beyond human fallibility. The world from which one can sensibly draw comparative evidence to bear on American political development—western democracies over the past century—is vastly smaller and less diverse than the world that would have to exist if one were to control for all relevant factors. The real world is a very restricted laboratory for conducting the kinds of tests that would yield watertight conclusions about macrosocial events like socialism. All that one may do is use evidence that is available to develop and test hypotheses about causal processes. We compare in several ways, across and within countries, in order to isolate as far as possible the causal effects of particular factors. We also pay close attention to strategic choices of relevant actors—socialists and unionists—in trying to evaluate the consequences of their choices and whether they could have acted differently.

In the language of social science methodology, this study is applied social science. We are less interested in developing and testing generalizations than in understanding a particular outcome. We do not underestimate the virtues of "thick description" in understanding why socialism failed in the United States, but where we can, we try to be more rigorous, which means that we place the phenomenon in a comparative context. There is no shortage of hypotheses that have been developed by historians, political scientists, sociologists, and participants to explain why "it didn't happen here." However, there does appear to us to be a deficit of systematic testing of those hypotheses cross-nationally. Some readers will doubtless conclude that we have failed to be rigorous enough, while others will find that our attempts to compare are heavy-handed and overly positivistic. We are vulnerable on both counts, but hope that readers will allow us to plea-bargain by virtue of the intrinsic difficulty of the task we have set ourselves.

This book would not have been possible without assistance from many individuals along the way. We would like to thank Daniel Bell, Lewis Coser, Evelyne Huber, Robert K. Merton, Doug McAdam, Don Searing, Jürg Steiner, and John Stephens for criticism and advice. Over the years, many research assistants have worked with us. These include Jeffrey Hayes, Steve Wuhs, Lucy Kennedy, Jason Lakin, Marcella Ray, Stuart MacIntosh, Elizabeth Bucuvalis, JoEllyn Fountain, Kermit Blank, Ivan Llamazares, Jennifer Bednar, Richard Haesly, David Scott, Susan Glover, Tim Burch, Beth Fetrow, Lauren Lovelace, Carrie Lovelace, Leah Seppanen, and Claire Mock. We would also like to acknowledge with gratitude grants from the Earhart, Ford, Olin, and National Science Foundations. The Hoover Institution of Stanford University has provided a stimulating venue and research support for Lipset, as have the Center for Advanced Study in the Behavioral Sciences, the Institute of Public Policy of George Mason University and the Woodrow Wilson Center for International Scholars. For Marks, the Department of Political Science at the University of North Carolina at Chapel Hill and the UNC Center for European Studies along with the Center for Advanced Study in the Behavioral Sciences at Stanford and the UNC Institute for the Arts and Humanities have provided invaluable support. Our editors at Norton, Donald Lamm and Angela von der Lippe, have given us much useful advice, not the least of which is the suggestion for the title. Last but very far from least, we owe more than we can possibly acknowledge to Sydnee Guyer Lipset and Liesbet Hooghe.

IT DIDN'T
HAPPEN HERE

Chapter 1

≡

AN EXCEPTIONAL

NATION

The United States, as noted by Alexis de Tocqueville and Friedrich Engels, among many visitors to America, is an "exceptional" country, one uniquely different from the more traditional societies and status-bound nations of the Old World.[1] The term "American exceptionalism," first formulated by Tocqueville in the 1830s, and since used in general comparative societal analyses, became widely applied after World War I in efforts to account for the weakness of working-class radicalism in the United States. The issue even gave rise to debates within the Communist movement in meetings of Comintern bodies in the 1920s, in particular between Jay Lovestone and Joseph Stalin, the secretaries of the American and Soviet parties.[2]

For radicals, "American exceptionalism" meant a specific question: Why did the United States, alone among industrial societies, lack a significant socialist movement or labor party?[3] This question bedeviled socialist theorists from the late nineteenth century on. Engels tried to answer it in the last decade of his life.[4] The German socialist and sociologist Werner Sombart dealt with it in a major book published in his native language in 1906, *Why Is There No Socialism in the United States?* The question was addressed by the Fabian H. G. Wells in *The Future in America*, which came out the same year. Both Lenin and Trotsky were deeply concerned with American exceptionalism, for it questioned the inner logic of Marxism, expressed by Karl Marx in the preface to *Capital:* "The country that is more developed industrially shows to the less developed the image of their future."[5] And there is no questioning the fact that, from the last quarter of the nineteenth century on, the most developed country has been the United States.

In trying to explain the absence of a socialist movement, many socialist writers have described America in terms not dissimilar from those of Tocqueville. The great Frenchman had noted in 1831 that the United States is "exceptional," qualitatively different in its organizing principles and political and religious institutions from those of other western societies.[6] Features of the United States that Tocqueville, and many others since, have focused on include its relatively high levels of social egalitarianism, economic productivity, and social mobility (particularly into elite strata), alongside the strength of religion, the weakness of the central state, the earlier timing of electoral democracy, ethnic and racial diversity, and the absence of feudal remnants, especially fixed social classes.[7] In this introductory chapter, we examine the way socialist intellectuals have seen the country when trying to explain the weakness of their movement.

The Inevitability of Socialism in America

As one historian has written, "Optimism is most usually the effect of an intellectual error."[8] The early socialist faith in the inevitability of socialism in America exemplifies this. In spite of the glaring weakness of socialist parties in the United States, leading Marxists have believed Marx's dictum that the most developed capitalist country would lead the world into socialism. As Werner Sombart argued:

> If . . . modern socialism follows as a necessary reaction to capitalism, the country with the most advanced capitalist development, namely the United States, would at the same time be the one providing the classic case of socialism, and its working class would be supporters of the most radical of socialist movements.[9]

This position was entrenched in orthodox Marxism. Engels repeated it in 1893. Before he became the most influential revisionist of Marxist ideas, Eduard Bernstein acknowledged its implications for the United States: "We see modern socialism enter and take root in the United States in direct relation to the spreading of capitalism and the appearance of a modern proletariat."[10] Karl Kautsky, considered the leading theoretician in the German Social Democratic party, enunciated in 1902 that "America shows us our future, in so far as one country can reveal it at all to another." He elaborated this view in 1910, anticipating the "overdue sharpening of class conflict" developing "more strongly" in the United States than anywhere else.[11] The British Marxist H. M. Hyndman noted in 1904 that "just as North America is today the most advanced country economically and socially, so it will be the first in which Socialism will find open and legal expression."[12] August Bebel, the political leader of the German Social Democrats, stated unequivocally in 1907: "Americans will be the first to usher in a Socialist republic." This belief, at a time when the German party was already a mass movement with many elected members of the Reichstag, and the American Socialist party had secured less than 2 percent of the vote, was based on the fact that the United States was "far ahead of Germany in industrial development." Bebel reiterated this opinion in 1912, when the discrepancy in the strength of the two movements was even greater, saying that America will "be the first nation to declare a Cooperative Commonwealth."[13] The French socialist Paul Lefargue, Marx's son-in-law, paraphrased his father-in-law on the flyleaf of his book on America: "The most industrially advanced country shows to those who follow it on the industrial ladder the image of their own future."[14]

American Marxists, though more aware of the problems facing their movement than their European comrades, also recognized that the assumptions of historical materialism required that the United States should be in the lead politically. Thus, at the Amsterdam Congress of the Socialist International held in 1904, the leader of the American Socialist Labor party, Daniel De Leon, whom Lenin considered a truly creative Marxist, stated, "Taking into consideration only certain cardinal principles [of Marxism], the conclusion cannot be escaped that America is the theatre where the crest of capitalism would first be shorn by the falchion of socialism."[15] And shortly thereafter, De Leon proclaimed to the 1906 convention of the Industrial Workers of the World (IWW) in Chicago, "If my reading of history is correct, the prophecy of Marx will be fulfilled and America will ring the downfall of capitalism the world over."[16]

The continued inability of socialists to create a viable movement in the United States was a major embarrassment to Marxist theorists who assumed that the superstructure of a society, which encompasses political behavior, is a function of underlying economic and technological structures. Many Marxists of the late nineteenth and early twentieth centuries understood their theory required them to believe that "the United States, of all the countries in the world, [was] most ripe for socialism."[17] Max Beer, whose fifty-year career in international socialism included participation in the Austrian, German, and British parties, described the anxiety among European Marxists created by the weakness of socialism in America, which they voiced in private discussions with each other. The United States was a "living contradiction of . . . Marxian theory," and raised fundamental questions about its validity.[18]

Statements that the United States had to be and would be the first socialist country declined after the Bolshevik Revolution in 1917, but one of its two major leaders, Leon Trotsky, took cognizance of Marx's statement in a 1939 publication intended for a popular American audience. He reprinted the sentence and then simply dismissed it with the comment that "under no circumstances can this . . . be taken literally."[19] Trotsky, of course, knew his Marxism and was well aware that the United States should be the first on the path toward socialism. By citing the statement he revealed that it was much on his mind. That he sidestepped it suggests he had no answer to the conundrum it posed for Marxists.[20]

The argument that American nonsocialist politics would prove to be the model for the European left was presented in full flower in 1940 by Lewis Corey, an early leader of the American Communist party. Corey wrote a series of articles on the topic in *Workers Age*, the organ of a neo-Communist sect, the Lovestoneites. As summarized by historian of American radicalism Harvey Klehr, Corey foresaw in prescient terms that

rather than being an exception, America was actually the model for capitalist countries. Only the positions in the race had been changed; European socialists could see in America the image of their own unhappy future. Far from being a unique or even only slightly different case,

America was the prototype for capitalism. In a curious reversal of roles, it was now the European socialists who could look across the ocean to see the future of their own movement.[21]

The conundrum remains. Although the United States is the most productive industrialized nation, it has never had a viable left-wing working-class party. Its trade unions, which have been weaker than those of most other industrial countries, have been steadily declining in membership since the mid-fifties. At the present time, less than one-sixth, under 14 percent, of the employed labor force belongs to unions. This is down from one-third in 1955 and is a level of organization lower than that of almost all other developed economies.

The comparison with the United States' northern neighbor is particularly striking. Canada has an economy structurally comparable to that of the United States, though, of course, much smaller. Its trade union movement currently encompasses over one-third of all employed people. The strength of its socialist movement, the New Democratic party (NDP), in opinion polls, has at times placed it in first place in a three-party race.[22] Over the past two decades, the NDP has governed four provinces, British Columbia, Saskatchewan, Ontario, and Manitoba, as well as the Yukon Territory, and remains in office, as of 2000, in the first two and the Yukon. It, however, declined in the 1990s, receiving twenty-one parliamentary seats and 11 percent of the vote in the 1997 federal election. The Parti Québécois (PQ), a statist and nationalist party, forms the government of Quebec. In the 1970s the PQ applied for membership in the Socialist International, but was rejected because the NDP already represented Canada. These differences within North America, between two wealthy industrialized countries, give renewed life to the issues of why socialism, trade unionism, and class consciousness are weak in the United States.[23]

It is ironic that Karl Marx's belief that the working class was destined to organize revolutionary socialist parties in every capitalist society was based on a mistaken perception of events in America. He overestimated the radicalism of the Workingmen's parties which operated in a number of eastern cities in the late 1820s and early 1830s.[24] His view of these parties was heavily influenced by *Men and Manners in America*, written by Thomas Hamilton, a British Tory who visited the United States in 1830.[25] An examination of Marx's notebooks reveals that he had copied a number of

Hamilton's statements describing the emergence of class consciousness as of 1830. This led him to anticipate the ultimate triumph of the American working class. Hamilton's description of what Marx termed "the first story of an organized political party of labor in the world's history" convinced him that American workers (and others) would create a class-conscious movement dedicated to the abolition of capitalism.

The Workingmen's Parties

Given their importance in shaping both Marx's general theory and his image of America, the Workingmen's parties of the 1830s deserve our attention. Most of the Workingmen's parties originated in the struggle for greater equality, particularly equality of opportunity. Concerned with fostering meritocracy, these parties demanded a state-supported mass educational system. The New York party went so far as to advocate a variant of Robert Owen's proposal that all children be required to attend public boarding schools from the age of six. This was to assure that they have a common environment for twenty-four hours a day, not simply during the school day.[26] The Workingmen's parties attacked the major parties for their lack of interest in labor and proposed a variety of reforms to upgrade workers' social, economic, and legal position.

The strong egalitarian commitment of the Workingmen's parties did not lead them to advocate socialism, collective ownership, or equality of result. Rather, they wished to open up opportunity for all and to reduce the advantages of those born to privilege.[27] In this sense, their leaders were premature social Darwinists, not Marxists. The parties secured sizable votes in state and municipal elections, as Marx was glad to note.

However, the Workingmen's parties declined quickly after their rapid ascent, a reversal that Marx never confronted or explained. One source of the movement's failure was "the taking up of some of its most popular demands by one of the old parties."[28] The Jacksonian Democrats responded to the electoral successes of this third-party movement by showing "greater concern than ever before for the various reform provisions of the Workingmen's program."[29] Although relatively strong in many local contests, the parties, like many subsequent efforts of minor left parties in America, proved unable to deal with the "presidential question"—the possibility that by nominating their own candidate, they would draw votes away from the more left-disposed major party nominee.

Although the Workingmen's parties disappeared in the early 1830s, Marx and Engels were to emphasize decades later that Americans "have had, since 1829, their own social democratic school."[30] But, as noted, Marx and Engels misinterpreted this episode of American history. The parties' ideology reflected the strong belief of many Jacksonian Americans in equality of opportunity, rather than equality of result. Like subsequent generations of Progressives and liberals, the Workingmen's parties protested the growth of private and public monopolies and limits on competition. They did not try to curtail free enterprise or inequality of income; instead they sought meritocracy within capitalism.

America as a New Society

In analyzing the prospects for socialism in America, Marx and Engels evaluated how and in what respects the United States differed sociologically from European societies. America was a new nation and society. It was the most democratic country and lacked many of the institutions and traditions of previously feudal societies. As a result, the United States had a "modern and purely bourgeois culture."

Recognizing after Marx's death that socialist movements were not emerging on a mass scale in the United States, Engels attributed the political backwardness of American workers to the absence of a feudal past. Thus, he wrote in 1890 that Americans "are born conservatives—just because America is so purely bourgeois, so entirely without a feudal past and therefore proud of its purely bourgeois organization."[31] Two years later, Engels noted, "It is . . . quite natural, that in such a young country, which has never known feudalism and has grown up on a bourgeois basis from the first, bourgeois prejudices should also be so strongly rooted in the working class."[32]

Along with many other commentators on the American scene, the famed German sociologist Max Weber also emphasized that the United States was the only pure bourgeois country; the only one that was not postfeudal, that was without "medieval antecedents or complicating institutional heritage."[33] Similar arguments were made in the 1920s by the most profound Communist theoretician, Antonio Gramsci, who pointed out that America was able to avoid the remnants of mercantilism, statist regulations, church establishment, aristocracy, and sharp status cleavages that postfeudal countries inherited.[34] Both Weber and Gramsci pointed to America's unique origins and consequent value system as a source of its economic and political development. These values encompassed both secular, liberal *laissez-faire* and America's distinctive, individualistic religious tradition, based on the dominance of the Protestant sects that, as Weber stressed, facilitated the rise of capitalism.[35] Gramsci emphasized that the "difference between Americans and Europeans is determined by the absence of 'tradition' in the United States, in so far as tradition also means passive residues of all the social forms eclipsed by past history."[36]

The ultimate source of authority in the American polity can be found in the Preamble of the Constitution, which starts with the words "We, the people of the United States." Populism is constrained, however, in the American experience, by constitutionalism. The Revolutionary Americans, having defeated a tyrannical king, feared the power of a unified, central state. They sought to avoid tyranny by checks and balances, dividing power among different political bodies, all subject to a Bill of Rights limiting government authority. The antistatist, antiauthoritarian component of American ideology, derived from Jefferson's Declaration of Independence, remains an underlying source of the weakness of socialism in the United States.

American radicals have generally been more sympathetic to libertarianism and to syndicalism than to state collectivism. Analyzing this tradition, historian David DeLeon notes that unlike Scandinavian social democracy, Fabian bureaucratic socialism, and Soviet communism, American radicalism has been permeated by suspicion, if not hostility, toward centralized power. The essence of this heritage—which has been expressed in both individualistic and communal forms—may be described as "antistatism," "libertarianism," or, more provocatively, "anarchism."[37]

This heritage may be seen in the behavior of the American labor movement. The ideology of the American Federation of Labor (AFL) was syndicalist for much of its first half century. The AFL's radical competitor, the Industrial Workers of the World (IWW), was anarcho-syndicalist. Both the AFL and the IWW regarded the state as an enemy and felt that government-owned industry would be much more difficult for workers and unions to resist than private companies. Samuel Gompers, the leader of the

AFL for four decades, emphasized that what the state can give, the state can take away, and concluded from this that workers must rely on themselves. Gompers and much of the old AFL were far from conservative. In 1920 Gompers described himself as "three-quarters anarchist."[38] As Daniel Bell, the foremost student of American socialism, has noted, the AFL was more militant than European labor movements before and immediately after World War I, as reflected in its greater propensity to strike and engage in violence.[39]

Richard Flacks, a founder and leader of Students for a Democratic Society (SDS) in the sixties, writing as a left-wing academic in the mid-nineties, has emphasized the ties between the radical, but nonsocialist, New Left and the antistatist tradition:

> The dominant spirit in the 60s was neither social-democratic nor statist/stalinist/leninist, but owed more to anarchist/pacifist/radical democratic traditions: Students and workers should claim voice in the institutions they inhabit; communities and neighborhoods should have democratic control over their futures; co-ops, communes, and collectives should be the places to try alternative futures and practice authentic vocation. . . . Here in short was a thoroughgoing critique of statism, advanced not by the right, but by young Black and White activist/intellectuals devoted to a decentralizing, devolutionary, radical-democratic politics.[40]

There is a striking similarity between the orientation of the IWW and that of the New Left, both of which emphasized individualism and antistatism.[41] The New Left's confrontational tactics, involving civil disobedience, also followed in the footsteps of the Wobblies. One of the most influential academic stimulators of the early New Left, William Appleman Williams, expressed his antistatism in his strong preference for Herbert Hoover over Franklin Roosevelt. He noted that Hoover did not propose to strengthen the power of the central state but favored "voluntaristic but nevertheless organized cooperation within and between each major sector of the economy."[42]

Another academic icon of the student New Left, the sociologist C. Wright Mills, admired the competitive, free-yeoman tradition of American free enterprise and decentralized politics. There is perhaps no more favorable portrait of the operation and consequences of the pre–Civil War

American economy and polity than the one presented by Mills. In much-exaggerated terms, he pictures early-nineteenth-century America as a near utopia. Property was widely and equitably distributed and provided security and protection against tyranny. Rapid and continuing social mobility meant that few remained propertyless for long. The early United States, in Mills' view, was virtually a libertarian society: "Political authority, the traditional mode of social integration, became a loose framework of protection rather than a centralized engine of domination; it too was largely unseen and for long periods very slight."[43]

These conceptions of the United States have been described by Irving Howe, the leading American socialist intellectual of the second half of the twentieth century, as the essence of "American exceptionalism," which, he writes,

has often taken the guise of a querulous anti-statism. . . . It can veer toward an American version of anarchism, suspicious of all laws, forms, and regulations. . . . Tilt toward the right and you have the worship of "the free market"; tilt toward the left and you have the moralism of American reformers, even the syndicalism of the IWW.[44]

Stratification

Pre–World War I socialists did not limit their analyses of the failure of socialism to cultural variables. The country's situation as an underpopulated overseas settler society also helped to produce an economy and class system far different from those in Europe. In the Old World, expropriation had driven peasants off the land and into the cities to become lowly paid workers.[45] Marx believed that in the United States, the proletarians had the opportunity to become independent producers. He stated in *Capital*: "The wage-worker of today is tomorrow an independent peasant, or artisan, working for himself. He vanishes from the labour-market, but not into the workhouse."[46]

Labor scarcity, which raised wages in America by comparison to Europe, was reduced by large-scale immigration. Marx noted, however, that at a time of great industrial expansion during and after the Civil War, the "lowering of wages and the dependence of the wage-worker are yet far from being brought down to the normal European level."[47]

Given Marx's conclusion, it is not surprising that in the 1890s Engels also cited economic growth and the prosperity of the United States as among the "very great and peculiar difficulties for a continuous development of a workers' party." In contrasting the situation in the two great English-speaking nations, he noted, "The native American workingman's standard of living is considerably higher than even that of the British, and that alone suffices to place him in the rear [politically] for still some time to come."[48] Two years later, he emphasized that in America, prosperity did not simply fill the coffers of the bourgeoisie but actually reached the workers.[49]

Marx and Engels also focused on social mobility, stressing, in the words of the former, that "though classes, indeed, already exist, they have not yet become fixed, but continually change and interchange their elements in a constant state of flux."[50] Similarly, Engels, like Tocqueville over a half century earlier, was struck by the American ideal of a nation "without a permanent and hereditary proletariat. Here everyone could become if not a capitalist, at all events an independent man, producing or trading, with his own means, for his own account."[51]

It is interesting that in 1846 Marx wrote that the political efforts of Americans to extend the opportunities to settle on free land and to become farmers represented a leftist demand, an effort to gain equal opportunity. As Michael Harrington notes, he saw "the Free Land movement . . . as the first form of the proletarian revolution . . . , as a movement based upon the living conditions of a class which necessarily must become communist. . . ."[52]

Marx's conclusion is significant since, as Harrington argues, he implied that the desire of ordinary Americans for individual upward mobility, and for the ownership of their own plot of productive land, reflects the same motivation found in support for socialism. He concluded that the mass of Americans who felt that the American system assured them of such opportunity actually believed they were living in an egalitarian society. This exceptionalist argument, like many others of Marx, was destined to reappear again and again in observations on America by foreign commentators, and by American socialists like Leon Samson and Michael Harrington, down to the present.

A number of observers have explained the weakness of class consciousness in America relative to Europe in terms of contrasting experiences and

perceptions of inequality. The foreign-born American socialist leaders
Victor Berger and Morris Hillquit emphasized the enduring historical
character of class awareness in Europe. It long predated the rise of socialism. As Berger put it in 1903, "The feeling of class distinction in America,
at least among native workingmen, has not the same historic foundation
that it has in Germany, France, or England. There the people were accus-
tomed for over a thousand years to have distinct classes and castes fixed
by law."[53] From the time of Marx and Engels, socialists have agreed with
Tocqueville that social class differences (as distinct from economic class
differences) were much weaker in America than in Europe. In the Old
World, people were placed in distinct classes by the society. Workers were
led to support labor parties in response to deep postfeudal divisions in
society. In the United States, by contrast, class was more of an abstraction
and socialists were faced with the prospect of persuading workers to think
in class terms.

Much of the European socialist discussion about social stratification in
America in the decade preceding World War I was based on Werner
Sombart's detailed 1906 study *Why Is There No Socialism in the United
States?*[54] And here again, we find a parallel to Tocqueville's account of
American exceptionalism. Sombart, who was then a socialist, wrote:

> America is a freer and more egalitarian society than Europe. In his rela-
> tionship to other people and to social institutions, and in his position in
> and to society . . . the American is also better-off than he would be in the
> contrasting European situation. For him "Liberty" and "Equality" . . . are
> not empty ideas and vague dreams, as they are for the European working
> class. . . . [In America] there is not the stigma of being the class apart that
> almost all European workers have about them. . . . The bowing and
> scraping before the "upper classes," which produces such an unpleasant
> impression in Europe, is completely unknown. . . . [The workingman]
> feels differently from his counterpart in a country where a person only
> begins to be considered a person when he is, if not a baron, then a reserve
> officer, a doctor, or a person on probation for a profession. . . .[55]

George Plekhanov, the father of Russian Marxism, for whom Lenin had
great respect, also saw American developments positively. He wrote
approvingly of Sombart's explanation for the weakness of socialism in

America, which focused on the "democratic character of North American political institutions; . . . the extremely favorable economic position of the North American worker compared to that of the European, and . . . a multitude of free lands which made it possible for the proletariat 'to escape to freedom' from capitalism."[56]

Like Sombart, many socialists recognized that although American capitalism resulted in the growth of inequality and the emergence of a highly privileged class, the income and life chances of the underprivileged also improved absolutely, given rising productivity and the widespread distribution of steadily cheaper items of mass consumption. Thus, H. G. Wells emphasized that while "a growing proportion of the wealth of the community is passing into the hands of a small minority of successful getters, [this] is masked . . . by the enormous increase of the total wealth." Although the proportion of total income in the hands of workers did not increase, their standard of life improved. Wells concluded that "the great mass of the population is not consciously defeated in the economic game. It is only failing to get a large share in the increment of wealth." Wells noted that even in "the filthy back streets of the East Side" of New York, people were much better off than their peers in London. "Common people" were much better clothed in America than in Europe.[57]

Leon Trotsky recognized this also. In his political autobiography, written at the beginning of his final exile in 1929, which otherwise contains few references to his personal life, Trotsky described, almost in awe, his experience of "an apartment in a workers' district" in New York, in the East Bronx, where he and his family lived for two months in 1917. "That apartment, at eighteen dollars a month, was equipped with all sorts of conveniences that we Europeans were quite unused to: electric lights, gas cooking-range, bath, telephone, automatic service elevator, and even a chute for the garbage. These things completely won the boys [his children] over to New York."[58]

Comparative living standards are still debated. Analysis of data from Birmingham, England, and Pittsburgh, Pennsylvania, from 1890 to 1913, suggests that the aggregate transatlantic wage gap was smaller than has sometimes been assumed.[59] But, as Michael Harrington recognized in reference to these data, native-born American workers were especially advantaged in a society of immigrants. Because immigrants took low-paying jobs, natives could move up, live well—and resist socialist blandishments.[60]

Writing in 1988, Richard Flacks concluded that "the stability and legiti-

macy of established authority in the United States has rested on its capacity to 'deliver the goods'—that is, to provide the material basis for viable
daily life."[61] And at the end of the twentieth century, this capacity, emphasized by Plekhanov, Sombart, Wells, and Trotsky, is still in evidence.
Distribution of wealth has grown more unequal, but consumption and the
overall standard of living have not. In absolute terms, the less privileged are
better off than before.

Although social and political class consciousness were seemingly inhibited by egalitarian social relationships, a relatively high standard of living,
and a belief in the existence of widespread opportunities for upward
mobility, these did not produce a docile working class, as Daniel Bell has
observed. Visitors to the United States around the turn of the century
commented on the greater "frequency and bitterness of industrial conflict"
in comparison to Europe, an observation that was statistically accurate.
They explained such behavior as another consequence of the peculiar
American social system, which emphasized meritocratic competition. One
analyst of the foreign traveler literature has aptly summarized these conclusions:

> Most of the European visitors explained industrial conflict as a result
> rather than a contradiction of the material and social democracy which
> typified the life of the American worker. The abundance of his life, they
> pointed out, added to the strength of his ambition for more. His self-
> reliance made him sensitive to his rights. Industrial conflict in America
> was a man-to-man fight, with no quarter asked or given, unmitigated by
> the tradition of subordination on the one hand, or of benevolence and
> responsibility on the other.[62]

The exceptional character of the American class structure was analyzed
in 1906 by H. G. Wells in a way which anticipated political theorist Louis
Hartz, writing half a century later. Wells, then an English Fabian socialist,
related the unique history and class structure of the United States to the
absence of both a socialist party and a true conservative, Tory one. In
Wells' view, two major European classes—subservient landbound peasants
and the aristocracy—were missing from the American scene. The absence
of the former meant that there was no "servile tradition," while the
absence of the latter minimized "state responsibility, which in the old

European theory of society was supposed to give significance to the whole." Wells stated:

> The American community, one cannot too clearly insist, does not corre-
> spond to an entire European community at all, but only to the middle
> masses of it. . . . This community was, as it were, taken off its roots,
> clipped of its branches and brought hither. . . . Essentially America is a
> middle-class become a community and so its essential problems are the
> problems of a modern individualistic society, stark and clear, unham-
> pered and unilluminated by any feudal traditions either at its crest or at
> its base.[63]

Racial heterogeneity and large-scale immigration were two obvious related differences between the United States and Europe.[64] The former was generally ignored as a source of socialist weakness by socialist writers; the latter received much more attention. However, Marx and Engels pointed to the role of ethnic diversity in undermining class consciousness by giving native-born white workers a privileged position, thus enabling the bourgeoisie to play workers of different racial and ethnic backgrounds against one another. In a letter written in 1870 to two friends in New York, Marx noted that in America the "working class is *split* into two *hostile* camps," native and foreign-born. He recommended to his correspondents that they should press for a "coalition among workers of different ethnic backgrounds."[65]

Engels, commenting on the same problem two decades later in 1892, emphasized that "your great obstacle in America, it seems to me, lies in the exceptional position of the native workers. . . . [T]he ordinary badly paid occupations [are left] to the immigrants, of whom only a small section enter the aristocratic trade unions."[66]

Americanism and Socialism

Richard Hofstadter has written that, "It has been our fate as a nation not to have ideologies but to be one."[67] Apart from the former Soviet Union, other countries define themselves as birthright communities, based not in ideology but in a common history. This, as Michael Ignatieff emphasizes, is rooted in "the people's pre-existing ethnic characteristics, their language, religion, customs, and tradition."[68] Americanism, however, is an "ism" or ideology in the same way that communism or fascism or liberalism are isms.[69] The American ideology, stemming from the Revolution, can be subsumed in five words: antistatism, laissez-faire, individualism, populism, and egalitarianism.[70] The implications of the latter two for socialism were spelled out by Hermann Keyserling and Leon Samson, writing in the late 1920s and early 1930s.[71] They argued that the movement had little appeal because the social content of socialism, with the big exception of property relations, is similar to what Americans think they already have, namely, a democratic, socially classless, anti-elitist society.

As Samson, a radical socialist, put it:

When we examine the meaning of Americanism, we discover that Americanism is to the American not a tradition or a territory, not what France is to a Frenchman or England to an Englishman, but a doctrine— what socialism is to a socialist. Like socialism, Americanism is looked upon . . . as a highly attenuated, conceptualized, platonic, impersonal attraction toward a system of ideas, a solemn assent to a handful of final notions—democracy, liberty, opportunity, to all of which the American adheres rationalistically much as a socialist adheres to his socialism— because it does him good, because it gives him work, because, so he thinks, it guarantees him happiness. Americanism has thus served as a substitute for socialism.[72]

Samson noted that conservatives, Republicans, and businessmen, whom he preferred to quote to illustrate his own observations, adopted language, concepts, and goals for American society which in Europe were voiced only by socialists. Writing in the early 1930s, he pointed out that Herbert Hoover took Europe as a negative model, saying that in America, "we resent class distinction because there can be no rise for the individual through the frozen strata of classes." Hoover and other conservatives emphasized meritocracy and equal opportunity as goals of the American system.

It is of interest to note that Gramsci also stressed that America's unique history resulted in a general value system, a conception of life, which he, too, dubbed "Americanism." The essence of Americanism is rationalism uninhibited by the existence of social classes and values derived from a feudal past. "Americanism" is not simply a way of life, it is an "ideology."[73] Unlike other nations, America is characterized by the complete ideological "hegemony" of bourgeois values, unaffected by feudalism.

> Americanism, in its most developed form, requires a preliminary condition . . . that there do not exist numerous [postfeudal] classes with no essential function in the world of production. European "tradition," European "civilization," is, conversely, characterized precisely by the existence of such classes, created by the "richness" and "complexity" of past history. One could even say that the more historic a nation the more numerous and burdensome are those sedimentations of idle and useless masses living on "their ancestral patrimony," pensioners of economic history. . . . America does not have "great historical and cultural traditions"; but neither does it have this leaden burden to support. . . .[74]

The conception of America as a classically liberal, antistatist society was elaborated after World War II by political theorist Louis Hartz, in much the same terms as H. G. Wells:

> [My] chief argument is that the Americans started almost clear of the medieval heritage, and developed in the utmost the modern type of productive social organization. They took the economic conventions that were modern and progressive at the end of the eighteenth century and stamped them into the Constitution as if they meant to stamp them there for all time. America is pure eighteenth century.[75]

A similar argument about the American and European systems was presented by socialist leader Morris Hillquit. In 1909, he noted that in America there was "no room for a Conservative Party in the European sense," i.e., a statist or Tory Conservative party. Like Wells, he argued that the Republicans correspond "to the [antistatist] Liberal parties of Europe," while the Democrats bear "some resemblance to the Radical [left liberal] parties of European countries."[76]

. . .

An American Labor Party

Marx and Engels repeatedly criticized socialists who were unwilling to work within the broader labor movement. They argue that the best course for socialists in America was to work within the broad stream of indigenous working-class organizations rather than to form their own exclusive socialist party. Lenin, in a preface to the Russian translation of Marx's and Engels' correspondence, pointed out that "What Marx and Engels most of all criticize in British and American socialism is its isolation from the labor movement."[77]

Engels argued on several occasions that it was vital for socialists to attach themselves to a broad-based, genuine working-class movement even if that movement did not accept socialist principles. In 1886 Engels wrote: "The first great step of importance for every country newly entering into the movement is always the constitution of the workers as an independent political party, no matter how, so long as it is a distinct workers' party."[78] In the same year, Engels again took up the issue, noting that the dominant tendency among socialists in the United States was to isolate themselves from the mainstream of the working-class, and build doctrinally pure, but small factions:

> It is far more important that the movement should proceed harmonious-ly, take root, and embrace as much as possible the whole American prole-tariat, than that it should start and proceed from the beginning on theoretically perfectly correct lines. There is no better road to theoretical clearness of comprehension than to learn by one's own mistakes.
>
> . . . A million or two of workingmen's votes next November for a *bona fide* workingmen's party is worth infinitely more at present than a hun-dred thousand votes for a doctrinally perfect platform.[79]

Not surprisingly, this criticism was also made by British socialists who supported the idea of a broad labor party based in the unions. While socialism was no stronger in Britain than in the United States prior to World War I, the labor movement was stronger in one important respect: the majority of socialists and unionists were able to cooperate within one party that represented workers as a class. In an article on the United States, the

Socialist Review argued that the structural and cultural barriers faced by socialists made it imperative for socialists to join with unionists in creating a unitary party, even if they had to sacrifice their ideological purity: "In no country is a fusion between the Socialist and Trade Union forces more necessary than in America."[80] This view was shared by Labour party leader Keir Hardie after his trip to the United States in 1908:

> I have lived too long . . . to have any faith in the prophecies concerning the coming collapse of the capitalist system. Capitalism has a power of adaption for which some of its Socialist opponents do not make sufficient allowance. The one thing that will bring Socialism soon is a big, genuine working-class movement around which the better element of American citizenship could rally. Unless this can be brought into being I am inclined to be doleful concerning the future of the Socialist Party in America.[81]

Sectarianism

A related feature of American radicalism that adversely affected working-class political mobilization was a propensity for sectarianism, for treating Marxism or other radical doctrines as absolute dogmas to be applied in all situations, behavior which Daniel Bell has stressed in his penetrating analysis of the failure of American socialism.[82] Michael Harrington also argues that "the great and abiding sin of American socialism has been sectarianism."[83] Much earlier, Engels referred to "that sectarian land, America," where purists could always count on support.[84] Marx, as well, "confessed to a certain suspicion of 'Yankee socialists' as 'crotchety and sectarian.' "[85] Engels repeatedly criticized the Socialist Labor party's first effort to create a Marxist working-class movement, for treating Marxist theory in a "doctrinaire and dogmatic way as something which has got to be learnt by heart and which will then supply all needs without more ado. To them it is a *credo* and not a guide to action."[86] In 1894, he criticized the Socialist Labor party for reducing "the Marxian theory of development to a rigid orthodoxy, which the workers are not to reach themselves by their own class feeling, but which they have to gulp down as an article of faith at once and without development."[87]

The Russians Plekhanov and Lenin reiterated the judgments of Marx and Engels about American radicals, pointing to political sectarianism as a cause of their weakness. In 1907, Lenin wrote, "The burden of all [Marx's and Engels'] numerous comments on the . . . American Socialists is the accusation that they have reduced Marxism to a dogma, to a 'rigid . . . orthodoxy' . . . [and] are incapable of adapting themselves to the theoretically helpless but living and powerful mass labour movement that is marching alongside them."[88] Ironically, in discussing differences between European and American socialism in 1906, Marx's grandson Jean Longuet noted that a rigidly orthodox Marxism was stronger within the American socialist movement than anywhere else, except in Russia.[89]

Why were American radicals so sectarian? On a sociological level, the sources of political orthodoxy were linked by Marx and Engels to America's religiosity, to the strength of Protestant sectarianism. Engels noted the United States was characterized by "common law, religion, and sectarianism."[90] Marx was particularly impressed with the role of religion in American life. Like Tocqueville, he saw its vitality as a consequence of competitive religious institutions and the absence of an established church: "North America is pre-eminently the country of religiosity. . . . We find that religion not only *exists* but displays a *fresh* and *vigorous* vitality."[91]

Religious and political sectarianism are thus likely to abound. Marx and Engels, like Tocqueville, emphasized political consequences flowing from the unique voluntary, sectarian, and congregational character of American religion. While Tocqueville emphasized the role of non-state-supported denominations in fostering politically relevant voluntary associations, Marx and Engels stressed how Protestant sectarianism underpinned competitive individualism and produced moralistic and political sectarianism in America. These, in turn, impeded collectivist politics.

The Political System

Most analyses of the prospects for socialism in America published in the late 1890s and early years of the twentieth century continued to emphasize that American democratic political institutions inhibited workers from recognizing their class situation. In much of Europe, socialist parties had gained strength while fighting for elementary political rights, particularly for the suffrage, which Americans had secured *prior* to industrialization. As

Karl Kautsky put it in 1904, "The struggle for freedom is very much superior to the effortless possession of a freedom that others have won before."[92] Lenin also stressed in 1907 that the United States, which is "in many respects the model and ideal of our bourgeois civilization . . .[has] no rival . . . in the extent of the political freedom and the cultural level of the masses of its population."[93] He emphasized that the weakness of socialism in America stemmed from "the absence of any at all big, nation-wide democratic tasks facing the proletariat." American socialism was weak precisely because it was dealing with "the most firmly established democratic systems, which confront the proletariat with purely socialist tasks." Correspondingly, Lenin noted that the German Social Democrats were powerful because they worked in "a country where the bourgeois-democratic revolution was still incomplete," where "military despotism, embellished with parliamentary forms [Marx's expression in his *Critique of the Gotha Programme*], prevailed, and still prevails."[94]

Generally, socialists were strong in countries "where the proletariat formed its party before the liberal bourgeois formed theirs." Morris Hillquit elaborated the argument that political freedom undermines class consciousness, noting, much like Lenin, that "paradoxical as it may seem, our very democracy has militated against the immediate success of socialism."[95]

[A] check to the progress of the socialist movement in the United States was to be found in the political institutions of the country: the working classes of the European countries were, as a rule, deprived of some political rights enjoyed by other classes of citizens, and the common struggle for the acquisition of those rights was frequently the first cause to draw them together in a political union. . . .

In the United States, however, the working men enjoyed full political equality at all times, and thus had one less motive to organize politically on a class basis.[96]

Max Beer, a leader of the Socialist International, also emphasized the absence of a middle-class democratic revolution that mobilized the working class: "In the Old World the rise and effervescence of Socialist Labour movements at various periods were, as a rule, the concomitant phenomena of middle-class upheavals, which, directly or indirectly, mobilized some strata of the working class," and "were accompanied by an inrush of Socialist ideas." These included the Reform Bill struggles in Britain, the revolutions of 1832 and 1848 in France and Germany, and the 1905 Revolution in Russia. But as Beer asserted, "In the United States middle class movements against a privileged hereditary upper class or personal monarchy could not arise, for these phenomena did not exist, and there was no need to mobilize the working classes for the fight."[97]

That bourgeois democracy, mass-based parties, and white manhood suffrage in America predated the emergence of a large-scale proletariat would not, in and of itself, prevent class political organization. However, as Sombart emphasized, the American electoral system by its focus on the presidency encourages two parties which compete among all strata "for electoral purposes" so that it is "extremely easy for the proletariat to belong to the traditional parties; . . . even the class-conscious worker need never go against the dictates of his intellect." He also argued that "[t]he politicians for reasons of prudence, try systematically to keep the masses in a good humour, for their success in elections is naturally dependent upon the votes of the population. The . . . circumstance that there are two major parties competing with each other now benefits the proletariat, as well as all lower social strata."[98]

The presidential system, and the two coalition parties which it seemingly helps to produce, has been seen as a major obstacle in the path of the Socialist party, an argument which is developed in detail in the next chapter. In discussing the reasons for an unexpectedly small Socialist vote in 1908, Hillquit unwittingly described the general conditions which prevail whenever a "third party" threatens to accumulate significant electoral support: "The Democratic party . . . revived all the slogans of its old time middle-class radicalism and re-instated the prophet of that brand of radicalism, William J. Bryan, in the leadership of the party. . . . [T]heir appeal to organized labor for active support of the candidates of that party, could not but be detrimental to the socialist campaign."[99]

This reaction by the Democrats accorded with responses to earlier efforts to create left third parties. The Workingmen's parties that had so impressed Marx had been absorbed by the Jacksonian Democrats, who had modified their politics in the cities where the third party had strength. Orestes Brownson, one of the Workingmen's party leaders, was the first, but definitely not the last, to suggest that radicals should work to make the Democrats a party of "social Democracy, as distinguished from political."[100]

The ability of the major parties, particularly the Democrats, to absorb radical protest within their electoral coalition was not simply a function of the sophistication of American politicians or the weak sense of solidarity of prospective American leftist voters. Rather, as Hillquit noted, it was inherent in the special electoral system of the United States; "since a new party rarely seems to have the chance or prospect of electing its candidate for governor of a state or president of the country, the voter is inclined in advance to consider its entire ticket as hopeless. The fear of 'throwing away' the vote is thus a peculiar product of American politics, and it requires a voter of exceptional strength of conviction to overcome it."[101]

Engels also noted other ways that America's political system contributed to the weakness of organized radicalism. In 1893, in listing factors preventing the growth of a workers' third-party alternative, he emphasized "the Constitution . . . which causes every vote for any candidate not put up by one of the two governing parties to appear to be *lost*. And the American . . . wants to influence his state; he does not throw his vote away."[102] He stressed the difficulty of creating a *third* party, where there was no second ballot (runoff), and concluded, during the period of the greatest strength of the Populists in the 1890s, that "there is no place yet in America for a third party," because of the size, complexity, and heterogeneity of the country.[103] "The divergence of interests even in the same class group is so great in that tremendous area that wholly different groups and interests are represented in each of the two big parties, depending on the locality."[104] Other factors which reduced potential support for "third parties" were dealt with by Sombart. He pointed to the "over-valuation of success" inherent in America's pure bourgeois achievement-oriented culture, which made "who won" the only question of interest in sports and economic and political life. As he emphasized: "The American prays before the god of Success, he strives to lead a life acceptable to his god. . . . [Since] all individuals are bent on success, each must aim to come ahead of the rest."[105] This focus on success, on winning every race in which one participates, "ensures a politics of majorities."

The Labor Intellectuals

Discussion of the weakness of socialism in the United States in the nineteenth and early twentieth centuries was dominated by socialist intellectuals. But during this period, the topic was also addressed by an academic school of institutional labor economics and labor history, established at the University of Wisconsin under John R. Commons and his student and successor Selig Perlman. Both men favored the limited, antipolitical, job-consciousness approach of the American Federation of Labor. Their lifelong study of organized workers led them to reject socialism as inappropriate to American conditions. Socialism seemed, to them, a dysfunctional ideology brought to workers by intellectuals. Commons and Perlman sought to explain why America was politically exceptional; why European-style class consciousness did not exist here. As Commons put it, "Labour movements in America have arisen from peculiar American conditions, and it is by understanding these conditions that we shall be able to distinguish the movements and methods of organization from those of other countries."[106] In spite of basic differences with the socialists in economic assumptions and political goals, their explanation included many of the factors emphasized by socialist writers. Commons and Perlman, like Lenin and Hillquit, argued that "universal manhood suffrage," which American workers secured "at least two or three generations before labour in other countries," was a major "cause of the lack of 'class consciousness' among American workers."[107] They noted: "In other countries, where the labor movement started while the workingmen were still denied the franchise, there was in the last analysis no need of a theory of 'surplus value' to convince them that they were a class apart and should therefore be 'class conscious.' "[108]

The American political system posed other barriers to socialism. Perlman repeatedly stressed that "the American political party system . . . [is] essentially different from the European." As conglomerate "guilds," the major parties could absorb third parties because they "are capable . . . of a flexibility of one hundred and eighty percent [sic] in their platforms, [and have] extraordinary dexterity at 'stealing the thunder' of the new party." Echoing a line of argument made by Engels three decades earlier, Perlman noted that American parties lack the strong party discipline found in parliamentary systems. As a result, congressional candidates can take any positions they wish in their constituencies; "although these 'guilds' are organized nationally, the managers of the local branches have practically unlimited discretion in the choice of the 'goods' they wish to handle locally." Perlman argued that the failure of efforts to build independent labor parties are primarily due to "this uncanny adaptability of the established American political parties."[109]

Prior to the Great Depression, the reluctance of the American labor movement to press for state welfare cannot, however, be attributed to the difficulty in organizing a labor party. The American antistatist tradition produced a union movement which in principle, though often not in action, refused to look to government to improve the position of the American worker. As Perlman put it, American workers perceived little choice "between an autocratic capitalist management of industry and a bureaucratic one by 'experts' appointed by the state."[110] This syndicalist, antistate view did not temper the militancy of the labor movement, for "labor leaders in this country have, on the whole, always been more aggressive against the employers, and have striven more relentlessly for full job control than have their radical rivals."[111]

Beyond these political factors, unique sociological conditions produced a special "psychology of the laboring man" in America. Commons and Perlman reiterated the argument made by Engels that in Europe a rigid stratification system stemming from feudalism produced class consciousness. In Britain, unlike America, "society, with its [explicit] hierarchy of classes, keeps labor together by pressure from the top."[112] The failure of American workers to think in class terms was reinforced by social heterogeneity and by greater opportunity to move occupationally and geographically. As Commons put it in 1908: "While promotion at the top weakens class solidarity, immigration and women's labor at the bottom undermine it."[113]

Twenty years later, Perlman noted the failure of the socialist expectation that with the "exhaustion of the supply of free public land, the wage earner . . . [would] become cooped up for good in the class of factory operatives." He pointed out that in an advanced industrial economy new opportunities for mobility were in fact "more varied and entail less hardship than the old opportunity of 'homesteading' in the West. . . ."[114] He went on to stress that class consciousness is inhibited by the fact that America as an open society has produced "the most heterogeneous laboring class in existence—ethnically, linguistically, religiously and culturally."[115]

Conclusion

American society and politics have, of course, changed greatly over time. The Depression of the 1930s produced a qualitative difference from previous eras. As Richard Hofstadter wrote, this era brought a "social democratic tinge" to the United States for the first time in its history.[116] The Great Depression gave rise to planning, the welfare state, and greatly extended government regulation in society generally.

The Depression Europeanized American politics and American labor organizations. Social class became more important as a source of party support.[117] Conservatives, increasingly concentrated in the Republican party, remained antistatist and laissez-faire, though many became willing to accommodate a somewhat more activist role for the state as envisaged in the Roosevelt New Deal. This accommodation, however, gradually dissolved after World War II, in response to long-term prosperity, which helped to produce a return to classic libertarian values, i.e., conservatism, American-style. The lessening of class tensions which reached their height in the Depression has been reflected in the marked decline in union membership since the mid-1950s and in the declining salience of class position for voting. Even before Ronald Reagan entered the White House, the United States had a lower rate of taxation, a smaller deficit as a proportion of GNP, a less-developed welfare state, and fewer government-owned industries than other western industrialized nations.[118]

It is obvious that America and the rest of the western world have changed greatly over the past two centuries. They have become industrialized, urbanized, and better educated. Central states have become more powerful. The postfeudal elements that existed in many European countries have declined enormously. In social structural terms, they have become more like America.

Not surprisingly, cross-national polls continue to reveal that Americans are much less favorable to an active role of government in the economy and large welfare programs than Canadians and Europeans. As compared to the citizens of other advanced democracies, Americans show a preference for private efforts in welfare as in business. They lead the world in philanthropic giving. As sociologist Nathan Glazer reports, "Non-public resources in American welfare are greater than is found in any other major nation."[119]

Similar conclusions about the left in the United States have been reached by Richard Flacks. In reviewing the left literature on the sources of radicalism, he also stresses the exceptional character of America. He sums up his analysis by saying that "*none of the conditions that the tradition of the left has theorized to be requisite for the emergence of either mass allegiance to socialism, or a party representing the majority of the working class have been present in the United States."* He argues that if one had sought to plan a society in order to minimize the prospects for a left movement, "one could not have done much better than to implement the social development that has, mostly unplanned, constituted America."[120]

In the succeeding chapters, we seek to put historical and sociological flesh on these generalizations about American exceptionalism in attempting to explain the special character of the American left, and why, above all, it has never taken a socialist or class-conscious form.

Finally, we raise again the conundrum for radicals arising from the belief that "socialism will in all likelihood come to fullest bloom in the New World."[121] Sombart was driven to challenge and worry about this conclusion by the fact that the United States "is a country with no socialism, despite its having the most advanced capitalist development."[122] He raised the specter that if socialism did not emerge in the world's most developed economy, the movement might decline in Europe, as countries there reached the productive heights attained by the United States.[123] We return to this issue in the final chapter.

=====

Chapter 2

THE AMERICAN

PARTY SYSTEM

The failure of the Socialist party is but one instance of the ineffectiveness of third parties in the United States over the last century.
Since the Civil War, just nine non-major party candidates in thirty-three
contests have polled more than five percent of the national vote in any
presidential election.[1] Only one non-major party has managed to exceed 5
percent of the total popular vote in two consecutive congressional elections, the Populists in 1894 and 1896.[2] This is not for want of contenders.
Roughly eleven hundred local, regional, and national parties have contested national or state elections since 1824, of which at least seventy-eight
have described themselves as "workers'," "labor," or "socialist." Over the last
century the nominees of the Democratic and Republican parties have on
average received almost 95 percent of the national vote in presidential
elections, a two-party oligopoly more complete and durable than in any
other modern democracy.

Given the remarkable dominance of the two major parties and the
inability of any challenging party to achieve major-party status, it is sensible to ask whether the socialist experience is part of a more general phenomenon rooted in the distinctive character of the American political

system. Both participants and scholars have argued that one or more of the basic features of the American polity—the plurality electoral system, the presidential selection process, party primaries, federalism, and flexible, nonprogrammatic parties—have inhibited socialism as a political movement by making it difficult for any minor political party to survive. Numerous analysts have also concluded that the American political system has undermined support for socialism quite apart from its effects on the viability of third parties. As noted earlier, both V. I. Lenin and the American labor economist Selig Perlman, among others, have suggested that the early attainment of suffrage for white males in America denied socialists the opportunity to lead workers in a broad movement for citizenship rights, as they had done in most European countries. Several writers have argued that federalism undercut support for socialism because it fragmented institutional power and denied workers a common set of political experiences.

In this chapter we draw on a variety of comparisons, both across and within societies, to evaluate the validity of these explanations. Some explanations we find implausible in the light of the evidence—including, particularly, the "gift of the suffrage" and federalism explanations. Though we find that the American political system does tend to reduce electoral support for third parties, including the Socialist party, this set of factors is not sufficient to explain the distinctive failure of the American Socialist party in comparison with socialist parties in other industrial societies. A number of nonsocialist third-party presidential candidates— Robert La Follette (1924), George Wallace (1968), John Anderson (1980), and Ross Perot (1992 and 1996)—have done better than any Socialist nominee.[3]

The Electoral System

The electoral system for Congress and the presidency is often cited as one of the main stumbling blocks for third parties in America. It is based on the plurality or first-past-the-post principle in which parties do not receive any representation unless they gain more votes than any other party within a constituency. The importance of this arrangement in creating a two-party

system at the expense of third or minor parties has been described by
Maurice Duverger:

> The simple-majority [plurality] single-ballot system favors the two-party
> system. . . . An almost complete correlation is observable between the
> simple-majority single-ballot system and the two-party system: dualist
> countries use the simple-majority vote and simple-majority vote coun-
> tries are dualist. The exceptions are very rare and can generally be
> explained as the result of special conditions.[4]

Plurality electoral systems convert votes into seats in a way that hurts
small parties if their limited support is spread across many constituencies.
Voters who might otherwise have backed a small or new party are dissuaded from doing so because they realize that a vote for it is almost invariably
wasted.[5] Their support for a third party may actually be self-defeating if it
reduces support for the lesser evil, the major party they prefer.

The effect of the plurality electoral system is evident in the experience
of the American Socialist party. Even during its peak years of electoral support, from 1912 to 1920, when the party gained between 3 and 6 percent
of the national vote in presidential elections, socialists were barely represented in Congress. Their only representatives were Victor Berger, who
represented a Milwaukee constituency in 1910, 1918, 1922, 1924, and
1926, and Meyer London, who was elected from the Lower East Side of
New York in 1914, 1916, and 1920.[6] In 1912, when the party reached its
high point, 6 percent of the presidential vote, it failed to elect a single representative to Congress.

It is tempting to stop here and ascribe the failure of third parties in the
United States since the Civil War entirely to the effects of plurality electoral systems. Indeed, this is part of conventional wisdom. But historical
comparison of the United States with European and other English-speaking societies raises serious doubts about an interpretation resting primarily
on the effects of the plurality electoral system.

Although proportional electoral systems are now the norm in Western
Europe, this was not always the case. Sweden had a plurality single-mem-
ber district electoral system up to 1907, as did Denmark until 1915, while
Britain, Canada, and most former Commonwealth countries continue to

have such systems.[7] Several other European states, including Germany until 1914, had electoral systems based on single-member districts.

Because they were newcomers, social democratic parties in these societies initially found themselves in the position of contesting elections as a minor party. As a result they were underrepresented in their legislative assemblies during their formative years. But each of these parties managed to overcome this barrier to establish itself as a major party or, in the case of Canada, as a durable and influential third party.

Two basic strategies can offset the disproportion arising from plurality electoral systems: first, third-party activists can focus their efforts selectively on constituencies in which they have some special source of strength, such as coal-mining areas in Britain; second, they can avoid splitting the left vote by making an electoral pact with the major party closest to them ideologically so that they do not compete in the same constituency. The American Socialists, however, refused on principle to make arrangements with "bourgeois" parties, an expression of socialist sectarianism which we shall examine in detail.

Most Western European social democratic parties placed less emphasis on socialist purity than did the American Socialist party. The British Labour party, for example, began as a small third party that was willing to ally with nonsocialists, contesting only those constituencies where workers were in a clear majority. This strategy, based on cooperation with the Liberals, meant that in its early years the Labour party was somewhat insulated from the effects of the plurality electoral system. In the general election of 1906, the first in which it gained significant parliamentary representation, the Labour party received twenty-nine (4.3 percent) of the seats in the House of Commons on the basis of 4.8 percent of the national vote. In the two subsequent contests before World War I, Labour continued to receive seats in rough proportion to its share of the national vote: forty seats (6.0 percent of the total) in January 1910 with 7.0 percent of the vote, and forty-two seats (6.3 percent of the total) in December 1910 with 6.4 percent of the vote. Its percentage of the vote in districts it contested was actually much higher. The party was subsequently aided by the waning of the Liberal party, and with the exception of 1918, Labour's share of parliamentary seats continued to keep more or less in pace with its proportion of the national vote.[8]

As a minor party competing in a plurality electoral system, the Danish Social Democratic party collaborated with the established party of the left, the Venstre, which was essentially a peasant movement. In 1895 and 1898, the Social Democrats were the fourth largest party, with 11.3 percent of the vote in 1895 and 14.3 percent in 1898. Yet in those elections they managed to gain eight and then twelve seats in the 114-member Folketing.[9] By World War I the party's willingness to cooperate with the Venstre enabled it to win one-fifth of the seats in the Folketing.

Since World War I, the Canadian Labor party, followed by the Co-operative Commonwealth Federation (CCF) and the New Democratic party (NDP), have suffered under Canada's plurality electoral system because they would not collaborate with a major party or even with other minor ones. However, the negative effect of plurality for these parties was moderated because they could take advantage of regional concentrations of support (particularly in the western provinces), and, on average, these yielded more than half the number of seats they would have received under proportional representation. The Canadian Labor party received on average only 1.6 percent of the national vote in elections it contested before the establishment of the CCF in 1932, and yet from the 1920s on it was always able to elect at least two representatives to the House of Commons.[10] From 1935 to 1988 the CCF/NDP received an average of 14.7 percent of the vote and 8.2 percent of parliamentary seats. Other third parties, such as the Progressives and the Social Creditors, also elected parliamentary representatives. In 1997, the NDP elected 7 percent (21) of the members of the House of Commons with 11 percent of the vote.

The wasted-vote thesis presumes that voters whose first preference is a minor party are dissuaded from voting for it because they realize that it has little chance of winning. Instead they act on their second preference, voting for the major party that they regard as the "lesser evil." Minor parties, however, can overcome the wasted-vote effect if voters do not have a strong preference for either major party and/or consider voting a symbolic or expressive act rather than a means to directly influence election outcomes.

These considerations suggest that there is nothing automatic about the effects of electoral systems on voting. The causal connections between electoral system and party performance involve party strategy and individual orientations, and these vary across time and place. For example, Ross Perot did not lose support during his revived 1992 campaign; in fact he, uniquely among American third-party candidates in this century, continued to gain votes as the election drew nearer. Survey evidence reveals that his supporters did not have a strong preference between the major party candidates and hence felt no pressure to desert Perot in the polling booth.

The experience of the German Social Democrats under the Kaiserreich appears to confound the wasted-vote thesis. Until 1912 the German party, like the American, refused to engage in deals with other groups and was, in any case, treated as a pariah by the left bourgeois parties. In the twelve elections between 1871 and 1907 the Social Democrats suffered severe underrepresentation under a majoritarian electoral system. Yet the period was marked by sustained growth in socialist electoral support.[11] The party's success is all the more noteworthy because its support was geographically diffuse rather than concentrated. Ironically, however, the very weakness of democracy in Germany helped the party to endure. The impotence of the Reichstag in controlling government policies devalued electoral outcomes. Elections were more symbolic expressions of popular preferences than means of determining governmental leadership. In addition, the Social Democratic party adapted to state repression and the social exclusion of workers in a highly stratified society by forming an extensive network of socialist unions, clubs, and societies that fostered strong class loyalty among its supporters—loyalties that provided a degree of immunity to the wasted-vote argument.

These examples suggest that the political failure of third parties in the United States cannot be explained simply by the way electoral rules have affected voters. In any case, as noted above, the Socialists did worse than a number of American nonsocialist third parties. In the next sections we examine the effects of three distinctive American institutions—the presidency, federalism, and restrictions on ballot access—and then consider how the relatively undisciplined and decentralized two-party system derives from these institutions.

The Presidential System

The election to the executive branch in the United States combines two features that are highly detrimental to third parties: the principle of plurality and the aggregation of national votes through the Electoral College. Neither of these features is unique to the United States. As noted, Britain, Canada, and other former Commonwealth countries have plurality elections, and France has adopted a presidential election system based on two rounds of voting at the national level.[12] However, among the industrialized democracies, only the United States combines these two features, electing its executive via a plurality electoral system with a single round of voting.

This makes it difficult, if not impossible, for a minor party in the United States to improve its national chances by cooperating with other parties to limit competition or by taking advantage of geographical concentrations of support. The first strategy is hard to carry through in the United States because the presidency is a unitary institution that cannot be divided easily among parties.[13] Building on local pockets of support, as happened in parliamentary systems, is almost certain to fail in the United States because the effective constituency for the election of the president is the country as a whole. Although it is mathematically possible for a third party to gain a balance of power in electoral votes if the major parties are closely matched, this is a remote and unprecedented possibility. The Electoral College has the well-known effect of turning even close popular elections into landslide margins of victory. Only one presidential contest since the Civil War, that of 1876, has been fought to within twenty Electoral College votes.

Given the separation of the executive and legislative branches of government in the United States, third parties are denied the prospect of gaining some executive influence as a coalition partner. Because of the enormous pressure toward party consolidation exerted by the electoral system, factional coalitions have always taken place within, rather than between, political parties. The American presidential system is thus an extreme version of "winner take all": the winning ticket emerges with a monopoly of the executive for four years.

It is possible to test the effect of the presidential electoral system. We hypothesize that extreme disproportionality of representation and skewness of reward in presidential elections are reflected in variations in minorparty voting across different electoral levels. Logically, the influence of the "wasted vote" should be greater as one moves up from local elections to congressional and finally presidential elections.

This is consistent with the fact that American Socialists did best at the city and local levels. The state of Wisconsin provides a revealing example. Despite participating in less than one-third of Wisconsin's House elections between 1904 and 1932, Socialists managed to gain more votes in the state than did their presidential candidate on four of seven occasions. In the three presidential election years (1904, 1908, and 1912) in which the Socialist presidential candidate, Eugene Debs, received a slightly higher share of the Wisconsin vote than the House candidates, the party put up only three, two, and three candidates, respectively, in the eleven House constituencies.[14] Even though most observers believed that Debs' candidacy increased Socialist support around the country, evidence from Wisconsin suggests that the party was weaker at the presidential level than at the local level.

While the absolute number of Socialist votes was generally higher in presidential election years than in midterm elections, the proportion of Socialist votes was higher in the latter. Socialist candidates did better when turnout was relatively low. This can be seen clearly when one compares two House of Representatives constituencies where the Socialist party was consistently strong over the first three decades of the twentieth century: Wisconsin Districts 4 and 5, located in Milwaukee (see Table 2.1). Analyzing patterns across each set of three consecutive elections beginning with a presidential election year yields sixteen cases.[15] On average, the share of Socialist votes in midterm elections was 5.8 percentage points higher than in presidential elections.[16]

Third-party congressional candidates, in general, tended to perform better in midterm elections. People's party candidates for Congress were more successful in 1894 (when three were elected) than in 1892. Milwaukee's Victor Berger was elected five times as congressional representative for District 5—in 1910, 1918, 1922, 1924, and 1926, all but one being a midterm election. State third parties, notably the Farmer-Labor party of Minnesota and the Progressive party of Wisconsin, elected a number of House members and senators in the 1920s and 1930s without being tied to presidential tickets.

The extent to which the American presidential system diminishes third-party support appears to vary with the perceived difference between the two major parties, as well as with the competitiveness of the election. Socialists themselves were, of course, well aware of this. In response to a heckler who shouted that a Socialist vote was a wasted vote, Eugene Debs is said to have responded, "That's right. Don't vote for freedom—you might not get it. Vote for slavery—you have a cinch on that."[17] Norman Thomas, who led the Socialist party from 1928, once remarked that when candidates with contrasting agendas are embroiled in a close electoral battle, potential Socialist voters are more inclined than usual to follow a second-best strategy, casting what they believe to be an effective vote, rather

Table 2.1: Socialist Party Election Results in
Wisconsin House Districts 4 and 5

Year	District 4	District 5
1900	6.0	5.2*
1902**	*15.1*	*18.6*
1904	24.0	27.6
1906	*29.6*	*28.1*
1908	24.7	27.8
1910	*36.7*	*38.3*
1912	32.6	36.3
1914	*35.1*	*34.9*
1916	32.7	36.9
1918	*41.8*	*43.7*
1920	38.6	45.5
1922	*44.5*	*53.3*
1924	31.8	41.6
1926	*35.2*	*48.8*
1928	22.1	38.2
1930	*36.2*	*40.4*
1932	20.4	23.3
1934	*20.7*	*24.6*

* Socialist Labor party.

** Non-presidential year results in bold.

Source: Robert A. Diamond, ed., *Congressional Quarterly's Guide to
U.S. Elections* (Washington, D.C.: Congressional Quarterly, 1965).

than following their first (Socialist) preference. Conversely, when potential third-party voters view the outcome of the major-party contest with indifference or when the voting appeal of one candidate far outstrips the other, they are somewhat more likely to follow their inclinations and cast an independent vote. As Thomas notes, "Gene Debs got his highest vote—6 per cent of the total—in 1912. Why? Partly, at least, because that year, voters were pretty sure that the winner would be Woodrow Wilson or Theodore Roosevelt, not William H. Taft, and they didn't believe that the difference between these two fairly progressive men was important enough to prevent their voting for their real preference, the outspoken socialist and labor man, the beloved Gene Debs."[18]

This factor is obviously one of many that influenced the Socialist vote in these years, but it is worth noting that the experience of subsequent elections up to 1924 is consistent with this hypothesis. In 1916, few workers or potential supporters of the Socialist party could be indifferent to the major-party contest for president, which pitted Woodrow Wilson, the engineer of the Clayton Act, which purportedly exempted unions from antitrust regulation, against Charles Evans Hughes, a Supreme Court justice, who was on record as endorsing antilabor injunctions. Furthermore, Wilson, unlike Hughes, was publicly opposed to American intervention in World War I, a position that was popular with Socialists and many of their major ethnic supporters, such as Jews and Germans.[19] In an extremely close presidential contest, the Socialist party's 3.2 percent share of the vote was little better than half that of the previous election.

In the 1920 presidential election, the Socialist party received a slightly larger share of the vote (3.4 percent) than in 1916, despite a very sharp decline in its membership base. Eugene Debs, still in prison for resisting American involvement in World War I, was the beneficiary of sympathy votes, but his cause was probably aided as well by the fact that Warren Harding was, as anticipated, the runaway victor in the major-party competition by a margin of 26 percent of the national vote; he won a greater share of Electoral College votes than any president since Abraham Lincoln.

The 1924 presidential election was similar to that of 1912. Many on the political left were indifferent to the candidates selected by the major parties, a factor that significantly bolstered the Socialist-supported third-party Progressive ticket headed by Republican Robert La Follette. In 1924 there was no lesser evil, because both major candidates were conservative. Both Calvin Coolidge, the Republican nominee, and John W. Davis, a Wall Street corporate lawyer, selected by the Democratic party, held views that converged against organized labor and Midwestern farmers. By gaining the support of farmers and workers who opposed both the major-party candidates, La Follette received 16.6 percent of the total presidential vote, the largest share for a third party in any election since the Civil War, until Ross Perot's performance in the 1992 elections. Contemporary observers noted that there probably would have been no third-party candidacy in 1924 if

William G. McAdoo, a Democratic front-runner who was sympathetic to labor, had been nominated instead of Davis.[20]

In all plurality electoral systems a third party is faced with a stark choice between political principles and its preferred policy outcomes because its electoral participation will normally draw votes away from competing parties that are ideologically closer to it. In the United States the force of this logic is accentuated in presidential contests because the electoral system creates a winner-take-all situation for the entire country.

Federalism

Another constitutional feature, federalism, has been conceived both as a source of weakness for third parties, especially socialist, and as a component of the political system which can encourage the emergence of viable minor parties. Two main lines of argument have been advanced for the first thesis. First, federalism, with the division of powers among the presidency, Congress, and the judiciary, undercuts attempts to portray the national state as a decisive instrument for economic and social change. Second, federalism weakens efforts to generate working-class consciousness or confirm socialist criticisms of American society as a whole because authority is fragmented into states. On the other hand, federalism may actually facilitate third-party efforts because, as in Canada, it provides smaller and thus more accessible political arenas for third parties that have little chance for success in the national political system.

The argument that federalism undermines the national state as an instrument of change was used by supporters of *laissez-faire* within the AFL to make the point that socialism is impractical and that it is more fruitful to seek improvements in working conditions through collective bargaining than by legislation.[21] This view was echoed by Selig Perlman, who stressed that because of the division of powers and, above all, federalism, "American governments are inherently inadequate as instruments of economic reform." Perlman concluded that it made more sense for workers to rely on labor unions rather than political parties to improve their working lives.[22]

The fragmentation of political authority in America undermined arguments in favor of legislative activity that appeared more compelling in centralized states such as Britain. In Britain, Sidney and Beatrice Webb argued from the 1890s on that legislation of working conditions had practical advantages over collective bargaining. According to their detailed analysis of the costs and benefits of political activity, unions should become involved in politics because that is the most effective way to pursue their economic goals. First, according to the Webbs, legislation bearing on employment conditions had the great advantage of being permanent: once it was achieved, such legislation was extremely difficult to reverse. Second, legislation had the virtue of universality: it covered all workers in a particular occupation or industry, whether they were union members or not.[23]

These grounds for an active political strategy were not nearly as convincing in the United States, particularly before the Great Depression of the 1930s. The task of gaining legislation is far more uncertain, complex, time-consuming, and expensive in the United States than in a unitary parliamentary democracy. As an American Federation of Labor observer at the 1899 British Trades Union Congress, T. J. Tracey, noted, a key difference between Britain and the United States was that "instead of having one Imperial Government to appeal to for relief, there were forty-five States to be won over to their side, each requiring separate and distinct propaganda work."[24] When unions attempted to gain favorable legislation in individual states, they had to contend with state courts. Employers were often able to thwart regulatory policies on the grounds that they impinged on their constitutional right to do what they wished with their property. More often than not, unions discovered that legislation was effective only when they had the organizational resources to ensure that it was enforced. Laws could be rendered inoperative simply by inadequate state inspection.

Some contend that the power of the courts chiefly explains the business-oriented strategy of the AFL from the turn of the twentieth century. Political scientist Victoria Hattam notes that judicial interpretation eviscerated many labor laws and led AFL activists to prefer economic action over political reform. Her conclusion is that the AFL's strategy of business unionism "was the product of the distinctive institutional structure of the American state rather than the consequence of the party system, workers' aspirations, or the composition of the work force."[25] However, there are good reasons for believing that while the courts diminished the appeal of labor legislation, they could not have been responsible for the strength of voluntarism in the AFL. The courts made labor legislation difficult, but not impossible. In the early 1900s and beyond, the American Federation of

Labor continued to pursue legislation on a variety of fronts, includin[ ]
and women's labor and health and safety standards, where there was si[ ]
icant public support and where the potential benefits of authoritative co[ ]
trol outweighed the difficulty of achieving it.[26]

Business unionism involved general opposition to third-party political
activity and resistance to socialism and the Socialist party in particular. The
reasons for this stretch far beyond the unwillingness of judges to rule in
favor of labor legislation. Labor leaders who opposed political regulation of
working conditions justified this on the grounds that it threatened to
undermine their self-reliance, and would introduce an intolerable measure
of state interference in their activities, dividing their members into exclusive political camps.[27] The fact that there was always a risk that labor legislation would be ruled unconstitutional or would be otherwise blocked in
the courts made it a risky strategy. This, however, cannot explain why AFL
leaders did not respond by intensively pressuring the courts (as they did in
reaction to the mounting tide of labor injunctions in the 1900s) or why
they rejected independent political activity.

Another line of argument maintains that federalism weakened the
Socialist party by denying it a national focus of oppression against which it
could campaign. According to Theodore Lowi, "Even as the economy
became national, through national markets and exchanges, the states
remained the source and the focus of politics. There was, in effect, no national pattern of law, legitimation, or repression to confirm a socialist critique."[28]
Lowi argues that if workers were to develop a generalized critique of capitalism it was necessary for them to have a common set of political experiences,
and this did not happen because the separate states and cities were the effective units of governance for workers.

The history of working-class mobilization in Australia, Canada,
Germany, and Switzerland runs counter to Lowi's thesis about the
American experience. These countries, like the United States, have federal
constitutions. In fact, the authority of constituent states or regions in each
of them is *greater* than in the United States and yet their polities have
entrenched social democratic parties.[29] The Australian case is particularly
instructive because regional Labor parties were extremely successful both
before and after 1901 when the colonies came together to form a federal
government. After confederation, the Australian Labor party (ALP) adopted a two-tier organization reflecting the federal division of powers in the

910 the ALP, with 50 percent of the national vote,
labor administration in the world. It is telling that
ally speak of the Australian Labor parties in the
c into chapters covering each federal state.[30]

f socialism in the United States to federalism
nce of a strong social democratic party depends on
common national experiences. However, the record of the ALP
indicates that geographical diversity is no bar to the success of a social democratic party. During much of Australian history, political parties have been able to harness a variety of grievances in different parts of the country. Support for radical political movements everywhere in the industrialized world has been particularly strong among groups of workers who, for one reason or another, live in isolated communities, cut off from the larger society. The radicalism of hardrock miners, lumber workers, sailors, and coal miners, for example, is rooted in their experience of economic and social exploitation in geographically and/or socially segregated areas.[31]

One may argue that in America, federalism actually helped the Socialists because it split the country up into small constituencies. Although it was very difficult for the Socialist party to convince its potential supporters that it had a real chance in presidential elections, this was not necessarily the case in state or city elections. Given the geographical concentration of socialist support in a few states, radicals could argue that votes in these units could give them control of meaningful executive and legislative positions.[32] Social democratic or near social democratic movements were able to win statewide elections and/or major party primaries in North Dakota, Oklahoma, Minnesota, Wisconsin, California, Oregon, and Washington between 1918 and 1940.

The earliest example occurred in North Dakota. The Nonpartisan League (NPL), which was founded by former members of the Socialist party in 1916, captured the North Dakota Republican party and, after winning the state election, put into effect an ambitious agrarian program of state credit banks, extensive state services for farmers, and state ownership of public utilities, terminal elevators, flour mills, packing houses, and cold storage plants. It also legislated a maximum eight-hour day and an extensive package of labor legislation. Cases such as this, which include left-party administrations both at the state level and in a variety of cities (discussed in more detail in Chapter 3), do not fit easily with the strong version of the federalism argument, which claims that socialism failed in America because it could never be realized in a federal setting.

From a cross-national perspective, the relationship between regime type (federalist or unitary) and social democracy appears open-ended. Australia, Germany, and Canada have seen labor and social democratic parties implement social democratic reforms in federal settings. In the latter, the Cooperative Commonwealth Federation (CCF), along with its successor the New Democratic party (NDP), acquired and maintained control in Saskatchewan from 1944 to 1964, from 1971 to 1982, and again from the late 1980s to the present; in British Columbia from 1972 to 1975 and during the 1980s and 1990s; in Manitoba from 1967 to 1977 and from 1981 to 1986; and in Ontario from 1990 to 1995. In Quebec, the separatist Parti Québécois, which petitioned unsuccessfully to be admitted to the Socialist International (the application was opposed by the NDP), has governed the French-speaking province from 1976 through 1985 and again from 1994 to the present. Although the Canadian social democrats have never held federal power, provincial governments controlled by them have enacted major reforms, including the first government medical system, strongly pro-union legislation, and a variety of statist economic and welfare policies. The Canadian federal system has undoubtedly helped the cause of a third party representing labor and radical agrarians because it has allowed for a regional footholds and real political power in what otherwise would have been a predominantly two-party system. Since the early 1920s, Liberals and Conservatives held the great majority of seats in the federal parliament until the 1993 and 1997 elections, when two regionally based parties, the Bloc Québécois and the right-wing Reform party, became the two largest groups after the dominant Liberals in the House of Commons.

To sum up, federalism may either help or hinder minor parties in western democracies. Although American political culture in general has been antistatist, federalism has engendered considerable diversity of political experience, from racist government in the south, to laborism in some industrialized areas, to agrarian radicalism in the Wheat Belt. Both the successes of third-party candidates at the local and state levels in the United States and the experience of socialists in other federal societies suggest that the overall failure of American socialists cannot be explained by the federal character of the American political system.

.   .   .

The "Gift of the Suffrage"

Many scholars and socialists have pointed to the "gift of the suffrage," the fact that white males were given the right to vote without having to campaign for it, as an important explanation for the weakness of socialism and, more generally, of working-class political consciousness in America. Because the suffrage was extended to white males before industrialization, the lower classes were never melded into a cohesive, class-conscious block by their shared exclusion from the rights of political citizenship. There is some truth to this observation, but there is a more general relationship which underlies this. The key to the development of labor and socialist parties was the extent to which other political parties were able to build support among labor before the development of the working-class parties. Key here is the timing of a mature and broadly-based party system, rather than manhood suffrage per se.

The experience of the left in Australia and Switzerland is revealing. Although widespread suffrage was achieved relatively early in these countries, it did not lead workers to identify with non-working-class parties. A critical intervening variable is the extent to which an early stable party system develops as a result of manhood suffrage. If one does not, as in Australia and Switzerland, then early manhood suffrage is perfectly compatible with a strong working-class party.

Given its similarity to the United States as a new society and a former British colony, Australia is particularly revealing. In Australia, male suffrage seems to have contributed to the meteoric rise of state Labor parties once they were established in the early 1890s. In the first election it contested, in 1891, the New South Wales Labor Electoral League won over one-fifth of the vote, and by the first decade of the twentieth century, Labor parties had participated in every state government except that of Victoria. These gains were capped in 1910 when the Australian Labor party secured half the national vote.

One of the challenges in making comparisons such as this is that other causal factors vary. Working-class culture and class traditions were more deeply rooted in Australia than in the United States, which was a much more heterogeneous society both in terms of class and national origins. Immigration to Australia in the nineteenth century was preponderantly British and working-class, and had a significant Chartist component. The extension of manhood suffrage in the major Australian colonies in the 1850s put into effect the chief political demand of the British Chartist movement. Chartist demands for social regeneration and a moral economy, though unfulfilled, continued to have great influence in Australia through the second half of the nineteenth century. Further, a class vision of society was not alien to the large majority of those who worked on farms in Australia. In contrast to the United States, where most farms were owned by independent farmers, in Australia most who worked on farms were wage laborers. Only huge farms could survive in the harsh conditions of the Outback, and the workers who were employed there saw their interests as fundamentally similar to those of urban workers. Indeed, some of the most bitter strikes took place in the large sheepshearing farms of the interior.

Alongside these social and cultural contrasts are some party-political differences that appear to be powerful in explaining divergent social democratic outcomes in the two societies. By the time social democratic parties were established in the United States, the Democratic and Republican parties had already laid deep roots among urban workers. Because manhood suffrage occurred prior to the creation of working-class parties in the 1880s, the social democrats had to compete for the allegiance of workers who had already developed party-political loyalties in an established party system.

In Australia the situation was very different. There was no stable Australian party system before the country formed a federal polity at the beginning of the twentieth century. Instead there was a mosaic of weakly institutionalized parties based on shifting cleavages and allegiances that varied from state to state. Efforts on the part of the existing protectionist and free-trade parties to tie local organizations into national coalitions were greatly hampered in the years before Australia became united. The dominating political issue up to the early 1890s, when labor parties were first established, was land redistribution, which, however, never became the focus of a stable pattern of party-political cleavage. As a consequence of the late crystallization of party loyalties, the development of a stable party system followed, rather than preceded, the establishment of labor parties. The period of national awakening and political mobilization following the formation of the Commonwealth coincided with the establishment of the national Australian Labor party. This greatly aided labor's claim to represent the country's national aspirations. Instead of having to find its niche in an already structured political landscape, the Australian Labor party was the principal creator of the party system.

In line with its self-defined national role, the Australian Labor party emphasized unifying populist themes as much as or more than class conflict in competing for electoral support. To the extent that class-specific appeals were used, they were posed in extremely broad terms, and even this diffuse class vocabulary took second place to populist national appeals, particularly for racial exclusion. "Outpourings that might pass for ideology were soon hard to distinguish from nationalist thought," wrote Frank Farrell. "Concepts of working-class opposition to monopoly capitalism merged with a concern for the conditions of the 'masses' or the 'people.' Laborist ideology quickly incorporated city, craft, and rural labor, the 'little man' on the land, and anyone disposed to think of themselves as a 'battler' or a 'dinkum Aussie.' "[33]

At its 1905 conference, the ALP dedicated itself to two broad goals: first, "the cultivation of an Australian sentiment based upon the maintenance of racial purity and the development in Australia of an enlightened and self-reliant community," and second, "the securing of the full results of their industry to all producers by the collective ownership of monopolies and the extension of the industrial and economic function of the State and Municipality."[34]

Swiss experience reinforces the Australian example. Manhood suffrage was in place in Switzerland by 1848, well before the emergence of a large urban working class, yet the Swiss Social Democratic party performed quite strongly in national elections, receiving 6.9 percent of the vote in 1896, rising steadily to 20.1 percent in the last election before World War I, and ranging between 20 and 30 percent in the period since 1918. The party was aided by the fact that, as in Australia, no cohesive party system developed in the decades following the introduction of manhood suffrage. The Swiss party system reflected the decentralized character of the political system: the orientation of political parties varied appreciably from one canton to another.[35] The Social Democratic party was the first party to be organized along national lines.[36]

The cases of Australia and Switzerland compel us to pay attention to contextual factors in evaluating the consequences of early manhood suffrage in America. What appears to be crucial is not the mere fact of early suffrage, but its role in channeling workers within the major political parties and their city-based political machines. Early suffrage opened up the possibility of early participation by the less privileged in the American political system, but the character of that involvement was influenced by existing structures of political opportunity and the responses of workers to competing sources of identification and cleavage. Because workers were just one group among many, they had to ally with others to achieve their political objectives, which could be achieved most directly within the major parties. Workers sought political access just as the Democratic and Republican parties looked for new constituencies, a marriage of convenience that, as Amy Bridges has argued, led workers into cross-class alliances: "Workers became Republicans and Democrats not as the result of 'symbolic' or 'ritualistic' activities but in the service of quite objective working-class goals."[37]

In the absence of any shared political exclusion, the economic position of workers was just one potential source of cleavage. With the introduction of white manhood suffrage and other democratic reforms in many states in the 1820s and 1830s, radicals who were affiliated with fledgling trade unions and traditional groups of notables vied with a new class of professional politicians to gain control of the Jackson–Van Buren Democratic party. The success of the professionals resulted from their ability to forge a mass-based party relying on town and ward organizations that appealed at least as much to ethnocultural issues as to economic concerns. In the Jacksonian climate of democratic politics, attempts to mobilize workers through craft unions were viewed as backward-looking because they were not oriented to the task of creating broad election-winning coalitions.[38] The major parties competed for the support of workers in terms of ethnicity, religion, and cultural background, and these sources of mobilization reduced the salience of social class. Workers tended to participate in politics as members of divergent ethnic, religious, and cultural groups rather than as workers or artisans sharing specific economic grievances.

The weakness of class as an organizing principle of American politics was reinforced by the residential communities that workers formed. Ira Katznelson has stressed that party political groupings were based far more on spatial community than on occupation or economic class. Political parties had few, if any, direct connections with trade unions. As a result, "politics in the antebellum city came to be defined in the main, not as a politics of capital and labor, but as a politics of competition between ethnic-territorial communities from which capital was absent."[39]

This pattern of party mobilization was further institutionalized after the Civil War in the political machines that were strongest precisely where workers were most concentrated, in the larger cities and particularly in New

York and Chicago. Tammany Hall in New York and its functional equivalents elsewhere provided patronage, favors, and political access that cut across class. The deep roots of the political machine in the life of local communities tied even recent immigrants to the political process and posed a formidable barrier to subsequent attempts to mobilize workers along class lines.[40]

By the time socialist parties came on the scene in the last decade of the nineteenth century and trade unionists began to debate the issue of independent representation, the Democratic and Republican parties had been entrenched among large sections of labor for several decades. As an official of the United Mine Workers of America lamented, American workers "possessed the franchise fully enough, but did not use it in the right way. The Democrats and Republicans adhered to their parties as closely as to their religion. . . . Many of us think it just as easy to get the most bigoted Roman Catholic and Protestant to kneel down at the same altar to pray as to get the workers to vote together."[41]

The existence of democratic rights in America compelled socialists to focus narrowly on workers' economic interests and to emphasize economic exploitation in their attempts to attract workers away from established parties and existing channels of political expression. Radicals and socialists had strong support among many groups of workers in individual industries and labor unions, but economic grievances were far less inclusive than grievances rooted in shared political exclusion. Working-class radicals found their greatest support among particular groups of workers who were unable to form viable labor unions or whose unions were beaten down in the process of economic development. But despite socialist predictions that all workers would come to share common grievances as capitalism advanced, many of the most skilled and organized groups of workers found that they could defend or even improve their wages, hours, and working conditions through sectional or craft unionism.[42]

When workers had the opportunity to participate in the political system, they were subject to a variety of influences that integrated them into existing political channels. A venerable tradition in political theory links the act of participating in the political system to the development of loyalty to institutions. Although a sudden increase in participation may be destabilizing, the opportunity to participate and the belief that one's involvement is worthwhile tend to be related to satisfaction with the political system. As Gabriel Almond and Sidney Verba observed in their classic comparative study of political culture, "Those who consider themselves competent to participate are also more likely to believe that a democratic participatory system is the proper system to have."[43] The electoral reforms of the Jacksonian era multiplied the numbers of locally elected officials, instituted direct election of governors and presidential electors, and shortened terms of office. Logically, it would appear that these evolutionary measures serve to legitimate the democratic regime in the eyes of the populace and to encourage participation through existing channels.

In sum, early suffrage for white males molded the American working class indirectly by allowing native workers and repeated waves of immigrants to be influenced by established political institutions, above all the Democratic and Whig-Republican parties. As a result, workers were integrated into a party system based on ethnicity, religion, and residential community more than class or work community. Workers were drawn into the pragmatic game of coalition building in a polity dominated by two diverse and porous political parties that competed for their votes by appealing across class lines to a variety of nonclass sources of loyalty.

Ballot Access

The institutional barriers to third-party electoral success in the United States have included, from the 1890s on, the complicated and time-consuming process of gaining access to state ballots. Whereas major party candidates are automatically listed on ballots, minor parties have had to meet a series of regulations and hurdles adopted by individual state legislatures dominated by the major parties themselves. A number of states, including Montana, California, and Oklahoma, require that minor parties gain the signatures of 5 percent of the state's registered voters. Some states, e.g., Tennessee, demand an absolute number of signatures; others, including New York, have added a provision requiring a certain number of signatures from each county; in South Carolina, signatories have to list their precinct and voter registration numbers.

Perhaps as vexing for minor parties mounting national campaigns is that the deadlines for meeting such requirements vary from state to state. Petitions have to be circulated by one date and filed by another, sometimes several months before the election itself, in some cases only shortly before.

Thus, a minor party is effectively presented not with one national nomination process, but with almost as many as there are states to be contested, each with its own bureaucratic oddities.[44] Because these provisions are enforced by hostile major-party supporters, minor parties face the additional possibility that they will be denied access to the ballot on a technicality, as happened to the Socialist party in New York in 1946, when petitions collected in each county of the state with the requisite fifty signatures were held invalid because in some instances the canvasser inadvertently misstated his own district.[45]

The logic of ballot access under a plurality electoral system has given rise to strange bedfellows. Since the Democratic party usually had the most to lose when Socialists were on the ballot, it was the Democratic party rather than the Republican party that most frequently sought to deny the Socialist party a place on the ballot. Norman Thomas recounted that the Socialist party was thrown off the ballot in New York in 1946 not by " 'reactionary' Republicans, but 'liberal' Democrats, with the full knowledge and consent of such professedly ardent liberals as Herbert Lehman, formerly governor and then candidate for the United States Senate, and James Mead, candidate for governor. . . ."[46]

Ballot exclusion was a continual source of frustration for Socialists, but it cannot explain the failure of socialism in America. The political restrictions faced by the Socialist party were not particularly imposing when compared to the suppression of socialists and their organizations in several European countries in the pre–World War I decades, as we detail in Chapter 7. Socialists generally succeeded in their efforts to gain access to the ballot, as did many nonsocialist third-party candidacies, including relatively large movements, like George Wallace's American Independent party in 1968 and Perot's independent candidacy in 1992, his Reform party in 1996, and smaller movements, such as Henry Wallace's Progressive party in 1948, John Anderson's independent candidacy in 1980, and the Libertarian and the Natural Law parties in the 1980s and 1990s.

Party Flexibility

The American political system not only punishes small parties but also provides strong incentives for ideological diffuseness within the major parties.

The electoral system, the separation of the executive branch from the legislature, and the primary nomination system have combined to encourage major parties to undercut third ones by adopting parts of their platforms when they threaten to be successful in order to "steal their thunder."[47] The dampening effect of these factors may be exemplified by the role they played in various American elections contested by Socialists from the turn of the century to the 1930s, and by comparisons with Canada.

Majority government in any democratic society requires forming coalitions among competing interest and value groups. Under the American system there is a strong incentive to make those coalitions *within parties before elections* rather than across parties after elections, as in polities that have proportional representation. Given the high degree of geographical, ethnic, and social diversity of American society, coalition-building produces open and opportunistic political parties.[48] As James MacGregor Burns has observed, "Majoritarian strategy assumes that in the end politicians will rise above principle in order to win an election."[49]

Although the plurality electoral system is a powerful stimulant in creating ideologically diffuse catchall parties, such parties are clearly not unique to the United States. All political parties operating in plurality electoral systems are subject, in some degree, to the pressures discussed above. However, anyone who has observed American political parties from a comparative standpoint can hardly fail to be impressed by the exceptional degree of ideological diffuseness, permeable channels of recruitment, internal dissonance, and electoral opportunism of the Democratic and Republican parties.[50] These characteristics are the outcome of unique American conditions, particularly the separation of the executive and legislature and the primary nomination system. Because the executive and legislative branches are divided, party unity in the legislature is not necessary to sustain the government in office. In contrast to parliamentary systems where parties tend to be tightly disciplined to support their leaders and policies, the division of powers in America allows legislators wide latitude to vote as they wish, reacting to their constituents and financial backers. With this in mind, Nelson Polsby has noted that "the analogies to parliaments which predominate in intelligent conversation about Congress do the powers of our national legislature less than justice. For unlike parliaments the world around, the American Congress dissolves neither itself nor the government when it has serious disagreement with its Executive."[51]

Party labels have rarely impeded members of Congress from representing the interests or value groups that predominate in their individual constituencies, even when doing this brings them into conflict with others in their own party. In America, congressional politics is essentially local, as the late Speaker of the House Tip O'Neill observed. The United States is unique among polities with plurality electoral systems in that the electoral pressures toward building diverse coalitions have not been countered by the need to build coherent, tightly disciplined parties in order to sustain a parliamentary majority to keep the executive in office.

The innovation of the popular nomination primary from the early years of the twentieth century has reinforced this tendency by providing opportunities for ideologues to join and take over segments of either party. In the United States, in contrast to other democracies, party elites are not able to control access to the spoils of party candidacy. In seeking the broadest possible support, they must tolerate varied opinion within their ranks. This creates a constant lure for frustrated minority candidates or potential ones to campaign for political office within one of the major parties. In addition, it may be more rewarding for an ideological group to capture the label of a major party than to run its own candidate.[52]

This strategy has been used with considerable success by radicals who have sought to organize a party within one of the major parties, as in the case, already noted, of the Nonpartisan League in North Dakota and other midwestern states from 1916 on. Further examples are the Farmer Labor League in Oklahoma in 1923, the Commonwealth Federation in Oregon and Washington in the 1930s, and Upton Sinclair's End Poverty in California (EPIC) gubernatorial campaign in 1934. The Communists followed this strategy, operating sub rosa among the Democrats in the late 1930s and the 1940s as have a number of small radical groups that emerged from the New Left.

Political analysts from Werner Sombart to the present have pointed to the permeability of the major parties and the possibilities of advancement within them as an important factor reducing third-party strength. Not only are radicals induced to vote for one of the major parties rather than throw their vote to a candidate less likely to achieve office, but their leaders have the option of trying to gain office by working directly within a major party. And, as noted, the major parties themselves are vulnerable to takeovers by activist minorities by virtue of the primary system, which greatly weakens the hold of the established party leadership over recruitment into the party hierarchy.

Given the ideological diffuseness of the major parties in the United States, the lack of party discipline in Congress, and the institutional porousness of the major parties, third parties have faced formidable competition at every level of American government. Minor-party candidates have repeatedly sought to gain political office, but in no other democracy has the duopoly of the two major parties over political representation been so complete. Significant third-party movements have generally emerged in the United States when groups, interests, or factions believe that they are being ignored by both major parties—that neither party is "the lesser of two evils."[53] But after the dissidents have demonstrated their support base, one or both of the major-party coalitions may respond by coopting elements of the minor-party program or by nominating candidates who speak the language of the protest. Third parties have typically had the bittersweet experience of gaining some of their legislative demands while losing the basis for continued organization as a separate party. Richard Hofstadter described this experience with the metaphor of the bee that dies after having stung.[54]

The Workingmen's parties that emerged during the late 1820s provide historical testimony. The major legislative demand of the Workingmen's parties, the ten-hour day, was passed into law by major-party administrations in Rhode Island, New Hampshire, Maine, New Jersey, and Connecticut, states where artisans and workers were particularly concentrated. In New York, where limits on the workday were achieved only later through strikes, the labor movement pressured the state government into abolishing imprisonment for debt, halting restrictive voter registration regulations, and weakening the militia system. Given the opportunism of the major parties in the search for votes, participation in party politics was frustrating for those who sought to sustain a "pure" radical alternative to the major parties. Sean Wilentz describes the decline of the Workingmen's movement as "beset by invasion, deflection, co-option, and eventual ruin at the hands of outsiders and their radical pawns."[55]

In 1872, the Democratic presidential nomination of Horace Greeley, social reformer and member of the pre–Civil War Fourierist socialist movement, undermined the effort of the American affiliate of the First International, the National Labor Union, to run David Davis for the presidency as a labor candidate. A quarter of a century later, the most sustained and successful effort to build a left third party which appealed to farmers and workers, the People's party, failed when the Democrats absorbed it by accepting much of the Populist program and nominating a militant advocate of agrarianism, William Jennings Bryan, for the presidency.

Party Flexibility and the AFL

Party permeability and the competition of major-party candidates for labor support helped to lure the American Federation of Labor away from a third-party strategy into a policy of trying to influence the major parties by "rewarding friends" and "punishing enemies." The AFL was the only union federation among those in western industrialized societies not to give its support to a working-class political party. This greatly weakened the organizational and financial base of third-party efforts in America. Canada, Great Britain, Australia, and New Zealand stand by way of contrast. Each had radical or working-class parties that were eventually institutionalized with the backing of the major unions. The syndicalist and antistatist orientation of the AFL reflected American culture, but was also a practical response to constraints and opportunities in the American political system.[56]

Many unionists were by no means convinced of the desirability of working within the major parties prior to the formation of the AFL, but came to accept this approach as they experienced the disappointments of third-party political activity, particularly their failure to elect Henry George mayor of New York in 1884. However, American unions scored some successes in influencing the major parties in the years approaching the turn of the century. AFL unions were particularly pleased with the Democratic party's nomination of William Jennings Bryan as presidential candidate in 1896. Bryan's platform included both anti-injunction and anti-immigration planks specifically directed to gain the support of organized labor.

Bryan was nominated again by the Democratic party in 1900 and 1908 and made a strong and evidently successful pitch for the union vote in competition with the Socialist party. Democratic efforts to woo the AFL intensified. With Woodrow Wilson's administration and the Clayton Act (1914), the AFL could point to results as a justification of its policy. The Wilson administration enacted several prolabor measures, including workmen's compensation, child labor legislation, a progressive income tax, and legislation regulating the working conditions of seamen, and in addition appointed William B. Wilson, an official of the United Mine Workers of America, as first secretary of labor. Even unions that were sympathetic to socialism were drawn into the orbit of two-party competition in support of the Democratic party. In the 1916 presidential election, when Wilson was opposed by the anti-union Charles Evans Hughes, many socialist-leaning unions, including the influential Machinists Union, chose to support Wilson rather than Allan Benson, the candidate of the Socialist party.

The AFL turned to independent third-party activity in the 1924 presidential election, but this decision and the federation's unwillingness to stay the course thereafter illustrate how labor's orientation to independent party politics was conditioned by the major parties. Essentially, the AFL supported an independent ticket because the possibility for cooperation with the Democrats was doomed by the nominee and platform of the 1924 convention. As noted above, the Democrat John W. Davis ran against Calvin Coolidge on a platform that ignored the demands of labor and agrarian groups, and thus encouraged them to support a third candidate, progressive Republican senator Robert La Follette, who was also endorsed by the Socialists. La Follette and the unions, however, insisted that he and his running mate, Democratic senator Burton Wheeler, were "independent" candidates and their decision to run did not involve a commitment to establishing a third party or the acceptance of statist doctrines. The AFL's position was clear:

The Republican convention nominated candidates unacceptable to labor. . . . The Democratic convention nominated candidates unacceptable to labor. . . . There remain the candidacies of Robert M. La Follette and Burton K. Wheeler, the first an independent Republican, the second an independent Democrat running as such. . . . Cooperation hereby urged is not a pledge of identification with an independent party movement or a third party, nor can it be construed as support for such a party, group, or movement except as such action accords with our nonpartisan political policy. We do not accept government as the solution of the problems of life. Major problems of life and labor must be dealt with by voluntary groups and organizations of which trade unions are an essential and integral part. Neither can this cooperation imply our support, acceptance or endorsement of policies or principles advocated by any minority groups or organizations that may see fit to support the candidacies of Senator La Follette and Senator Wheeler.[57]

It was evident that the AFL had no intention of organizing a permanent third party. Its 1923 convention had overwhelmingly defeated a motion calling for a labor party, and to make sure that no one misunderstood the federation's position toward cooperation with the Socialists, Samuel Gompers wrote in its official organ in September 1924 that "our support of Senator La Follette does not in any way, or to any degree, identify us with or commit us to doctrines advanced by any other group that may be supporting the same candidates. These candidates have the support of minority groups . . . with which we are and have been in the sharpest kind of disagreement. We shall continue to oppose these doctrines at all times. . . ."[58] Gompers explained the shift from the AFL's previous policies, which largely involved support of Democratic candidates, on the grounds that the "situation is entirely different from the previous campaigns. Here we have practically no choice, one [party] is no nearer to us than the other."[59] The Socialists, though unhappy with the anti-third-party position of La Follette, Wheeler, and the AFL, cooperated completely with the campaign. Their organization helped get the ticket on the ballot in many states.

In retrospect, it would appear that the close to five million votes secured by the Progressive ticket were more than should have been expected in a period marked by economic prosperity, in which "the business interests were apparently more thoroughly entrenched, in both political power and public esteem, than at any time since the days of Harrison and McKinley." Economic and social factors were simply not "strong enough to compel changes in voting behavior and to remold party lines."[60]

The Democratic party secured only 28.8 percent of the presidential vote in 1924, compared to 16.6 percent for the hastily organized Progressives, and ran behind the latter in twelve states. The Democrats learned their lesson. As George Sould noted, "The Democratic party did not thereafter repeat its mistake of 1924; it took pains [in succeeding elections] to nominate men who might enlist labor support—Alfred E. Smith [in 1928] and Franklin D. Roosevelt [in 1932]."[61] The Democrats "realized that in order to survive they would have to appeal to the agrarians and urban workers, providing a distinctive alternative to the Republicans."[62]

The political orientation of the major parties created the large left-third-party movement in the 1920s: "Rejected by the Republicans and ignored by the Democrats, precisely because the labor and agrarian forces appeared so weak, many of their leaders turned to serious consideration of a third ticket."[63] But once these groups had demonstrated that they could drain away significant support, their object had been accomplished and they returned to operating as pressure groups within the major parties. The hard fact was that organized labor and agriculture wanted to be effective, and to have friends rather than enemies in high office. The 1924 Progressive campaign did not produce third-party members in Congress, except in Minnesota, where the Farmer-Labor party was a strong state party. Senators La Follette and Wheeler were members of the Republican and Democratic party, respectively. Fiorello La Guardia was reelected on the Socialist party ticket from New York, although he continued to sit in the House of Representatives as a Republican.

In 1928, both major parties chose as their nominee for president the candidate most acceptable to the unions: Herbert Hoover, then regarded as a great humanitarian and progressive who favored collective bargaining, and Alfred E. Smith, who as governor of New York had a strong prolabor and liberal record. As a result the AFL formally refused to endorse either major-party candidate; as historian Vaughn Bornet points out, "neither one of them [was] recognizable as an 'enemy.'" Smith campaigned more vigorously for labor's vote than Hoover. He strongly opposed the use of the injunction against labor, stressed the unequal distribution of income, discussed the problems of the unemployed (pledging to remedy them by public works), and reminded unionists of the "accomplishments of the Wilson administration." As a result, "almost invariably any outspoken partisanship of the A.F. of L. leaders, unions and organizations was exerted for Governor Smith." The Socialists, therefore, "considered [Smith] their chief competitor" and concentrated their fire on him.[64]

Roosevelt and the Protest of the 1930s

With the coming of the Great Depression in the 1930s, a sharp increase in protest and anticapitalist sentiment threatened to undermine the existing political system and create new political parties. The findings of diverse opinion polls, as well as the electoral support given to local radical, progressive, and prolabor candidates, indicate that a large minority of Americans were ready to back social democratic proposals. It is significant, then, that even with the growth of class consciousness in America, no national third party was able to break the duopoly. Radicals who operated within the two-party system were often able to achieve local victories, but these accomplishments never culminated in the creation of a sustainable third party or left-wing ideological movement. The thirties dramatically demonstrated not only the power of America's coalitional two-party system to dissuade a national third party, but also the deeply antistatist, individualistic character of its electorate.

We will discuss the politics of the 1930s in some detail because it furnishes an excellent example of the way the American presidential system has worked to frustrate third-party efforts. Franklin D. Roosevelt played a unique role in keeping the country politically stable during its greatest economic crisis. But he did so in classic or traditional fashion. He spent considerable time wooing those on the left. And though many leftists recognized that Roosevelt was trying to save capitalism, they could not afford to risk his defeat by supporting a national third party.

Powerful leftist third-party movements emerged in Minnesota, Wisconsin, and New York.[65] In other states, radicals successfully advanced alternative political movements by pursuing a strategy of running in major-party primaries. In California, Upton Sinclair, who had run as a Socialist for governor in 1932 and received 50,000 votes, organized the End Poverty in California (EPIC) movement, which won a majority in the 1934 Democratic gubernatorial primaries. He was defeated after a bitter business-financed campaign in the general election, after securing over 900,000 votes. By 1938, former EPIC leaders had captured the California governorship and a U.S. Senate seat.[66] In Washington and Oregon, the Commonwealth Federations, patterning themselves after the social democratic Cooperative Commonwealth Federation of Canada, won a number of state and congressional posts and controlled the state Democratic parties for several years.[67] In North Dakota, the revived radical Nonpartisan League, still operating within the Republican party, won the governorship, a U.S. Senate seat, and both congressional seats in 1932, and continued to win other elections throughout the decade.[68] In Minnesota, the Farmer-Labor party captured the governership and five house seats. Wisconsin, too, witnessed an electorally powerful Progressive party backed by the Socialists.

The Socialist and Communist parties grew substantially as well. In 1932 the Socialist party had 15,000 members. Its electoral support, however, was much broader, as indicated by the 1932 presidential election, in which Norman Thomas received close to 900,000 votes, up from 267,000 in 1928.[69] The Socialist party's membership increased to 25,000 by 1935. As a result of leftist enthusiasm for President Roosevelt, however, its presidential vote declined to 188,000 in 1936, fewer votes than the party had attained in any presidential contest since 1900.[70] The Communist party, on the other hand, backed President Roosevelt from 1936 on, and its membership grew steadily, numbering between 80,000 and 90,000 at its high point in 1939. According to Peggy Dennis, whose husband was to become the national secretary of the party in the 1950s, Communists played major roles in "left center" winning electoral coalitions in four states and had significant influence in thirty-one others, mainly within the Democratic party.[71] Although her estimate may be exaggerated, considerable evidence attests to the Communist party's great strength within other parties in California, Minnesota, New York, and the state of Washington.[72]

National surveys suggest that the leftward shift in public opinion during the 1930s was even more extensive than indicated by third-party voting or membership in radical organizations. Although large leftist third parties existed only in Minnesota, New York, and Wisconsin, three Gallup polls taken between December 1936 and January 1938 found that between 14 and 16 percent of those polled said they would not merely vote for but "would join" a Farmer-Labor party if one was organized. Of those interviewees expressing an opinion in 1937, 21 percent voiced a readiness to join a new party.[73]

If the Great Depression, with all of its attendant effects, shifted national attitudes to the left, why was it that no strong radical movement committed itself to a third party during these years? A key part of the explanation was that President Roosevelt succeeded in including left-wing protest in his New Deal coalition. He used two basic tactics. First, he responded to the various outgroups by incorporating in his own rhetoric many of their demands. Second, he absorbed the leaders of these groups into his following. These reflected conscious efforts to undercut left-wing radicals, to preserve capitalism.

Franklin Roosevelt demonstrated his skill at co-opting the rhetoric and demands of opposition groups the year before his 1936 reelection, when demagogic Senator Huey Long of Louisiana threatened to run on a third-party Share-Our-Wealth ticket.[74] This possibility was particularly threatening because a "secret" public opinion poll conducted in 1935 for the Democratic National Committee suggested that Long might get three to four million votes, throwing several states over to the Republicans if he ran at the head of a third party.[75] At the same time several progressive senators "like La Follette, Cutting, Nye, etc. . . . [were] flirting with the idea of a third ticket," and as a result Roosevelt was concerned that the 1936 election might witness a Progressive Republican ticket, headed by Robert La Follette, alongside a "Share-Our-Wealth" ticket.[76]

To prevent this, Roosevelt shifted to the left in rhetoric and, to some extent, in policy, consciously seeking to steal the thunder of his populist critics.[77] In discussions concerning radical and populist anticapitalist protest, the president stated that to save capitalism from itself and its opponents he might have to "equalize the distribution of wealth," which could necessitate "throw[ing] to the wolves the forty-six men who are reported to have incomes in excess of one million dollars a year."[78] Roosevelt responded to the "share-the-wealth clamor" by advancing tax reforms designed to stop "an unjust concentration of wealth and economic power."[79] Attacking "the perpetuation of great and undesirable concentration of control in a relatively few individuals over the employment and welfare of many, many others," he singled out "the disturbing effects upon our national life that come from inheritance of wealth and power."[80] The president promised to raise income and dividend taxes, to enact a sharply graduated inheritance tax, and to use tax policy to discriminate against large corporations. Huey Long reacted by charging that the President was stealing his program.[81]

President Roosevelt also became more overtly supportive of trade unions, although he did not endorse the most important piece of proposed labor legislation, Senator Robert Wagner's labor relations bill, until shortly before its passage.[82] The bill "threw the weight of government behind the right of labor to bargain collectively, and compelled employers to accede peacefully to the unionization of their plants. It imposed no reciprocal obligations of any kind on unions."[83]

Raymond Moley, an organizer of President Roosevelt's "brain trust" who later defected from the administration, emphasized that the president, through these and other policies and statements, sought to identify himself with the objectives of the unemployed, minorities, and farmers, as well as "the growing membership of the Congress of Industrial Organizations (CIO), Norman Thomas' vanishing army of orthodox Socialists, Republican progressives and Farmer-Laborites, Share-the-Wealthers, single-taxers, Sinclairites, Townsendites [and] Coughlinites."[84]

Beyond adopting leftist rhetoric and offering progressive policies in exchange for support from radical and economically depressed constituencies, President Roosevelt also sought to recruit the actual leaders of protest groups by convincing them that they were part of his coalition. He gave those who held state and local public office access to federal patronage, particularly in Minnesota, Wisconsin, and New York, where strong statewide third parties existed. Electorally powerful non-Democrats whom Roosevelt supported included Minnesota governor Floyd Olson (Farmer-Labor party), New York City mayor Fiorello La Guardia (American Labor party), and Nebraska senator George Norris (Independent), as well as Wisconsin governor Philip La Follette and his brother, Senator Robert La Follette, Jr. (both Progressive party).[85] This strategy had an impact. In 1937, Philip La Follette's executive secretary told Daniel Hoan, the Socialist mayor of Milwaukee, that a national third party never would be launched while Roosevelt was "in the saddle," because Roosevelt had "put so many outstanding liberals on his payroll [that] . . . any third party movement would lack sufficient leadership."[86] The president told leftist leaders that he was on their side and that his ultimate goal was to transform the Democratic party into an ideologically coherent progressive party in which they could hope to play a leading role.[87] A few times he even implied that to secure ideological realignment, he personally might go the third-party route, following in the footsteps of his cousin Theodore Roosevelt.

Franklin Roosevelt ran his 1936 presidential campaign as a progressive coalition, not as a Democratic party activity. Arthur M. Schlesinger, Jr., has described Roosevelt's tactics as follows:

> As the campaign developed, the Democratic party seemed more and more submerged in the New Deal coalition. The most active campaigners in addition to Roosevelt—Ickes, Wallace, Hugh Johnson—were men identified with the New Deal, not with the professional Democratic organization. Loyalty to the cause superseded loyalty to the party as the criterion for administration support. In Minnesota, the Democratic ticket thus withdrew in favor of the Farmer-Labor ticket; in Nebraska, Roosevelt ignored the Democratic candidate and endorsed George Norris; in Wisconsin, the New Deal worked with the Progressives; in Massachusetts,

the administration declined to back James M. Curley, the Democratic candidate for senator. It was evident that the basis of the campaign would be the mobilization beyond the Democratic party of all the elements in the New Deal coalition—liberals, labor, farmers, women, minorities. To do this required the elaborate structure of subsidiary organizations and committees which Roosevelt began urging . . . as early as January 1936.[88]

Roosevelt was reelected by an overwhelming majority in 1936—he carried every state except Maine and Vermont. Yet his second term proved much less innovative than his first. This was due, in part, to several Supreme Court decisions during 1936 striking down various New Deal laws as unconstitutional and the president's subsequent inability to mobilize popular protest against the Court. Reacting to a perceived shift in the public mood to the right, particularly from 1938 on, Roosevelt substantially reduced his reform efforts. The change, however, did not lead to a loss of leftist support. The Communist party, following its Soviet-dictated Popular Front policy, actively opposed efforts in a number of states to create independent radical anti-Roosevelt political campaigns. Sounding like a moderate liberal group, it increased its membership, formed large front groups, and generally expanded its influence in the labor movement.[89] On the assumption that the 1937–38 recession had undermined Roosevelt's prestige, Wisconsin governor Philip La Follette attempted in 1938 to create a new third party, the National Progressives of America. The president responded with a renewed effort to co-opt such opposition. He told Harold Ickes in May 1938 that he hoped to handle the problem by "a little confidential . . . talking with [Philip's brother], Wisconsin Senator Bob La Follette."[90] As Ickes wrote in his diary:

What he indicated that he would say to La Follette was that their Progressive movement was all right, if they didn't get too far out.

He has it in mind, as 1940 approaches, to make overtures to the La Follettes and the Farmer-Labor group in Minnesota. He would be willing to make a deal with the La Follettes as the result of which Bob La Follette could go into the next Cabinet as Secretary of State. . . . [T]hen Phil could go into the Senate and this would take care of both of them. . . .

[The President further indicated that] [s]omething also could be done to bring in the Farmer-Labor group.[91]

The midterm elections in November 1938, however, made it unnecessary for President Roosevelt to react to a possible electoral threat from the left. Both the Wisconsin Progressive party and the Minnesota Farmer-Labor party suffered crushing defeats, losing most of their congressional seats, and Republicans badly defeated both Philip La Follette in Wisconsin and Elmer Benson in Minnesota in their gubernatorial reelection campaigns.[92] Although unhappy about the Republicans' gaining eighty-one seats in the House, eight seats in the Senate, and thirteen governorships, the president wrote a post-election letter to his friend Josephus Daniels, ambassador to Mexico, in which he noted that some good things had occurred: "We have on the positive side eliminated Phil La Follette and the Farmer-Labor people in the Northwest as a standing Third Party threat."[93]

But subsequently, President Roosevelt made an effort to win maximum support for his third-term race by integrating non-Democratic reformers into the party. In June 1939, Roosevelt told Henry Wallace and Harold Ickes of his desire to work out an alliance between Wisconsin Progressives and Democrats whereby the Democrats would support Progressive Bob La Follette for reelection as senator and the Progressives would back a Democratic gubernatorial candidate with progressive views. Roosevelt thought that "in this way Wisconsin [could] be won" for the Democratic presidential ticket.[94] In Minnesota, the Democratic National Committee, with Roosevelt's backing, worked to link the weakened Farmer-Labor party with the Democrats, hoping that the two could eventually be merged.[95]

Roosevelt's efforts to enlarge and maintain his coalition were not limited to his dealings with those to his political left. A major part of his electoral and congressional support came from southern whites and Catholics. Thus, although Roosevelt was probably more open to sympathetic discussions with black leaders and more supportive of their requests than previous presidents, he refused to press for measures—such as an antilynching bill—that were likely to alienate white southerners.[96] Similarly, Roosevelt's dependence on Catholic support made him unresponsive to the left's concerns during the Spanish Civil War. Although the left urged support of the Loyalist cause, Roosevelt, aware of the pro-Falangist leanings of the Catholic part of his coalition, insisted on maintaining an embargo on the supply of arms to both sides even though this hurt the Loyalists more, since Franco's forces had other sources of supply.[97]

Although party divisions became more class-based, efforts to build a national left-wing third party failed. This cannot be explained by any absence of protest or popular support for radical efforts. Several developments attest to the growth of class conflict and the vigor of anticapitalist feeling that resulted from the Great Depression: mass demonstrations of the unemployed, the aggressive tactics and radical views of farm groups, widespread militancy and disdain for private property exhibited by many groups of workers, leftist views expressed by large minorities in the opinion surveys, and, finally, the strong and disparate electoral support given to leftist third parties and organized factions within the major parties in New York, Washington, Wisconsin, Minnesota, Nebraska, North Dakota, Oregon, and California.[98]

President Roosevelt recognized that the long-range interests of his coalition and the Democratic party were best served by encouraging radical groups, whether inside or outside the party, to feel as though they were part of his political entourage. Thus, as we have seen, he showed a willingness to endorse local and statewide third-party or independent candidates and give them a share of federal patronage. In return, they were expected to support the president's reelection. Time and again between 1935 and 1940, meetings to lay the basis for a national third party went awry because those involved recognized that the bulk of their constituencies favored reelecting the president. And in the last analysis, most radical, labor, and minority-group leaders supported the president as well. Certainly these leaders objected to particular Roosevelt policies, to his compromises with conservatives, and, in some cases, to his refusals to back their group or organization in some major conflict. Nevertheless, they concluded that a government in which they could play a part, which had shown some responsiveness to their concerns, and which acknowledged their importance was far preferable to a Republican administration with strong links to business.

The economic crisis of the 1930s was more severe in the United States than in any other large society except Germany. It presented American radicals with their greatest opportunity to build a third party since World War I, but the constitutional system and the brilliant way in which Franklin Delano Roosevelt co-opted the left prevented this. The formation of such a party in Canada, where socialist and labor movements had been weak prior to the 1930s, suggests that under other political conditions discontent could have been channeled into a viable third party.

.   .   .

Comparison with Canada

In Canada the ability of relatively weak labor and socialist groups to elect representatives to provincial legislatures and the federal House of Commons prior to the 1930s reduced the pressure on them to back one of the two major parties, the Liberals or the Conservatives. By virtue of the parliamentary system, Canadian socialists could focus on elections within single constituencies, rather than in the nation as a whole, without having to suffer a negative tailcoat effect as a result of their inability to win head-of-government elections. Their legislative representatives formed a distinct opposition party in some provinces and in the federal House of Commons, and on more than one occasion socialists were the fulcrum party, when neither the Liberals nor the Conservatives could muster a majority. As early as 1900, for example, two socialists held the balance of power in the British Columbia legislature and "were able to exact a great deal of prolabor legislation as their price for not bringing the government down."[99]

Canada's parliamentary system facilitated the success of agrarian and social democratic third parties following an economic downturn in the early 1920s. J. S. Woodsworth was elected as an Independent Labor party (ILP) member to the House of Commons from Winnipeg and remained in the House for the next two decades as the leader of Canadian socialism. He led a group of two members, who were formally recognized in the House as a national party.[100]

In 1926, the tiny Labor group, with the backing of third-party United Farmer MPs from Alberta, held the balance of power in a House almost equally divided between Liberals and Conservatives. They were able to secure the first old-age pension act in Canada in return for keeping the Liberal government in office. But perhaps more important than these policy achievements was the fact that the party could use its representation in Parliament to publicize its existence. In the words of a Canadian historian, the party "used Ottawa as 'a great broadcasting machine for working class education.' "[101] These activities were extremely important in preparing the way for the formation of Canada's first effective national socialist party, the Cooperative Commonwealth Federation (CCF), which was founded in 1933. The handful of socialist and left-wing farmer MPs elected from Alberta and Manitoba in the twenties were able to play a crucial part in creating the CCF. As Martin Robin notes, "A small group of independent MPs, favored by House rules which recognized their independence and facing disciplined major parties, could effectively claim a separate party existence and use parliament for propaganda and legislative purposes."[102]

In the mid-thirties, the new Cooperative Commonwealth Federation secured significant representation in the provincial legislatures of British Columbia (where it had seven seats), Manitoba (seven seats), and Saskatchewan (ten seats). It also captured seven federal constituencies with 8.9 percent of the national vote in the 1935 election to the House of Commons. Many Canadian labor leaders, particularly those active in the CIO-affiliated Canadian Congress of Labor, backed the socialist party.

Although the CCF had only a small number of MPs until the end of World War II, it was present in all the parliamentary debates as an independent force. Historian Gad Horowitz notes that: "in Canada once a third party elects even a handful of MPs, it is in the national limelight. . . . [Its leader shares] the limelight with the prime minister and the leader of the opposition."[103]

During the 1930s and early 1940s, Canadian social legislation moved in the same direction as American social legislation, although with much less fanfare. The dominant Liberal party, under MacKenzie King, reacted to the presence of the CCF in what has been described as "antagonistic symbiosis." The left party initially advocated reforms, some of which the larger one eventually implemented. Thus, support for a third party was not seen as wasted, but rather as the effective way in which people could press the major party (or parties) to move in the direction they favored. Prime Minister MacKenzie King told M. J. Coldwell, who succeeded Woodsworth as national leader of the CCF, that "the CCF has performed the valuable function of popularizing reforms so that he could introduce them when public opinion was ripe."[104]

The presence of a socialist party in Parliament identified King and the Liberals with the center; in the United States, however, the absence of a party to the left of Roosevelt and the Democrats enabled them to take on the aura of the left party, the prolabor party. King once described socialists as "Liberals in a hurry," but he "had to answer to the arguments of socialism, and in doing so he had to spell out his liberalism." As a result of this difference, the mood of King Liberalism was conservative and defensive. There was no "feeling of high adventure, sense of iconoclasm, genuine 'radicalism' about it; the young men who became New Dealers in the United States became CCFers in Canada."[105]

Pro-CCF labor leaders explained the differences between their political strategy and that of their American peers by the absence of a primary system in Canada. Unlike Americans, they could not work within the major parties to nominate and elect prolabor members of Parliament who could then support prolabor positions even if this conflicted with the program of their party leaders. A bulletin published by the Canadian Labor Congress noted that American congressmen can vote independently of their party line. Hence, treating each candidate individually, regardless of party, makes far more sense in the United States than in Canada, where political parties are cohesive groupings. Canadian socialist labor leaders did not have to make the painful choice which confronted Walter Reuther and other American socialist labor leaders, who realized that if they were to influence events they would have to abandon the Socialist party and join the New Deal coalition.[106]

There is no way to estimate whether as many, or possibly more, Americans would have been as prone to help form a socialist party during the thirties as Canadians did under a different party and electoral system. The fact that close to a fifth of Americans indicated approval of a farmer-labor or labor party in polls taken during the 1936–38 period, a much larger proportion than were voting for the CCF, may be taken as evidence in this direction, but responses to such hypothetical questions are hardly conclusive. Still, it may also be noted that in July 1942, when the Roper-Fortune poll asked: "Do you think some form of Socialism would be a good thing or a bad thing for the country as a whole?" a quarter of all Americans replied that it would be "a good thing," compared to 40 percent who answered, "a bad thing" and 34 percent who said they did not know. The presidential system, the "Roosevelt factor," clearly cannot be ignored in any explanation of why the 1930s seemingly had little impact on the structure of the polity.

Conclusion

In this chapter we have engaged in a variety of comparative analyses—across societies and within them—to evaluate explanations for the failure of American third parties in general and the failure of the Socialist party in particular. We have argued that basic rules of the political game in the United States—the plurality electoral system, the presidency, the separation of powers, and primaries—sustain a two-party duopoly at the national level. The American political system creates incentives and disincentives for two, and only two, broad, porous, ideologically diffuse national political parties. The effort of the Socialist party to survive as a third party alongside the two major parties was doomed by institutional arrangements over which it had little or no power. From this standpoint the fate of the Socialist party may be regarded as a particular example of the inability of all minor-party attempts to survive in competition with the major parties.

But our understanding of the failure of socialism in America cannot stop here. Why were socialists unable—or unwilling—to shape one of the major parties in their own image? The question is all the more pertinent because an important source of two-party duopoly has been the extraordinary porousness of the major parties. To explain why only two parties dominate does not explain why one of them was not socialist in orientation.

The same comparative standpoint that explains two-party duopoly in the United States also reveals that social democratic parties were able to break into established two-party systems elsewhere. Taking advantage of formidable social, political, and organizational resources, social democratic parties managed to overcome considerable systemic barriers in all industrial democracies except the United States. Why could the American Socialist party not do the same? To do this one needs to turn to socialist and labor strategy in the context of American society and culture.

One must also explain why the Socialist party did not match the performance of other third parties. Since the Civil War, Socialist electoral performance has been eclipsed by the Greenbackers with more than a million votes in the midterm elections of 1878, the Populists with over a million votes (8.5 percent) in the 1892 presidential election and 1.5 million votes in 1894, La Follette's 16.6 percent of the presidential vote in 1924, and the post–World War II presidential candidacies of George Wallace, John Anderson, and Ross Perot. No socialist candidate has ever become a vehicle for major protest in the United States. Voters in the country of classical liberalism, antistatism, libertarianism, and loose class structure have not turned to statist or class-conscious parties even when under severe economic stress. While socialist factions have been influential within some state parties, none has ever been able to dominate a national campaign of the major parties. The same cannot be said of the more conservative or libertarian groups. Barry Goldwater, Ronald Reagan, and Newt Gingrich led successful takeover efforts by these factions within the Republican party.

Some writers have argued that basic features of the American political system—federalism and early suffrage—weakened the cause of socialism quite apart from any effect they had on third parties generally. Our comparative analysis leads us to reevaluate the influence of these factors.

The effect of federalism for socialism is double-edged. It weakened the state as an instrument of reform and denied to socialists the possibility of organizing against national exploitation. Yet federalism also allowed socialists the possibility of electoral success and executive control in political units much smaller than the country as a whole. The gift of the suffrage appears to be a more convincing explanation for socialist weakness. Suffrage for white males prior to industrialization helped integrate labor into the mainstream parties along ethnic and religious lines and thereby diminished class as a source of party-political cleavage. The strength of the major parties within organized labor and the relative weakness of the class cleavage narrowed the political space available to the Socialist party in the early years of the twentieth century. But we have also shown that the effects of early suffrage depend upon other aspects of the society, including the degree to which a stable party system is already in place, the cultural heterogeneity of labor, and the level of prior class consciousness, which was relatively high in Australia and Europe and low in the United States.

The explanation presented here is not elegant, but it does reflect the sensible supposition that neither political, sociological, nor cultural factors alone are sufficient to explain the weakness of socialism in America. While the character of the political system accounts for the failure of third parties, it does not explain the particular weakness of socialist compared to other protest presidential candidates. It is necessary, as noted in Chapter 1, to emphasize the unique classically liberal (libertarian), anti-statist, and individualistic American value system and more equalitarian social class (status) structure in trying to account for the absence of socialism as a major force in America. One must also come to terms with the organizational setting in which American socialists strategized. In Chapter 3 we look for sources of socialist weakness in the character of American unionism and in Chapter 5 we examine how socialists responded to this.

THE SPLIT BETWEEN

UNIONS AND THE

SOCIALIST PARTY

Marx and Engels stressed that one of the greatest weaknesses of the socialist movement in America was its isolation from the mass of workers, and, in particular, its separation from established labor unions. In elaborating this critique, Marx and Engels were actually diagnosing an exceptional and enduring characteristic of American political development, namely the continuing division between organized labor and political parties seeking to represent workers as a class. Many socialists and unionists struggled to overcome this division, but they never succeeded in bringing the major union movement, the American Federation of Labor and later the AFL-CIO, to support an independent working-class political party. In this chapter we suggest that this split reflected American values and the domination of craft unions in the American labor movement. These factors appear more powerful than the character of the American political system in explaining the absence of a socialist or labor party in the United States.

The separation of political from economic organization distinguishes the left in the United States from that in every other industrialized democracy. In contrast to trade unions in Germany and other European societies, American unions were established autonomously from left-wing political parties and remained free from party-political control, though some were socialist-led and others, particularly the Congress of Industrial Organizations, had a strong covertly Communist wing. In the United States, as in other English-speaking societies, unions of skilled craft workers were already well established by the time socialist parties emerged in the last quarter of the nineteenth century. But unlike labor organizations in these societies, American unions never created their own national labor party. The AFL and the AFL-CIO have opposed independent party activity, preferring to exercise political leverage through the two major parties, particularly the Democratic party. This has given rise to a revealing contrast in language: in America the term "labor movement" merely refers to unions, while in other English-speaking societies it encompasses working-class economic and political organizations.

The split between unions and the Socialist party helps to explain why a party that appeared to be on an upward trajectory in the years before World War I could not consolidate its support over the following decade. Until the end of the Great War, the electoral performance of the party measured up well against that of socialist parties in other English-speaking democracies. Ironically, the United States was the only one of these countries in which a party campaigning under a socialist banner was able to gain as much as 6 percent of the national vote (for Eugene Debs in 1912). In addition, eleven hundred socialists were elected to various state and local positions (including seventy-four town and city mayoralties) on the eve of World War I. This compares favorably with the performance of socialist or labor parties in Canada, Australia, New Zealand, and Great Britain. The British Labour party received 7 percent of the national vote in December 1910, competing in seventy-eight constituencies (11.6 percent of the total).[1] In Canada, socialist or labor parties had some strong regional bases, particularly in British Columbia, where the Socialist party received 22 percent of the vote in the provincial elections of 1909, but these groups contested very few national constituencies. Their best national result was 0.1 percent of the vote in 1911, contesting five constituencies (2.3 percent of the total). The story is similar for socialist groups in Australia and New Zealand. Labor parties were exceptionally strong in these countries; correspondingly, parties that described themselves as socialist were marginal.[2]

The membership of the American Socialist party was tiny by comparison with those of leading working-class parties in Britain and Australia. U.S.

Socialist party membership peaked at 118,000 in 1912 and 109,000 in 1920, low figures compared to the 1.9 million members of the British Labour party in 1912 or the 250,000 Labor party members in New South Wales alone. Despite Eugene Debs' public rejection of electoral success as a political goal, the party was far more effective in gaining votes and electing representatives to various local and state offices than it was in building a solid organizational base. While labor parties in other English-speaking democracies were developing strong roots in the working class and labor unions, American Socialists were battling within and against mainstream unions.

Before World War I, the underlying organizational weakness of the Socialist party was overshadowed by its solid electoral gains and the belief that these would continue. But the official declaration of Socialist opposition to the war in 1916 subjected the party to tremendous social and political pressures. The antiwar policy itself reflected the absence of union influence in the party. And because the party lacked solid union support, it was ill equipped to build a stable, financially secure organization. As a result, the 1910s were a roller-coaster ride for the party. This was a period of great successes interspersed with equally significant failures. In 1914, Socialists had created a diverse electoral coalition with substantial backing among American-born workers in western states; but by 1920, Socialist support came mainly from immigrants, particularly German, East European, and Russian (Jewish) immigrants in the large midwestern and eastern cities. Neither coalition lasted. Electoral gains were followed by electoral busts, and from the 1920s on the party was a mere shell of its former self.

Party organization may seem an unlikely place to locate the fate of the American Socialist party. There is little systematic discussion of nitty-gritty party organization in the vast literature bearing on the failure of American socialism. To this day, the best treatment remains Nathan Fine's work published in 1928, *Labor and Farmer Parties in the United States 1828–1928*.[3] Fine delved into the details of Socialist party organization, noting not only that the party was relatively weak in numbers, but that it was highly unstable. In a memorable passage he noted tersely: "The rank and file of the Socialist Party in truth made, and then, unfortunately, unmade it. But it was not altogether the same rank and file."[4] "Not altogether the same rank and file" is the subtheme of this chapter.

Was the Socialist party to blame, or were unions in the United States different from those in Western Europe and other English-speaking

democracies? We believe that both questions can be answered affirmative-
ly. In this chapter, we examine the character of American unions, and we
find that they were distinctive in ways that led them away from socialism.
In Chapter 5 we discuss Socialist strategy toward unions, and we conclude
that Socialists themselves made some basic mistakes.

The Distinctive Character of American Unionism

The unwillingness of most American unions to support a socialist or labor
party is related to broad features of American society and politics: the domination of craft unions in the labor movement; antistatist values; the distinctive character of the U.S. electoral and presidential systems; the resultant
strength and porousness of the major parties; and the cultural, religious, and
ethnic diversity of the American working class. In this section we analyze
the distinctive organizational character of American unions, and in the following section we focus on cultural sources of union opposition to the creation of a labor party.

The Structure of American Unionism

In broad terms one can distinguish two types of unionism: *exclusive* unionism that is based on skilled groups of "craft" workers who attempt to
improve their working conditions mainly by limiting the inflow of
unskilled workers into their job territory (e.g., through apprenticeship regulations) and *inclusive* unionism based on less skilled workers who attempt
to improve their working conditions by mobilizing large numbers to pressure employers and/or gain political representation. Every labor movement
is composed of some mix of these types of unionism.[5] A distinguishing feature of the American labor movement is the extent to which one of these
types—exclusive unionism—predominated.

Exclusive unionism was challenged briefly by the Knights of Labor, a
broad-based labor movement based on a loose alliance of local assemblies of
skilled and unskilled workers. Founded in 1869, the Knights grew swiftly
during the 1880s to encompass some 700,000 or more workers at its peak
before declining with equal swiftness in the early 1890s. Unlike the AFL, the
Knights sought to include workers at all skill levels across a variety of indus-

tries. The movement was highly decentralized and lacked the centralized control of strike funds that was the mark of durable unions that were being established in the AFL and abroad. Organizationally incoherent, the Knights were poorly positioned to resist an employers' backlash that intensified in the 1890s. Concluding her sociological analysis of the Knights, Kim Voss observes, "After the Knights of Labor disintegrated, the American labor movement once again became the domain of a small group of skilled workers, organized primarily along craft lines. As such, it was increasingly out of step with labor movements on the other side of the Atlantic. Consequently the failure of the Knights marks the moment when, from a comparative perspective, the American labor movement began to look exceptional."[6]

From the 1890s, union movements in English-speaking and continental European societies became more diverse and more inclusive as large industrial unions composed of unskilled workers grew strongly alongside older, more exclusive unions. In the United States, the older unions remained predominant. In Britain, for example, no less than five of the ten largest unions in 1910 were inclusive industrial unions. In the United States, the only inclusive unions among the top ten were the United Mine Workers and the Garment workers.[7] From the establishment of the American Federation of Labor in 1886 to World War I, exclusive craft unions accounted for at least three-quarters of the total membership of the federation in any year. With the rapid postwar expansion of unionism among textile workers, steelworkers, and other workers in heavy industry, the proportion of craft unionists declined, but it still remained in excess of two-thirds through the 1920s. Industrial unions appeared to be in ascendancy when the CIO split from the AFL in 1935, but craft or occupational unions continued to encompass the bulk of the American labor movement. At its pre–World War II peak, in 1941, the CIO encompassed fewer than 3 million workers out of the 8.3 million organized in the country.[8]

The conflict among unions over political representation is linked to organizational differences within the labor movement. Powerful craft unions inside the American Federation of Labor sustained the business unionism that dominated the labor movement as a whole. Industrial unions, which were more sympathetic to a class-based party, remained a minority, albeit a vocal one. This tension within the American labor movement provides a key to understanding both the repeated attempts to develop an independent class-based party and their ultimate failure.

The differences between craft unions and industrial/general unions are centered in the job characteristics of their members, differences in membership, and, above all, their contrasting labor market strategies. In each of these respects, craft unions can aptly be described as closed or exclusive organizations.[9] They restrict membership to skilled workers in a particular occupation, leaving the vast majority of lesser-skilled workers to their own resources. Their focus in the late nineteenth and early twentieth centuries was on organizing the so-called aristocrats of labor, relatively skilled workers who tended to be the most educated and have the highest-status, best-paid jobs, e.g., printers, carpenters, and cigar workers. The strategy of such unions was exclusive in the sense that they attempted to improve conditions of employment by restricting the supply of labor available to employers, making it difficult for them to hire workers who had not been apprenticed in the craft. These unions were not simply bargaining agents for workers concerning wages and employment conditions, they were, in addition, concerned with the organization of production on the shop floor. Their strategy emphasized the boundaries between their craft and other types of labor, and this led them to battle employers over a wide range of "control" issues, including apprenticeship regulations and traditions of craft autonomy.

On the one hand, they fought employers on issues having to do with control over production and the supply of labor, but on the other hand, they were vitally interested in excluding unskilled workers from their job territory. Although workers in exclusive unions were often conscious of their status as labor aristocrats, they did not shy away from conflict if their vital interests were affected. Craft unions could be extremely militant. They have been involved in long and bitter strikes. But their militancy was part of the struggle to remain above the unskilled proletariat, to preserve their niche in the division of labor rather than to abolish the division of labor itself. Their motivating fear was that of losing their craft and, as a result, being driven down into the ranks of the unskilled.

Craft unions in the AFL, led by the Carpenters, the International Typographical Union, and the Cigar Makers' International Union in the years before World War I, viewed political activity as a secondary strategy to be undertaken only under exceptional circumstances. To the extent that craft unions campaigned for legislation regulating working conditions, this was intended to complement rather than replace their efforts in the labor market. In their eyes, the main challenge was to consolidate union organization

Table 3.1: Types Of Unionism

	Exclusive Unionism	Inclusive Unionism
Composition	**Craft** and other skilled workers in a particular occupation	**All grades** of workers, unskilled as well as skilled, in a particular industry
Labor Market Strategy	**Internal Restriction:** Attempt to control the supply of labor in a given job territory	**External Pressure:** Inability to control supply of labor; Attempt to pressure employers by force of numbers
Membership Strategy	**Exclusionary:** Defense of apprenticeship regulations and other barriers to entry in relevant labor market(s)	**Encompassing:** Expansionist effort to encompass all who work for given employers
Political Resources	Relatively **small membership thinly spread** across country	Relatively **large membership geographically concentrated** depending on location of industry
Political Orientation	**Weakly politicized:** Political activity viewed as marginal to regulation of working conditions	**Highly politicized:** Focus on gaining improvements in working conditions through legislation

and pressure employers in the labor market rather than to create independent labor representation. Craft unions were convinced that they could achieve their goals through occupational organization in the labor market. In this sense they were syndicalist. Many socialists viewed craft unions as irrational because they combined militancy and voluntarism, occupational consciousness and sectionalism, yet these ambiguities were a response to the opportunities and constraints that faced these unions in the labor market.

When such unions edged further into politics from the early 1900s on, they did so in self-defense. They were impelled to mobilize politically to fend off mounting threats from the courts, to counter the political mobilization of employers in the open-shop drive, and to restrict immigration. From the 1890s, state courts issued a series of injunctions against unions restraining strikes on grounds of conspiracy. The legal pretext for constraining unions was the antitrust provisions of the Sherman Act (1890). In 1902 the Executive Council of the AFL responded with an intense political effort to contain "flagrant, unjustifiable, outrageous" antilabor injunctions.[10]

The obvious advantages of joint action on these issues led unions, even in the AFL, to expand their national political organization. In this respect, developments in the United States testify to the strength of underlying commonalities in western societies in this period. By the second decade of the twentieth century, unions in the United States, as well as in Britain and Germany, were deeply involved in politics. But exclusive craft unions in the AFL, unlike their compeers across the Atlantic, continued to view political activity in narrow instrumental terms and to reject independent third-party activity.

The main impetus toward an aggressive political strategy within the ranks of labor has come from industrial or general unions composed of broad ranks of skilled and unskilled workers in a particular industry or grouping of industries. The kinds of tactics that such unions have at their disposal are quite different from those of exclusive craft unions. Workers who lack clearly defined skills are not able to control their supply of labor at its source and bargain with employers from an institutionalized position of moderate strength. Instead they use force of numbers to pressure employers into concessions or try to induce governments to legislate improvements in workers' welfare. Because such unions are not usually able to tinker with the labor market from the inside, they have focused on enforcing changes externally, through legislation and by threatening employers with a complete shutdown of their enterprises. What industrial unions could not achieve through the subtle exclusionary policies followed by craft unions they made up for by organizing all workers in a particular industry and using force of numbers to put maximum pressure on employers.[11]

Industrial or general unions, as noted, are inclusive in the sense that their membership strategy is encompassing. Both exclusive and inclusive unionism politicize the labor market by introducing power relations in place of the impersonal logic of competition. But inclusive or "open" unions have had to introduce political considerations in a more explicit way, by force of numbers rather than by controlling the supply of labor. This led them into the vanguard of unions campaigning for a third party and political regulation of the labor market. "The new 'open' unions . . . had the motivation to engage in independent political activity because their inclusive recruitment strategy fostered a class consciousness which encouraged members to see politics in class terms." Robin Archer adds that "the new 'open' unions also had the resources to engage in independent political activity because their large memberships could potentially be translated into large numbers of votes, and because these votes were often geographically concentrated and so could be translated into parliamentary seats."[12]

Although the AFL was dominated by exclusive unions, it contained some active industrial unions. The latter consistently campaigned for a more political strategy. Five early industrial unions affiliated with the AFL—the United Mine Workers, the Brewery Workmen, the Amalgamated Clothing Workers, the Western Federation of Miners, and the Ladies Garment Workers—provided the bulk of third-party support among labor before the 1930s. This is revealed in the distribution of delegates in critical votes at AFL conventions. While the aggregate membership of these industrial unions never amounted to more than a quarter of the total membership of the AFL, these unions provided around one-half to three-quarters of overall support for left-wing causes and independent labor party initiatives at AFL conventions, including the 1894 vote on the issue of independent political representation for labor (49.1 percent of the total vote in favor), the 1902 vote proposing political organization to secure for labor "the full equivalent of its toil" (54.1 percent of the total vote in favor), the 1911 vote condemning the National Civic Federation and labor's connection with it (77.4 percent of the total vote in favor), and the 1915 vote opposing a resolution that political regulation of hours is impractical and undesirable (59.5 percent of the total vote against).[13]

Left political and ideological votes in AFL conventions became an endangered species in the 1920s as the leadership clamped down on political dissent, but the one major vote in this period, on nationalization of the railways in 1920, confirms the contrast between inclusive and exclusive unions. Nationalization was supported by 29,159 delegate votes to 8,349 opposed and 1,507 abstaining. Given the high level of support for nationalization, in this case it is most revealing to examine where the opposition came from. All but 320 of opposition votes came from officials in the following exclusive, craft-dominated unions: Hod Carriers, Carpenters, Glass Bottle Blowers, Lathers, Musicians, Plasterers, Plumbers, Steam and Operating Engineers, Theatrical Stage Employees, Teamsters, and Tobacco Workers.[14]

Understandably, socialists campaigned for the introduction of industrial unionism as a general principle within the AFL. A leading spokesman was James Maurer, the leader of the Reading, Pennsylvania, Socialist party and a prominent union activist. At the 1910 Socialist convention he sponsored a minority left-wing motion, supporting the Socialist International's condemnation of "class collaborationist craft unions" and backing "Industrial Unionism as a principle and as an indispensable part of the class struggle, without endorsing any particular organization." The resolution also called on all party spokesmen "to carry . . . the message of common action against the common enemy and of Industrial Unionism generally."[15] He also fought for the principle within the AFL and succeeded in getting the Pennsylvania Federation, which he headed from 1912, to endorse industrial unionism and to back an IWW strike in Patterson, New Jersey, in 1913.[16] Although an AFL officer, Maurer was reluctant to oppose the Wobblies. He wrote that he "never hesitated to go into any kind of struggle where the workers are fighting . . . and I never cared what they called themselves. If they were IWWs, I was with them. . . . Where I differ from them [typical AFL leaders] is that I refuse to fight my own class."[17]

The pro-Socialist industrial unions were flanked by a few craft unions which were impelled into radical politics by their weakness in the labor market. Various groups of artisans, the largest of which were boot and shoe workers, machinists, and carpenters, found their skills, job control, and traditional work practices drastically eroded by economic forces beyond their control. The radicalism of these workers was a response to the failure of pure and simple unionism to secure a niche in the division of labor in the face of decisive economic change.

Industrial and declining craft unions provided the basis for labor parties in the cities. In Milwaukee the Brewery Workmen took the lead, in Reading and Minneapolis, the Machinists, and in New York the garment unions. But the unions that provided the core support for class-based politics—inclusive unions of unskilled and skilled workers and unions of craft workers in retreat—continued to form a minority within the AFL.

Inclusive Unions in Britain and Australia

The hypothesis that the predominance of exclusive unionism within the AFL influenced its orientation toward the creation of a labor party can be gauged from a comparative perspective.[18] Britain is a particularly revealing case for contrast with the United States. In both countries, unions were deeply rooted before the efforts to build mass working-class parties, and craft unions were dominant within the early movement. In Britain, the New Model Unions, which arose from the 1850s and which marked the institutionalization of British unionism, were established to defend job territories that had survived the ongoing division of labor, or, as in the case of engineering and spinning, were created in the process of mechanization in the old crafts. Such unions were never as preponderant as in the United States. Alongside them there were large inclusive unions of coal miners and weavers, and from the time of the upheaval of New Unionism in 1888–89, they were joined by a number of industrial unions composed of dockers, gas workers, and diverse groups of unskilled workers. By our calculations, these unions made up 38.5 percent of the affiliated membership of the Trades Union Congress (TUC) by the turn of the century, and by 1913 their share had risen to 55 percent.[19]

The political sympathies of these unions were influenced by their historical connections to the major parties. The Textile Workers continued to lean toward the Conservative party until the early 1900s, while elements of the Miners' Federation retained strong Liberal sympathies after affiliation with the Labour party in 1909. But even when these unions did not support the Labour Party, they were committed to union political representation and revealed to other unions what could be achieved given sufficient determination and resources.

Socialist sympathies ran deepest among the new unions created in 1889–90. Such organizations played a role well beyond their proportion in the union movement as a whole in supporting the Labour Representation Committee (renamed the Labour party in 1906). Several of the largest unions that affiliated with the fledgling LRC when it was established in 1900–01 were industrial or general unions. These included the United Builders' Labourers, the National Union of Dock Labourers, the Dock, Wharf, Riverside, General Labourers' Union, the National Union of Gasworkers and General Labourers, alongside the older Amalgamated Railway Servants. Together, these and other smaller unions representing semiskilled and unskilled workers accounted for 47 percent of the total union membership affiliated with the LRC when it was first established.[20] Over the next two years, before the lessons of the *Taff Vale* court case (which found unions liable for the losses incurred by employers in strikes) had boosted the cause of labor representation, the ranks of the LRC were swelled by other large inclusive unions, including the United Builders' Labourers, the National Amalgamated Union of Labour, and, largest of all, the United Textile Factory Workers' Association.[21]

The thesis that inclusive unions have fundamental commonalities across different national contexts is supported by John Laslett's comparison of the political activities of the Lancashire Miners and of Illinois District 12 of the United Mine Workers of America. Laslett presents evidence that both unions made strenuous efforts to regulate their members' working conditions through legislation, exhibiting, in Laslett's words, "an identical set of political beliefs."[22] The key difference between these unions lay in the structure of political opportunities in the United States and Britain: "In Lanarkshire and in southern Illinois it was the nature of the party system, and the different methods that the miners used to manipulate that system so as to secure their goals, that influenced their political choices."[23] Although these unions adapted to contrasting political circumstances in different ways, "the evidence suggests that as regards trade union democracy, miners' control over the work process, and the desire for far-reaching social change, the aims of miners on both sides of the Atlantic were very similar."[24]

A similar pattern of inclusive union support for an independent party can be seen in the development of the Australian Labor party. Several unions representing miners, dockers, and particularly farm laborers and other rural workers were prominent in the creation of state labor parties from the early 1890s. Chief among these was Australia's largest union, the Australian Workers Union. This organization, which began as a pastoral union and expanded into a general union for all rural workers, became the backbone of the Labor party where it was otherwise weakest, in the rural areas. In New South Wales, "by the end of the nineties, the AWU and Labor party executive were virtually indistinguishable. All the prominent Labor politicians held, or had held, positions in the AWU by then, and relied heavily on the union for a power base."[25] These included three men, J. C. Watson, W. A. Holman, and W. M. Hughes, all of whom became Labor premiers.

The contrast in the relationship of inclusive unions and exclusive unions with the Labor party is revealed in the comparison of Victoria, where unionism remained dominated by exclusive, craft unions, with New South Wales. In Victoria the Labor party was weak both in organizational and electoral terms, while in New South Wales the party had an extensive organization based in the unions and experienced early and continued electoral success.[26]

Robin Archer has extended this line of analysis in his comparison of working-class support for independent political activity in the United States and Australia by tracing independent labor politics to the efforts of new inclusive unions. In addition, Archer argues that one of the new unions, the shearers' union, was "able to provide a bridge between the union movement and aggrieved small farmers; just the group with whom the American unions most needed to form an alliance."[27]

American Antistatism and Labor

The unwillingness of the leadership of mainstream American unions to support an independent labor party in collaboration with Socialists reflects cultural dispositions grounded in American history. American culture was forged in an egalitarian, antistatist, individualistic revolution. The dominant strain in American culture contrasts sharply with more ascriptive, communitarian, and paternalistic cultures of European societies. Through the nineteenth and early twentieth centuries, mainstream values in the United States were considerably more liberal, in the classical sense—i.e., individualist and antistatist—than those of any European society. The sharpest social cleavages in the United States have been racial and ethnic, whereas those in European societies were more explicitly class-based. In Europe, language and culture have been powerful sources of identity in ethnically segmented societies, such as Belgium, Switzerland, and the Netherlands, but ethnolinguistic groupings in these societies were territorially based, and within each of these groupings, class was a more powerful source of political cleavage than in the United States. American culture is distinctly different from the cultures of European societies in which collectivist, class-based movements of the political left were strengthened by rigid social cleavages and wide status differences.

A culture does not, of course, uniquely determine the responses of individuals to their environment; rather it constitutes a "bounded rationality" that helps to shape the way an individual comes to terms with new challenges and uncertainties. A culture can be conceived of as a "prism" of shared norms through which the responses of individuals to social institutions are refracted. It makes no sense, therefore, to argue about the causal primacy of institutions versus culture. The great traditions of American working-class resistance to capitalism—republicanism, populism, and unionism—have interpreted (and reinterpreted) cultural themes of equality, individualism, and antistatism under different historical circumstances. Several observers have remarked on the affinity between the sectarianism and moralism of the Socialist party, and particularly of its longtime leaders Eugene Debs and Norman Thomas, and the pietistic moralism of Protestant sects. As historian David DeLeon contends, "Social democracy, communism, and other relatively authoritarian movements that rely upon coercive centers of state power" have run against deep libertarian currents in American culture and as a result have never succeeded in developing deep roots.[28] "Statist radicalism" in its various forms has been an ephemeral influence in American politics, while "the black flag [of anarchism] has been the most appropriate banner of the American insurgent."[29]

Prior to the Great Depression, the American labor movement, from mainstream unions in the AFL to the radical Industrial Workers of the World, opposed programs to extend the role of the state. The IWW, which believed that social revolution could be achieved by a grassroots labor uprising, was anarcho-syndicalist, while the AFL's philosophy came close to syndicalism. Both rejected socialism on antistatist grounds.

In her book on the American Federation of Labor, Julie Green traces the shifts in AFL political strategy in response to pressure from the rank and file, employers' campaigns, court decisions, and the opportunities that were available to labor leaders to gain influence in the Democratic party. "Amidst all the changes that AFL politics had undergone since the nineteenth century," Green observes, "those in control of the Federation remained quite consistent in their attitudes to the state. As Gompers [who presided over the AFL from its establishment in 1886 to his death in 1923 with the exception of a single year] pronounced in 1898, 'Our movement stands for the wage-earners doing for themselves what they can toward working out their own salvation. But those things that they cannot do for themselves the Government should do.' According to this formula, labor should seek only limited legislation to establish unions' right to strike, picket, and boycott; to free trade unions from unfair competition with cheaper labor sources (thus the AFL worked to restrict immigration and convict and child labor); and to make the government itself into a model employer."[30]

Until the Depression of the 1930s, the AFL was opposed to state provision of old-age pensions, compulsory health insurance, minimum wage legislation, and unemployment compensation, and from 1914 on was against legislating maximum hours for men. As Selig Perlman put it, American workers perceived little choice "between an autocratic capitalist management of industry and a bureaucratic one by 'experts' appointed by the state."[31] This syndicalist antistate view did not temper the labor movement, for "labor leaders in this country have, on the whole, always been more aggressive against the employers, and have striven more relentlessly for full job control than have their radical rivals."[32] The American labor movement was not opposed to political action, but it entered politics chiefly to create rules that would allow it to operate effectively in the labor market.[33] It sought, above all, to protect "its legal right to strike and to bargain collectively," as well as to secure legislation assuring minimum standards for all workers, with respect for issues like "safety and health . . . and workmen's compensation."[34]

Samuel Gompers exemplified the distrust of the state among unionists. In commenting on an article written in 1908 by the American syndicalist theorist William English Walling attacking the idea of a labor party, Gompers stressed that he agreed with the basic syndicalist supposition that unions were the kernel of the new society and should stay free of party-political entanglements.[35] Although he never had apocalyptic hopes for massive social and economic revolution brought about by a general strike, Gompers shared with syndicalists the assumption that unions were more vital institutions than political parties. As Christopher Tomlins has observed, "The leaders of the AFL . . . avoided involvement in reform politics, embracing instead the prospect of a new social and political order based on the harmonious interaction of workers voluntarily associated in their various trades and callings. . . . Not only were [unions] the sole means whereby American labor as a whole could be defended, they were also the only appropriate institutional mechanism through which the ultimate liberty of American workers could be achieved."[36] Commenting on syndicalists who were making gains in several European countries, Gompers observed that "nine tenths of their work [is] just the same as that of the A.F. of L."[37]

The 1930s witnessed a change in the political and ideological behavior of much of organized labor. The American movements became deeply involved in political action, largely in support of the Democratic party. The CIO and sections of the AFL adopted political programs calling for a high level of government involvement in planning the economy as well as sharp increases in welfare and health programs.

These changes reflected the impact of the Great Depression in undermining traditional American laissez-faire beliefs among large sectors of the population, and in bringing about acceptance of the need for state action to reduce unemployment, assist those adversely affected by the economic collapse, and support trade unionism. Analyses of public opinion polls and election results noted that class factors had become highly differentiating variables. Samuel Lubell, who conducted in-depth interviews of many voters, concluded that the electoral support for Roosevelt and New Deal programs constituted "a class-conscious vote for the first time in American history. . . . The New Deal appears to have accomplished what the Socialists, the IWW and the Communists never could approach. It has drawn a class line across the face of American politics."[38] However, as discussed in Chapter 2, this period provided a classic instance of the flexibility of the major parties in the face of potential third-party opposition. Support for a third labor or socialist party was siphoned off by Roosevelt and the Democratic party.

Antistatism made American labor wary of the potential benefits offered to unions and workers by labor parties in other predominantly English-speaking, industrialized societies. Apart from their demand for protection from punitive legislation, a demand shared by American unions, labor parties in Britain, New Zealand, and Australia campaigned for various state welfare measures, including unemployment compensation and health insurance, for an expanded governmental role in the labor market involving legislation of minimum wages and maximum hours, and government ownership of basic industry. Such demands were not as appealing to American workers as they were to workers elsewhere. The antistatist strain in American culture led many unionists to continually oppose reforms that were central to the political programs of labor parties.

Attempts to Establish a Labor Party

Since the founding of the American Federation of Labor in 1886, there have been repeated attempts to establish a labor party to represent American workers as a class in national politics. While none of these has been successful, the idea of a labor party has attracted substantial minority support, particularly among industrial unions represented in the AFL and among craft unions representing workers in declining sectors of the economy.

As a broad-based movement encompassing workers in a variety of industries and crafts, the Knights of Labor pursued an expressly political strategy. In 1886, unions affiliated with the Knights and the AFL, along with various radical groups, established United Labor parties which succeeded in electing several local tickets in eastern and midwestern cities.[39] In these years American unions appeared to be in advance of those in Britain in advancing independent labor representation. On returning from their visit to the United States in 1886, Karl Marx's daughter and son-in-law, Eleanor and Edward Aveling, wrote: "The example of the American working man will be followed before long on the European side of the Atlantic. An English, or, if you will, a British Labour Party will be formed."[40] *Reynolds' Newspaper*, the British working-class organ, admonished the Trades Union Congress to model its newly formed Labour Electoral Association after the United Labor party. As it turned out, however, the United Labor party was undermined by a series of disputes between Henry George, the head of the party, and socialists who accused George of being too accommodating toward his old party political rivals. But the new party faced a greater obstacle. The major parties were spurred to enact labor laws which met several of the unions' immediate demands, a response to third parties which has occurred frequently and successfully in American political history.

In the early 1890s the most severe economic depression of the nineteenth century made many unionists sensitive to the potential benefits of broad-based independent political cooperation with other hard-pressed groups. In these years, a number of socialist and union leaders attempted to build a bridge between their own efforts for a labor party and the sharp rise of agrarian radicalism among poorer farmers and sharecroppers, particularly in the south and west, as expressed in the populist Farmers' Alliance. In February 1892, delegates from several AFL unions, including the Mineworkers and Machinists, met in St. Louis with representatives from farmers' organizations and the Knights of Labor to express their support for the People's party launched the year before. The movement appealed most strongly to economically threatened small farmers and artisans. Its chief support among organized workers was from shoe workers, metal miners, and machinists, each of whom, political scientist Michael Rogin points out, "faced a similar threat, as the rapid introduction of machinery undermined their autonomy, reduced their income, and devalued their skills."[41]

Although Samuel Gompers was critical of union support for Populism on the grounds that it detracted from labor market activity, the 1892 AFL convention in Philadelphia adopted two planks of the Populist platform: government ownership of the telegraph and telephone systems, and the popular initiative and referendum. More broadly, the convention instruct-ed members of the Executive Council "to use their best endeavors to carry on a vigorous campaign of education . . . in order to widen the scope of usefulness of the trade union in the direction of political action."[42]

At its next convention, the AFL came close to establishing a labor politi-cal action committee along the lines of the still small, but promising, Labour Representation Committee in Britain. An eleven-plank program was adopted which included demands for compulsory education; a legal eight-hour day; abolition of sweat shops; municipal ownership of street cars and gas and electric plants; nationalization of telegraphs, telephones, railroads, and mines; the referendum; and, most controversial of all, the "collective ownership by the people of all means of production and distrib-ution" (Plank Ten). The preamble to the program urged American unionists to follow the example of British unionists, who "by the light of experience and the logic of progress [have] adopted the principle of independent political action."[43] The program was to be referred back to the membership of individual unions, who would instruct their delegates how to vote at the next convention. Although the convention narrowly voted against referring the program back with their "favorable recommendation," a motion con-taining the program was passed by a vote of 2,244 to 67.[44]

In the following months the eleven planks found support in many unions. Only the Bakers' Union rejected them as a whole, while the International Typographical Union was one of only two unions to reject the socialist-sounding Plank Ten. Despite considerable pressure for a political strategy, the results of the 1894 convention in Denver were ambiguous. Instead of submitting the program as a whole to a vote, the preamble and individual planks were taken up one by one. With the exception of the pre-amble, which was rejected, and Plank Ten, which was amended to refer to the abolition of the monopoly system of landholding rather than public ownership, all the remaining planks were adopted. However, majorities for individual planks did not add up to a supermajority for all eleven planks, and when the platform was voted on as a whole it was rejected by 1,173 votes to 735. At this convention, AFL president Samuel Gompers, who orchestrated the fight against independent political action, was defeated for reelection by John McBride of the United Mine Workers, who had argued in favor of a labor party.

However, support for independent labor representation weakened as the Labor-Populist movement dispersed into its constituent elements, and the failure of the political program to win wholehearted AFL approval turned some leading socialists away from the organization. Thomas J. Morgan, the Chicago machinist who introduced the political program, left the AFL in 1895 on the grounds that most union leaders were incorrigibly conservative and that the AFL would, in any case, be superseded as labor became more revolutionary.[45] At the 1895 AFL convention, the pure and simple conception of unionism was dominant. Gompers was again elected president, a position he went on to hold for the rest of his life. His emphasis on voluntarism was made official by the passage of a resolution that "party politics whether they be democratic, republican, socialistic, prohibition, or any other, should have no place in the convention of the A.F. of L." Only 158 out of 1,618 voting dissented.[46]

Despite growing Socialist electoral strength from 1902 to 1912, support within the AFL for independent labor representation fluctuated wildly. At the 1902 convention a resolution introduced by Max Hayes, a leading socialist in the International Typographical Union, requiring the AFL to "advise the working people to organize their economic and political power to secure for labor the full equivalent of its toil and the overthrowal [sic] of the wage system and the establishment of an industrial cooperative democracy," was narrowly defeated by a vote of 4,897 to 4,171, with 309 abstaining.[47] At the next convention, however, socialist resolutions along similar lines were decisively rejected.

Over the next few years, the Gompers doctrine, rewarding labor's friends and punishing its enemies regardless of party affiliation, funneled support to the Democratic party as President Taft and the Republican party ignored union demands for protection from injunctions. At a special meeting in 1906, representatives from fifty-one AFL unions drew up a Bill of Grievances and established a national organization to focus the movement's legislative activity. The name of the organization—the Labor Representation Committee—was the same as that used by British unions, but the resemblance was superficial. The AFL participated in election campaigns as a pressure group and, unlike the TUC, still refused to take any steps toward an independent party. British unions, while supporting friendly major-party candidates (mainly Liberals) in constituencies they could not win alone, also ran their own Labour party candidates in strongly working-class districts.

The failure of this new effort to break Republican control of the House of Representatives in the 1906 congressional elections or limit the use of injunctions raised hopes that the AFL would become more sympathetic to the creation of a labor party. In the wake of the Supreme Court's 1908 union-weakening decision on the *Danbury Hatters* case, which made the Sherman Antitrust Act applicable to unions, even moderates began to consider drastic remedies. John B. Lennon, treasurer of the AFL and a stalwart business unionist, threatened that "if the wage-workers in this country become thoroughly convinced that there is no policy to pursue except that of independent politics, they will pursue it with a vim and determination and effectiveness that has never been dreamed of by the workers of any country in the world."[48] Over the next decade, the demand for independent labor representation came up directly or indirectly at several AFL conventions. The high point of the challenge to the AFL's "pure and simple" unionism coincided with the Socialist party's peak in 1911 and 1912, when several well-known Federation leaders, including John Lennon of the tailors and James O'Connell of the machinists, were defeated in election contests in their unions by candidates supported by Socialists. In 1912, Max Hayes, the longtime proponent of independent labor representation, challenged Gompers for the presidency of the AFL and received a little less than one-third of the vote. Without ever marshaling a majority of AFL delegates behind the idea, supporters of a labor party became entrenched in some of the largest industrial unions, including the United Mine Workers, the Brewery Workers, and the Ladies Garment Workers, and regularly polled up to one-third of the votes at AFL conventions.

After World War I there was a flurry of third-party activity as a number of labor organizations hoped to emulate the success of the British Labour party in breaking through to major-party status. The experience of the war revealed the possibilities of state control in the economy, summed up by the term "war socialism." The United States was actively involved in World War I for less than twenty months, but in this relatively short time industries of direct concern to the war effort, water and rail transport, the mines, and the telephone and telegraph systems chief among them, were brought under direct state control, while various others, including the munitions industries, were subject to extensive regulation.[49] Demands for the socialization of industry were taken up by several unions, including the United Mine Workers, the Railway Brotherhoods, and organizations in the needle trades. In 1918 and 1919, state labor parties were formed in Illinois and New York with the support of the United Mine Workers and the Ladies Garment Workers, respectively. In December 1919 these state parties convened a national meeting to form a Labor party of the United States. Fifty-five affiliates of the AFL were represented, including the United Mine Workers, the Ladies Garment Workers, the Amalgamated Clothing Workers, the Brewery Workers, the Cigarworkers, Bricklayers, Carpenters, Painters and Molders, Bakers, Quarry Workers, Fur Workers, Glass Workers, and the sixteen unions composing the independent Railroad Brotherhoods. In emulation of Woodrow Wilson's "Fourteen Points" doctrine for international peace, the platform of the party was entitled "Labor's Fourteen Points," a combination of liberal-progressive and socialist demands for equal rights for women, an inheritance and graduated income tax, proposals for federal action on unemployment, the eight-hour day, a minimum wage, public ownership of the nation's utilities and resources, and "democratic management" of industry and commerce.[50]

The Labor party sought to enlist Robert La Follette as its presidential candidate, but failed to do so, mainly because he was wary of campaigning on a ticket that included socialist demands. In the presidential election of 1920 the party, renamed the Farmer-Labor party, gained just 300,000 votes for a ticket headed by Parley Parker Christensen, a progressive, with the socialist printer Max Hayes as his running mate. The Socialist party, which had refused to join with the new party, received over three times as many votes (3.5 percent of the total) for its perennial presidential candidate, Eugene Debs, who ran from a prison cell. He had been convicted of sedition in 1918 for his antiwar activities.

In the presidential election of 1924 the AFL threw its weight behind the Progressive ticket of Senators Robert La Follette and Burton Wheeler. This was the first and only time that the AFL deserted both major parties to support a third party. Socialists, who had altered the constitution of their party two years before to permit cooperation with a labor party, hoped that this marked the beginning of a new era of unity between the political and industrial wings of labor. As Morris Hillquit observed, "For the first time in the political history of our country, all forces of the organized labor movement are united in support of an independent candidate for the President of the United States."[51] Similar hopes were shared by several unions that had been active in setting up a labor party in 1919, and both the United Mine Workers within the AFL and the Amalgamated Clothing Workers under Sidney Hillman from outside made large financial contributions to the venture.

But the appearance of unity during the 1924 presidential election masked fundamental differences in goals between the unions and the Socialists. The leadership of the AFL, and Samuel Gompers in particular, saw their backing of La Follette as a one-shot affair to punish the Republican and Democratic parties for summarily rejecting the AFL's Bill of Grievances and adopting tickets that were clearly unsympathetic to organized labor. The Republican party stood by Calvin Coolidge, who as president had helped roll back labor's gains from the war, while the Democratic party passed over William G. McAdoo, who as federal railroad administrator in 1917–19 had been sympathetic to labor, in favor of corporate lawyer John W. Davis. As noted in the previous chapter, neither La Follette nor the AFL saw the election of 1924 as the start of a permanent challenge to the two-party system. The AFL's political campaign committee made this absolutely clear in declaring that "cooperation hereby urged is not a pledge of identification with an independent third party nor can it be construed as support for such a party, group or movement, except as such action accords with our nonpartisan political action."[52]

La Follette received nearly five million votes or 16.6 percent of the national total, the second-highest share for a third party since the Civil War.[53] The Progressive party won only one state, Wisconsin, but came second in eleven others, including California. However, only around one million votes came from industrial areas; the rest were mainly from the farming states. Viewed as an experiment of independent left-wing political action, it was possible to conclude that this campaign was a success, especially given its late start and lukewarm support by the AFL. Among labor parties in the Anglo-American societies only the Australian Labor party gained a greater share of the vote in its first contested national election (18.7 percent in 1901), and that was after more than a decade of intense activity at the state level. But most unions within the AFL judged the performance of the party in terms of electing friends in high places. By this standard, the experiment was a failure.

Although a few unions continued to voice their support for independent labor representation through the 1920s and 1930s, its backers were never able to gain the support of even a third of the delegates at AFL conventions. From 1935 on, the chief sources of support for a labor party were to be found in the CIO, the newly formed Committee for Industrial Organization (later the Congress of Industrial Organizations).[54] As noted in the previous chapter, in 1936 the garment unions of New York State, with the help of Labor's Nonpartisan League, then dominated by John L. Lewis of the United Mine Workers and the CIO, established the American Labor party (ALP) as a statewide organization designed to win socialist and labor votes for Roosevelt's reelection. In the New York State elections of 1938 the party received more than 1.2 million votes. The ALP was modestly successful in New York only because it endorsed Franklin Roosevelt. Many of its members, who had largely been active in the Socialist and Communist parties, hoped the ALP would turn into to a truly independent labor party after the Roosevelt presidency.

Following Roosevelt's third electoral victory in 1940, CIO head John L. Lewis, who had opposed Roosevelt's reelection and advised the Republicans to nominate Herbert Hoover, favored a third-party venture, as did the now anti-Roosevelt Communists active in the many CIO affiliates. The Communists turned against Roosevelt and the antifascist Popular Front strategy they had been following after the Stalin-Hitler pact of August 1939. They now opposed anti-Nazi policies. In that year the CIO convention authorized its Executive Board to "give serious consideration . . . looking toward the formulation of a program which would guarantee and assure an independent political role for organized labor."[55] But this initiative was impeded by the growing conflict between Lewis and the pro-Roosevelt, pro-Allied majority of the CIO. After Lewis was replaced as head of the CIO, the Communists returned to enthusiastic support of Roosevelt and opposition to a labor party following the German attack on the Soviet Union in June 1941.

The Consequences of the Party-Union Split

The failure of the American Socialist party to gain the steady support of mainstream unions influenced the organizational strength, stability, and political orientation of the party. In the remainder of this chapter we analyze the effects of the party-union split in two ways. We compare the American party with socialist and labor parties in other countries and we trace the experience of cities within the United States where the party managed to buck the national trend and gain union support at the local level. Both kinds of comparison confirm our claim that the party-union split decisively weakened the American Socialist party.

Socialist Party Organization

The most obvious—and most devastating—consequence of the rift between the Socialist party and labor unions is that it severely undermined party organization. The American Socialist party existed in isolation from the mass of organized workers. By the turn of the twentieth century, in its fourteenth year of existence, the AFL encompassed 750,000 workers. By 1913 the figure was 2.5 million. For its part, the Socialist party's membership never exceeded 118,000 even at its peak in 1912.

The force of this contrast is all the greater because union membership tends to be far more intensive than party membership. Almost all unions were built on occupational communities, close-knit groupings of workers that expressed shared norms. Some occupational communities reflected distinctive ways of life.[56] Coal miners, for example, formed extremely solidaristic occupational communities because they were socially isolated from the wider society, worked under dangerous conditions in which group trust was necessary for survival, and shared, in many cases, a history of industrial conflict with employers. Such workers lived in close connection with each other both at work and at home. Coal miners were exceptional, but in the days before unions could enforce membership legally, unions were strongest when based on an occupational community that enabled them to instill union membership as a social norm.

The financial commitment of unionists far exceeded that of party members. Unions struggled to improve the working lives of their members on a daily basis, and their monthly or weekly membership dues were often set at a higher level than the annual membership dues of the party. Given the deep roots that unions had in the working class, their extensive membership, and their relative financial strength, American Socialists could ill afford a split.

The strength or weakness of party organization mattered far more in the pre–World War I period than it does in the contemporary era of mass media and direct advertising. In most industrial societies, workers' parties were the first mass organizations to arrive on the political scene. They sought to mobilize huge numbers of supporters to offset the disadvantage of being outsider parties representing less privileged sections of the population. Political parties have a wide range of functions. They are a vital means of information about the issues of the day. Their meetings and newspapers connect supporters and potential supporters to the polity. They are instrumental in getting their supporters to the polls. But in many countries they have been far more than this. Socialist parties once constituted what one might today call a counterculture. They were part of a working-class community based in pubs, libraries, political meetings, and social organizations of almost every kind. Labor unions were also at the core of this community. For many workers in Western Europe or in other English-speaking democracies, there was no sharp line dividing their union from the party. The two were fused within an overarching movement and way of life.

Unlike socialist parties abroad, the American Socialist party was not part of an inclusive working-class community, and was never able to enlarge its membership by encompassing workers who might enroll simply because they were members of a labor union. One upshot of this was that the American Socialist party remained a small and vulnerable organization in an age of huge organizations and mass movements. It was a minnow in an age of whales. As the political scientist Leon Epstein has observed, "In the first decade or so of the twentieth century, American socialists built a party that was not far behind the growing strength of the new British Labour party. Moreover, the Socialist Party of America was avowedly socialist in a way that British labour was not until 1918. What the American socialists did not have, however, was the trade union base the new British party secured in 1900. This made the American movement more purely socialist but also, in the long run, much smaller."[57]

Even at its peak in the years before the war, when a large number of Socialist candidates were elected to various local, state, and national political offices and the party secured the votes of 6 percent of the electorate, the membership of the party never exceeded 0.12 percent of the population. The contrast with other leftist working-class-based parties is sharp. Working-class parties that were closely allied to unions, as in Britain, Germany, Australia, and Sweden, could tap human and financial resources that were literally tens of times greater than those available to a party that was isolated. In its early years the British Labour party was electorally weak, yet organizationally strong. Union affiliation with the party provided a membership that, as Table 3.2 details, ran into the hundreds of thousands from the year of its birth. Henry Pelling concludes his history of the establishment of the Labour party by pointing out that despite limitations of party strategy, "by 1903 the new party machine was in existence, and whatever the political views of its officers, it soon began to build up among them a vested interest in its maintenance. The officials of the great trade unions had made up their minds in favour of a distinct party of their own, and so long as their industrial strength continued to grow, the strength of the political organization would also increase."[58]

The contrast is equally sharp with Australia. In New South Wales alone, the Labor party estimated its membership at over one quarter of a million in 1914. Links between unions and the Labor party were probably closer than in any other liberal democracy (Britain included), and this has been viewed as a critical ingredient in the meteoric rise of the party in the first decade of the twentieth century. Variations within Australia confirm the importance of party-union links. In New South Wales and Queensland, where the dominant pattern of close collaboration between politically active unions and state labor parties was strongest, the Labor party soon became a mass organization with a large membership and vote. In contrast, the Labor party in Victoria lacked deep roots in the union movement, and as a result it was not able to create a strong organizational base. With a weak and under-financed central organization, the Victoria Labor party was a party of parliamentarians rather than a mass party.[59]

The extraordinary weakness of American Socialist party organization is evident from Table 3.2. The French Socialist party, which, like the American, faced a union movement that was largely syndicalist and opposed to independent party political representation, still managed to encompass a larger membership than the American Socialist party in a country with a smaller population. Measured on a per capita basis over the period as a whole, the American Socialist party was less than half as encompassing as the French Socialist party, one-twentieth the level of organization of the German party, and one-seventieth that of the British Labour party.

We do not have comparable data at the individual level, but the aggregate figures set out in Table 3.2 suggest that the American party had higher

Table 3.2: Social Democratic/Labor Party Membership

	United States Socialist Party of America		Great Britain Labour Party		Germany Sozial-demokratische Partei		France SFIO	
	Member-ship (1,000s)	Members per 1,000 pop.	Member-ship (1,000s)	Members per 1,000 pop.	Member-ship (1,000s)	Members per 1,000 pop.	Member-ship (1,000s)	Members per 1,000 pop.
1900			376	9.1				
1901			469	11.3				
1902			861	20.5				
1903	16	0.2	970	23.0				
1904	21	0.3	900	21.1				
1905	23	0.3	921	21.4			35	0.9
1906	27	0.3	998	23.0	384	6.3	40	1.0
1907	29	0.3	1072	24.5	530	8.5	53	1.3
1908	42	0.5	1159	26.3	587	9.3	57	1.4
1909	41	0.5	1486	33.4	633	9.9	58	1.5
1910	58	0.6	1430	31.8	720	11.1	69	1.7
1911	85	0.9	1539	34.1	837	12.8	70	1.8
1912	118	1.2	1895	41.7	970	14.7	73	1.8
1913	96	1.0			983	14.7	75	1.9
1914	94	1.0	1612	35.5	1086	17.1	93	2.3
1915	79	0.8	2093	46.2	516	8.6	25	0.6
1916	83	0.8	2220	49.2	433	7.7	26	0.7
1917	80	0.8	2465	54.9	243	4.6	28	0.7
1918	82	0.8	3013	67.3	249	5.0	16	0.4
1919	109	1.0	3511	78.8	1012	21.9	133	3.4
1920	27	0.3	4360	98.2	1180	27.5	180	4.6
1921	13	0.1	4010	89.9	1221	27.8	50	1.3
1926	12	0.1	3388	74.6	806	15.4	111	2.7

Sources: United States: Nathan Fine, Labor and Farmer Parties in the United States 1828–1928
(New York: Rand School of Social Science, 1928), p. 326.

Britain: Maurice Duverger, Political Parties: Their Organization and Activity in the Modern State, trans. by
Barbara and Robert North (New York: John Wiley, 1954), pp. 68–69.

Germany (1906–1914): Dieter Fricke, Die Deutsche Arbeiterbewegung 1869–1914: Ein Handbuch über
ihre Organisation und Tätigkeit im Klassenkampf (Berlin: Dietz Verlag, 1976), p. 245.

rates of membership turnover than even the French Socialist party. Averaging annual aggregate membership declines provides a rough yardstick for comparison. The American party comes out on top with 12.5; the French has a score of 11.3, while the figures for the British Labour and German Social Democratic parties are 2.3 and 7.5, respectively.

The weakness of union-party links contributed to the fragility of the organizational base of the American Socialist party. This line of argument is developed in Maurice Duverger's classic analysis of party development. Explaining the organizational weakness and instability of French socialism as compared with the more stable party structure in England led Duverger to note: "The English workman who is a member of a Trade Union, itself integrated within the Labour party, is surely bound to his party by a tie very much stronger than binds the French workman for whom Trade Union activity and political activity involve different organizations. It would seem that the superposition of loyalties brings about a reinforcement of each individual tie: there is multiplication as well as addition."[60]

A parallel observation can be drawn from Adam Przeworski's and John Sprague's analysis of socialist party electoral performance across seven Western European societies.[61] They conclude that strong ties between unions and social democratic parties decrease the costs of pursuing a cross-class electoral strategy. Where workers are tied to social democratic parties by virtue of their membership in unions, they will be more likely to vote for the working-class party even if it dilutes its proletarian appeal with planks designed to attract middle-class groups. Serious union-party ties reduce losses inherent in a cross-class electoral strategy.

Socialist Subculture

The absence of strong union-party links in the United States not only hurt the American Socialist party directly, it also arguably weakened class consciousness. Unlike proletarians in more stratified, postfeudal European societies, American workers rarely felt themselves part of a class subcul-

France: Duverger, *Political Parties*, pp. 68–69.

Population figures were derived from Paul Kennedy, *The Rise and Fall of the Great Powers* (New York: Vintage Books, 1987), p. 199. Intermediate years between censuses were calculated on a straight-line basis.

ture, nor have they been part of an encompassing labor movement based in a myriad of educational, leisure, and fraternal organizations reinforcing social class.

The separation of unions from the political left in the United States reflects antistatist elements in American culture, but over the long term it is possible to regard values themselves as influenced by political institutions. As Adam Przeworski argues: "Political parties along with unions, churches, factories, and schools forge collective identities, instill commitments, define the interests on behalf of which collective actions become possible, offer choices to individuals, and deny them."[62]

In the United States, basic social, economic, and political institutions undermined class consciousness by reinforcing the multiplicity of contending, cross-cutting cleavages based on religion, ethnicity, and race. The Socialist party's appeals to inclusive working-class consciousness were countered by the efforts of craft unions, which dominated the AFL, to segment labor organization into specific trades or occupations. Craft unions were less ambitious than the Socialist party in that they did not try to remake American workers in a new mold, but adjusted their organizations to the particularities of labor markets and preexisting cultural loyalties and prejudices, including above all the divide between native and immigrant workers.

Working-class consciousness was also weakened, as Ira Katznelson has emphasized, by the split between orientations in the workplace and in residential communities. This tension, which Katznelson describes in terms of "city trenches," helps one understand a paradox in American political development. American workers fought strikes with employers as intense as any in Western Europe. On a variety of indices, including the volume and violence of strikes, American workers were as aggressive, or as Daniel Bell has noted, even more militant, than workers in other western societies. Yet, industrial conflict rarely deepened class consciousness. Moreover, at home, according to Katznelson, workers tended to view their interests in ethnic, religious, or community terms:

> Over a long period of time, the stark division in people's consciousness, language, and action between the politics of work and the politics of community became a tacit mechanism in the selection of alternatives. . . . The system of city trenches has produced a working class unique in the West: militant as labor, and virtually nonexistent as a collectivity outside

the workplace. Workers have thus tended "to oppose capitalists rather than capitalism."

It is not surprising that there have been attempts to challenge this urban class system through working-class socialist or laborist parties that would appeal to workers as workers both in the community and in the laboring portions of their lives.[63]

The split between work and community reflects the ethnic heterogeneity of the workforce and the distinctive organizational basis of American labor. Although workers were subject to the pressures of capitalism and industrialism in the workplace, these were mediated by cultural, religious, and ethnic identifications.[64] At the same time, American workers "made themselves" by creating organizations to defend or improve their economic and political conditions. This was reinforced by relatively fluid status cleavages alongside a value system emphasizing individualism and social mobility. In light of this, it is not surprising that American working-class organizations were much less able than their European counterparts to channel proletarian activity along class lines. The overall impression of American working-class culture and organizational life is one of richness, diversity—and fragmentation.

Socialist Orientations

The division between mainstream unions and the American Socialist party also affected the ideology of the party, reinforcing radical tendencies and weakening reformism. The reason for this is that blue-collar workers organized in unions have generally been more likely to press for material improvements under capitalism than have intellectual radicals belonging to socialist parties. Correspondingly, socialist parties that have had significant union wings have been subject to significantly greater reformist pressures than those where party intellectuals did not have to compromise with blue-collar unionists. This tension between the reformism of manual workers and the radicalism of the socialist intelligentsia is well known and often remarked upon by writers and activists. It is a major theme in the development of labor movements across industrialized societies in the nineteenth century and first decades of the twentieth century, and was often mentioned by Samuel Gompers in his condemnation of the American Socialist party.

Their split with the unions put the American Socialists in some strange company—alongside the Russian Bolshevik party and far removed from the labor parties of Australia, Canada, or Britain. Lenin made a conscious decision to insulate the Bolshevik party from union influence on the grounds that unions would stray from revolutionism toward "economism," i.e., compromise with capitalism. In the United States, the split was only partially intended, but the result was similar. It is a paradox of American political development that this country is the only English-speaking democracy in which unions played a marginal role in socialist strategy. In a political system that demands a broad-based reformist party, American socialists, as we detail in Chapter 5, created one of the most radical socialist parties in the world.

What might have changed if the party had forged an alliance with mainstream unions? Perhaps the best known example of how growing union influence could lead a radical socialist party toward reformism is that of Germany, where a steady rise in union membership and influence relative to intellectuals in the Social Democratic party from the 1890s on gradually pushed the party away from its revolutionary origins. The debate centered on political use of strikes. Most party leaders viewed a general strike as a potent weapon in their political arsenal, but union leaders, above all Carl Legien, the head of the socialist Free Union movement, urged that the strike was an economic weapon that should be reserved for unions. Even in Germany, the home of the largest socialist party in the world before World War I, and a beacon for orthodox Marxism, unions came to shape the labor movement as a whole. Party membership rose toward the million mark by 1913, but union membership exceeded 2.5 million. In 1893, union membership was one-eighth of the Social Democratic vote; by 1907 it had risen to one-half. Intellectuals continued to dominate socialist theorizing, but leaders of blue-collar unions exerted considerable influence over major decisions.

The influence of unions was decisive in the debate that took place in every socialist party about whether to support engagement in World War I. Socialist parties were deeply torn over the issue. Internationalism and pacifism were rooted in socialist ideology, and many party leaders and most socialist intellectuals refused to support a war among capitalist imperialist powers. But because the mass of workers and their unions in countries on both sides of the conflict were determined to support the national cause,

working-class parties threw their weight behind the war effort. In the
United States the decision about participation in the war came later, when
the ghastly nature of trench warfare was evident. As in Europe, the debate
pitched intellectuals against workers, but the union presence in the party
was too weak to swing the outcome. Nathan Fine, writing a decade later,
observed bluntly that the party's decision at the St. Louis convention in
April 1917 to oppose U.S. entrance into the war was "due primarily to the
fact that unlike the parties of Europe, the Socialist Party of the United
States in 1917 was not a mass movement." According to Fine, the party's
"absence of control over the trade unions with their bread-and-butter
demands, its lack of political strongholds and a large organization to con-
serve, all this made the American party primarily a party of propaganda and
education."[65]

Union-Party Links at the City Level

The hypothesis relating the weakness of the Socialist party to the strength
of links between the party and labor unions can be illustrated by comparison within the United States. Like many unions and the Democratic and
Republican parties, the American Socialist party was highly decentralized,
permitting variations in party-union relationships in a number of towns
and cities.

The Socialist party in Milwaukee was probably the closest approxima-
tion within the United States to the model of an integrated working-class
movement in which party organization was entrenched within unions. The
Milwaukee party was rooted in a subculture of singing societies, carnivals,
group picnics, a Sunday school, a party newspaper, and much else.[66] This
reflected the German origins of many socialist activists and their prior
experience of union-party links within the dense socialist subculture of the
German Social Democratic party. Unions in the Milwaukee Federated
Trades Council were closely intertwined with the party, so much so that
while socialists and unionists had formally autonomous organizations, historians speak of the two effectively sharing membership, policies, and
goals. Sally Miller notes: "The Milwaukee party as it developed was much
more in the image of European social democratic parties than reflective of
American political organizations."[67]

Victor Berger, the acknowledged leader of the Milwaukee socialist movement, opposed attempts to commit the American Federation of Labor to socialist resolutions at its annual conventions in favor of a gradualist strategy in which socialists would work on behalf of unions and thereby show how a strong Socialist party could assist unions in the labor market. In this respect, Berger was close to British leftists who deemphasized socialist policies to gain union support for common objectives. As Berger put it, "I do not propose to run the trade unions into a political machine nor the Socialist party into a trade union. However, I want the trade union to be part of the same movement as the political party. . . . [T]his is the Wisconsin idea."[68]

Although it never became the dominant stream of American socialism, this strategy was influential. Several AFL unions were led by socialists, including the garment worker organizations, in which Jews from Eastern Europe were dominant, and the Brewery Workmen, a union composed predominantly of German immigrants that had its headquarters in Milwaukee. The major newspaper of the socialist movement in Milwaukee, the *Social Democratic Herald*, which Berger edited, proclaimed on its masthead that it was the "Official paper of the Federated Trades Council of Milwaukee and of the Wisconsin State Federation of Labor."[69]

Socialist practice in Milwaukee, denigrated by left-wing intellectuals as municipal socialism, or "sewer socialism," was concerned above all with showing that socialists could run an efficient and honest city government while aiding unions and the underprivileged. In their first successful mayoralty campaign in 1910, the Milwaukee Socialists advocated free medical care, public works for the unemployed, and "public ownership and operation of public service enterprises," including a wood and coal yard, an ice plant, city services for plumbing in homes, a slaughterhouse, four markets and storage houses, a stone quarry, taxation of big corporations, banks and trust companies, and encouragement of labor unions.[70] They accomplished little of this ambitious program because of constitutional restrictions on the jurisdictions of cities.[71] Daniel Hoan, Socialist city attorney and subsequently long-term mayor, was able, however, to bring a rate-reduction case against the privately owned street railway and to force it to cut prices and conform to various safety and health regulations.[72] The Socialist administration also enacted policies to benefit union labor—for example, by compelling building contractors for city construction projects to permit union organization in Milwaukee.[73]

Subsequent Socialist administrations countered patronage politics by instituting meritocratic civil service standards in the police, fire, parks, and recreation departments. They also were able to apply socialist principles with the adoption of municipal ownership of the electric and street car utilities, municipal marketing of basic foods, and municipal banking. Led by Meta Berger (Victor Berger's wife) and Frederick Heath, who were elected to the Milwaukee school board in 1909, Socialists built coalitions with nonpartisans to gain direct election of school board members, expand appropriations for education, promote continuation schools for young workers, establish vacation schools, and provide medical and dental programs and free lunches for children.[74] In the 1930s, Mayor Hoan succeeded in building the first cooperative housing project in any American municipality.

Another facet of Milwaukee socialism was its acceptance of fiscal constraints and its overriding concern with efficiency. Socialist city governments were fiscally conservative. Property taxes under successive Socialist mayors from 1910 to 1940 were actually lower than in the period before and after their administrations.[75] The Socialists reacted to the fact that a large proportion of workers, and in particular families of German immigrants, owned their own houses. In their concern with efficiency, their emphasis on the role of government in the provision of public services, and their belief that socialism would gradually gain in strength as it was seen to work in practice, the Milwaukee Socialists followed a strategy of gradualism that closely resembled that of Sidney Webb and the British Fabians.

The strength of union-party connections in Milwaukee was reflected in the ambivalence of the local party's reaction to American intervention in World War I. At the national level the Socialist party had been adamantly opposed to the war, a policy that was very much in line with the views of most German-Americans living in Milwaukee, and it reiterated this position after the Congress voted to go to war in April 1917. But the Milwaukee union organization, the Federated Trades Council, never wholeheartedly accepted this position, and in 1918 explicitly embraced President Woodrow Wilson's war aims and the war bond drives. Socialist unions in Milwaukee and elsewhere were pressed to support the war (or at least not oppose it); as we will see in the subsequent chapters, the cost of repression and persecution for opposition could be high.

The Milwaukee Socialist party was torn between these contradictory pressures. Victor Berger, who was both Austrian-born and a leader of the

national party, signed an antiwar proclamation and opposed American intervention, but Mayor Hoan attempted to sidestep the issue. Under threat of
expulsion, he reaffirmed the Socialist party's antiwar position, but also
spoke at patriotic meetings. Typical of his efforts to straddle both sides, he
organized a preparedness parade as a "National Civil Demonstration."[76]

The war weakened Socialist organization in Milwaukee, as will be docu-
mented later. The labor base of the party, the close connection with the
local unions, was never as strong after the war as before. The cultural and
organizational roots of the party in the German immigrant population
declined, as Milwaukee Germans deemphasized their ethnic distinctive-
ness in the process of Americanization, sharply enhanced by the war. But
the dissolution of the party was a gradual process.[77] In the post–World War
I era, the Milwaukee party fared much better than local Socialist parties
that had never developed strong trade-union roots. Between 1920 and
1926, Socialists won approximately 45 percent of seats in common council
elections. Victor Berger was reelected to Congress in 1922, 1924, and
1926, and Mayor Hoan remained undefeated until 1940.

In Reading, Pennsylvania, the Socialists had major-party status from
1910 on, when they elected James Hudson Maurer to the state assembly
and were victorious in subsequent years in the mayoralty and some local
council contests. As in other centers of Socialist strength, success was associated with a strong link to the organized labor movement. Almost all of
the party's leadership and candidates were trade unionists.[78] David
Shannon notes that "the nature of the Socialist organization in Pennsylvania made it almost a labor party."[79] Maurer was active in both the AFL
as president of the Pennsylvania State Federation of Labor from 1912, and
in the national Socialist party as the representative of Pennsylvania in the
party's National Executive Committee, as candidate for governor in 1906,
and as representative in the state legislature for several terms.[80] According
to Shannon, Maurer "saw himself representing two constituencies, the
party and labor." Typical of his policies were a campaign to abolish the
Pennsylvania state police, which he regarded as a "strikebreaking" force, and
a threat to lead a general strike if the legislature failed to support a workmen's compensation bill.[81]

Like the Milwaukee party, the Reading organization was able to involve
its members in a wide range of activities, including card parties, debates,
picnics, a socialist orchestra, and singing, drama, and sport groups. The

party owned a publishing company that published a weekly newspaper, the *Reading Labor Advocate*, that was also the official organ of the local labor council; ran a small cigar factory (among its brands of cigars was the "Karl Marx"); and owned a three-story building in downtown Reading that housed both the party and local unions. In 1929 the party purchased a plot of land that became "Socialist Park," providing a lucrative source of revenue as well as a venue for socialist activities. Between 1928 and 1936, years in which the Socialist party was extremely weak nationally, the membership of the Reading party increased from 570 to 2,350, in the latter year accounting for around one-sixth of the entire national membership.

In his overview of Reading socialism, William Pratt emphasizes that the encompassing character of the party organization at work, at home, and in a wide variety of leisure activities provides a key to explaining its success: ". . . Reading socialism was more than a political movement. In fact, to many of its hard core, it was almost a complete way of life."[82]

From the 1910s, socialism and unionism were very closely interconnected in another electoral stronghold, New York City. Analysis of membership records reveals the high degree of overlap between union and party membership. In his study of the social background of enrolled Socialists in 1915, Charles Leinenweber finds that no less than one-quarter of registered Socialists were garment workers. Garment workers were the largest occupational grouping in every district where the Socialist party had significant support: the Lower East Side, Brownsville, and the Bronx. The heavily Jewish unions were among the party's staunchest supporters. Beyond ethnicity, New York Socialists were disproportionately drawn from skilled workers in industrial unions. Leinenweber observes: "The movement was working class, but represented organized, predominately skilled sectors of the working class, not unorganized and unskilled. Thus the movement was underlaid by trade unions, making the Socialist party de facto a labor party."[83]

The importance of a union base for socialism is confirmed in regression analysis of variations in Socialist voting at the county level in the state of New York. Sari Bennett summarized her findings for the period 1900 to 1912: "Intensely unionized areas with a small number of unions—characteristics of industrial unions—were predisposed to favor socialism and an appeal for the reformation of capitalist society. . . . [T]hree factors—industrial unionism, lengthy strikes, and urban-industrial change—created an environment in which the electorate could be persuaded to the socialist point of view."[84]

The experience of the political left in Minneapolis further illustrates the effect of prior union mobilization on Socialist success. In 1908 the Minneapolis branch of the International Association of Machinists swung its support to the Socialist party as a consequence of a bitter struggle against employers culminating in a strike in which machinists were attacked, jailed without being charged, and shot at by special police hired by the local open-shop organization, the Citizens' Alliance. Thomas Van Lear, the leader of the International Association of Machinists, fought mayorality campaigns in the 1910s that were effectively run through the union. In Minneapolis, David Paul Nord notes, "The Socialist party gradually became more broadly based in the labor movement, but always the machinists remained at the center of power."[85]

The vote for the Socialist party increased step by step with the political mobilization of the Machinists and other unions in the polarized situation that developed in Minneapolis from the 1910s. In the mayoral race of 1910, Van Lear gained more than ten times the vote of the previous Socialist candidate two years before, and after a second narrow defeat in 1912, he was elected to office in 1916. During these years, Van Lear welded together a coalition of machinists, other organized workers (including the teamsters who were fighting to gain union recognition), and municipal reformers who supported socialization of the city's corrupt utility companies. Ethnic factors, in this case Scandinavian, were also supportive of the movement.

As mayor, Van Lear was backed by only four Socialist aldermen in a twenty-six-member city council. Consequently, he could obtain little in the way of legislation. However, he "kept up the struggle with utility corporations," bringing "suit on behalf of the city" to reduce rates.[86] He also appointed a Socialist, who was a longtime member of the Machinists, as chief of police. Under Socialist control, the police helped to check the power of employers in strike situations.

By the time Van Lear began serving as mayor in early 1917, the issue of American intervention in the war was beginning to undermine the relationship of unions to the Socialist party. While the national party reaffirmed its antiwar stand, Van Lear and most unionists were drifting in the opposite direction. As in Milwaukee, organizational survival forced the Socialist-linked unions to support or at least not oppose the war. Responding to the passage by the Minnesota State Federation of Labor convention of mid-1917 of a prointerventionist resolution, the Socialists attacked the AFL as "hopelessly reactionary." In the following year, Van Lear was thrown out of the Socialist party. Nord observes that "the defection of the labor movement, not the attacks of loyalty groups, was the blow that wrecked the Socialist party in Minneapolis."[87] Leaving aside the question of whether to blame unions or party for the split, it is apparent that union support for the Socialist party had been a critical element in its success. Once the connection was broken, the Minneapolis Socialist party was marginalized. The importance of union-party links is reinforced by the subsequent success of the union-supported Minneapolis Municipal Nonpartisan League, and later the Minnesota Farmer-Labor party, which elected state-wide nominees for senator and governor during the twenties and thirties.[88]

The mutually supportive ties between local Socialist parties and unions affiliated with the AFL in Milwaukee, Reading, New York, and Minneapolis were exceptional within the larger national picture of the Socialist party. They provided the party with resources, both human and financial, that were lacking in most other areas of the country. This is not to say that other factors were absent. As has been mentioned and will be elaborated on in the next chapter, socialism in these cities was ethnically based. Concentrations of German, Jewish, Scandinavian, and other immigrant groups with a social democratic tradition were important sources of support for radical working-class politics.

The experiences of the party in Milwaukee, Reading, New York, and Minneapolis suggest that generalizations about the positive effects of union-party links for socialist organization, derived from the experience of other industrial societies, hold up for the United States as well. The American Socialist party was most entrenched and its support was most durable where it was able to build a base in the labor movement. In the cities discussed above, socialism became something of a way of life, embracing labor unions within an encompassing subculture. Under such circumstances the political obstacles to a third party were less decisive because the party was more than simply a machine for winning elections. These local parties were strong because they could draw on the diverse sources of commitment that exist in unions and class-related community organizations.

The Socialist party was most successful in cities where it took on the characteristics of a labor party, but such cases were few and far between in the country as a whole. Without the support of the Socialist party or AFL at the national level, these city labor parties remained interesting, but isolated, experiments with little influence on the shape of politics in the broader society. Even at their height, as Richard Judd has noted, socialist city administrations formed "small islands of authority in a sea of bourgeois power."[89] And most important, they were unable to transfer their local electoral strength to support for the party nationally, or even (for the most part) for state elections. Even unions led by Socialists would not waste their influence with the two major parties by voting for a hopeless nominee for president, or even governor.

Before World War I, alliances between local labor unions and socialist parties were at least tolerated by their national organizations. Unionists and Socialists who wished to cooperate at the local level could take advantage of the highly decentralized character of their respective organizations. Support for both the party and the unions declined during the 1920s, but it may be noted that Milwaukee, Reading, New York, and Minneapolis remained centers of socialist or left-third-party (the Farmer-Labor party in Minnesota) strength until the emergence of the New Deal and the Congress of Industrial Organizations in the 1930s.

Conclusion

In the United States, alone among the English-speaking democracies, the major working-class-oriented party operated in isolation from the mainstream of the union movement. Not only was the Socialist party established autonomously from the American Federation of Labor, but, for the most part, the two organizations were locked into intense mutual hostility. This harmed the party in several ways. It severely weakened the party's membership and resource base. The Socialist party never became a mass party, but remained a small organization spread thinly across a very large country. Like other socialist parties it lacked powerful or rich supporters, but unlike them it could not draw on mass organization to even the balance. Organizational weakness was associated with instability. The party appealed to members more on ideological than on interest grounds, and as a result its membership fluctuated wildly over time. The native-born party of 1912, with its disproportionate strength in western and southwestern states, was unrecognizable in the largely immigrant, city-based party of 1920. The weakness of ties with mainstream unions also shaped key Socialist policies, for it gave socialist intellectuals unusual sway within the party. The absence of entrenched unions was obvious in the party's costly decision in 1917 to oppose the country's participation in World War I. Finally, and more speculatively, the union-party split weakened class consciousness over the long term, for it aborted the possibility of a solitary labor movement which would integrate workers' economic and political concerns within one house.

These outcomes were disastrous for the Socialists, given the high cultural and institutional barriers to their success. The socialist project was always going to be an uphill battle in a culture characterized by individualism and antistatism and a polity dominated by two entrenched and opportunistic political parties. The Socialist party had both the most ambitious goals among the parties it competed with, and the least chance of gaining political power in the foreseeable future. A strong and durable organization would have given the party a better base on which to weather the reverses and electoral disappointments it was bound to suffer. One cannot replay history to investigate what might have happened had the party been better prepared to meet the challenge of American culture and political institutions, but the comparisons we have made in this chapter—both cross-nationally and within the United States—suggest that, had the party been able to gain majority union support, it would have been stronger and more durable and would have pursued more practical policies. Given the obstacles it faced, the Socialist party could ill afford to be isolated from unions with membership and resources many times greater than its own.

Chapter 4

IMMIGRANTS AND

SOCIALISM

Double-Edged Effects

Several streams of argument link the fate of the Socialist party in the United States to the influx of newcomers to the country from every part of the world. First, immigration created an extraordinarily diverse labor force in which class coherence was undermined by ethnic, racial, and religious identity. The importance of this has been noted by many observers of the American labor movement, including Marx and Engels. Ethnic diversity hurt socialists, who appealed to workers along class lines, and helped Democrats and Republicans, who had no inhibitions in making ethnic appeals. The difficulties faced by socialists were aggravated because craft unions in the American Federation of Labor (AFL) were also organized along ethnic lines, encompassing native workers and "old" immigrants from Northern Europe and largely excluding "new" immigrants from Southern and Eastern Europe, along with Chinese and African-Americans. In conceiving of workers as a cohesive class, socialists were struggling against the ethnic affinities of most workers and their organizations, as well as against individualistic and egalitarian values in American culture.

A second stream of generalization about immigration analyzes the political affinities of particular groups of immigrants. Two conflicting views have dominated this discussion. On the one hand, some have argued that immigrants were a vital source of support for socialism. These writers point out that socialism was largely imported by immigrants from Germany and Northern Europe in the second half of the nineteenth century. Germans, Jews, and Finns were prominent among socialist activists. From 1917, immigrant groups who opposed American involvement in World War I made up the overwhelming majority of members of the Socialist party. Conversely, other writers have emphasized that the vast bulk of immigrants were never attracted to the Socialist party. These analysts seek to explain why the party failed to gain the allegiance of the poorest, most vulnerable sections of the population.

A third line of argument centers on the role of Catholicism as an impediment to socialist success. The Socialist party never succeeded in appealing to Catholic immigrants, a notable failure given that Catholics constituted a majority of the industrial workforce in the critical decades around the turn of the twentieth century when the country was undergoing rapid economic development. This cannot be explained by saying that Catholics were inherently opposed to socialism, for they played an important role in Australian and British labor party movements. But the American socialists stressed anticlericalism far more than socialists in other English-speaking countries. By so doing they alienated a large section of the working-class population which had values that were otherwise favorable to collectivist planning and statist welfare policies.

Fourth and finally, socialism was widely perceived to be a foreign import into the United States. Although most immigrants were not socialist, and most socialists were not immigrants, many socialists were immigrants, most visibly in cities like New York, Chicago, and Milwaukee, where Jews and Germans were concentrated. The fact that socialism was introduced into America by German speakers, and was disproportionately supported by foreign-accented workers and intellectuals in the largest urban areas, allowed its opponents to attack it as fundamentally un-American.

Ethnic Diversity

Marxists appeal to workers on the basis of class, arguing that the most important fact shaping a person's life is whether that person owns capital or is paid to labor by someone who does. According to the classic socialist credo, all other group identities are secondary to the basic division between capitalists and workers. Hence, the strength and durability of class identity in relation to other forms of group solidarity—ethnic, cultural, religious—is of the utmost importance. Socialists framed their appeal to workers in class terms, and one may inquire into the success of their appeal by examining the extent to which class dominated contending sources of identity.

By this yardstick, American society was extremely unpropitious for socialism. Almost everyone who has studied the prospects for class solidarity among American workers, from Marx and Engels on, has stressed the fact that the United States is a nonfeudal, immigrant society with an extraordinarily high degree of ethnic, religious, and racial diversity.[1] The American working class in the early twentieth century was composed largely of immigrants.[2] The United States Immigration Commission reported in 1911 that barely one-fifth of wage earners had native white parents, while almost three-fifths were of immigrant origin.[3] Economist Simon Kuznets estimates that from 1840 to 1930 the foreign-born and native-born of foreign or mixed parentage grew thirteenfold, from less than three million to more than forty million. By 1930 roughly one-third of the total population was of foreign stock.[4]

Immigration to the United States was extraordinarily heterogeneous, even by comparison with other major settler societies. Table 4.1 compares immigration to the United States with immigration to Canada, Argentina, and Australia. More than three-quarters of immigrants to Australia and Canada came from Britain in the years 1911 to 1915. Immigration to Argentina was dominated by Southern Europeans, in particular Italians and Spaniards. In contrast, no country, or even region, is preponderant as a source of immigrants to the United States in this period.

The composition of the immigrant population became markedly more diverse from the end of the nineteenth century. In every decade from the founding of the Republic up to 1890, persons from Northern and Western Europe (including Germany) formed at least 70 percent of the new arrivals, but over the next ten years newcomers from these countries constituted just under half of the total, and from 1900 to 1920, less than one in four immigrants came from Northern or Western Europe.[5] As a result, from the 1890s, the labor force in the United States became the most ethnically heterogeneous in the world.

Table 4.1: Immigration by Region of Origin, 1911–1915

Region of Origin	Country of Immigration *(% of total from each region/ absolute number of immigrants from each region)*			
	United States	Argentina	Australia	Canada
British Isles & United States	21.03%	1.00%	89.52%	79.80%
	743,542	9,003	553,355	965,354
Developed Western Europe[1]	11.35%	4.43%	4.94%	5.45%
	401,334	39,932	30,523	65,950
Southern Europe[2]	32.10%	88.44%	1.81%	5.16%
	1,134,401	797,952	11,149	62,478
Eastern Europe[3]	26.77%	6.13%	.93%	7.12%
	946,257	55,308	5,762	86,124
Asia[4]	3.51%	0%	2.71%	2.21%
	124,169	0	16,766	26,774
Other Countries[5]	5.24%	0%	.09%	.26%
	185,095	0	552	3,021
Totals	3,534,798	902,195	618,107	1,209,701

[1]Belgium, Denmark, Finland, France, Germany, Netherlands, Norway, Sweden, Switzerland

[2]Greece, Italy, Portugal, Spain

[3]Poland, Russia, Serbia, Turkey in Europe

[4]China, India, Japan, Syria, Turkey in Asia, Other Asian Countries

[5]Africa, Central America, Mexico, Oceania, Pacific Islands, South America, West Indies

This shift in the origins of immigrants deepened the rift between "old" immigrants from Britain and Northern Europe, who were often skilled and able to assimilate quickly into the larger society, and "new," less skilled, entrants from Southern and Eastern Europe.[6] The earnings of "old" settlers were comparable to native-born whites, while "new" immigrants earned substantially less, on account of their relative lack of industrial skills and experience and their poor fluency in English, as well as overt discrimination by those who had arrived earlier or who had been born in the United States.[7]

Friedrich Engels commented in 1892 that the American "bourgeoisie" consciously exacerbated conflict among workers to deflect pressure away from themselves.[8] But he was also aware that ethnic and racial divisions were major obstacles to the creation of a class-conscious workers' movement irrespective of ruling-class strategy. Nine months after his statement that divisions among workers played into the hands of the ruling class, Engels noted that workers were riven into "the native-born and the foreigners, and the latter in turn into (1) the Irish, (2) the Germans, (3) the many small groups, each of which understands only itself: Czechs, Poles, Italians, Scandinavians, etc. And then the Negroes. To form a single party out of these requires quite unusually powerful incentives. Often there is a sudden violent *élan*, but the bourgeois need only wait passively, and the dissimilar elements of the working class fall apart again."[9]

A contemporary socialist, Mike Davis, has argued forcefully that these divisions were intensified because ethnic, cultural, religious, and racial cleavages overlapped and reinforced one another.[10] The rapid increase in Irish Catholic immigration from the 1840s led to a Protestant reaction and a Catholic counterreaction that were expressed in mutually exclusive subcultures encompassing education, work, and leisure—from Catholic schools and fire companies to Protestant temperance associations. Conflict among ethnic groups was intense. Volunteer fire companies, little more than organized ethnic gangs, fought over city turf, setting fire to their opponents' property as well as fighting fires on their own. Such conflict was particularly violent in the labor market, for this was where ethnicity becomes entangled with economic competition. From the late 1830s, Irish immigrants entered labor markets formerly dominated by Germans, British, and African-Americans. They were successful partly because they were willing to work for lower wages than former immigrants and even former slaves, and partly because the Irish had a strong sense of community that allowed them to forcefully exclude competing workers, in particular blacks.

African-American workers felt the full force of ethnic mobilization in the industrial north in the second half of the nineteenth century. In the 1830s, African-American freemen were employed as laborers and artisans in a wide range of occupations. The mobilization of new immigrants into exclusive ethnic castes and their systematic, frequently violent refusal to tolerate blacks in the workplace effectively excluded them from many

Table 4.2: Immigration to the United States by Decade, Region, and Race, 1841–1940

| Decade | Total in 1,000s | Region (%) | | | | | |
		Northern & Western Europe	Southern & Eastern Europe	Canada & Newfoundland	Total White	Latin America & Caribbean Islands	Asia & Middle East
1841–50	1,713	93.0	0.3	2.4	95.7	1.2	0.0
1851–60	2,598	93.6	0.8	2.3	96.7	0.6	1.6
1861–70	2,315	87.8	1.5	6.7	96.0	0.6	2.8
1871–80	2,812	73.6	7.7	13.6	94.9	0.7	4.4
1881–90	5,247	72.0	18.2	7.5	97.7	0.7	1.3
1891–00	3,688	44.6	51.9	0.1	96.6	1.0	2.0
1901–10	8,795	21.7	69.9	2.0	93.6	2.1	3.7
1911–20	5,763	25.3	50.0	12.9	88.2	6.0	4.3
1921–30	4,107	32.5	27.5	22.2	82.2	14.4	2.7
1931–40	528	38.7	27.2	20.5	86.4	9.7	3.0

Sources: U.S. Bureau of the Census, Historical Statistics of the United States, Colonial Times to 1957, Series A 9-22, A 34-50, C 23-38, & C 228-295 (Washington, D.C., 1960); U.S. Bureau of the Census, Historical Statistics of the United States, Colonial Times to 1970, Series A 9-22, A 44-50, C 23-28, & C 228-295 (Washington, D.C., 1975).

kinds of employment. A survey of African-American employment in Philadelphia in 1856 found that "less than two-thirds of those who have trades follow them . . . on account of the unrelenting prejudice against their color."[11] By the end of the antebellum period, African-American workers were virtually excluded from mechanic and artisanal occupations and much manual labor because white workers made it almost impossible for black apprentices, journeymen, or laborers to work alongside them or for employers to hire such workers.[12]

Fierce and prolonged discrimination against African-Americans produced a distinct underclass that was regarded as a race apart from white workers and their unions, and which, as a result, was excluded from their political projects, including socialism. Those who were the most exploited and who had the least to lose in militant class struggle—namely blacks—were distant from the political concerns of the working class as a whole. White workers were often as motivated to keep African-Americans out of their job territories as to battle employers directly for better conditions.

In the antebellum period, the principal split among white Americans was between Protestant nativists and Irish Catholic immigrants. In the decades around the turn of the twentieth century, a resurgence of militant anti-Catholicism, allied to nativism, divided the working class between Protestants and then mainly Southern European Catholics. These ethnic-religious subcultures—old-immigrant Protestant on the one side; new-immigrant Catholic on the other—were solidified politically in the Republican and Democratic parties. The Republican party expressed Protestant moralism allied to market-driven individualism, while the Democratic party accepted cultural diversity and communitarian remedies.

Such ethnic heterogeneity created a patchwork of conflicting party-political allegiances and weakened the chances that labor unions would back a new labor party. Immigrants from Britain, native stock, and Northern European Protestants were predominantly Republican, while Irish Catholic and Eastern and Southern European workers were largely Democratic.[13] Opponents of third-party political activity within the American Federation of Labor contended that labor was too diverse in its political sympathies to be bottled up in a single party. If workers were alienated from the movement because it was associated with such a party, unions would suffer a loss of bargaining power.[14]

Class-based conflict was not absent, nor even particularly weak, in the pre–World War United States. When one looks at patterns of conflict in the workplace, the United States ranked toward the top in both strikes (in relation to the size of the workforce) and in labor violence among industrial democracies.[15] But class consciousness in the workplace was secondary to ethnicity as a basis for organization and political activity. As noted, this argument has been elaborated by Ira Katznelson in his examination of how ethnicity and class played out in the workplace and in residential communities. Katznelson contends that experiences in the workplace led workers to class-based unions, but neighborhood patterns produced ethnic-based political affiliations. In America, "links between work and community-based conflicts have been unusually tenuous. . . . What is distinctive about the American experience is that the linguistic, cultural, and institutional meaning given to the differentiation of work and community . . . has taken a sharply divided form, and that it has done so for a very long time."[16]

The contrast with European societies could hardly be stronger. In an age before the institutionalization of border controls and passports, Europeans saw considerable movement of peoples among their countries (as well as mass emigration). In the pre–World War I era, a large number of Irish worked in England, Poles in Germany, and Belgians in France. In Catholic countries, the church supported Catholic unions as a counterweight to socialist unions, but ethnic and religious cleavages in the working class did not overwhelm class solidarity or the ability of socialist parties to mobilize workers politically by class appeals. In several European countries, socialist parties drew on an entrenched working-class subculture, from pubs, to working-class newpapers and presses, to choral societies and labor unions. Socialist parties were the first mass parties to develop in Europe, and they were immensely strengthened by their subcultural roots. The United States was no melting pot; distinct subcultures flourished, but these were ethno-religious, not class-based. When they sought communal sustenance in the New World, successive waves of immigrants depended on their ethnic-familial connections, and moved into distinctively ethno-linguistic neighborhoods. Successive waves of newcomers from different combinations of countries and continents shaped and reshaped the meaning of ethnicity for new arrivals as for those who arrived earlier. Ethnic identity was not an innate mark of birth, but was created as groups adjusted to the New World and conceptions of "them" and "us." To distinguish themselves from Catholic Irish, Protestant Irish delved deep in their history to conceive of themselves as "Scotch-Irish." Catholic Irish struggled against stereotypes of "new" immigrants from the 1840s on, but had established union leaders defending job territories by the time of the new influx of the 1890s. Among the wave of "new" immigrants, Hungarians, Czechs, and Poles were labeled "Slav," a term that meant little or nothing to them in their homelands.

Immigration decisively shaped the character of American unions because unions were on the front line in adapting to a heterogeneous workforce. The collective expression of ethnicity through unions was particularly marked in the United States.

Even when they adhered to the principle of internationalist socialism, or simply inter-ethnic solidarity, American union leaders (often first-generation immigrants themselves) could not ignore the culture of the peoples whom they were addressing. In the absence of social welfare legislation, it was at the level of the ethnic community that immigrants found the resources indispensable to their successful adaptation to the New World. Unionization, when it took place, proceeded from this social fabric or was doomed to failure.[17]

Unlike political parties that can tailor their appeals to half the population, unions must strive to recruit a goodly majority of the workers in the relevant occupation or industry if they are to bargain effectively with employers. But, within limits, unions can define the occupation or industry they wish to organize, and the fateful decisions made by the leaders of the American Federation of Labor, the dominant union movement from the 1890s through the 1920s, were motivated by the fear that "old" immigrants and their labor markets would be overrun by "new" immigrants.[18] This fear reinforced the exclusivity of craft union strategy described in the previous chapter. Instead of conceiving of their role as defending labor as a class, the AFL represented native workers and old immigrants in relatively homogeneous unions. Demands for restriction of immigration intensified the basic tension between native Americans and "old" immigrants who dominated organized labor, and the "new" immigrants who remained outside the labor movement.[19]

The presumed cultural inferiority of the new immigrants, and their lack of previous experience with unionism, or in many cases even with industrialism, confirmed the prejudice on the part of many AFL leaders that the new immigrants were difficult or impossible to organize. Despite the success of some unions, most notably the United Mine Workers, which recruited 100,000 Polish and East European miners in Pennsylvania in the great anthracite coal strike of 1902, most organized skilled workers believed that their best policy was to defend their narrow job territories against incursion rather than build more inclusive organizations. It is no accident that the term "job territory" was invented in the United States.

Differences between largely unorganized immigrants and organized labor were reinforced by nativism and racism. The primary loci of these prejudices could be found in the antagonism between Protestants and Catholics and in anti-Chinese sentiment. One can gain an idea of the extreme bitterness of such racism from alarmist contemporary accounts of how Chinese immigration would threaten American workers and undermine American culture. Samuel Gompers himself coauthored a vitriolic pamphlet on the subject which was published in 1902 by the AFL, entitled *Meat vs. Rice: American Manhood vs. Asiatic Coolieism: Which Shall Survive?*[20]

Divisions within labor were reinforced by the economic effects of immigration. Immigration introduced successively less affluent and less skilled classes of newcomers while improving the lot of old immigrants. The first generation generally occupied the lower rungs of the economic ladder, and this allowed second-generation offspring and other native-born whites to rise into skilled and managerial positions. This pattern continued into the 1920s.[21] Isaac Hourwich, an authority on immigration, asserted in his pre–World War I study of the phenomenon: "It is only because the new immigration has furnished the class of unskilled laborers that the native workmen and older immigrants have been raised to the plane of an aristocracy of labor."[22]

The thrust of our argument is that in the critical decades before World War I, ethnicity provided a stronger basis than social class for political attachment. But this does not mean that ethnicity eliminated radical working-class political activity. In the first place, in urban areas where immigration was slight or gradual, or where class organization was already entrenched, there was the possibility that class could trump ethnicity. Second, where ethnicity and class identity coincided, one would expect to see increased potential for class conflict.

John Cumbler provides some evidence for the first of these expectations in his study of two contrasting industrial cities in Massachusetts: Lynn and Fall River.[23] Workers in Lynn responded to the steady decline of the city's shoe industry in the late nineteenth and early twentieth centuries by adopting militant trade unionism. Housing patterns and community organizations were also class-based. In Lynn, a relatively small and steady stream of new immigrants were integrated into existing working-class institutions. Fall River, by contrast, lacked class traditions, and it experienced a rapid and large influx of immigrants in the 1890s. Portuguese and Polish workers who poured into the town were excluded by established English, Irish, and French Canadian workers. The predictable result was an ethnically splintered town with little evidence of working-class solidarity.

Many case studies of successful local socialist organizations in the United States stress the importance of an ethnically homogeneous population, either native or immigrant. Richard Flacks observes that socialists were particularly strong in communities with experience of "communication and shared social understanding among people with shared ethnicity or other sub-cultural membership."[24] John Bodnar reaches a similar conclusion in his examination of immigration in Steelton, Pennsylvania: "Ironically, while ethnicity was somewhat of a divisive force before 1930, it was actually laying the basis for the type of cooperation that would be necessary for the eventual triumph of the CIO. The reliance on the ethnic community taught newcomers the value of confronting social problems and economic difficulties with large, formalized institutions and organizations rather than with isolated kin."[25]

Analyzing the reasons for the long-term success of socialism in Reading, Pennsylvania, William Pratt concludes: "The Reading movement enjoyed advantages that many other local Socialist movements in America did not. Its membership was made up almost entirely of the predominant native ethnic stock of the city—the Pennsylvania Dutch. This being the case, local Socialists were never stigmatized as foreigners. . . . The small percentage of recent immigration reduced the chances of ethnic conflict."[26] In evaluating the reasons for the election of Socialist mayors in three small midwestern industrial cities—Canton, Illinois; Elwood, Indiana; and Marion, Indiana— Errol Stevens emphasizes that the population of each was almost exclusively native-born.[27] The same factor is noted by Garin Burbank, in his assessment of the factors underlying Socialist support in Oklahoma, the state which provided the party with its highest prewar percentage vote and per capita membership.[28] In analyzing radicalism among hard-rock miners, Melvyn Dubofsky points to "ethnic similarity": "Those workers who filled the young industrial cities of the West shared a tradition of union organization, a common language and a certain amount of ethnic similarity."[29]

The role of ethnic homogeneity is, however, not limited to communities or occupations which were preponderantly native-born or of English-language foreign origin. The major sources of Socialist electoral and membership strength among immigrant communities were also in culturally homogeneous populations. The Germans of Milwaukee and the Jews of the Lower East Side of New York were the only groups to elect Socialists to Congress. In New York, as noted in previous chapters, the Socialist party was really successful only in predominantly Jewish areas.[30] Fine points out that Milwaukee socialism rested above all on "the fact that they had a stable German proletarian element as the backbone of their movement."[31] The party was, however, able to attract considerable support in the one predominantly Catholic Polish ward after reaching major-party status in German districts.[32]

A comparison of Italian immigrants in Argentina and the United States confirms the hypothesis that ethnic homogeneity was an important ingredient in socialist support. In Argentina, Italian immigrants composed the majority of the Buenos Aires working class and were active as leaders and members in large radical unions and political movements, both anarchist and socialist. Italians in Buenos Aires lived in a relatively ethnically homogeneous environment, much like that of Germans in Milwaukee. Italian immigrants in New York began to join unions after 1910, often those in which socialists were strong, as in the garment trades. But they did not respond in large numbers to socialism and were underrepresented in labor organizations. Marlene Terwilliger, comparing the political activity of Italians and Jews in New York, suggests that one reason for the continuing unwillingness of Italians to join the party was that "even when in political agreement, [they] were never 'at home' in the New York Socialist Party, which was preponderantly Jewish."[33]

The view that immigration is the key to understanding the weakness of socialism in America is challenged by the fact that it was precisely during the years of greatest immigration, in the decade before 1914, that class conflict was most acute and the Socialist party strongest. Despite some claims that immigrants were underrepresented in the Socialist party before World War I, membership data indicate that this was not so. A study by the party of the ethnic composition of its membership in 1908 revealed that 29 percent were foreign-born, a proportion not very different from the ratio of immigrants in the industrial working population.[34] In 1910, white immigrants made up 31 percent of all those occupied in mineral extraction, manufacturing, transportation, and trade.[35]

This objection does not touch on the basic argument we are making, for immigration not only brought millions of individuals to America with particular propensities to support or oppose the Socialist party, but it shaped the working class as a whole. Mass immigration spurred ethnic identities and racial exclusion that sliced the American working class into exclusive communities with diverse political affinities. As we show below, some of these ethnic groups were inclined to socialism. The point that cannot be stressed too often is that the extraordinarily diverse waves of immigration from the 1840s to the 1920s created an equally diverse working class. In the first two decades of its existence from 1901, the American Socialist party was an amalgam of native and immigrant groups, but was never a class-based party. Its leaders developed an ideological appeal that actually on occasion drew a greater proportion of the population to socialism than in other English-speaking societies before World War I, but the party always lacked a solid class base. American workers were riven by ethnic particularisms that made it difficult, if not impossible, to unite them behind the notion of a working-class party.

Immigration profoundly affected American unions in a way that reinforced this outcome. The dominant majority of AFL unions responded to mass immigration by defending native workers and old immigrants against the incursion of new workers. They fought on two fronts: bargaining militantly with employers and seeking to increase the scarcity of labor in their job territories by constraining the influx of newcomers. The result was an effective but sectional movement that never saw itself as the representative of the working class as a whole and never adopted the idea that the workers would be best served by a separate party.

Immigrants

Did the Socialist party fail because it was unable to gain the support of the mass of immigrants? Which groups of immigrants supported socialism, and why were American radical parties dominated by immigrants, particularly in the early years and during and after World War I? These two lines of questions have shaped the study of immigrants and socialism in the United States. The key to understanding how immigrants fit into an explanation of the failure of the Socialist party is that there is no contradiction in the answers to the two questions. On the one hand, as we detail below, the Socialist party was unable to attract the vast majority of immigrants, a decisive failure given that immigrants formed the bulk of the working class. By and large, immigrants adhered to traditional values and were far removed from socialism. On the other hand, when one looks at the kinds of individuals who did support socialism, immigrants—in particular Jews, Finns, and Germans—are present in disproportionate numbers. Only a minority of immigrants were socialists, but, for extended periods of time, most socialists were immigrants.

Immigrants as Radicals

In early-twentieth-century America, many socialist strongholds were populated by newcomers from abroad: Germans in Milwaukee, Finns and Scandinavians in Michigan and Minnesota, and East European Jews in New York City.[36] Several of the most influential socialist unions were made up largely of immigrants, including the German-dominated Brewery Workmen and the Jewish-controlled garment workers' organizations. The only Socialist party members elected to Congress in the United States were two immigrants who represented districts predominantly inhabited by members of their own ethnic group. An Austrian-born Jew, Victor Berger, who emphasized his Teutonic background, was elected to represent the largely German Fifth District of Milwaukee from 1911 to 1913 and 1919 to 1929, while Meyer London, a Russian-born Jew, was sent to Congress from the predominantly Jewish Lower East Side Ninth District of New York from 1915 to 1919 and again from 1921 to 1923.

German immigrants introduced socialism to America. Both the American section of the First International and the Socialist Labor party (SLP), founded in 1876 as the Workingmen's party, were formed mainly by the German-born. For many years the SLP "was a small Turnverein whose members hassled over old world politics."[37] Early meetings were conducted in German.[38] Under the leadership of Daniel De Leon, a Jewish immigrant from the West Indies, the SLP tried hard to Americanize itself and to recruit among the native-born. But, as Henry George noted contemptuously, "they have also greatly crippled freedom of speech among themselves by determining to conduct their discussions in the English language."[39]

Morris Hillquit reported that at most only 10 percent of the members of the SLP were American-born during the last two decades of the nineteenth century. The overwhelming majority, including most of the party's leaders, were foreign-born non-English-speakers.[40] The dangers this posed were recognized by De Leon.[41] According to a report written by the most important leader of the party to the 1893 Zurich Congress of the Socialist International, socialism in America was thereby weakened:

> [The fact that] the apostles of the Social Revolution were at first mostly men of foreign birth, who landing here equipped with learning and experience of older civilizations were not deceived by appearances, but whose foreign birth was used by schemers and corruptionists to pull the wool over the eyes of the American proletariat and induce it to look upon Socialism as an exotic plant, has contributed not a little to retard the progress of the movement here. . . .[42]

The impression of strong immigrant support for the Socialist party is confirmed in quantitative analyses of voting for the Socialist party candidate Eugene Debs in the presidential elections of 1912 and 1920 across six eastern and midwestern states: Illinois, Minnesota, New York, Ohio, Pennsylvania, and Wisconsin. These states had high concentrations of foreign-born and provided a significant share (42 percent in 1912 and 59 percent in 1920) of the total vote nationally for the Socialist party in its peak years. Our quantitative analysis, which is reported in detail in the appendix to this chapter, shows that the Socialist vote at the county level varies significantly in response to a county's immigrant makeup—positively with the presence of Russians (Jews), Nordic immigrants (Finns, Swedes, Norwegians), and Germans (1920) and negatively with Irish and Germans (1912). The proportion of immigrants in a county predicts Socialist voting more powerfully than the proportion of wage earners or the degree to which a county was urban.[43]

No group has been regarded as more firmly entrenched in supporting American socialism than settlers from Germany. The participation of Germans in national and municipal socialist politics is detailed by many case studies of eastern and midwestern towns and cities where the Socialist party was particularly successful.[44] In 1920, Germans were disproportionately socialist—largely as a result of their opposition to American involvement in World War I. But, surprisingly, we find that in 1912, Germans were *less* likely than other citizens to vote Socialist. Many socialists were German in 1912, but German immigrants as a whole tended to be less socialist than the population as a whole.

The leadership of Germans in the American socialist movement has been linked to the political sources of emigration from Germany, particularly in the wake of the defeated democratic revolution of 1848, and the later repression of the German Social Democratic movement in the late 1870s and early 1880s. The German Social Democratic party was the strongest socialist movement in the world before World War I, and many newcomers brought their ideological sympathies to America.[45] German immigrant support for the Socialist party has also been linked to the fact that many Germans experienced industrialism before leaving their homeland. As Gerald Rosenblum, a student of immigration, observed, "It was primarily those immigrants with industrial backgrounds who added to the radical cohorts in this country. Germans were conspicuous in this regard."[46] Conversely, the larger number from rural areas were not attracted to socialism in America.

Although Germans continued to play a determining role in some cities, particularly Milwaukee, their predominance within the socialist movement as a whole declined with the establishment of the Socialist Party of America.[47] In 1901, the party, which resulted from a merger between the Social Democratic party, a predominantly native-born radical group led by Eugene Debs, and a largely foreign-born spinoff from the Socialist Labor party, succeeded in gaining support among both native Americans and old immigrants. The new party thus fulfilled the hopes of Marx and Engels for a predominantly native, largely working-class party. From its founding, the great majority of the delegates to its conventions were American-born.[48] Until American entry in World War I, the Socialist party secured its highest share of votes in states with relatively few foreign-born residents: Oklahoma, Nevada, Montana, Washington, California, Idaho, Florida, Arizona, and Texas.[49]

The impression of minimal German participation in the American Socialist party before World War I is confirmed in our statistical analysis of the presidential election of 1912. Despite the continued prominence of German immigrants in a number of towns and cities where socialism was strong, by 1912 there is no positive association between the percentage of the population who were German immigrants and Socialist voting at the county level. While there is a simple correlation between the proportion of the German immigrant population and Socialist support, the positive association disappears once we control for the proportion of wage earners, urban dwellers, and the presence of other ethnic groups. (See Table 4.4 in the appendix to this chapter.)

How can this finding be accounted for in the face of extensive case study evidence of German-American support for socialism in cities and towns such as Milwaukee and Minneapolis? A breakdown of counties according to the degree of industrialization and urbanization helps to solve the puzzle. In urban counties and counties with a significant percentage of wage earners, the relationship between the proportion of German immigrants in the population and Socialist voting is positive. However, in rural counties and in counties where there were few workers there is a significant negative relationship between the proportion of German immigrants and Socialist voting. The reason for this can be found in the divide between Catholics and Protestants back in Germany. In Germany, rural areas tended to be conservative and disproportionately Catholic, whereas urban areas were more likely to be secularized and Protestant. This pattern apparently held among German migrants to America. (See Table 4.5 in the appendix to this chapter.)

A study of the German working-class community in Chicago also documents that the radical influence of the first wave of German immigrants was declining by the early 1900s.[50] As German immigrants self-consciously tried to Americanize, the distinct German subculture of newspapers, festivities, theater, picnics, and clubs of all kinds that underpinned socialist organization declined. The old socialist German-language newspaper, *Arbeiter-Zeitung*, which explicitly rejected American culture and values, was increasingly viewed as old-fashioned and out of touch with American conditions.[51] While the socialist subculture of German immigrants could sustain and regenerate itself in a few cities that were densely populated by Germans, such as Milwaukee, in most other areas it eroded.

The negative association between Socialist voting and the presence of German-born in rural areas was sharply reversed in 1920. (See Table 4.5 in the appendix to this chapter.) Concentrations of Germans in nonurban counties became positively and significantly associated with Socialist voting. The extraordinary shift from 1912 to 1920 testifies that Socialist opposition to American intervention in the war mobilized support in German immigrant areas far more effectively than any previous party policy. An analysis of German-American support for the party in Wisconsin outside of Milwaukee during these years concludes, "Sympathy for the fatherland and reaction to repression rather than finely developed class consciousness were the main reasons for the success of outstate Socialism."[52]

Jews have been regarded, along with Germans, as the immigrant core of the Socialist party. Socialist leaders were disproportionately Jews, and Jews were active across the spectrum of non-Jewish labor and social democratic organizations.[53] The electoral successes of the Socialist party in New York City in the 1910s, which included the election of a congressman and a number of state legislators, were rooted in first-generation Jewish immigrant settlements on the Lower East Side.[54] Socialism was exceptionally strong in the sweatshops in the clothing industry, where, as Paul Buhle has observed, "socialists quickly formed the leadership of large sections of the workforce, and remained for many generations eminently respectable, indeed widely considered necessary for the stabilty of both labor and capital."[55]

The strength of Jewish support for the Socialist party is confirmed in our data analysis. There is a highly significant relationship between the proportion of Russian immigrants (a surrogate for Jews, since the Census does not inquire into religion) and the percent voting Socialist at the county level for both the 1912 and 1920 presidential elections.[56] Jewish immigrants tended to live in urban working-class counties where Socialist voting was higher than elsewhere, but the effect of concentrations of Russians is strong even when controlled for urbanism and occupational status. This result is particularly impressive because New York City, the prime setting for Jewish socialism, is not included in our data analysis.[57]

A review of the background of socialist immigrants suggests that most had first come into contact with radical working-class movements in their country of origin or at least had extensive experience as industrial workers.[58] Gerald Rosenblum hypothesizes that the prior urban and industrial experience of immigrant groups explains the extent to which they were radical in U.S. cities.[59] Herbert Gutman argues along similar lines in his overview of the way in which tradition and custom shaped working-class behavior.[60] Jews are a classic instance, for many of them were, in Morris Hillquit's words, "ready made Socialists" by the time they arrived in America.[61] The combination of an overtly anti-Semitic regime in Russia and a large impoverished Jewish proletariat produced strong support for socialist organizations and trade unions.[62]

The link between prior experience and orientation toward socialism is supported in the contrast between southern Italians and northern Italians. The relatively small proportion of Italian immigrants who came from the more urban and industrialized northern part of the country were much more likely to join the Socialist party and AFL unions than their brethren from the rural south. A survey of 24,594 male workers taken by the U.S.

Senate Immigration Commission in 1910 indicated that 39.8 percent of the small group of northern Italians, most of whom were from urban backgrounds, belonged to unions, compared to but 10.6 percent of southern Italians.[63] Most southern Italian immigrants had been poor peasants who emigrated to earn enough money in America to improve their economic prospects on their return to Italy.[64] To the extent that we hear of the labor activities of southern Italians it is because they furnished support for militant strikes led by the anarcho-syndicalist Industrial Workers of the World (IWW), much as southern Italian workers backed anarchist groups at home. The distinctive character of southern Italian radicalism grew out of extreme economic and cultural "backwardness." Overpopulation, heavy taxation, poor land, and inadequate markets for agricultural produce pushed suffering beyond toleration. Such conditions and the oppression of the landowners (along with their clerical supporters) promoted anarchism rather than labor-socialism.[65]

Finnish immigrants combined a rural background with very high levels of support for socialism. During the greatest inflow, from 1893 to 1914, just one in eight Finnish newcomers was from a city.[66] However, Finnish socialists tended to come from southern and eastern Finland, precisely the impoverished rural areas that were to provide strong backing for socialism.[67] Finnish immigration never reached the absolute levels of German or Jewish immigration and so had a smaller impact on American society and socialism; nevertheless, in proportional terms, Finns supplied the highest levels of Socialist support of any ethnic group.[68] Membership in the Finnish Socialist Federation grew from 2,500 in 1906 to 13,677 in 1912 to a peak of 17,000 in 1914. The latter figure is all the more remarkable in light of the fact that the total number of Finnish immigrants enumerated in the 1910 Census of the United States was 129,700.[69] Table 4.4 in the appendix to this chapter confirms the strength of Socialist voting in counties with concentrations of Finnish immigrants.[70] By 1914 almost as large a proportion of Finns were Socialists as Socialists were Finns. This is the only immigrant group about which this can be said.

Socialist opposition to American intervention in World War I alienated large numbers of native and English-origin workers while it mobilized immigrants from Central and Eastern Europe who, for various reasons, either supported Germany or were opposed to an alliance with czarist Russia. After the Bolshevik Revolution, many Eastern European immigrants turned to the Socialist party in solidarity with workers in their countries of origin. They affiliated to the party via their own foreign-language federations, which by 1915 numbered fourteen. As a result of losing the bulk of its native-born and "Anglo-Saxon" supporters who resented its opposition to the war and opposed the Bolshevik revolution, the Socialist party essentially became a party of immigrants based in a few midwestern and eastern states.

The foreign-language federations provided 16,000 out of the party's 118,000 members in 1912; by 1915 the number had risen to between 25,000 and 30,000 out of a total of some 80,000; and by 1919 the federations encompassed more than half the party's 110,000 members.[71] In 1916, thirteen out of the fifteen socialist daily newspapers in the United States were printed in a language other than English.[72] The federations had an autonomous status within the party. In 1914, the party National Committee voted explicitly that "the Language Federations have full charge and jurisdiction of the language locals, and of all propaganda in the particular language."[73] The result, as Charles Leinenweber notes, was that they "were never integrated into the party."[74]

The separation of the language federations from the daily life of the party did not mean that they did not contribute to it. The Socialist Yiddish-language daily *Forward* had a circulation of 200,000 before the United States entered World War I. It was a profitable enterprise which donated large sums to the party's coffers. Finnish socialists also gave generously to the Socialist party.[75] But though the members of the Finnish Federation formed 10 percent or more of the total membership of the party from 1912 on, they, unlike the Jews, produced no leaders of consequence.[76]

The strength and autonomy of the foreign-language federations contributed to the Communist-Socialist split of 1919. Several federations supported the Bolsheviks and their call for an underground party and immediate mass action. Centrist leaders of the Socialist party, including Morris Hillquit and Victor Berger, who argued that the democratic character of the United States should be weighed heavily in determining party strategy, were attacked by the federations and their Bolshevik supporters as being too cautious. The new American Communist party, affiliated with the Third International, was made up largely of non-English-speaking federations. Of the thirty thousand members of the Communist party in 1919, all but four thousand belonged to language federations representing individuals from Eastern Europe and Russia.

By the end of World War I the Socialist party was a fragmented organization incapable of responding coherently to mounting radicalism expressed in a national wave of strikes and in widespread efforts to build a farmer-labor party. The strength of the foreign-language federations, their autonomy within the party, and their obsession with events outside the United States exacerbated factionalism and contributed to the destruction of the Socialist party.

Conservative Immigrants

A very different picture of the role of immigrants is suggested when one examines the orientations of the masses of immigrants living in America rather than the makeup of the Socialist party. Marcus Hansen, a leading immigration historian, has emphasized that "the weight of immigrant political influence has historically been felt on the side of conservatism."[77] He concludes that most immigrants saw the United States as a land of greater freedom and opportunity than the countries they had left, "and with the enthusiasm of converts they praised the Republic and the material blessings it offered."[78] Hansen, of course, was aware of the role that immigrants played in the socialist, as well as other radical, movements, a phenomenon which he, like scholars cited earlier, related to the fact "that many of them had been Socialists in the country of their birth." Hansen, however also reported that "more immigrant Socialists were lost to the cause in the United States than were won from the ranks of the newcomers."[79] Along similar lines, Oscar Handlin stated unequivocally that "the process of immigrating" itself fostered a "conservatism alien to the dominant trends in American life." As he notes:

Perhaps the most prevalent myth about immigrants links them with radicalism, but nothing could be farther from the truth. The overwhelming majority were exceedingly conservative in politics, as in other forms of social expression. The peasant origins of many, and the comparative backwardness of the societies from which they emigrated, bred a submissiveness which was not shed in the crossing. In fact the very process of emigration fostered it. Forms, ways of doing things, which in the old country needed no justification, in the new, had to be bolstered continually by a rigid traditionalism. Thus, the Polish or Italian peasant, transplanted to Warsaw or Naples, might become a socialist or anarchist, but in Chicago or Cleveland, he was so preoccupied with defending what was familiar that disruptive influences made no impression upon him. Migration froze development.[80]

Richard Hofstadter has also stressed the influence of the peasant background of most early-twentieth-century immigrants, noting that they were "totally unaccustomed to the active citizen role." Insofar as they participated in politics it was largely for "concrete and personal gains," not "high principles."[81]

Handlin, Hofstadter, and political scientist Martin Shefter have pointed to the fact that urban city machines, mainly Democratic, won the allegiance of immigrant communities by providing them with services, representation, and avenues of mobility before Socialists appeared on the scene.[82] New immigrants from Southern and Eastern Europe were rarely interested in socialism.[83] Gerald Rosenblum notes that the " 'job consciousness' of the foreign born was quite consistent with the unionism practiced in the AFL."[84]

The fact that many did not view themselves as permanent *settlers* in the United States, but as *sojourners* who planned to return to Europe, also helps to explain their lack of interest in social reform or American politics generally. Studies of several "new immigrant" groups, particularly the Italians, Slavs, and Greeks, emphasize that many, if not most, often came with the intention of making enough money in a few years to return home to buy property.[85] The 1911 Immigration Commission found that for every one hundred Southern and Eastern Europeans admitted to the United States between 1907 and 1911, forty-five went back (for "old immigrants" the corresponding figure is thirteen). In the case of Italians, no fewer than seventy-three departed for every one hundred who arrived.[86]

Lack of interest in socialism also reflected the socioeconomic gains experienced after coming to the United States that enabled many "sojourners" to return to their native land. In general, wages for given occupations in America were much higher than in Southern and Eastern Europe. Further, most newcomers experienced an economic boost by simply switching from the agrarian to the industrial sector.[87] As Daniel De Leon put it, no matter how bad things were in America, they were better than in the overseas homeland. He suggested that late-nineteenth-century immigrants were not attracted to the socialist movement because the American "standard of living is, on the whole, superior to the European. As a result of this, a portion of the immigrants to this country who, at home laboured under the most wretched conditions, feels greatly relieved with wages that had already caused grumbling among the natives, and is consequently, alienated, at least temporarily, from Socialist thought. . . ."[88]

Most turn-of-the-century European socialist analysts accepted the proposition that immigrants gained by going to America. Belgian socialist leader Emile Vandervelde reported after a trip to the United States in 1904 that "no one seriously disputes that, all in all, American workers have a position very much superior to that of the European worker." [89] German socialist Ludwig Quessel produced statistical evidence that the real wages of Americans were increasing—which he attributed to the power and influence of labor unions. Morris Hillquit, writing the first major history of American socialism in 1910, also stressed that his party suffered because "the American working men still enjoyed some actual [economic] advantages over their brethren on the other side of the ocean. . . . [T]hey had yet before them the example of too many men who before their very eyes rose from the ranks of labor to the highest pinnacles of wealth and power; they were still inclined to consider labor as a mere transitory condition."[90] More recently, the major post–World War II Socialist leader and theoretician Michael Harrington reiterated this theme: "It is true that many of the immigrants, even though living under objectively degrading conditions, saw their lot as improved compared to the old country. They thus had an impression of relative betterment, not relative deprivation."[91]

A questionnaire survey of foreign-born workers in the building trades administered by the Michigan Bureau of Labor and Industrial Statistics in Saginaw in 1892 provides limited empirical evidence that these interpretations correspond to the actual sentiments of immigrants. Over three-quarters said that conditions in the United States were superior to those in their native country.[92]

Catholic Opposition to Socialism

No discussion of the influence of immigration on American socialism can ignore the special role that Catholic institutions and parishioners played. Catholicism has helped to shape socialist parties in many capitalist societies during much of the twentieth century. Catholicism retained into the modern era values formed in medieval times, including disdain for materialism, profits, and usury (interest). It emphasized "conservative" or Tory communitarian values and the responsibility of the well-to-do, the state, and the church for the underprivileged. While Protestantism has been more individualistic, Catholicism has been more group-oriented or collectivistic.

The countries of the Protestant Reformation were more disposed than Catholic countries to accept the competitive and individualistic values of industrial and urban societies. Protestant values, as Max Weber and many others have emphasized, contributed to the rise of industrialization and capitalism. Conversely, the medieval communitarian values that Catholicism retained helped to foster the growth of the welfare state and stratum- or class-based organization. One might expect, therefore, that Catholicism would lead to support for socialism and Protestantism to rejection.

In fact, as we know, the opposite seems to have occurred. In countries with predominantly Catholic populations, such as France, Italy, and Spain, strong lefts emerged, which, however, were identified with secularism, anticlericalism, and atheism, derivative from the French Revolution, while practicing Catholics backed rightist and antisocialist parties. In Protestant societies the predominant religious denominations were not rejected by the bourgeois left. The clerical-secular divide did not foster strong Christian parties. Hence, socialists did not suffer from religious antipathy directed against the left. This pattern can be seen most strikingly in Germany, where socialism flourished primarily in the Protestant areas in the east, e.g., Prussia, while in western Germany, the Catholic Church, as in Latin Europe, repeatedly condemned atheistic materialistic socialism and weakened the appeal of the Social Democratic party.

The situation was quite different in Great Britain and Australia, where Catholic clergy, supportive as elsewhere of communitarian values, were able to accept their labor parties. In these countries statism and class consciousness were not identified with Marxist anticlericalism. Religious nonconformist Protestants played an important role in the British Labour party. Irish Catholic trade unionists helped to organize and lead the Labor party in Australia. Leaders of both parties downplayed any antireligious feelings they harbored.

In the United States, however, as discussed in Chapter 5, socialists were more ideological and sectarian than in the democratic European and

Australasian countries, and antireligious and even anti-Catholic sentiments were openly expressed by many radicals. American socialists thus undermined their appeal to a rapidly growing portion of the working class— Catholic immigrants, a group that was otherwise sympathetic to collectivism and welfare. By the turn of the century, Catholics constituted the bulk of new immigrants and the backbone of the American industrial workforce and trade union membership. Politically, most became part of, and loyal to, the Democratic party, which in urban industrial areas supported the aspirations of the new immigrants in the economy and polity.

In contrast to the situation in Australia and Britain, the church would not tolerate its followers supporting the Socialists. The American hierarchy openly and actively resisted socialism, while at the same time endorsing trade unionism and welfare reforms.[93] G.D.H. Cole, writing about America before World War I, noted, "At the very least, the growing political strength of Catholicism was of great influence in keeping the Trade Unions aloof from any movement wearing a socialist label or 'tainted' with classwar doctrine or materialist philosophies of action."[94] Catholics, especially the Irish, constituted the largest single identifiable ethnic group in the AFL.[95] David Saposs estimated that before World War I, "the majority of . . . members of unions were Catholics."[96] As of 1928, Selig Perlman reiterated that "Catholics . . . are perhaps in the majority in the American Federation of Labor."[97] Of greater significance perhaps is the fact that the large majority of AFL union officials were Catholics. Marc Karson reported that of "the eight vice-presidential offices in the AFL Executive Board from 1900 to 1918, Catholics numbered at least four during any one year." He also noted that his "incomplete" enumeration of presidents of AFL international unions during this period located "more than fifty Irish Catholics" among them, none of whom were Socialists.[98] Following the lead of the Vatican, which had strongly condemned socialism in the papal encyclicals of 1891 and 1903, the American Catholic Church, as noted, took a very active role both in denouncing socialism to its congregations and in influencing the AFL to adhere to Catholic social views. The hierarchy endorsed both the sanctity of property rights and "pure and simple" trade unionism.[99] The following reaction was typical of many of them:

In Milwaukee, Archbishop Sebastian Messmer . . . left no doubt in the minds of Milwaukee Catholics as to what their attitude should be toward the Socialist party. "The private ownership of property," the Archbishop warned his flock, "is supported by the gospel apostolic teaching, and the rules of the Church, and is a divine ordination, not to be changed by the hand of man. . . . A man cannot be a Catholic and a Socialist. . . ."[100]

It was clear to AFL leaders that Catholics would not be allowed by the church to belong to any organization that endorsed a so-called materialistic ideology.[101] A Jesuit wrote in 1908 that if the AFL were to support socialism it would "immediately burst asunder. The great majority of the AFL are Christians and Catholics. . . ."[102] It is not surprising, therefore, that the founding and three-decade president of the AFL, Samuel Gompers, although a Jew, worked hard to convince Catholic Church leaders that he was sympathetic to their outlook.

The success of the Catholic Church in preventing most of its working-class parishioners from supporting the Socialists cannot be attributed to successful propaganda. Catholic opposition to socialism in the labor movement went beyond mere propaganda or church homilies. There were a number of organizations, such as the Catholic Workingmen's Association, the Catholic Workingmen's Welfare Federation, the Central Society, and the Militia of Christ for Social Service, formed in 1910, that concentrated on combating radical influence. The latter group, the Militia, was the most important. Its chief objective was "to cultivate the aspiration of the workers to better their conditions through organization in conservative trade-unions. . . ." Its directorate included heads of major AFL international unions.[103] David Saposs noted:

> It counted among its members the leading Catholic labor leaders, and had the approval of Gompers and the handful of other non-Catholic conservative labor leaders. The Militia of Christ was an auxiliary of the Church. It had large funds at its disposal. It was manned by an able staff. It immediately became a formidable factor in the battle against radicalism. It issued literature and retained a corps of propagandists and lecturers. In addition, it routed outstanding labor leaders and priests, who had distinguished themselves in labor affairs, on tours where they spoke to working class audiences against radicalism and for the conservative brand of laborism.[104]

Socialists frequently blamed Catholic activity for their failure to mobilize more workers.[105] In 1912 the Socialist magazine *The Masses* complained that "the American Federation of Labor is getting more and more in the hands of the Militia of Christ."[106] In New York City, where a strong Socialist party organization made little headway in recruiting Catholics, "organizers contended before the party's Executive Committee that they could not organize Catholic workmen owing to the strong anti-Socialist attitude of the Catholic clergy."[107]

But as noted, all this occurred while Catholic organizations and clergy strongly supported trade unionism and social reform. The foremost pre–World War I American Catholic analyst of socialism, Father William Kerby, professor of sociology at Catholic University, argued in 1904 that "social reform was the only effective defense against the Socialist crusade."[108] He and other Catholic spokesmen lauded Pope Leo XIII's labor encyclical and advocated strong unions and welfare legislation, such as minimum wage laws. In the words of Bishop William Stang of Fall River, Massachusetts, workers required "a sound insurance system, indemnifying not only against accidents, but against reverses of life, such as sickness, loss of work, old age. . . ." Such policies, noted Bishop Stang, "would give the laboring classes what at the present time [1904] they need the most, security of existence, and would keep them from drifting into socialism."[109] Catholic social activists advocated the welfare state long before it became a viable political program in the polity at large, calling for legislative enactment of the eight-hour day, state support for the unemployed, public housing, and the like, all before World War I.[110]

Given such support for welfare reforms and unions, one might ask why American Socialists were unwilling to follow labor parties in Britain and Australia that took pains to avoid anticlericalism or atheism. The answer in part lies in the fact that Marxism was enormously influential in the American Socialist party.

From its founding, the British Labour party had close links with religious groups, particularly with nonconformist Protestant sects, such as Methodists. In contrast, while the Socialist party of the United States included many dedicated Protestants, a large portion of the party was overtly antireligious and anti-Catholic. Some Socialists went far beyond the anticlerical views of European Marxists.[111] The most widely read Socialist newspaper, *The Appeal to Reason*, which had a national circulation of more than three-quarters of a million in 1913, frequently attacked the Catholic Church for supporting capitalism and opposing socialism.[112] Its editor, J. A. Wayland, "repeatedly denounced Catholicism with scarcely less vigor than capitalism itself."[113] Shortly before his death in 1911, Wayland helped to found *The Menace*, a weekly that became the leading anti-Catholic organ in the country, reaching a circulation of a million. *The Menace* concentrated week after week on exposing Catholic conspiracies, charging among other things that the Knights of Columbus were dedicated "to a war of extermination against all heretics."[114] Even very liberal Catholics such as Monsignor John Ryan, a strong advocate of a full-fledged welfare state and a militant supporter of trade unionism, who stated that socialism in its pure form was a progressive system that did not fall under the condemnation of the church, insisted in 1909 that Catholics "were not morally free . . . to affiliate with the Socialist Party of America because the movement it represented was inherently antireligious."[115] A year later, Arthur Preuss, editor of the *Catholic Fortnightly Review*, posed the question to Socialist leader John Spargo: "Tell us, if we were to put you and yours in power, would you confine your activity strictly to the economic territory, speaking no word and lifting no hand against the moral principles, doctrine truths, or religious institutions we hold sacred?" But as a historian of the Catholic pro-union organization Catholic Social Action observes:

> To these questions the American Socialist movement never returned satisfactory answers. The party's resolution of 1908 that socialism was "not concerned with matters of religious belief" was not accepted by Catholics at face value. They noted that in the vehement debate on the resolution the more uncompromising Socialists damned the proposal as a monstrous lie and the plank finally carried by only one vote. Ryan not incorrectly observed that the circumstances surrounding the plank's adoption "strongly suggested that some of the members voted for the resolution solely as a matter of good tactics."[116]

What so disturbed Monsignor Ryan was that an amendment to this resolution, introduced by Morris Hillquit, passed by only one vote, 79 to 78, after heated debate. The controversial motion stated: "The Socialist movement is primarily an economic and political movement. It is not concerned with institutions of marriage or religion." A close analysis of the transcript of that convention suggests, however, that it passed only because "the party's Right had maneuvered by parliamentary means not to allow a vote on the original report."[117]

The opposition of Irish Catholic union leaders to the Socialist party was reinforced by the links between the Irish and the Democratic party.[118] Summarizing socialist support in New York, historian Melvin Dubofsky concluded that Irish workers had little inclination toward socialism because "they were amply represented in Tammany Hall. The Irish immigrant link to the Democratic machine, well established by the end of the nineteenth century, was at floodtide in the Progressive era when Boss Charles Murphy grafted modern social reforms onto the old ward-heeling Tammany structure."[119] Although the AFL was officially nonpartisan in politics, it followed the principle that had been adopted in 1906 of "reward your friends and punish your enemies." In practice, this "made the Federation a political auxiliary of the Democratic party in the northern industrial centers."[120] In these cities, the Democratic party was largely dominated by Irish Catholics, the same group that controlled the AFL. To have endorsed Socialist party candidates would have pitted Irish labor leaders against Irish politicians, a prospect clearly not to be welcomed by the Catholic Church or Irish leaders in general.

The conclusion that Catholicism played a major role in inhibiting the growth of socialist strength within the American labor movement does not win uncritical acceptance among scholars. Labor historians Philip Taft and Gerald Grob both reject it.[121] Grob argues that American labor ideology reflected the middle-class aspirations of American workers, and that union leaders recognized that endorsement of socialism would undercut their appeal. Thus he concludes that "the antisocialist position of American trade unionism and the antisocialism of the Catholic Church tended to parallel each other, although for somewhat different reasons." Catholic opposition to socialism, therefore, "served to reinforce that which already existed within the framework of trade-union ideology."[122] Grob's argument is reasonable. There are many sources of socialist weakness in America beyond Catholic opposition. As we have seen, during its early years, a good part of the membership of the AFL was ready to support socialist principles in resolutions and to vote for socialist candidates for union office. At the 1902 AFL convention, a socialist resolution was defeated by only a few hundred votes, 4,897 to 4,171. Even if, as Victor Berger argued, only two thousand of these votes were cast by committed Socialists, the close result indicates broad socialist support.[123] In 1912, Max Hayes, a moderate socialist, representing the International

Typographical Union, ran for president of the AFL against Gompers, and secured over a quarter of the delegate vote.[124]

Not surprisingly, however, the unions that Socialists controlled, or in which they had significant influence, were largely ones in which Catholic immigrants were outnumbered by those of Jewish or Northern European Protestant background. These included the Clothing Workers, the Brewery Workers, the Boot and Shoe Workers, the Carpenters, the United Mine Workers, and the Western Federation of Miners. Only the Boot and Shoe union contained a significant number of Irish Catholics, although the English and native-born predominated within it.[125] Among miners, socialist strength was largely among the English-speaking non-Catholic elements, rather than the "new immigrants."[126]

The American working class was primarily composed of Catholic immigrants in the two decades preceding World War I, when the country was industrializing rapidly. Vigorous Catholic opposition to socialism can hardly be exaggerated as a reason for the failure of the Socialist party. Yet this wound was partly self-inflicted. The histories of the British and Australian labor movements reveal that Catholics could support non-Marxist labor parties. By rejecting the labor party model, American socialists sustained their principles, but lost Catholic support. The two decades before the United States entered World War I were a make-or-break period for American socialists, and the Catholic Church proved to be a major stumbling block.[127]

The Attitudes of Socialists to Immigration

The failure of the pre–World War I Socialists to recruit significantly among the millions of "new immigrants" has also been attributed to the party's hostility toward immigration. Some scholars have argued that the party discouraged new immigrants and unskilled workers in a bid for trade union support. Charles Leinenweber concludes that "as a consequence of this exclusive focus, the Socialist party remained out of touch with large segments of the American working class. . . ."[128]

The party was bitterly divided over the question of unrestricted immigration. Following the lead of the AFL, many socialists supported restrictions on entry on the grounds that a flood of unskilled and poor newcomers would lower the living standard of native-born and old-immigrant workers.[129] Native and assimilated skilled workers viewed new immigrants as an economic threat, and moderate party leaders wanted to maintain close ties with the AFL. On the other hand, many, though not all in the left wing of the party, saw new immigrants as a reservoir for revolutionary politics. In 1910, after years of bitter debate, the party convention by a vote of 55 to 50 adopted a compromise resolution introduced by Morris Hillquit:

> The Socialist Party favors all legislative measures tending to prevent the immigration of strikebreakers and contract laborers, and the mass importation of workers from foreign countries, brought about by the employing classes for the purpose of weakening the organization of American labor, and of lowering the standard of life of American workers.
>
> The party is opposed to the exclusion of any immigrants on account of race or nationality, and demands that the United States be at all times maintained as a free asylum for all men and women persecuted by the governments of their countries on account of their politics, religion or race.[130]

Rhetorically, as this resolution makes clear, the party took the high road, rejecting exclusion on racial grounds while allowing the restriction of immigration in practice.[131] The Socialist party included many who were bigoted against non–Northern European elements, and this, no doubt, reflected norms in the wider society. As noted earlier, the most popular Socialist paper, *The Appeal to Reason*, was openly hostile to Catholic immigrants.[132] "Capitalists," its editors wrote, "were conspiring to bring in the lowest scum of Europe, that they may have cheap labor."[133] Victor Berger, who for a long time was the party's sole congressman, though himself foreign-born, frequently attacked the presence of "coolie labor" from Asia. He emphasized in an article in the Milwaukee *Social-Democrat Herald* in 1907: "The kernel of the question, after all, is whether the United States and Canada are to remain a white country [sic] or become peopled by a yellowish black race with a white admixture."[134] In a speech to the House of Representatives in 1911, he extended his concerns to include "modern white coolies," that is, "Slavians, Italians, Greeks, Russians and Armenians," who have "crowded out the Americans, Germans, Englishmen and Irishmen."[135]

Others in the party also succumbed to racism, rejecting Asian immigrants and American Negroes even more strongly than newcomers from Southern and Eastern Europe. Speaking about Asians, the prominent

American Marxist, Ernest Untermann, emphasized that racial conflict would continue after class conflict ended: "The question as to what race shall dominate the globe must be met as surely as the question as to what class shall own the world." Herman Titus, a left-wing leader from Seattle, argued that "racial incompatibility was a fact, and no amount of Proletarian Solidarity or International Unity can ignore it. We must face the facts."[136]

Beyond detailing the diverse reactions of different groups of immigrants to the socialist movement, and the way in which the Socialists responded to the issue of immigration, it is important to note how immigrants shaped the American movement.

"Foreign" Nature of the Party

Foreign-born American socialist leaders have been charged by some analysts of radical history with being so intent on European events that they neglected American issues. This is the position taken by Robert Alexander, who has argued: "It is obvious . . . that the radical parties have been unduly concerned with events in other countries. In part, of course, this was because immigrants have played such an important role in the radical movement. . . . Yet in spite of this periodic emphasis on 'Americanization,' the radical movement has remained fundamentally oriented toward European questions and developments rather than American ones."[137]

Although immigrants as a group played a much smaller role in the pre-1914 Socialist party than in the late-nineteenth-century movement, the leadership of both was disproportionately foreign-born, a fact stressed by historians. John Laslett points out that "save for a few outstanding exceptions such as Eugene Debs . . . most of the socialist leaders were immigrants from continental Europe who brought over with them an unwanted ideology and were unable to operate effectively in the pluralistic framework of American politics."[138]

Foreign-born members of the party, both outside and within the language federations, devoted a considerable part of their energies to discussing events abroad. Rosenblum attributes this to the ghetto structure of immigrant society, to the fact that the federations were "operating within the bounds of an ethnic subsystem."[139] At the 1912 Socialist party convention, some delegates expressed the view that the foreign language federations' continued focus on European events demonstrated their failure to integrate into the party.

Variations in national origin contributed to factional disputes within the Socialist party.[140] Before the war, the two most visible and influential immigrant groups, the Germans of Milwaukee and the Jews of New York, generally backed the more moderate or right-wing elements, as did the largely native-born Pennsylvania Dutch (Germans) of Reading. A referendum to recall left-wing IWW leader Bill Haywood as a member of the Socialist party National Executive Committee in 1913 for purportedly advocating violence drew support mainly from New York, Massachusetts, Pennsylvania, and Wisconsin.[141] Conversely, the left-wing radicalism of the language federations during and after World War I reflected conditions in their homelands. The Latvian Federation, for example, took a left-wing line, opposing all forms of religion and demanding land nationalization.[142] Disputes in Europe were carried directly into the American Socialist party, as when one of the two Polish federations endorsed the revolutionary followers of Rosa Luxemburg, while the other supported Josef Pilsudski's right-wing nationalist Polish Socialist party.

The fact that so many Socialist leaders and supporters were immigrants enabled the party's enemies to attack it as a foreign group. Opponents labeled the Socialist party an alien influence. Writing in 1912, Peter Roberts, a student of immigration, stated: "Everywhere the bugaboo of socialism is associated with the foreigner. Operators and members of the leisure class again and again say: 'They are dangerous—they are socialists and Anarchists.' "[143] The visible presence of Jews within the leadership and membership of the party also facilitated the use of anti-Semitism against it.[144]

Socialists were acutely aware of the debilitating effects of an ethnically divided working class. Some attempted to overcome the problem by emphasizing internationalism and industrial unionism.[145] This attitude, found particularly on the left of the party, was expressed by Bill Haywood's famous statement in Lawrence that "there is no foreigner here except the capitalists. . . ."[146]

The most explicit and successful appeal to new immigrants by American radicals was that of the Industrial Workers of the World (IWW), the revolutionary industrial union organization. The IWW focused on the most exploited workers, irrespective of their racial or immigrant status. In the words of George Speed, an IWW organizer on the West Coast, "One man is as good as another to me; I don't care whether he is black, blue, green, or yellow, as long as he acts the man and acts true to his economic interests as a worker."[147] Many of the activists in the Wobblies were labor agitators who could quickly respond to industrial conflict wherever it emerged beyond the reach of established AFL unions. Most of the great strikes in which the IWW was involved were explosions of discontent among unskilled and semiskilled immigrant workers who did not join, or were excluded from, AFL unions— Hungarian machinists in Bridgeport (1907–8), Hungarian, Croat, Slovenian, Austrian, and Serb steelworkers in McKees Rocks (1909), Italian, Austrian, Russian, and Turkish textile workers in Lawrence (1912), southern Italian and Eastern European Jewish textile workers in Paterson (1913).

These strikes began as spontaneous outbursts by previously unorganized workers, and in each case they were met by heavy-handed opposition on the part of employers, who attempted to exploit differences among unskilled immigrant workers and mostly native or old-immigrant skilled workers.[148] Concessions won by workers at the height of a strike were difficult to sustain when the strike was over and employers could settle scores with local militants. Although the Wobblies were optimistic that new immigrants would help constitute a radical mass movement, their efforts came to naught. The immigrants who participated in strikes to remedy intolerable conditions rarely remained within the radical organization. The IWW gained membership with each spontaneous uprising, but its peak paid-up membership in 1912—the same year as the American Socialist party reached its high point—was a little over eighteen thousand. The union was committed to revolutionary syndicalism, but, as Thomas LoFaro notes, "almost every IWW-led strike—Lawrence, Mass., 1912; Patterson, N.J. of the same year—was inspired by the desire for immediate material gain, better wages and working conditions, and shorter hours, and not for the purpose of precipitating any revolutionary upheaval."[149]

Conclusion

We have analyzed the effects of immigration for socialism by examining how it interacted with other aspects of American society and politics. Immigration, particularly in the critical period from the 1890s, created an enormously diverse working class at a time when labor unions were being formed and consolidated. Immigration decisively shaped the AFL, and the AFL, in turn, reinforced ethnic divisions within the American working class. When ethnicity and class coincided or overlapped, conflict in the workplace could be intensified. Some of the most violent strikes in any western industrializing society took place in the United States between new immigrant workers and their native bosses. But the overall consequence of ethnic divisions among workers was to weaken the drive for a labor or socialist party representing workers as a class.

This is not to deny that several groups of immigrants, particularly Russian Jews, Finns, Germans, and Eastern Europeans, brought to America political experiences that predisposed them to socialism. Many, and from 1917 most, party members were immigrants. But the debate about the role of particular groups within the Socialist party cannot overlook the hard fact that while many Socialists were immigrants, relatively few immigrants were Socialists.

The strength of the pre–World War I Socialist party among both foreign-born and native-born workers demonstrates that class-conscious radicalism could emerge in America, particularly in times of economic transition and after cyclical economic downswings. But viewed cross-nationally, the extent of such support was limited. Much as the syndicalist AFL and the anarcho-syndicalist IWW rejected statism while engaging in militant class action, workers resisted socialist appeals. Ethnic and religious diversity clearly weakened support for socialism.

Racial divisions exacerbated tensions within the working class. The situation of African-Americans resembled that of lower strata in postfeudal Europe in that they were locked into an explicitly inferior social position and were economically oppressed, with few prospects for upward mobility. But relatively few African-Americans turned to socialism or joined unions. An important reason for this is that they were simply ignored by skilled white workers, who were dominant in the AFL and to a lesser extent in the Socialist party. Moreover, the great majority of African-Americans who lived in the South were denied the right to vote or the freedom to engage in racially relevant protest politics. Efforts to create a racially integrated movement foundered on deep-seated intolerance and suppression. Even the Socialists ignored them, although some, led by Eugene Debs, tried to challenge such orientations.

Ethnic and racial divisions among American workers were reflected in labor organizations. The AFL was dominated by skilled native workers who fiercely defended their job territories against the influx of new immigrants and African-Americans. This deepened ethnic/racial antagonisms and undermined the efforts of some unionists to create a labor party which would represent workers as a class. Rather than being moderated by labor organization, in the United States ethnic divisions were often strengthened by the rift between white skilled workers entrenched in the AFL craft unions and unorganized immigrants outside. Socialists made little headway in overcoming such divisions.

Ironically, therefore, Socialists failed to recruit precisely among the ethnic and racial groups whose communitarian values or socioeconomic position should have made them most receptive to socialist appeals: African-Americans and the "new" immigrants, predominantly Catholics, and to a lesser extent the Greek Orthodox. The values most linked to "American exceptionalism," in this case the rejection of statism, the commitment to individualism and meritocracy (equality of opportunity), were rooted in the white American Protestant majority. African-Americans and the rapidly growing population from Southern and Eastern European backgrounds, whose values were antithetical to individualism and Protestant sectarianism, and were most congruent with socialist and welfare state beliefs, were not available to the American socialists.

These outcomes did not simply flow from the structure of American society. Socialists themselves, as we shall see in more detail in the next chapter, contributed to their failure by following ideologically rigid policies. The American Socialist party was one of the most orthodox Marxist parties in the democratic world. We have argued that orthodoxy contributed to anti-Catholicism within the party. Samuel Gompers and most of the AFL leadership were far more successful in their appeals to Catholic workers than the Socialists.

The failure of American socialists to find a base among Catholic workers, as well as blacks, occurred precisely when American society was experiencing the economic and class strains endemic in rapid industrialization which gave birth to significant class-conscious movements elsewhere in the modernizing world. In the following chapter, we consider how sectarianism and ideological purity undermined American socialism.

. . .

Appendix

The statistical analysis presented in this chapter is based on county-level data for six states: Illinois, Minnesota, New York, Ohio, Pennsylvania, and Wisconsin.[150] These states were selected because they have large immigrant populations and exhibit wide variation along important contending variables, including proportion of rural/urban population, the presence of industrial manufacturing, and the distribution of native/immigrant population. These states include a significant proportion of the total number of immigrants in the groups we discuss. In 1910 they encompassed 59 percent of immigrant Germans in the United States, 39 percent of the Finns, 51 percent of the Irish, 60 percent of the Italians, 55 percent of the Norwegians, and 65 percent of the Russians. In addition, these states were of considerable substantive importance in terms of overall support for the Socialist party: they provided 42 percent of the total Socialist vote in 1912 and 59 percent in 1920.

Using counties in these six states as the units of analysis allows us to match census data for 1910 and 1920 with election returns for the 1912 and 1920 presidential elections. The census data are from *Historical, Demographic, Economic and Social Data: United States 1790–1960* (ICPSR 0003) and election data are from *U.S. Historical Election Returns, 1788–1984* (ICPSR 0001). We constructed two datasets, one combining 1910 census variables with 1912 election returns and a second matching 1920 census variables with 1920 returns. For 1910 the total number of counties in the six states under analysis is 475; for 1920 there is one additional case because New York County became two counties, New York and the Bronx. Because the data on the number of wage earners in manufacturing are available only in the 1920 census returns, these data are matched to the 1910 census returns by combining Bronx County and New York County into one case. In addition, since data on rural/urban population are not available in machine-readable form for 1920, we matched the 1910 census data to the 1920 dataset by designating all the population in Bronx County as urban. Data on religious affiliation by county are obtained from the Census of Religion for 1916. Since these data are not available in machine-readable form, we entered the data for Roman Catholics, Jews, and "Total Religious Affiliation" for each county. Protestants are defined as the total affiliated minus the number of Catholics and Jews. We checked the influence of these religion variables at various points in our analysis below, but do not include them in Table 4.4 because they have little influence on the remaining coefficients.

These data, in ratio form, are analyzed using OLS regressions to explore the relationship between concentrations of specific ethnic groups and voting for the Socialist party. The independent variables (number of foreign-born immigrants, wage earners in manufacturing, and urban population) are divided by the total county population in order to mitigate the influence of population. The dependent variable (number of votes for the Socialist party) is divided by the total number of votes cast in the county for the presidential election. Although there has been some debate over the possibility of biased estimates when using ratio variables, Firebaugh demonstrates that while the use of ratio variables may lead to biased correlation coefficients, no systematic bias is introduced by the use of ratio variables in regression equations.[151] In addition to OLS, we also estimated the parameters using weighted least squares. The weight was constructed as a function of the residual of the OLS equation, i.e., the absolute value of the residuals is regressed on the predicted value from the OLS equation with the weight calculated as the reciprocal of the square root of this predicted value.[152] Since the WLS results do not vary substantially from those reported in Table 4.4 using OLS for ease of presentation, we have chosen to report the OLS results.

It is worth emphasizing that the regression coefficients presented here should be interpreted in terms of the impact of the percentage of a given ethnic group on the percentage of Socialist voting across the counties under study rather than as a measure of how individuals voted. To translate aggregate results such as those presented here into statements about individual behavior demands information about contextual effects that is unavailable from the historical record.[153] However, it is possible to control for some important contending influences on Socialist voting at the county level, and we utilized census data in an attempt to do this on a systematic basis.

Table 4.3: Ethnic Profiles of States, 1910 and 1920

1910	Ill.	Minn.	N.Y.	Ohio	Pa.	Wis.
Total population (thousands)	5,638	2,075	9,113	4,767	7,665	2,333
% Urban	61.7	41.0	78.8	55.9	60.4	43.0
% Rural	38.3	59.0	21.2	44.1	39.6	57.0
% Foreign-born whites	21.3	26.2	29.9	12.5	18.8	22.0
% English	5.0	2.2	5.4	7.3	7.6	2.7
% German	26.5	20.2	16.0	29.3	13.6	45.5
% Irish	7.8	2.9	13.5	6.7	11.5	2.7
% Italian	6.0	1.8	17.3	7.0	13.6	1.8
% Russian	12.4	3.2	20.5	8.2	16.7	5.8
% Finnish	0.2	4.9	0.3	0.7	0.2	1.1
% Norwegian	2.7	19.4	0.9	0.2	0.2	11.1
% Swedish	9.6	22.5	2.0	0.9	1.6	5.0
% Socialist vote (1912)	7.1	8.2	4.0	8.7	6.9	8.4

1920	Ill.	Minn.	N.Y.	Ohio	Pa.	Wis.
Total population (thousands)	6,485	2,387	10,385	5,759	8,720	2,632
% Urban	67.9	44.1	82.7	63.8	64.3	47.3
% Rural	32.1	55.9	17.3	36.2	35.7	52.7
% Foreign-born whites	18.6	20.4	26.8	11.8	15.9	17.5
% English	4.5	2.3	4.9	6.4	6.5	2.4
% German	17.0	15.4	10.6	16.5	8.7	32.9
% Irish	6.2	2.1	10.2	4.3	8.8	1.7
% Italian	7.8	1.5	19.6	8.9	16.1	2.4
% Russian	9.8	3.3	19.0	6.4	11.6	4.7
% Finnish	0.3	6.0	0.4	0.9	0.2	1.5
% Norwegian	2.3	18.6	1.0	0.2	0.2	9.9
% Swedish	8.7	23.1	1.9	1.1	1.4	5.0
% Socialist vote (1920)	3.6	7.6	7.0	2.8	3.8	11.5

Sources: Bureau of the Census (1910; 1920); *Congressional Quarterly* (1985).

Note: Ethnic groups are a percentage of foreign-born whites (other percentages are based upon total population).

Table 4.4: Immigrant Support for Socialism, 1912 and 1920

1912

	Intercept	Wage-earners	Urban	German	English	Russian	Nordic	Irish	Italian	R^2
Overall	.022	.265	.050	-.123	.643	.491	.399	-2.343	.163	.45
	(5.976)	(5.969)	(4.442)	(2.347)	(1.780)	(2.868)	(13.86)	(9.375)	(1.122)	
Illinois	.018	.065	.044	-.029	.998	1.531	-.036	-1.902	-.137	.50
	(4.669)	(0.735)	(2.774)	(0.311)	(2.108)	(4.622)	(0.387)	(3.334)	(0.908)	
Minnesota	.065	.825	-.022	-.563	4.273	-.108	.244	-4.215	-.647	.51
	(1.730)	(3.523)	(0.048)	(1.813)	(1.351)	(0.135)	(1.890)	(2.542)	(0.565)	
New York	.006	.127	.043	-.009	.337	.375	.145	-.975	.065	.48
	(0.747)	(1.475)	(1.887)	(0.049)	(0.753)	(1.824)	(0.572)	(3.119)	(0.294)	
Ohio	.022	.355	.081	-.195	1.504	.055	.397	-3.493	.500	.63
	(3.710)	(2.734)	(2.633)	(1.093)	(1.881)	(0.075)	(0.694)	(2.673)	(0.920)	
Pennsylvania	.012	.259	.013	.617	1.006	.797	.493	-2.863	.643	.42
	(1.108)	(2.587)	(0.368)	(1.345)	(0.797)	(1.939)	(1.380)	(3.985)	(1.867)	
Wisconsin	.006	.104	.042	.130	-.277	1.015	.321	-1.648	-.231	.43
	(0.286)	(0.630)	(1.435)	(0.835)	(0.252)	(1.524)	(2.960)	(1.080)	(0.559)	

Table 4.4: Immigrant Support for Socialism, 1912 and 1920 (cont.)

1920

	Intercept	Wage-earners	Urban	German	English	Russian	Nordic	Irish	Italian	R^2
Overall	-.004	.163	.013	.502	-.203	1.076	.494	-1.234	.272	.53
	(1.342)	(4.811)	(1.533)	(7.433)	(0.564)	(6.333)	(17.38)	(4.258)	(2.222)	
Illinois	.005	.040	.007	.148	.479	1.579	.075	-1.287	.219	.62
	(2.823)	(1.060)	(0.987)	(2.242)	(1.871)	(5.496)	(1.358)	(2.885)	(3.662)	
Minnesota	.024	.277	.036	-.383	-.289	.542	.477	-2.439	.256	.62
	(1.021)	(1.815)	(1.408)	(1.132)	(0.085)	(0.517)	(4.794)	(1.174)	(0.172)	
New York	-.003	.127	-.005	.287	.821	.874	.259	-.794	.498	.69
	(0.419)	(1.628)	(0.283)	(1.026)	(1.803)	(5.616)	(0.962)	(2.314)	(1.951)	
Ohio	.003	.091	.017	.014	.346	.573	.113	-1.662	.312	.63
	(1.376)	(2.319)	(1.791)	(1.618)	(1.026)	(1.263)	(0.666)	(1.921)	(1.791)	
Pennsylvania	-.001	.084	.022	.659	.173	.589	.046	-1.497	.375	.40
	(0.172)	(1.957)	(1.492)	(2.012)	(0.198)	(1.089)	(0.187)	(2.592)	(1.928)	
Wisconsin	-.003	.408	-.003	.931	-2.583	.699	.354	-3.308	.178	.43
	(0.123)	(1.929)	(0.079)	(2.809)	(0.973)	(0.516)	(1.926)	(0.789)	(0.278)	

Table 4.5: German-Born Support for Socialism by
Percentage of Wage Earners and Urban Population

	High-Wage-Earner Counties	Low-Wage-Earner Counties
1912	0.466	-0.144
	(1.236)	(2.785)
1920	1.776	0.444
	(3.912)	(6.585)
	Urban Counties	Rural Counties
1912	0.034	-0.147
	(0.200)	(2.703)
1920	0.868	0.451
	(3.942)	(6.660)

Note: Entries are multiple regression coefficients (with t-ratios in parentheses) from an equation which includes control variables for percentage wage earners in manufacturing (in urban/rural analysis), percentage urban (in high/low wage earner analysis), percentage of foreign-born English, Russian, Scandinavian, Irish, and Italian. High-wage-earner counties (N=50) are defined as counties with 15% or more wage earners in manufacturing and low-wage-earner counties (N=475) as less than 15% wage earners in manufacturing. Urban counties (N=87) are defined as counties with 50% or more of the population in towns of more than 2,500 and rural counties (N=388) as less than 50% of the population in towns of 2,500.

Chapter 5

SECTARIANS VS.

REFORMISTS

Were Socialists Undermined by Their Own Strategy?

"The Socialist party has never, *even for a single year*, been without some issue which threatened to split the party and which forced it to spend much of its time on the problem of reconciliation or rupture. In this fact lies the chief clue to the impotence of American socialism as a political movement. . . ."[1] So argued Daniel Bell, elaborating Marx and Engels' concern that one of the basic failings of American socialists was their penchant for sectarianism.[2]

The debate between those who argue that a major cause of socialist weakness lies in the policies of socialists themselves and those who focus exclusively on external constraints is beside the point. These views are not mutually exclusive: the question is one of evaluating their relative causal influence. Paradoxically, it may well be the case that socialist strategy was important because of—rather than despite—formidable external constraints. Since the barriers to the creation of a viable third party in the United States are so high, socialists were arguably better off working through one of the existing major political parties than trying to sustain an independent party. The considerable attention that historians of the Socialist party have given to questions of strategy, and their emphasis on the debilitating effects of conflicts within the party, reflect the limited freedom that socialist leaders had for strategic error. At stake was not merely electoral success or failure, but the existence of the party itself.

A principal criticism of the Socialist party has been that it was overly concerned with ideology, that it was inflexible and factionalized, and thus unable—or unwilling—to make the kinds of compromises necessary to build a viable electoral base. As noted in Chapter 3, the party alienated the leadership of the AFL and thus cut itself off from the major working-class organization in the country. Reiterating Marx and Engels, historian Mark Lause emphasizes the Socialists' "predisposition to ideological dogmatism."[3] This was reflected particularly in the party's opposition to the establishment of a labor party that would encompass both socialists and unionists.

These criticisms are countered by those who make the opposite case that the Socialist party failed because it was not radical enough. While most political analysts follow Engels in contending that socialists failed to win a mass following because they were overly concerned with ideological purity and were reluctant to work with nonsocialist groups, some have insisted that the party failed because it was too opportunistic. These critics argue that the party was too willing to encompass moderate or "progressive" elements and, as a result, became vulnerable to co-optation by nonsocialist forces.

These contrasting perspectives reflect the dilemma of political effectiveness versus ideological integrity faced by all radical political organizations. In America, this quandary is expressed in the choice between building a social movement and establishing a political party. The American political system induces political parties to build heterogeneous coalitions to gain a majority of the vote. Electoral competition pressures party leaders to temper rigid ideological stands. Social movements, by contrast, invoke strong moralistic passions that differentiate them sharply from other contenders. Emphasis on the intrinsic justice of a cause often leads to a rigid us-them, friend-foe orientation. There was persistent tension in the Socialist party between "opportunists" who saw a short-term need for political compromise to develop electoral strength and "sectarians" who stressed the moral aspect of the movement and believed that any goals short of complete social transformation were unworthy.

Criticisms of strategy are particularly relevant to the period of socialist decline after the party's peak around 1912, and again to its failure to grow during the Depression of the 1930s. Political structure can help explain the perennial weakness of the Socialist party and third parties generally, but it cannot account for the ebb in the party's strength in these two periods. The decade leading up to 1912 was viewed by Socialists as their takeoff period. Before 1912, contemporary observers—nonsocialists as well as socialists—were convinced that socialism had enormous potential, both as a movement and as a party.[4] By 1920, however, the party had not only failed to realize these expectations but was a mere shell of its former self. If one wishes to analyze the failure of the Socialist party from the standpoint of individual and collective responsibility, in terms of what could have been done differently, then the period between 1912 and 1920 is critical. The only other real chance for the Socialist party to establish itself as a major presence in American politics would come during the Great Depression.

Socialist Sectarianism and the AFL

If Socialists were to succeed in building a viable political party, they desperately needed the support of major labor unions. We have seen (in Chapter 3) that the task was a difficult one, given the cultural orientations of American workers and the organizational character of unions in the AFL. How did Socialists respond to this challenge? The party's sectarian bent was particularly evident in its peculiar relations with the labor movement and its unwillingness to cooperate in the formation of a labor party following the British model. Prominent leaders of the AFL in its first decades, such as Samuel Gompers, P. J. McGuire (the organizer of the Brotherhood of Carpenters), and Adolph Strasser (president of the Cigar Makers), had been involved in socialist and Marxist groups earlier in their career as unionists, but became alienated from them because of their emphasis on ideological purity and bitter internecine factionalism.[5] Gompers' attitude toward socialists was shaped by his early experience in leading a local union, the New York Cigar Makers. As part of a campaign to outlaw the manufacture of cigars in tenements, where employers exploited young women, the union worked vigorously to reelect the man who initiated the legislation, Republican Edward Grosse, a former member of the International Workingman's Association. The members of the Socialist Labor party (SLP) in the union denounced Gompers for backing a non-Socialist for electoral office and succeeded in defeating him in 1882 for reelection as president of the local. Gompers later wrote that the Socialists "were willing to see the cigar industry absorbed by tenement-house production unless that fate could be averted by socialism."[6] When Adolph Strasser invalidated the election in which the socialist Samuel Schimkowitz defeated Gompers, on the grounds that Schimkowitz was an employer, the Socialist Labor party in New York and other locals seceded and formed a competing union, the Cigar Makers Progressive Union. This action inflamed relations between Gompers, Strasser, and the Socialists.[7]

Yet, as William Dick notes, these and other quarrels with the Socialist Labor party in the 1880s did "not mean that men like McGuire and Gompers had abandoned their own socialist ideas completely. On the contrary, the evidence suggests that it was a long time before they gave up the Marxism they had been raised on as union men."[8] In 1886, Gompers was involved in Henry George's campaign for mayor on a Labor party ticket, which had the backing of both unions and socialists. George finished a close second in a three-man race, but soon afterward the socialists split from the Labor party.[9] To Gompers, the conflict "demonstrated how futile and hopeless was the attempt to form a labor party, when the difference between factions was so great, the difficulties of framing a platform acceptable to all so large, and the sentiment of solidarity so infantile."[10]

Although Gompers was to remain sympathetic toward radical ideologies for some years, he became convinced that any effort to mobilize a young struggling union movement in politics would prove disastrous.[11] Instead, Gompers followed what he considered to be the Marxist line of concentrating on union activity in the labor market, relegating political action to the future.[12] Unions, in Gompers' view, should avoid "all controversial questions upon which we might encounter a fatal rock of dissension. Rather let us postpone such measures, though many may see the justice of them, until a greater degree of unanimity is achieved."[13] This approach was bitterly attacked by the Socialist Labor party and later by a number of leaders of the new and larger Socialist party formed at the turn of the century, and many unionists responded in kind.[14]

Gompers' suspicions that socialists wished to dominate the AFL were further aroused in 1890 when Daniel De Leon and the Socialist Labor party insisted on affiliating with the federation. Gompers relates that he was so convinced of the justice of his position that in 1891 he "wrote a let-

ter to Fred [sic] Engels, whom I regarded as a friend of the labor movement, giving him an ungarbled account of the cause of the dissension."[15]
Although Gompers never knew it, Engels wrote letters to others indicating
his complete agreement with Gompers against De Leon. He never
answered Gompers' letter because he hoped to see him in Europe in order
to "settle the matter orally," a meeting which never occurred.[16] Engels
wrote to a friend, Hermann Schlüter, in America saying that "I should have
thought it would have been well to keep on good terms with Gompers,
who has more workers behind him, at any rate, than the SLP. . . ."[17] De
Leon went on to set up a dual union, the Socialist Trades and Labor
Alliance. Had American Marxists followed Engels' advice and worked with
Gompers from the start it is conceivable that a cooperative relationship
could have developed.

Similar hopes to win over the AFL were current among some socialists
in the late 1890s. Seymour Stedman, subsequently the Socialist party's
vice-presidential nominee in 1920, was "gravely disturbed" by the opposition of some of his comrades in the Social Democratic party (precursor to
the Socialist party) to Gompers' reelection as president at the 1898 federation convention. Stedman believed that Gompers could still be won over,
since he had told Victor Berger that "he would vote for the Social
Democratic candidates and advise his friends to do likewise." John Tobin,
the socialist president of the Boot and Shoe Workers' Union, "also declared
that Gompers had assured him that he would vote for the Social
Democratic party."[18]

Many in the Socialist party (SP), which was formed in 1901 as a merger
between the Social Democrats and anti–De Leonist Socialist Laborites,
rejected the AFL. Among these was the party's most prominent leader,
Eugene Debs, who had long battled with Gompers. The enmity between
the two men began during the Great Pullman Strike of 1894, when Debs,
as leader of the American Railway Union, had called for a general strike
against Gompers' opposition. Debs' antipathy to the AFL was deep; working in the AFL, he said, was as "wasteful of time as to spray a cesspool with
attar of roses."[19] Debs and other Socialists backed the revolutionary
Industrial Workers of the World (IWW) when it was established as a dual
union competing with the AFL in 1905. Debs' membership in the IWW
lapsed in 1908, but he continued to search for an alternative to the AFL. In
1914, Debs demanded the secession of the United Mine Workers from the

AFL and the creation of a "new industrial-union federation . . . which would draw to itself 'all the trade unions with industrial tendencies' . . . [so] that the 'reactionary federation of craft unions [could] be transformed within and without into a revolutionary organization.' "[20]

Debs summarized his contempt for the AFL in 1911 in the Socialist party magazine, the *International Socialist Review*:

> Not for all the votes of the American Federation of Labor and its labor-dividing-and-corruption-breeding craft unions should we compromise one jot of our revolutionary principles; and if we do we shall be visited with the contempt we deserve by all real Socialists, who will scorn to remain in a party professing to be a revolutionary party of the working class. . . .[21]

Other influential figures within the Socialist party, however, did attempt to bring the federation and the party into closer relations. In a discussion between Samuel Gompers and Morris Hillquit before the U.S. Commission on Industrial Relations in May 1914 concerning the relative merits of the AFL and the Socialist party, Hillquit argued that the two organizations had overlapping objectives and should therefore cooperate. Gompers replied by citing how Debs had repeatedly attacked the AFL as reactionary and had demanded that it be dissolved. When Hillquit argued that Debs did not speak for the party, Gompers inquired: "Do you regard that as the individual expression of opinion, when a man thrice the [presidential] candidate of a political party, urges that a movement be inaugurated to dissolve the only general federation of labor that ever existed for a period of time, such as the American Federation of Labor?"[22]

Most of the time, however, the majority of the Socialist party supported working within the AFL, hoping to move it toward socialism. Some major international unions, such as the United Mine Workers, the United Brewery Workers, the International Machinists Union, and the International Ladies Garment Workers Union, were influenced or controlled by Socialists.[23] In 1912, when Debs secured 6 percent of the vote for president of the United States, Socialist printers' union leader Max Hayes ran for the presidency of the AFL against Gompers and received 27 percent of the vote at the AFL convention.[24]

Yet, the large majority of activists in the AFL, including a number of former Socialists, were estranged from the party. After attending the 1909 AFL convention, Algie M. Simons, a prominent party intellectual and former editor of the *International Socialist Review*, claimed that two-thirds of the delegates were former members of the Socialist party or the Socialist Labor party. He reported, however, an "intense hatred against the Socialist party, combined with a perfect willingness to accept the philosophy of socialism."[25] Simons felt that the fault lay in the party's sectarian policies and abstract positions. In words resembling Engels' past comments about relations between the Socialist Labor party and the AFL, Simons wrote: "No one has denounced the defects of the American Federation of Labor more than I, but I am forced to recognize that it comes nearer to representing the working class than the Socialist party, and unless we are able to so shape our policy and our organization as to meet the demands and incarnate the position of the workers, we will have failed in our mission."[26]

The criticism that the AFL was dominated by craft unions that were little interested in organizing unskilled and immigrant workers is largely justified. But as Irving Howe has observed, the tactics used by leading socialists were self-defeating:

> Had the Debsians, as loyal though critical adherents of labor, stressed the need for industrial unionism and political involvement . . . they would have . . . probably increased their influence. But when they attacked Gompers for "class collaboration," without recognizing that unions are inherently agencies of both "class struggle" and "class collaboration," the Debsians threatened the unity of the labor movement—a movement that included as it had to strongly antisocialist elements. . . .[27]

Rejection of a Labor Party

Many Socialists were not simply unprepared to gain the support of the AFL unions but were opposed, in principle, to efforts to encompass unionists in a labor party. Many pre–World War I party activists opposed the idea on the grounds that there was no need for a new party, since the Socialist party was the American workers' party.[28] Some went further and denounced the notion of an inclusive labor party as a trap "designed by the capitalists to stop the growing vote of the Socialist party. A vote for a labor party was a vote for capitalism."[29]

There are a number of instances of Socialist opposition to such efforts.

In 1901, two hundred Socialists packed a meeting called by Chicago unions to form a labor party and succeeded in voting down the effort.[30] In 1903, reacting to the participation of California Socialists in an electorally successful Union Labor party in San Francisco, the National Executive Committee of the Socialist party resolved to expel anyone "compromising with a labor party." This threat was carried out when a major California party leader was expelled.[31] In 1904, Socialist delegates at a conference of four hundred labor leaders held in Colorado "to discuss the advisability of independent labor political action . . . defeated the motion for a union labor party."[32] In reaction to court action against United Mine Workers president John Mitchell in 1907, a resolution was introduced at that union's convention to "encourage, in spirit and in fact, the promotion of a national labor party." In the debate, Adolph Germer, a leader of the Socialist party and subsequently its national secretary, opposed the proposal on the grounds that there "already was a labor party in America . . . the Socialist party, which was committed to fighting the class struggle. . . ."[33] As historian John Laslett notes, "Germer reflected clearly the official policy of the Socialist party at this time, which feared that a broadly based labor party would be insufficiently radical in its program."[34]

Over the following years the Socialist party heatedly debated the issue of joining with the unions in a labor party. Moderates were accused of undermining the Socialist party and efforts were made to revoke their membership on the National Executive Committee. These attempts failed, yet they induced centrists such as Victor Berger and John Spargo to state publicly that they opposed a labor party.[35]

Debate was intensified in 1909 when Keir Hardie, past chairman of the British Labour party, visited the United States and criticized American radicals for their sectarianism.[36] Critics of the labor party idea, such as William English Walling, attacked Hardie and the British Labour party as opponents of democratic socialism. John M. Work, active in the Wisconsin party as a supporter of the moderate wing, was particularly dismissive: "The Labor party of Great Britain is less independent and further from socialism than the so-called Labor party of San Francisco and further than a hundred other abortive attempts of the kind we have had in the United States— attempts which have been indignantly cast aside by the good sense of the American working people."[37] The *International Socialist Review* carried articles by the English Marxist H. M. Hyndman, maintaining that "the Labour party in England today is the greatest obstacle to Socialist progress at home." Eugene Debs contributed to the debate by firmly stating his opposition to the labor party idea: "The Socialist party has already *catered far too much* to the American Federation of Labor, and there is no doubt that *a halt will have to be called*."[38]

Opposition to the establishment of a labor party became the dominant position within the Socialist party. In 1910, Victor Berger reiterated his view that unions should limit their activity to economic matters in deference to the Socialist party, which should "express the demands of the working class in the political field."[39] In the same year the National Executive Committee praised "the splendid work the Los Angeles comrades have done in averting the formation of a labor party as a rival to the Socialist party" and suspended the Arizona branch for helping to start a labor party.[40] In Washington, the state party did the same to locals and members for participation in a labor party convention.[41] At the 1913 AFL convention, Socialists opposed a resolution introduced by George Berry, the president of the Pressmen's Union, calling for the formation of a labor party.[42]

Efforts to create labor parties at the municipal level were generally regarded as opportunistic.[43] Where the Socialist party was strong, it inevitably recognized, in the words of Socialist mayor of Minneapolis Thomas Van Lear, that "socialism cannot be put in effect in any one city."[44] Municipal Socialist organizations that were able to win office were often centers of opposition to the Socialist party's left wing.[45] The latter found it hard to recognize that winning elections and holding office were not necessarily at odds with socialist principles. As noted, electorally successful Socialist parties such as those in Milwaukee, Minneapolis, Reading, and Schenectady were based on alliances with local labor movements.

In Milwaukee, the party found that the conditions for electoral success in the city did not jibe with the radical orientation of the national party. The city's Socialists ran an honest, efficient reform administration that was often out of tune with the evangelical radicalism of the national party led by Eugene Debs. Debs himself was little involved in building Socialist organizations at the local level and viewed attempts to develop reformist city machines as beneath the dignity of socialism. During the Socialist presidential campaign of 1916 he summarized his attitude as follows: "Let it not be supposed for a moment that on the part of the Socialists this is going to be a vote-chasing campaign. . . . We shall explain socialism and make our appeal to the intelligence, the manhood and womanhood of the people, and upon that . . . high plane, whatever the outcome, we are bound to win."[46]

The Milwaukee Socialists countered this by reiterating that reformist tactics pursued in cities such as Milwaukee were not mutually exclusive with radical goals. The balancing act between short-term reforms that could generate local electoral support and ultimate demands for the abolition of capitalism was a delicate one. After a successful mayoral campaign in 1910 in which the Wisconsin Socialists advocated a variety of practical reforms, these "moderates" were defeated for reelection in 1912, in part because even their campaign "seemed bent on insulting and driving away" nonsocialist voters. "The independents who alone could have salvaged victory from the fusionist attack were rebutted by Socialist opposition to the most acceptable of contemporary reform proposals. . . ."[47] One sympathetic contemporary observer noted: "The Socialists had a magnificent opportunity in Milwaukee, and simply frittered it away. . . . [T]he *spirit* of the Socialists, their fanatical class consciousness, their sectarianism, their fierce and bitter impossibilism—this it was that made them utterly intolerable."[48] Historian Floyd Stachowski notes that "Victor Berger, the architect of the Milwaukee Socialist movement, was guilty of driving away the very independent voters who had made Seidel's [1910] victory possible by ridiculing the 'goody-goodies' and 'church club men' . . . [and by] his talk of 'proletariat over capitalist' and 'revolutionary Socialist spirit.' "[49] In these years Victor Berger frequently referred to the benefits of allowing people to keep arms in their homes as a safeguard against capitalist perfidy.[50] As Frederick Olson emphasizes: "In the hopeful atmosphere of 1910 to 1912, when the Socialists throughout the nation were catching delightful glimpses of the promised land, it seemed unnecessary, almost treasonable, to give up sectarianism."[51] But Daniel Hoan was able to recapture the mayor's office for the party in 1916 by running on a moderate program of "home rule, public ownership of the utilities, resistance to the street-car company and enforcement of utility franchise provisions . . . and all measures necessary to aid organized labor."[52]

In Schenectady, the Socialist administration from 1911 to 1913 under the leadership of George Lunn was severely criticized by party members elsewhere for reformism in spite of Lunn's support of Debs and the national party. Lunn perceived the mission of his administration as one of applying "Socialist principles and methods" to secure "betterment of local conditions for the mass of the people."[53] The local party's platform affirmed the national party's program, called for municipal ownership of all public utilities as well as a public food market, sought to extend the educational system, and favored use of city resources to back trade unions. The Socialist administration put the city into the business of selling ice, coal, and groceries, policies ultimately blocked by court orders. It also provided free medical and dental care in working-class areas. Lunn walked the picket line in a number of strikes by AFL unions and prevented the use of strikebreakers. Lunn not only spoke in support of Debs' attacks on the "existing industrial order" but actively backed an IWW strike, for which he was praised in 1912 by Bill Haywood, the leader of the organization.

Three years after his defeat by a Democratic-Republican fusion ticket in 1913, discouraged by personal criticism and severe factionalism and bickering in the local organization, Lunn withdrew from the party. Although he insisted he was "as good a Socialist" as ever, Lunn ran successfully for Congress as a candidate of the Progressive and Democratic parties in 1916. A student of the Schenectady party's efforts, Chad Gaffield, comes to the conclusion that attacks on Lunn's Socialist party and mayoralty record as opportunistic and non-Socialist were "unfounded."[54]

In some other communities, Socialist mayors were expelled from the party shortly after taking office. The logic of electoral competition pressed Socialist candidates to campaign for the middle-class progressive vote alongside that of workers and unionists, but once in office, mayors often found themselves pressured by the party organization to confine appointments to members. Socialist mayors had to provide the local party with undated, presigned letters of resignation from their government positions so that the party would have the option of forcing its elected representative out of office if a dispute arose.

By 1913 the Socialist party had expelled a dozen of its representatives serving in public office.[55] In the state of Washington, for example, the left-wing state party refused to allow a Socialist state legislator to cooperate with labor and farmer representatives and censured him when he voted for a Progressive for speaker on the grounds that he should have nominated and voted for himself.[56] In Los Angeles in 1915 a lone Socialist councilman was forced to resign from the party because he voted for a Democrat for council president.[57] The party also purged prominent labor leaders on similar grounds. United Mine Workers vice-president and subsequent president

Frank Hayes resigned from the party after being threatened with censure for endorsing a non-Socialist prolabor candidate for sheriff in Colorado. John Walker, president of the Illinois Federation of Labor, was expelled from the party after he publicly endorsed Woodrow Wilson in 1916, stating that, as the head of the state federation, he had to go along with the policy adopted by the majority of the union membership. This argument was rejected by his party comrades.[58]

Events in two Ohio cities, Lima and Lorain, where Socialist mayors Corbin Shook and Thomas Pape were embroiled in conflicts with their local parties soon after taking office, illustrate the difficulty the Socialist party had in adapting to electoral success. Both Shook and Pape "opted for an efficient government that could perpetuate Socialist rule and develop Socialist sentiment in a more gradual manner" and followed the example of the party in Minneapolis and other reformist strongholds by appointing qualified non-Socialist progressives alongside party members to city posts.[59] Local left-wing Socialists supported by the state organization saw this as an attack on the integrity of the party and its commitment to government by workers. As the Lorain Socialists complained, it would "make the public infer that Pape [could not] . . . find a competent man among the three-hundred Socialists in Lorain. . . ."[60] The Lima and Lorain parties presented the pre-election resignations that Shook and Pape had submitted to their respective city councils, but neither accepted the resignations. Within a year of being elected to office, Shook and Pape shed their formal connections with the Socialist party and continued to run their city governments as nonpartisans. In the mayoral elections of 1913, the Socialist vote in Lorain dropped to 59 percent of its 1911 level and in Lima it fell almost 85 percent.[61]

The left wing of the party, which described municipal socialism as "sewer socialism," never offered a practicable alternative. Given the limited power of city governments, what were Socialist officeholders to do? As historian James Weinstein has observed, "When appealing for votes on a local level, both Left and Right pointed to the miserable conditions created by existing pro-capitalist governments, and both promised, if elected, to solve their city's most pressing problems."[62] The basic source of left-wing criticism of Socialist officeholders, according to Ruthenberg, was "an attitude which made the idea of Socialists holding public office under capitalism almost unbearable, and which caused many to view any practical activity of elected Socialists with extreme suspicion."[63] Although Socialists had a number of local electoral successes, on the whole they ignored local and regional issues and focused instead on national and international matters. It is interesting to note that even a leader of the centrist electorally oriented wing of the party like Morris Hillquit found occasion, when opposing Mayor Hoan in an inner-party struggle, to criticize "the 'practical' Socialists of Milwaukee, 'who believe in building modern sewers and showing results right away.' "[64]

Left-Wing Factions in the Major Parties

The refusal to join in a labor party reflects the inability of most American socialists to recognize the inherent difficulties of sustaining a viable third party, given the American constitutional and electoral system. The point was driven home negatively by Socialist party failures at the ballot box, and positively by the electoral successes of progressive and socialist-leaning movements, such as the Nonpartisan League (NPL) of the midwest in the 1910s, the Farmer Labor League in Oklahoma in 1923, Upton Sinclair's End Poverty In California (EPIC) movement, and the Commonwealth Federations in Oregon and Washington during the 1930s. Each of these was a reformist coalition that was prepared to operate *within* one of the major parties, rather than as a separate party, and was subsequently rewarded by winning one or more state-level primaries.

The basic case for this strategy was made by Edward Keating, a supporter of the North Dakota Nonpartisan League, who edited the railway unions' weekly, *Labor*: "We have something in America that they have in no other country in the world, and that is the primary. . . . The primary law renders the formation of new parties unnecessary for the reason that whenever the people wish to renovate one or both of the old parties they may do so by the simple expedient of taking advantage of the primary."[65]

The relationship of the Socialist party to the Nonpartisan League during and immediately following World War I illustrates the reluctance of the Socialists to adopt a flexible political strategy. By contesting party primaries in a number of midwestern states, the NPL was able to gain widespread electoral support. The NPL's platform was based on statewide programs of the Socialist party, yet the Socialists reacted negatively to the league's success and refused to collaborate with it.

The Nonpartisan League was organized in North Dakota in 1915 by a former Socialist party leader, A. C. Townley. Though the North Dakota Socialists supported IWW campaigns to organize farm workers and "opposed the farmer's perennial desire for cheap labor at harvest time," the state organization stood toward the right wing of the national party and was in favor of a program of immediate demands capable of mobilizing agrarian support.[66] To attract farmers who would not join the party because they shied away from socialist ideology, Townley pressed for the creation of a special "Organization Department," which conferred partial rather than full party membership.[67] Although Townley's strategy of recruiting those who were willing to follow the party's lead on agrarian issues was remarkably successful, the Socialist leadership decided to force him and his sympathizers out of the national organization.

Townley then established the Nonpartisan League, which adopted as its platform most of the immediate demands put forward by the Socialists.[68] Townley had not disavowed his socialist beliefs, but became convinced that the doctrinaire approach of his former comrades had made it impossible to build a viable radical movement in North Dakota. He also felt that while "many farmers were willing to accept the Socialist party," they could always be lured away by major-party nominees who were competing for their votes.[69] To counter this problem, the League entered its own slate in primaries of the North Dakota Republican party, the dominant force in the state. In the words of Robert Morlan, the NPL "endeavored to engage in direct political action without acquiring the disabilities common to third parties."[70] Its program proposed rural credit banks operated at cost, support of cooperatives and trade unions, and state ownership of public utilities and various industries serving farmers, including terminal elevators, flour mills, packing houses, and cold storage plants. This program closely followed the rural-oriented planks of the state Socialist party.[71]

The NPL's tactics were strikingly successful. By April 1916, a year after it was established, the NPL had recruited a membership of forty thousand. In its first electoral contest in 1916 the League elected the North Dakota governor and several state officials. In 1918 these posts were again captured by the League, along with control of both houses of the legislature. The NPL carried out a large part of its program, including a state-owned bank, a home building association providing loans at low rates of interest, a graduated state income tax that distinguished between earned and unearned income, a workmen's compensation act funded by employers, and state-owned flour mills, which produced Dakota Maid flour.[72] Not content with these, in 1919 the NPL, now in control of the state Republican party, proposed "a thoroughgoing system of state ownership, not merely a corporate or cooperative organization, working under state regulation."[73]

Although Townley sought to woo his former Socialist comrades into the NPL, the party would have none of it, and bitterly attacked the League. But the League's success undermined the Socialist party, and by 1917 most of the leaders of the North Dakota Socialist party had quit to join the NPL. Moreover, as Jackson Putnam notes, "The overwhelming majority of the League's organizers throughout the years were Socialists," and as such, "they did not abandon their beliefs."[74] Although the League suffered some electoral setbacks in the early 1920s, it elected a U.S. senator and a number of other state officials in 1922, and remained a potent force in state politics by winning the governorship in 1926 and most major state posts in the 1930s.

The NPL spread to several other states.[75] It gained control of the Democratic party in Idaho in 1918 and was extremely successful in Minnesota, where it nominated a congressman, Charles Lindbergh (the aviator's father), for governor in the 1918 Republican primary on a platform calling for even more state ownership than in North Dakota. Lindbergh received 150,626 votes to 199,325 for his conservative opponent, despite the fact that his congressional vote against the war made him vulnerable to charges of disloyalty.[76] The League's impressive primary vote led it to enter an independent slate in the November elections in alliance with the State Federation of Labor under the Farmer-Labor label. The new party elected twenty-four state representatives and eight state senators, while its gubernatorial nominee ran second to the Republican candidate, with the Democrats finishing a poor third. The tactic of first running in the Republican primary and then on a separate Farmer-Labor ticket in the general elections was repeated in 1920, when the NPL increased its vote and elected a congressman and forty-four state legislators.[77] By 1922, the NPL and the unions no longer went through the primary process.[78] In the election of that year, Henrik Shipstead was elected U.S. senator as a League-backed third-party Farmer-Labor candidate, as were three congressmen and seventy state legislators. Their nominee for governor lost by only fourteen thousand votes.[79] In 1923 the new Farmer-Labor party captured its second U.S. senator's seat by a vote of 290,165 to 195,139.[80]

In spite of, or perhaps more accurately because of, such ballot-box suc-

cesses, the Socialist party viewed the Nonpartisan League as an opportunistic rival and rejected offers of cooperation. At its special convention in
April 1917 held to respond to the American declaration of war, the party
received a report on the NPL by a prowar leader, John Spargo, which
described it as a "movement in the direction of Socialism" and concluded
"that cooperation on the national level was unthinkable, but cooperation
and boring from within on the local level would be possible if Socialist
Party restrictions on membership cooperation with other political organizations were liberalized."[81] The convention rejected this advice and voted
114 to 56 for a resolution which stated:

> [T]he purpose of the Socialist movement being the emancipation of the
> working class from economic servitude, rather than the election to office
> of candidates, it is, therefore, declared . . . that to fuse or to compromise
> is to be swallowed up and utterly destroyed; that they [SP local units] be
> urged to maintain the revolutionary positions of the Socialist party and
> maintain in the utmost possible vigor the propaganda of Socialism,
> unadulterated by association of [sic] office seekers. The social revolution,
> not political office, is the end and aim of the Socialist party. No compro-
> mise, no political trading.[82]

An amendment to the party's constitution that would have allowed
party members to "vote as they thought best when no Socialist candidate
was in the field" and to permit branches to cooperate with other political
groups on a local level was also defeated. In reporting on the convention,
Gerald Friedberg notes that "every other socialist party in the world at that
time permitted the freedom sought in this amendment," and that as a
result of this action, "the SP was isolating itself from every possible attachment."[83] As a result of this policy the Socialists lost almost all of their
members and leaders in North Dakota, Minnesota, and other states where
the NPL became strong.[84] In the spring of 1918, the North Dakota
Socialist party totally collapsed.[85]

In Minneapolis, Socialist mayor Thomas Van Lear and most union leaders
who had previously backed the party decided to follow North Dakota's lead
and joined with others to form the Working People's Nonpartisan Political
League, as a labor counterpart to Townley's farmers' Nonpartisan League.[86]
The program of the Working People's League called for socialization of "the

forces of wealth production" in the country as a whole and municipal ownership of utilities, street railways, telephones, and gas and electric light
plants.[87] The Socialist party, however, rejected the tactic and continued to
run local candidates in opposition to the league, with little success.[88]

Writing in 1909, party centrist Morris Hillquit acknowledged that many
European socialist parties entered into "political alliances with other parties," a strategy related to the practice in some countries of holding a second ballot in districts where no candidate secured an absolute majority in
the first contest. He concluded that where there were "no second ballots in
general elections, there seems to be no reason or excuse for any deviation
from the general socialist principle of absolutely independent politics."[89]
Hillquit and other socialists did not understand that the logic of the
American electoral system is fundamentally similar to a two-ballot system.
Party factions, which in a two-ballot system would be separate parties, can
contest primaries and then coalesce with other factions in the subsequent
general election, or run independently as third candidates. This was the
strategy of Nonpartisan Leaguers, both in putting up candidates in major-
party primaries and, as happened in Minnesota after they lost in the primary, running their own third-party candidate. It is interesting to note in this
connection that Friedrich Engels, writing in 1895, identified the second-
ballot system as an advantage for a socialist third party, since voters were
not so concerned on the first ballot with the possibility of wasting their
vote on a candidate who could not win.

The Socialists never came to grips with the unique character of
American electoral politics. Their focus was on the ultimate justice of their
cause, and they ignored the strategic context of the American political system. Certainly they never systematically exploited opportunities for influence given by the American political system, particularly within the major
political parties. Socialists tended to see politics in terms of absolute right
and wrong, and it was difficult for them to envisage a strategy that
involved institutionalized coalitions with non-Socialists. By participating in
major party primaries, in the fashion of the NPL, the Socialists could have
enlarged their potential electoral support by cooperating with unionists in
the AFL's Labor Representation Committee and with sympathizers in the
Nonpartisan League. They refused to do so. The issue was to return during
World War I and the 1930s.

.   .   .

World War I and the Socialists

The sectarian character of the Socialist party was acutely demonstrated by its response to World War I and the Russian Revolution. Before 1914, along with other socialist parties, the American Socialists opposed foreign wars as imperialist conflicts fought on behalf of capitalist class interests. Yet socialists in the European democracies engaged in the war soon abandoned their commitment to internationalism and supported their government's war effort. The American Socialists were bitterly upset by this "betrayal" and condemned their comrades in the belligerent nations who went along with war mobilization. Opposition to the war became a rallying call for the American party. Its 1914 campaign slogan was "Every socialist ballot is a protest against war." The party's one congressman, Meyer London, advocated "a general strike to stop shipments of food and ammunition" to the warring powers in May 1915.[90] In the same month the party adopted a new section to its constitution, by 11,041 to 782, which stated: "Any member of the Socialist party, elected to an office, who shall in any way vote to appropriate moneys for military or naval purposes, or war, shall be expelled from the party."[91]

The party continued its opposition after the United States declared war in April 1917. In so doing, it was actually to the left of the leading Western European socialist parties. Few antiwar minority movements within European socialist parties took as stark an antiwar position as the American Socialists in rejecting wars of "national defense" and in refusing to support reparations for Belgium, which had been invaded by Germany. [92]

Several factors converged to reinforce socialist opposition to the war. Many on the right of the movement had defected to the Democratic party before 1917 in response to the prolabor and progressive policies of the Wilson administration. This defection was countered by the entry of immigrants, who by 1917 had become a major element in the national party. The proportion of members who were foreign-born increased from less than 5 percent in 1912 to 35 percent by 1916, largely from countries that had little sympathy with the Allied cause.[93] By the time of the party's St. Louis convention in 1917 and its fateful debate about war policy, many pro-Allied members had voted with their feet and left.

Most important, as we have argued above, Socialist opposition to American intervention in the war was never countered by unions with strong links to the party. Daniel Bell has pointed out that "the American Socialist Party was a heavily doctrinaire party, more so than most of its European counterparts because of its lack of commitments to the labor movement. With none of the strings of responsibilities which held the European socialists, the party, reacting by formulas, branded the war 'imperialist' and then stood apart from it."[94] Trade unions in each of the combatant societies were determined to support the war effort and undermined the abilities of socialist parties to take a different line. The demands of unions for collective bargaining, legal security, and influence over public policy were a brake on the radical inclinations of socialist movements. Other European socialist parties that were antiwar, the Russian Bolsheviks and the Serbian Socialists, also had weak links to their respective national trade union movements. American unions, in contrast to the Socialist party, shifted almost unanimously to support the war after being initially opposed. James Weinstein observes that "not a single international union took a consistent antiwar stand. Most of the socialist-led unions supported the war effort, at least officially."[95] The only unions that continued to openly back the party were the significantly Jewish Amalgamated Clothing Workers and the International Ladies Garment Workers. Most Socialist union leaders felt that they could not endanger their organizations by following a policy that was both unpopular and liable to lead to government repression.

The consequence of the decision to oppose the war was not lost on contemporaries. A number of Socialist leaders, including Louis Waldman, William English Walling, and A. M. Simons, argued that the party could have maintained and even strengthened itself had it followed the policy adopted by the European socialist parties and the AFL.[96] There is a tragic side to this episode: the Socialists' determination to pursue an ethical policy led to an organizational collapse from which they never recovered. The antiwar policy is the prime example of the party's penchant for viewing politics in black-and-white terms while ignoring the strategic consequences of its actions. Irving Howe has driven home the point that the decision was reckless because it did not take account of the likely outcome: "A nonrevolutionary movement cannot afford the indulgence of revolutionary postures: it loses out as a party of reform, it proves itself ineffectual as a voice of revolution."[97] By opposing intervention in the war, American Socialists put themselves in the camp of revolutionaries like the Russian Bolsheviks, but they were not prepared for the repression that would surely come.

What would have happened if the Socialists had followed a more pragmatic strategy of conditional support for American intervention in the
war? Such hypothetical questions can never be answered definitively, but
one can turn to comparative analysis in an attempt to give a plausible
answer. Three kinds of cases are instructive: the experience of socialist parties elsewhere, the experience of American labor unions, and the experience of the Socialist party in the United States at the municipal level. The
implication that emerges from each of these supports Milton Cantor's
claim that "had American Socialists imitated their overseas brothers, their
party might well have adjusted to wartime exigencies, retained its reform
constituency, and survived."[98]

In the major warring societies of Western Europe, the socialist parties
that were drawn into the war effort gained significant electoral support. In
Britain, the Labour party increased its share of the vote from 6.4 percent
in 1910, the last general election before the war, to 21.4 percent in 1918,
the first vote after the war. The growth of socialist support in France,
Germany, Italy, and Belgium between prewar and postwar elections ranged
from 5 to 12 percentage points. In New Zealand, the Labour party's vote
increased from 9.6 percent in 1914 to 24.2 percent 1919. The only country, apart from the United States, in which the left was weakened during
the war was Australia, where a Labor party that already had significant
electoral support governed for the duration of hostilities. While the
Socialist vote in the United States fell by almost half during the war, socialists in France, Germany, Italy, and Belgium increased their share of the vote
in absolute terms by 10 percent on average, from 26.5 to 36.6 percent.

In these countries, World War I deepened class consciousness and transformed socialist parties into major governmental players. The key to war
strategy in each of the combatant societies was mobilizing labor to the
maximum extent both in the armed services and in industry, and this led
one government after the other into a policy of appeasing labor representatives and bringing them into decision-making at the highest level.
Moreover, the policies adopted by wartime governments had more than a
passing resemblance to socialism, for, at a minimum, they involved far-
ranging government control over the munitions industry, coal and steel,
and transport. Socialist policies that, before the war, had appeared to many
as utopian, were being put into practice by governments of various ideological stripes in the urgency of total wartime mobilization.

The experience of labor movements in Europe during the war was paralleled by that of the AFL. Union membership in America grew from a little over three million in mid-1917 to nearly 3.5 million in mid-1918, over four million in mid-1919, and over five million a year later, a level of organization that was to be exceeded only after 1935. Unemployment was virtually eliminated, since the demand for labor grew as men were taken out of the labor force to fight in Europe. Unions were helped also by the strenuous efforts of the government to gain their cooperation in the huge tasks of mobilizing workers, coordinating transport, energy, and munitions production, and enforcing industrial peace. Labor organization was greatly aided by the efforts of several government commissions, including, from May 1918, the War Labor Board, which mediated labor disputes and extended union standards to regulated industries.

An indication of the extent to which labor was now regarded as a legitimate participant in the country's life and politics is revealed in the extreme reaction of the administration to an editorial in *The Nation* attacking Samuel Gompers as the representative of the government on a tour of Europe to evaluate labor conditions. Banning the offending issue of *The Nation* from the mail, the solicitor to the postmaster general explained to Oswald Garrison, the magazine's editor, that Gompers "has rendered inestimable services to this government during this war in holding labor in line, . . . while this war is on we are not going to allow any newspaper in this country to attack him."[99] Gompers and the American Federation of Labor had finally achieved the legitimacy they desired, one which went beyond even that accorded to them by the first Wilson administration.

Given the distance between AFL unions and the Socialist party, union commitment to help in the American war effort could not sway the party. The split with organized labor had momentous consequences for Socialist policy. As noted, most socialists in Britain, France, and Germany were initially deeply opposed to participating in the war, but intense pressure, exerted through unions, eventually swamped the internationalism and pacifism of socialist theoreticians and intellectuals. To gain an idea of what might have happened in the United States had there been an alliance between Socialists and unionists, it is revealing to examine the experiences of those towns and cities in America where the Socialists had developed strong local ties with unionists. Tensions arising from the War were particularly acute in Minneapolis and Milwaukee, the only major cities with

Table 5.1 Socialist/Labor Vote Before and After World War I

	Last Election Before World War I (%)	First Election After Outbreak of World War I (%)
Countries Involved from Beginning of War		
France	38.8 (1914)	43.9 (1919)*
Germany	34.8 (1912)	43.5 (1919)**
Italy	22.8 (1913)	34.3 (1919)
United Kingdom	6.4 (1910)	21.4 (1918)
Belgium	29.5 (1914)	36.6 (1919)
Overseas Countries		
Australia	48.5 (1913); 50.9 (1914)	43.9 (1917)
New Zealand	8.8 (1911); 9.6 (1914)	24.2 (1919)
United States	6.0 (1912); 3.2 (1916)	3.4 (1920)
Neutral Countries		
Denmark	29.6 (1913)	28.7 (1918)
Finland	43.1 (1913)	47.3 (1916)
Netherlands	18.5 (1913)	25.0 (1918)***
Norway	26.3 (1912)	32.1 (1915)
Sweden	30.1 (1914)	36.4 (1914); 31.1 (1917)
Switzerland	20.1 (1911)	10.1 (1914); 30.9 (1917)

* Total for 1914 includes the Radical Socialist party, the Socialist Republicans, and the Socialist party. Total for 1919 includes these parties plus the Independent Socialist vote (1.8 percent).

** Total for 1919 includes Independent Social Democrats.

*** Total for 1918 includes Social Democratic Workers, Socialist, and Communist parties.

Source: Thomas T. Mackie and Richard Rose, *The International Almanac of Electoral History* (New York: Free Press, 1974).

Socialist mayors in 1917, in a number of small midwestern communities where the party was well entrenched, and in New York City, where the party had strong links with some unions.

The strength of the prowar socialist faction in Minneapolis reflected the close ties of the local party to the labor movement, especially the Machinists Union, of which Mayor Van Lear was a member. The national

Machinists Union organization had come out in support of American intervention in 1917. The local labor movement, including many socialist leaders, came to realize that their connection to the national AFL was more vital to them than that with the Socialist party.[100]

Deserted by organized labor, which was its major bulwark, the powerful Minneapolis Socialist party split and lost much of its membership to the newborn Working People's Nonpartisan League.[101] In Milwaukee, the wartime record of Mayor Daniel Hoan and of Socialist officials in the Wisconsin labor movement suggests that party-union ties had a similar effect in the party's most enduring center of electoral strength. In 1917 the Wisconsin AFL reversed its initial antiwar position to one of support for the government, and a number of Socialist union officials accepted appointment to the state and county councils of defense.[102] As the war progressed, "the unions, benefiting from the excellent organizing opportunities, were driven from the antiwar position of the Socialists."[103] Victor Berger and the Milwaukee party continued to oppose the war after America's entry, but Mayor Hoan grew ambivalent. He wrote early in 1917 that although he opposed American involvement, "if war would come, then the loyal support and assistance of every citizen will be absolutely necessary."[104] Although tensions between unions and the Socialist party were evident in Milwaukee, an outright split was avoided because the local party was willing to compromise with the union position, and the city's labor groups were themselves subject to conflicting pressures because they were based largely in the German ethnic community, which was antiwar.

In New York City, the Socialist party, with the support of the powerful Jewish garment unions, elected seven aldermen in 1917.[105] The largest socialist labor organization, the United Hebrew Trades, dropped its antiwar position in March 1918 following the announcement of Wilson's nonannexationist Fourteen Points on the heels of the democratic February Revolution in Russia.[106] While the Socialist aldermen supported measures to prevent war profiteering and opposed sale of war stamps as especially onerous for the poor, they did not come out in opposition to the war itself and actually voted for a number of prowar resolutions.[107] However, the New York party continued to oppose American intervention in the war and rejected the policies of their elected officeholders. In a June 1918 referendum, twenty-seven of the twenty-nine branches of the New York Socialist party went on record as opposing the Third Liberty Loan.[108]

Initially, Socialist resistance to the war appeared to strengthen the party. Millions of nonsocialist Americans opposed entry, and once the United States declared war in April 1917, their only vehicle for expressing continued opposition was voting Socialist. Thus the war gave the party a new burst of strength. In the 1917 municipal elections, it averaged an unparalleled 21.6 percent of the vote in New York, Milwaukee, Canton, Buffalo, Chicago, Cleveland, Dayton, Toledo, Reading, and nine other cities.[109] Morris Hillquit, running for mayor of New York, received 21.7 percent of the vote, while in local contests for judicial office in Chicago, the Socialists secured 34 percent.[110] Eugene Debs exuberantly observed that there was "nothing in all its [the party's] past career to be compared to the sweeping political victory achieved this year."[111]

In the following year the party's electoral record was mixed because of the outbreak of war hysteria and political persecution. In several centers where the party had had support among old-stock Americans, including most of the western states, it was virtually eliminated, while in other regions, particularly Minnesota, Wisconsin, and New York, where opposition to the war was ethnically based, the party was strengthened. Although the number of elected Socialist state legislators increased from twenty-nine in 1916 to thirty-two in 1918, these came from a narrower base, four states instead of nine, two years earlier.[112] Party membership, which had fallen below 80,000 in 1915 (from more than 118,000 in 1912), increased during the war largely among persons of German and Eastern European background, reaching 108,504 in 1919.[113] Yet a year later, the party was a shadow of its former self: it had only 26,766 members and was financially bankrupt.[114] Hillquit noted that the party was "completely wiped out" in several states where it had formerly been strong and had significant support only in a few eastern and midwestern states.[115]

Prior to the war the Socialist party had a culturally diverse membership encompassing both immigrants and the native-born. It was strongly supported in several immigrant enclaves, but, proportionally, its greatest strength came from agrarian and mining states in the west and midwest with predominantly native-born electorates. The party received more than 10 percent of the vote in Arizona, California, Idaho, Montana, Nevada, Oklahoma, and Washington in the 1912 presidential election and more than 6 percent of the vote in Florida, Idaho, Nevada, Oklahoma, Washington, and Wisconsin in the 1916 presidential election. The party's antiwar position was most vigorously supported by its two main ethnic bastions: Germans in Wisconsin and Jews in New York. Many Germans rejected American intervention on account of their attachment to their mother country, while many Jews were opposed because of their hostility to czarist anti-Semitism.[116] The party's antiwar policy attracted a large following from Eastern European communities, but it led to the eventual destruction of its backing among native-stock Americans in the rural west, southwest, and midwest. By 1918, Socialist support came overwhelmingly from immigrants in a few industrial centers.

The end of hostilities saw renewed attempts on the part of many unionists and former Socialists to build an American labor party. An Independent Labor party formed by the Illinois Federation of Labor in 1918 received over fifty thousand votes for its mayoral candidate in Chicago, John Fitzpatrick, in the election of the following year. The central labor federations of New York City and forty-five other communities voted to organize labor parties during 1919, and in November a National Labor party was formed by delegates from central city bodies and local unions from forty states.[117] This effort was supplanted by a larger convention held in December which decided to establish a Farmer-Labor party to contest the 1920 elections.[118] However, the Socialist party rebuffed overtures from the Farmer-Laborites for a joint campaign.[119] Most Socialist leaders, including moderates Victor Berger and Morris Hillquit, opposed an alliance even though party membership had dropped considerably and many Farmer-Laborites were socialist sympathizers.[120] The 1920 convention of the Socialist party took just one minute to vote down a resolution calling for cooperation with other groups.[121] A number of prominent Socialists, however, resigned to join the fledgling labor party. Membership losses were heaviest in the western states, where Socialists, as Stanley Shapiro points out, were "never a part of the superheated, European-oriented intellectualism of the eastern establishment."[122] In resisting efforts for a more inclusive left-wing party, the Socialists again ignored Engels' advice that the first step in America should be to mobilize workers in their own unions and party, even if this meant programmatic compromise.

The institutional isolation of the Socialist party in the United States clearly influenced the way the country's radicals approached the issue of whether or not to support national involvement in war. Opposition to an ongoing war meant subjecting themselves to public disgrace, ostracism, and quite possibly prosecution. Socialists across the Atlantic with organization-al or political positions to lose tended to go along with their countries' mil-itary efforts. In contrast to socialist parties in Western Europe, with their close links to trade union movements, the American Socialist party con-tained relatively few individuals who felt constrained to support the war in order to retain union support.

It is difficult to overestimate the consequences for the party of its oppo-sition to the war. The party had narrowed its geographic base and lost its native-born support; it was less oriented to events in the United States and more driven by events in Russia, and in the process had reinforced the pro-paganda that the party was unpatriotic and un-American. The Socialist party was viewed as in, but not of, America.

Contrasting Perspectives

The dominant line of intellectual criticism of the Socialist party has been that it was overly ideological, sectarian, and driven by factions. But some have argued almost the opposite—that the party was overly reformist. They cite its opposition to unlimited immigration, its failure to appeal to African-Americans, its lack of vision at the municipal level, and its purge in 1912 of proponents of extralegal methods, including supporters of the Industrial Workers of the World (IWW).

Byron Dixon concludes his detailed analysis of Socialist party policies on race and immigration issues before 1920 by stating that in its efforts to gain support the party was "quite willing to sacrifice . . . [its] ideology." He sees the betrayal of principle in the Socialist party as "a reflection of a larg-er weakness that explains its long-term failure . . . [its lack of] an analysis embracing the most exploited members of society within an ideology com-mitted to revolutionary change."[123]

There is no question but that the pre–World War I Socialist party com-promised with the racist and nativist sentiments prevalent among American workers. Many party members and leaders, including spokesper-sons for the party's left wing, openly expressed such views. The best that can be said for the Socialists is that some members, including their princi-pal spokesman, Eugene Debs, openly advocated a racially and ethnically egalitarian society. But the struggle for religious and racial equality was regarded as secondary to the class struggle itself. American Socialists followed Karl Marx in believing that evils such as anti-Semitism and race and gender discrimination would disappear under socialism.

The Socialist approach to municipal administration has been discussed earlier. It is true that Socialist city governments were basically reformist, but it is difficult to envisage what a revolutionary municipal administration could do other than follow efficient prolabor, welfare policies much as Communist urban politicians did in Italy, France, and Finland after World War II.

The policy that critics of reformism have most closely linked to the party's decline is the expulsion of those who opposed electoral methods in favor of violence at the party's 1912 convention.[124] The move was led by Victor Berger and Morris Hillquit, who were on the center right of the party, but it gained support from a wide spectrum of Socialists who perceived that the revolutionary rhetoric of supporters of the Industrial Workers of the World, the Wobblies, was an electoral liability. Even Eugene Debs, who initially backed the IWW and saw himself as a unifier within the party, wrote in the *International Socialist Review* that he strongly opposed "any tactics which involve stealth, intrigue, and necessitate acts of individual violence for their existence. . . . American workers are law-abiding, and no amount of sneering and derision will alter that fact. Direct action will never appeal to any considerable number of them while they have the ballot and the right of industrial and political organization."[125] In January 1913, William Haywood, leader of the IWW and chief advocate in the party of revolutionary action, was recalled from the National Executive Committee of the Socialist party by a referendum.[126]

It is possible to argue that the attack on the pro-IWW anarcho-syndicalists within the party is yet another example of the American Socialists' insistence on principle and lack of political expediency. Several European socialist parties were able to house a wider range of reformist and revolutionary currents than the American organization. If American Socialists had been less stubborn, it is argued, they might well have profited from these examples.[127]

The expulsion of the revolutionary syndicalists has also been criticized on the grounds that it relinquished the task of unionizing workers to the AFL, which, as we have seen, was a craft-dominated organization unsympathetic to immigrant and unskilled workers. In his biography of Eugene Debs, Nick

Salvatore writes that after the expulsion of the revolutionary wing, "the best opportunity in Debs's career to unify the Socialist movement and to re-orient the labor movement along industrial lines passed."[128] Although Debs continued to attack the leadership of the AFL, no major efforts to create unions for the unskilled were undertaken until the Great Depression and the emergence of the Committee for Industrial Organization, later the Congress of Industrial Organizations (CIO). Sympathetic with the left wing, Salvatore writes, "Berger and Hillquit consistently clung to their narrow approach to labor, even in the face of opposition from their own supporters. . . . Trailing after a bankrupt policy and following it with such severe blinders that they could not perceive important changes in the culture and attitudes of working people, Berger, Hillquit and their allies stringently limited Socialist options."[129] Salvatore sees Debs' unwillingness to confront the forces led by Berger and Hillquit as a personal failure that weakened the party.

Could the Socialists have helped to create a more encompassing union movement based on industrial unions if they had been more tolerant of the revolutionary faction? Should the party have created dual unions in opposition to the AFL or should it have deepened its links to existing unions? As discussed earlier, Socialists were deeply divided on this question, with the result that their efforts were contradictory and often self-canceling. Many, including Debs, supported industrial unions, such as the Western Federation of Miners, and helped establish the IWW, which targeted the most unskilled, exploited workers. But the results were disappointing. Even though the AFL focused its efforts on skilled, native workers, it was by far the largest labor organization from the 1890s on. The dual industrial unions that were established by Socialists and, later, Communists, alienated existing AFL unions and were, in any case, ineffective. Mike Davis, a radical critic of the AFL, nevertheless observes that "the Socialist left wing—many of whom angrily withdrew from the party after Big Bill Haywood was purged in 1912—adopted an almost exclusively industrial perspective that focused on the allegedly imminent revolutionary potential of the immigrant and unorganized workers. . . . [But] their syndicalism proved to be only a temporary tactical palliative for the needs of the unorganized factory proletariat."[130]

Historian Ira Kipnis interprets the expulsion of the revolutionary syndicalists as a prime cause of the precipitous decline in the membership of the Socialist party after 1912.[131] His argument, however, exaggerates the extent to which the 1912 convention represented a move to the right by the party and ignores the considerable increase in left-wing influence following defections of the right to the prolabor Wilson administration elected in 1912. Eugene Debs, who stood with the party's left on most issues, reported that the "spirit of the [1912] convention was perfectly revolutionary."[132] Debs may have been led to this view because the convention chose him as its presidential nominee against the opposition of both the centrist faction, headed by Morris Hillquit, and the rightist one, led by Victor Berger.[133] Moreover, important areas of left-wing strength, such as Oklahoma and Texas, continued to grow until they were faced with wartime repression. Gerald Friedberg confirms Debs' impression that the party moved considerably to the left after 1914: "Under the impact of 1914–16 developments, the left . . . experienced a rebirth of stature and power. . . . [L]eft wing influence was more and more decisive in determining official party positions, including dramatic reversals of pre-war policies."[134]

A comprehensive explanation for the loss of Socialist support between 1912 and 1916 must take into account the considerable number of voters and party members attracted to Woodrow Wilson and the Democratic party. Ironically, the historical record demonstrates that Socialists, as critics of opportunism asserted, proved vulnerable to the appeal of progressive non-Socialist political leaders. But this weakness repeatedly reinforced rather than reduced the party's propensity for sectarianism.

Socialist Sectarianism in America:
A Comparative View

Those who stress the rightist tendencies of the party as the source of its failure ignore the comparative evidence. While the American Socialist party, like socialist parties in Western Europe, had left, center, and right factions, on balance it was considerably more radical than these parties. The American Socialist party's right and center were more Marxist, at least in rhetoric, than those in continental Europe and used far more revolutionary language than comparable factions in other Anglo-American societies. European socialists occasionally made the point that those on the left of the American party more closely resembled the revolutionary anarcho-syndicalists of Europe than they did continental left-wing Marxists. Some American left-wingers had ideological links to De Leonism, which opposed any

reforms short of the abolition of capitalism. For this reason, they consistently rejected what they called "'truckling' for votes."[135] Debs, the party's most
prominent spokesman and its five-time presidential candidate, while clearly
an advocate of electoral politics, used revolutionary Marxist rhetoric in his
campaign speeches and in 1914 called for an amalgamation of the Socialist
party with the ultrasectarian De Leonist Socialist Labor party.[136]

In discussing differences between European and American socialism in
1906, Marx's grandson Jean Longuet noted that orthodox Marxism was
stronger within the American socialist movement than anywhere else
except in Russia.[137] And in the czarist empire, of course, socialists were not
operating in a democracy. Morris Hillquit observed in 1909 that socialist
parties in Europe "often combine with other progressive parties for the
attainment of common purposes," while "the socialists of America have in
fact on every occasion declared themselves against all forms of political
combination or cooperation with other parties."[138] In general, European
socialist visitors to America before World War I recognized that American
socialists were exceptionally radical.[139]

The contrast between socialism as practiced in Britain and in America
was especially sharp, as H. G. Wells observed during a trip to the United
States. Socialism in America, he wrote, is "far more closely akin to the revolutionary socialism of the continent of Europe than to the constructive and
evolutionary Socialism of Great Britain. . . . It is . . . altogether anarchistic
in spirit."[140] British socialists were disturbed that their American comrades
refused to follow their lead in joining with the unions in a mass-based
labor party and repeated the advice Engels had given a quarter of a century
earlier—that it was more important to have a large labor-based movement
than a small ideologically correct socialist party.

This was apparent to Henry Pelling, an English scholar who wrote a history of the American labor movement: "American Socialism was for the
most part more dogmatically Marxist. . . . The British observer who examines the record of the American Socialists is struck not only by their dogmatism but also by their lack of political responsibility. . . . American
Socialism produced many powerful works of literature, and it is remarkable how many of these works envisaged a catastrophic, rather than an
evolutionary, process of transition to Socialism."[141]

John Spargo, who had been active on the left of the British socialist
movement, and as a consequence was regarded as an intransigent, found his

place among the moderates of the Socialist party without any noticeable change in views after emigrating to America in 1901.[142] The rigidly Marxist British Social Democratic Federation (SDF), led by H. M. Hyndman, denounced by Engels for archsectarianism, regarded itself as the British counterpart of the Socialist party of America.[143] The leaders of the more moderate, but still quite left, Independent Labour party were annoyed by the tendency of American Socialists to identify with the SDF rather than themselves. Lawrence Moore observes that "British socialists in the Labour party . . . felt a kinship with very few of the American socialist leaders. From their point of view, the insistence by the latter on strict socialist independence thwarted in advance the attempts to win over American labor."[144]

Many on the right of the American party, including Victor Berger and Robert Hunter, rejected the revisionist views of German theoretician Eduard Bernstein. Berger, attacked by his left critics as the "American Bernstein," remained, according to Moore, "much closer to [the official Marxism of] Bebel and Kautsky than to any of the German revisionists."[145] There can be no doubt that Berger, as the ideological leader of the electorally most successful section of the party, Milwaukee, was a moderate and gradualist within the context of American socialism. Nevertheless, he frequently suggested that the people should be armed. In 1905 he proclaimed: "Friedrich Engels once said: 'Give every citizen a good rifle and fifty cartridges and you have the best guarantee for the liberty of the people.' Thomas Jefferson held the same views exactly. . . . With the nation armed, the workingmen are not in danger of being shot down like dogs on the least provocation."[146] And, on July 31, 1909, in a signed article in the Milwaukee *Social-Democratic Herald* that was later used against him and the party, Berger emphasized that Socialists "Should Be Prepared to Fight for Liberty at All Hazards":

> . . . In view of the plutocratic law-making of the present day, it is easy to predict that the safety and hope of this country will finally be in one direction only—that of a violent and bloody revolution.
>
> Therefore, I say, each of the 500,000 Socialist voters, and of the two million workingmen who instinctively incline our way, should besides doing much reading and still more thinking, also have a good rifle and the necessary rounds of ammunition in his home and be prepared to back up his ballot with his bullets if necessary.
>
> This may look like a startling statement. Yet I can see nothing else for the

American masses today. The working class of this country is being pushed hopelessly downward. We must resist as long as resistance is possible. . . .[147]

Although Berger, like others on the center and right of the party, reject-ed the Industrial Workers of the World and worked within the AFL, his opposition to World War I led him to reassess his views. He wrote in 1918, "I am beginning to believe that the IWW (or some labor organization that will succeed it but that will inherit its matchless spirit) is destined to take the place of the American Federation of Labor in our country and fulfill the mission in which the American Federation of Labor has failed."[148]

Morris Hillquit, though clearly moderate or centrist in the American context, was viewed by most British socialists as "foolishly sectarian."[149] His approach illustrated the paradox of American socialism, part movement, part party. Richard Fox points out that "many contemporaries . . . Americans and Europeans—considered him a thoroughgoing revolution-ary, many others with equal assurance labeled him a reformer."[150] This con-tradictory evaluation can be understood in comparative context. "For while Hillquit was not a 'revolutionist' in the special sense of 'dual unionist' which that term acquired in America, he was a 'revolutionary' as the authoritative spokesmen of European Social Democracy understood the term."[151] The American party was regarded by the European Marxists as a genuine revolutionary party, and "Hillquit was rewarded with recognition as their 'revolutionary' collaborator."[152]

During the early 1930s, a strong left wing reemerged within the Socialist party, largely based on young people who were reacting to the economic crisis of capitalism. They treated Hillquit's theoretical writings as "their bible."[153] Dennis McGreen observes that Hillquit "won their respect and often political support" because they considered his basic position "radical and uncompromising."[154] An indication of why Hillquit was regarded as a radical Marxist can be found in his theoretical work *From Marx to Lenin*, published in 1921. In discussing how a newly elected social-ist government would deal with the anticipated efforts of capitalists to use the armed forces and the police against the regime, Hillquit argued that the socialist state would probably need to use the "repressive force of gov-ernment" to maintain itself against "the forces of surviving capitalism aim-ing at its overthrowal."[155] While the "dictatorship of the proletariat" during the period of the "transitional Socialist state . . . is frankly a limited form of democracy . . . it is a higher form than the democracy of the bourgeoisie, because it means the actual rule of the majority over the minority, while the latter represents the rule of a minority over the majority."[156]

Although Hillquit believed with Marx that the United States was one of the few countries where "workers can achieve their goal [political power] by peaceful means," he would also write in a 1909 book, *Socialism in Theory and Practice*, "that by abusing our written Constitution, the American courts seem determined to force the People into the paths of violent revolution."[157] As Fox notes: "Hillquit was certain that the class *conflict* which socialists and non-socialists alike observed in America would lead to intensifying class *struggle* by means of which the working class, growing constantly more numerous and more prosperous in absolute terms, would attain political power."[158] The image of Hillquit as a reformist comes not only from his support for working within the AFL, but also from his conviction that Socialists should press for attainable reforms. This view, Fox points out, flowed from his "experience among the impoverished immigrants of New York's Lower East Side, who confronted capitalism . . . in the form of relentless poverty, hunger, and tuberculosis."[159]

The European view that the American Socialist party was on the left of the international movement was reflected in Lenin's polemical writings. In attacking opportunists and revisionists, Lenin singled out European Social Democrats such as Eduard Bernstein, the German revisionist Alexandre Miller, and Arthur Henderson, leader of the Independent Labour party, but in America Lenin's target was Samuel Gompers, the nonsocialist leader of the American Federation of Labor. Lenin praised Eugene Debs on a number of occasions and rarely attacked other Socialist party leaders. Hillquit and many others in the United States were placed in the center, not the reformist right. Before America's entry into World War I, Lenin believed that the American Socialist party, unlike most European ones, was capable of becoming a truly revolutionary party.[160]

In Retrospect: Why
Pre-1920 Socialist Strategy Failed

We have presented diverse evidence indicating that the strategy of the pre-1920 Socialist party hurt its chances of achieving major party status. Most

Socialists never fully realized the difficulty of the task they faced and so were unwilling to make the compromises that were necessary to give their party a fighting chance. They were unwilling to work patiently within the American Federation of Labor to build an organizational base in the working class that might have strengthened the party electorally. They blocked attempts to create a more encompassing labor party, fearing this would dilute socialist ideology and control. They criticized municipal Socialist administrations in towns and cities that offered the best hopes of building a regional base for subsequent expansion. They shunned efforts to create farmer-labor or labor parties, even in circumstances where such a strategy appeared promising. Finally, the Socialist party came out in opposition to American entry into World War I although the party was utterly unprepared for the mass hysteria and repression that party moderates warned would follow.

A number of writers who have noted these decisions have concluded that if the party had been less factionalized and more pragmatic it could have become an electorally viable party. But given our comparative analysis of the constraints on the Socialist party resulting from American antistatism, the weakness of social class, the country's political system, and ethnic diversity stemming from immigration, we have to be more circumspect. As mentioned earlier, in most of Europe, strong postfeudal class awareness encouraged greater worker solidarity with labor or socialist parties.

Given the strength of structural and cultural impediments in the United States, it does not make sense to emphasize mistakes in strategy or extremist ideologies as the crucial factors affecting Socialist support. The failure of socialism in America was overdetermined. The only realistic possibilities that presented themselves were for the creation of a labor party along the lines of those in other English-speaking democracies and/or the contestation of primaries within the major parties. But a strategy adapted to the particular circumstances of American society and culture was regarded by most Socialist leaders, as well as followers, as unprincipled, even if it might promise electoral success. They believed that whatever its short-term setbacks, socialism was destined to be the future for capitalist society, in America as elsewhere. Only later, in the 1920s when the party was in severe decline, did Socialist leaders such as Norman Thomas come to the conclusion that if the party was to survive it would have to adopt a more flexible approach, which meant making alliances with nonsocialist groups and dropping any ambitions for a socialist-dominated union movement.

Yet, as we note in the next chapter, in spite of the earlier failures, such a strategy was not followed during the Depression years, when Socialists had a last chance to build a viable movement.

Regardless of the possible effects of alternative strategies, it is evident that the American socialist movement was more sectarian and intransigent than those of other industrial countries. But reaching such a conclusion, as many historians of the movement have done, begs the question of why sectarianism has been more prevalent in the United States than elsewhere.

Whereas socialist or labor parties in most European and Anglo-American societies had to adjust to the existence of affiliated union movements oriented to improving conditions within capitalism, the American Socialist party, as we have seen, was relatively isolated from the major labor groups. The absence of party-union ties meant that the American party was spared the steady push toward reformism exerted by unions in countries such as Britain, Australia, Germany, and Sweden. Even in countries where socialist parties created unions, the parties soon found themselves dwarfed by labor organizations having several times as many members backed by relatively huge financial resources. Where socialist-controlled unions were reasonably effective as bargaining agents, they soon realized that it was worth struggling to improve conditions under the existing system of wage labor without pooling their resources for the final battle to eradicate capitalism. Only parties without union links thought otherwise. Like the Russian Bolsheviks, the American Socialist party was isolated from the inherently broad reformist stream of trade unionism.

The relationship between reformism and unions can be seen within the United States as well as in international comparisons. We have noted that reformism was strongest among local parties closely connected to unions, as in Milwaukee, Minneapolis, and Schenectady. These examples suggest that the causal influence between reformism and union links runs in both directions: reformists within the party were more sympathetic to the idea of local labor parties encompassing unions, while the union connection reinforced reformism in the local party.

A more general source of socialist sectarianism can be found in the influence of Protestant sectarianism, as discussed in Chapter 1. The sectarian denominations have fostered a variety of moralistic responses from prohibition to militant anti-abortion efforts and recurrent opposition to war. All but one war the United States has fought from 1812 to Vietnam has triggered an antiwar movement.[161] The sole exception is World War II, which began when the country was attacked. Like members of many other American movements, the country's socialists acted as if it were better to be right than effective. As Robert Alexander has noted, the propensity of American radical groups "to split on questions of doctrine and personality . . . [in ways comparable] only to similar trends in the Protestant churches . . . [helps] to explain why Marxist radicalism has never become a major force in United States politics."[162]

Pietistic moralism has been countered in major party politics by the need to compromise in order to form electorally viable coalitions to contest elections. Both the Democratic and Republican parties restrain moralism and extremism in order to appeal to diverse groups of voters. But social movements, including those oriented around nativism, racism, abolitionism, populism, prohibition, and socialism, have been far less restrained in voicing moralistic and, most important, sectarian impulses. Given the influence of religious sectarianism on American values, it is not surprising that the American socialist parties have been more sectarian than socialist parties in other industrialized nations, and have been relatively unwilling to compromise their ideological convictions.

Chapter 6

SOCIALIST

SECTARIANISM AND

COMMUNIST

OPPORTUNISM IN THE

THIRTIES

The Great Depression presented the Socialists with their final opportunity to build a viable political party. Rampant poverty, mass unemployment, widespread bankruptcies, and the public's general uncertainty about the future gave the Socialists grounds for believing that they could finally create a durable mass movement. With the establishment of the Committee for Industrial Organization (later the Congress of Industrial Organizations) in 1935, leftists finally had an industrial union movement with which they could work. The membership of unions grew from a little more than three million in 1927 (11.3 percent of the nonagricultural workforce) to over eight million in 1939 (28.6 percent of the nonagricultural workforce). Socialists expected similar gains.

Yet this was not to be. The Depression years saw spurts of growth, followed by periods of decline, in the membership of both the Socialist and Communist parties. Support for the Socialist party increased in the early thirties, while the Communists reached their zenith during the second half of the decade and again during the wartime alliance with the Soviet Union. However, the Socialist party declined from 1934 onward, while the Communist party became a minuscule organization by the end of the

1940s. Neither party was able to capitalize on Depression-born discontent and the radicalization of a significant segment of the population. By 1940, each party's presidential nominee received fewer votes than at the height of national prosperity in 1928. The two-party system remained intact, and the working-class and the trade-union movements had become even more closely tied to the Democratic party.

This outcome demonstrates anew the barriers third parties face in the American political system. A turn to the left on the part of the Democratic party under Franklin Delano Roosevelt in the early thirties placed radicals in an almost impossible situation, for they faced the starkest possible choice between ideological purity, i.e., supporting a socialist alternative, and policy effectiveness, which would involve supporting FDR. Leftists devised various ways of dealing with this dilemma, from outright opposition to the New Deal, to splitting their votes between third-party candidates at the state and local level and Roosevelt at the national level, to burrowing into the Democratic party from within. But no strategy could effectively counter the efforts of Roosevelt to muster leftist support behind the Democratic party.

Yet there are also grounds for believing that the leftists hurt themselves. At the beginning of the postwar period, Socialists modified their dogmatic refusal to work with nonsocialists when, in 1923–24, they endorsed the "independent" Progressive candidacy of Robert La Follette for president. Although he received almost 17 percent of the vote, the AFL and various farm groups, which had also backed him, decided against further involvement in such efforts. The failure of the campaign to create a mass third party, however, revived the disdain of Socialists for cooperating with others. In spite of a marked shift to the left within the trade union movement, the Democratic party, and the electorate as a whole during the 1930s, Socialists remained dogmatically independent. Throughout the Depression decade, Socialists continued their traditional approach of seeking to build a left party, following what can only be described as a sectarian strategy. They opposed all cooperation with left-wing and labor-union elements who worked with the Democratic party.

Before World War I, as we have seen, the labor movement was split by enmity between Socialists and mainstream unionists. From the 1920s the political wing of the labor movement was itself divided between mutually antagonistic Socialists and Communists. An already weakened movement was divided into yet weaker factions by battles worthy of giants. The Communist party, which had bitterly attacked Socialists as too reformist and opportunistic following the post–World War I split, shifted in 1936 to a policy of building progressive "left-center coalitions," largely within the Democratic party. This strategy was followed from 1936 to 1939 and again from 1941 to the outbreak of the Cold War, thus placing the Communists well to the right of the Socialists.

The Socialist Party

With less than eight thousand members and relatively few large branches, the Socialist party was in a poor position to take advantage of burgeoning mass discontent at the start of the Depression. Still, by 1932, membership had doubled to fifteen thousand, and Norman Thomas secured close to 900,000 votes, or 2.5 percent of the total, in the presidential race that year, up from less than 1 percent in 1928. Circulation of party newspapers grew from 300,000 in 1928 to 700,000 in 1932, and over two hundred new locals were formed in 1931 and 1932.[1] In communities such as Milwaukee, Reading, Bridgeport, and New York City, where the party had retained strong organizations through the 1920s, electoral support grew substantially.

The Wisconsin Socialists greatly increased their representation in the state legislature, and won the mayoralty in Racine for the first time. Milwaukee's Socialist mayor, Daniel Hoan, was reelected in 1932 with 63 percent of the vote, his strongest showing ever. The Milwaukee Socialists also captured twelve of the twenty-seven council seats, and nine of the twenty posts on the county board under a program of municipal ownership of public utilities, municipal banking, a six-hour day for city employees, and city marketing of milk and fuel.[2]

Bridgeport, Connecticut, fell under Socialist control for the first time in 1933.[3] Socialist victories in Reading were stymied only by collaboration between the two major parties. In New York City, in 1932, Morris Hillquit secured 251,656 votes as candidate for mayor, which was more than twice the New York City vote for Norman Thomas as presidential nominee.[4] Local Socialist candidates received a substantial vote in a number of other cities as well. Once again, the party received significantly greater support at the local than at the national level, an outcome which reflected a perennial disability for a third party in the United States. Many voters who preferred a Socialist or other third-party candidate to the major-party nominees felt impelled to cast their presidential ballot for the "lesser of two evils," in this case, Franklin Delano Roosevelt.

Socialists were bitterly disappointed by the vote for Thomas in 1932. Shortly before the election, the National Campaign Committee had anticipated that the vote would "substantially better the 2,500,000 vote mark which straw votes indicate will be cast for Norman Thomas." This prediction was not far from that made by a sample of political journalists.[5] Thomas himself, in a postelection talk to Socialist party organizers, acknowledged that the vote fell below his expectation: "Evidently those men and women in various parts of the country who candidly assured me that while they believed everything I said, they were going to vote for Roosevelt just to be sure to 'get Hoover,' were even more numerous than I thought."[6] Frederick Olson noted: "The Socialists had failed to reckon with the tendency of American voters to turn from one major party to the other in time of economic crisis, rather than to a third party."[7]

While Thomas put the greatest responsibility for the failure of the party on pressures stemming from the American electoral system, in May 1933 he wrote in a confidential letter to the party's national secretary that much as he liked "the name Socialist," it confused people because it was associated with foreign countries in which governments calling themselves socialist held power. He suggested that perhaps the time had come to drop the name "socialist" and convert the Socialist party into a "farmer-labor" party.[8]

The years 1932–1933 were the high point of Socialist strength during the Depression. The party declined in the succeeding years for two reasons: Roosevelt and his New Deal program were immensely appealing for many leftists, and the Socialist party itself was weakened by endemic factionalism.

Internecine warfare within the party during the 1930s attested once again to the Socialists' penchant for ideological purity.[9] The early thirties saw the revival of a militant left wing—largely based on young recruits—that sought to give the party a revolutionary cast and favored a united front with the Communists. The militant left was bitterly opposed by the Old Guard, composed primarily of party veterans who were largely European and self-educated, centered in electoral and union strongholds. As Daniel Bell notes of this group, they "defensively emphasized the 'working-class' character . . . of [the party's] origin and thinking."[10] The Old Guard opposed revolutionary rhetoric and cooperation with the Communists. This was the major schism, but there were several other factional conflicts. Thomas sadly commented: "We multiply parties, leagues, would-be parties, and God knows what."[11] At times there were at least six different organized factions and subfactions. Thomas himself played an active role in these disputes, aligning himself in the first half of the decade in the Debs tradition with the left-wing militant faction.[12]

Debates within the party during the early thirties revealed anew the propensity of American Socialists to isolate themselves from the mainstream of national politics. There was intense disagreement on "the road to power" to be taken by the minuscule organization.[13] The ultimately dominant Militant group was wedded to a universalist Marxist perspective. Its leaders hoped to work with Communists in a United Front, tended to favor extraparliamentary methods, and rejected cooperating with trade union leaders.[14] Like the earlier Socialist leftwings, the Militants were less concerned with gaining votes or offices than with publicizing the goal of socialism.[15] In 1934, the party convention adopted a new Declaration of Principles which stated: "If the capitalist system should collapse in a general chaos and confusion . . . the Socialist party, whether or not in such a case it is a majority, will not shrink from the responsibility of organizing and maintaining a government under the workers' rule."[16] The statement also declared that the party "will meet war and the detailed plans for war already mapped out by warmaking arms of the government, by massed war resistance, organized so far as practicable in a general strike of labor unions and professional groups in a united effort to make the waging of war a practical impossibility and to convert the capitalist war crisis into a victory for Socialism."[17] Although Norman Thomas and Daniel Hoan were privately unhappy with the revolutionary rhetoric of the declaration, they publicly supported it and thus facilitated its adoption by a convention vote of 99 to 47.[18] It was subsequently approved by 55 percent of those voting in a membership referendum.[19]

As this indicates, the majority of Socialists stood on the far left in the first years of the Roosevelt administration, sharply attacking the New Deal as state capitalism and as a system for institutionalizing scarcity. Yet both the left and right wings of the now tiny party favored trying to build a new mass third party.[20] Norman Thomas and the left-wing Militant faction

wanted a labor party which would "be national, working class in composition, independent of the major parties and federated."[21] Thomas emphasized, however, that the "Socialist Party never again ought to go into a
coalition like that of 1924, when we endorsed La Follette for President."[22]
In contrast, the right-wing Old Guard, which was centered in the increasingly pro-Roosevelt garment unions, was more prepared to make whatever
compromises were necessary to induce the union movement toward some
form of independent political action.[23]

Given these disagreements, the Old Guard finally withdrew from the
party (or was forced out) in 1936 and formed the Social Democratic
Federation. It was now free to support Roosevelt for president.[24] The with-
drawal (or expulsion, as the Old Guard defined the situation) brought in
its wake a 40 percent fall in Socialist party membership, a sharp decline in
influence within the various garment unions, and loss of control over various party institutions such as the Jewish *Daily Forward*, the *New Leader*,
and the Rand School (a party educational center in New York).[25]

The split, however, did not bring unity to the shrunken party. Instead of
two factions, the party now had three: the old Militants, who moved "right"
(as did the Communists); the Clarity caucus, which pressed for "revolutionary" tactics; and an Appeal group, composed largely of Trotskyists and
members of the youth movement, that was even farther to the left. The
Trotskyists had joined the Socialist party in 1936 in response to an invitation from Thomas on behalf of the party to unify all radicals who "believe
that the times require another American Revolution."[26] The Trotskyists, the
only group to take advantage of the invitation, entered largely to build a
faction, which could, they anticipated, absorb the party's left and withdraw
to form a new, truly revolutionary, Leninist party. They left the Socialist
party within a year and took most of the youth organization with them.

Internal peace was still not in store for the party. It remained bitterly
divided on how to work with statewide labor and progressive parties in
Wisconsin and New York, and over whether to cooperate with trade
unions which enthusiastically supported prolabor Democrats in local campaigns. There was also dissension on foreign policy issues.[27]

But the most important factor weakening the party was the attraction of
Roosevelt and his New Deal. When Norman Thomas was asked in the later
years of his life why the Socialists failed to take advantage of the
Depression, his answer was clear-cut: "It was Roosevelt in a word."[28]

The problem that Roosevelt posed for the Socialists was simple. His economic and trade union policies had great appeal to the poor, to the unemployed, to African-Americans, and to trade unionists and their leaders.[29] These programs, along with his rhetoric, which turned increasingly populist and anti-business, attracted voters who had been to the left of the Democrats.[30] Trade unionists and former Socialists were offered significant roles in the administration and the Democratic party. Roosevelt and his close advisers ingratiated themselves personally with progressives and leftists, regardless of party.[31] As noted, they worked with and supported the state candidates of the Wisconsin Progressives and Minnesota Farmer-Laborites. In New York, the state in which Norman Thomas had received his largest vote in earlier elections, the formation of the American Labor party allowed Socialists and other leftists to vote for Roosevelt in 1936 without formally endorsing the Democrats. The creation of near-socialist movements within the Democratic party in Oregon, Washington, and California drained the Socialist party in the west of almost all its members and leaders. Most of the intellectuals who had publicly backed Thomas in 1932 went over to Roosevelt.

The pressures to work within the Democratic party, following Roosevelt's election and his sponsorship of progressive and prolabor policies, "forced Socialists to choose between building a party or movement."[32] One longtime socialist intellectual, Upton Sinclair, presented the party with a dilemma in 1933 when he changed his voting registration from Socialist to Democratic, though he continued to pay Socialist dues.[33] The California and national Socialist parties rejected Sinclair's efforts to work as a Socialist within the Democratic party and expelled him on September 20.[34] Socialists bitterly attacked him and his End Poverty in California (EPIC) movement, which sought to run candidates in the Democratic party primaries. Norman Thomas insisted that Sinclair's chances of winning the Democratic gubernatorial nomination in 1934 were "very small."[35] He maintained that while some of Sinclair's proposals "had merit, the EPIC program was not socialism . . . [and] would not work; thinking it was socialism, the people would be harder to convince the next time around." A member of the Socialist National Committee who wired congratulations to Sinclair when he won the Democratic primary was forced to resign.[36] But most Socialists in California disagreed. Jerry Voorhis, subsequently a Democratic member of Congress but then still a party member, wrote to

Thomas, "The Sinclair movement is the nearest thing to a mass movement toward socialism that I have heard of in America."[37] Socialist party activists in California from all ideological wings resigned in order to back Sinclair. Party membership in California fell by over 90 percent between 1933 and 1935.[38]

Sinclair was not the only party leader who recognized that Roosevelt had opened the door for Socialists to work within the major political organizations. Abraham Cahan, the four-decade-long editor of the Socialist Jewish *Daily Forward*, proclaimed in October 1933 that "President Roosevelt has earned the gratitude of every thinking man in the country. He should be a Socialist, if anybody is entitled to membership in our party he is." Thomas replied by saying he "would second Cahan's nomination of FDR for membership in the Socialist party if Roosevelt would propose to nationalize coal mining and banking."[39] Expressing the opinion common among many Socialists, the Executive Committee of the Colorado Socialist party wrote to Thomas that many Socialists wanted to support the New Deal, "on the ground that Roosevelt is putting into effect most of the 1932 Socialist Platform."[40] Although Thomas was opposed to Upton Sinclair's plan to work within the Democratic party, he suggested privately in January 1934 that the party concentrate only on opposing anti–New Deal Democrats in the congressional elections of that year and that it should not nominate a presidential candidate against Roosevelt in 1936.[41] But after much discussion and debate, Thomas finally decided to run again in 1936, feeling that the party would disappear organizationally unless it nominated candidates.[42] This decision was strongly opposed by trade union leaders who were party members. Two garment union presidents, David Dubinsky and Max Zaritsky, resigned from the party early in 1936 to back Roosevelt.[43]

Thomas' opposition to Roosevelt was based on a deep-rooted belief that a socialist movement could not be built through support of major-party candidates, that the Socialists must educate the population, and that reforms could not eliminate capitalist unemployment and war. He saw the New Deal as "an elaborate scheme for stabilizing capitalism through associations of industries that could regulate production in order to maintain profits."[44] The main issue in 1936 according to Thomas and the party was "Socialism versus Capitalism."[45]

Ironically, however, many left-wingers in the party also urged that the party not nominate a presidential candidate, "fearing it would alienate labor completely." These included two leaders of the left Militant faction, Paul Porter and Leo Krzycki; two "firebrands" of the National Executive Committee, Powers Hapgood and Franz Daniel; and two leaders of the more radical Revolutionary Committee, Francis Hanson and William Chamberlain.[46]

The decision to oppose Roosevelt in 1936 delivered a death blow to the party. Thomas secured only 187,342 votes nationally, fewer than the party had attained in any presidential contest since 1900.[47] Membership plummeted from 21,951 in 1934 to 11,711 by the middle of 1936.[48] The party's decision to present an independent electoral ticket destroyed its remaining influence in the labor movement.[49] As noted, the New York–based garment union leaders withdrew to back Roosevelt. Various Socialists, including militants like Franz Daniel and Powers Hapgood, had warned that a Socialist presidential campaign would mean cutting "ourselves off from the labor movement." Leo Krzycki of Milwaukee, national chairman of the Socialist party and national vice-president of the Amalgamated Clothing Workers, resigned from the party under union pressure to support Roosevelt.[50]

Roosevelt's impact on union leaders, even early in his presidency, is revealed by a speech given by Van Bittner, a miners' union leader, at a union convention in the mid-1930s:

> Early in 1933 I visited the White House with . . . Philip Murray, and our old friend John Lewis, and Tom Kennedy. . . . At that time our union did not have enough members to pay the officers and during the course of that interview with the President he said this, "Boys, go home and have a good night's sleep because if I don't do anything else during my administration as President of the United States I am going to give the miners an opportunity to organize in the United Mine Workers of America."
>
> Well, for a week I just was in sort of a daze. . . . [C]ertainly after that I was for the President, and nothing he has done since would cause me to be against him.[51]

A semiofficial biography of Sidney Hillman, an important leader of the CIO and president of the Amalgamated Clothing Workers, who had been a longtime member of the Socialist party, boasted about his "intimacy" with the president, claiming that he "was numbered among the dozen or so of Americans who were the President's most trusted political friends."[52] United Mine Workers and CIO president John L. Lewis complained to his

biographer in 1940 that his ability to organize labor opposition was contin-
uously undermined by the president's tactic of co-opting CIO leaders:

> He has been carefully selecting my key lieutenants and appointing them
> to honorary posts in various of his multitudinous, grandiose commissions.
> He has his lackeys fawning upon and wining and dining many of my peo-
> ple. At proper intervals he has unveiled to them the glory of admission to
> the White House and permitted them to bask in his presence. . . .
>
> In a quiet, confidential way he approaches one of my lieutenants, weans
> his loyalty away, overpowers him with the dazzling glory of the White
> House, and appoints him to a federal post under such circumstances that
> his prime loyalty shall be to the President and only a secondary, residual
> one to the working-class movement from which he came. . . .[53]

Notwithstanding Lewis' sometime opposition to FDR, the administration's
economic policies pursued before and during World War II increased employment and thereby union membership.[54] Roosevelt's effort to create the
American Labor party (ALP) in New York State illustrates his conscious concern with winning socialist unionists for his coalition. New York, particularly
New York City, had a long history of electorally strong radical movements:
hundreds of thousands of the state's residents regularly voted for leftist third-
party candidates. The ALP was to nominate Roosevelt and other New Deal
Democrats on its own ballot, thus permitting Socialists and others on the left
to vote for Democratic candidates on a non-Democratic third-party slate.[55]
James Farley and Edward Flynn, Democratic party leaders, initially opposed
this proposal because they believed it might create a rival party. However, at
the urging of Sidney Hillman, Fiorello La Guardia, and Eleanor Roosevelt,
President Roosevelt told Farley to order Democratic party clubs to help gather the petitions necessary to put the new party on the ballot.[56]

Coalition tactics such as these led many union officials to resign from
the Socialist party. Many who left, including Sidney Hillman and David
Dubinsky, worked actively to recruit radicals for Roosevelt. Hillman
described his rationale at a 1936 union meeting:

> We have had a policy, which was not to endorse either of the two politi-
> cal parties, and that if we took a position it should be along Socialist
> lines. The position of our organization is known: that we are for a labor

party. We are today bound . . . to help bring about a labor or farmer-labor party—what is commonly known as independent political action. But [since Roosevelt took office in 1933,] things have happened. . . . We have participated in making the labor policy of this Administration.

We know that the defeat of the Roosevelt Administration means no labor legislation for decades to come. . . . I don't know whether legislation would put all the unemployed back to work, but we do know in our industry that the reduction in hours took in 50,000 . . . and with improvement in business and farm income we would have 175,000 in our industry. A change in the Administration raises a definite question whether the Amalgamated would have to fight completely on its own and not get the support which it enjoyed under the NRA [National Recovery Administration].[57]

As noted earlier, David Dubinsky, head of the International Ladies Garment Workers, resigned from the Socialist party early in 1936 after twenty-five years of membership.[58] He explained this emotionally difficult decision in strong terms:

Franklin Delano Roosevelt is the first truly progressive President we have had in this generation. The NRA . . . has . . . given positive and concrete help to the labor movement. . . . We must bear in mind that all enemies of labor are now combining against the New Deal, against FDR, and that means against labor. . . . An FDR defeat, therefore, must be avoided at all costs.[59]

The political orientation of Socialist union leaders during the 1930s reflected organizational imperatives. The New Deal gave unions the opportunity to grow; Roosevelt was intensely popular among their members. As a result, Socialist union leaders undermined efforts to create a national Farmer-Labor party, even though this was directly contrary to Socialist policy. Thus in 1933, when the Socialist party, backed by the Minnesota Farmer-Labor party, called a Continental Congress of Workers and Farmers to launch a national Farmer-Labor party, the attempt failed because of opposition from three labor leaders who, at that time, were Socialists: Emil Rieve of the Hosiery Workers, David Dubinsky of the International Ladies Garment Workers, and Sidney Hillman of the Amalgamated Clothing Workers.[60]

Writing about the drastic decline in Socialist support in the 1936 elec-

tions, Norman Thomas concluded that "the defection of socialist supporters, interested primarily in unemployment relief and social security, was to
have been expected. The relief might ideally have been more adequate,
and the social security legislation much better even under capitalism, but
there it was, and the masses were resolved not to go back to Hoover!"[61]

As former Marxist Will Herberg noted:

> The New Deal had brought vast ideological confusion in socialist ranks.
> Almost overnight, socialists, who had been proclaiming for years that any
> government under capitalism [must] be a capitalist government funda-
> mentally inimical to the workers and that nothing good could be hoped
> for from the old capitalist parties, became enthusiastic supporters of the
> Roosevelt regime, many—yes, many Militant "socialists"—even accepting
> appointive office under it in some of the New Deal agencies that were
> springing up in Washington. No more shattering blow to socialist
> morale—based as it was on the mystique of intransigent class struggle—
> could be imagined. It left socialist principles in a state of utter chaos.[62]

Between 1936 and 1940 the Socialist party continued to decline.
Though reduced to seven thousand members, the majority of the party
continued at the 1938 convention to insist that it run its own candidates
against any capitalist candidate. Furthermore, the majority, against the
advice of Norman Thomas, also opposed "the outright entry of the Socialist
Party [as an organization] into labor parties, such as the ALP in New York
and the Farmer-Labor Political Federation in Wisconsin."[63]

In Oregon, which had the largest Socialist state membership propor-
tionate to population in the country during the mid-thirties, the formation
of the broader social democratic Oregon Commonwealth Federation
(OCF), stimulated by the successes of the Cooperative Commonwealth
Federation in Canada, also led to a severe loss in leaders and members.
When the OCF decided in 1938 to operate within the Democratic primaries, the *Socialist Call* denounced the OCF for "political opportunism."
But though the Socialist party withdrew its support, the formerly Socialist
state chairman and executive secretary of the OCF, Monroe Sweetland,
and many other members chose to leave the party for the OCF.[64]

In Michigan, the Socialist party insisted on running a candidate for governor against incumbent Democrat Frank Murphy, who had strongly backed

the United Automobile Workers, one of the few unions in which the Socialists still had strength. This caused a serious problem for the activists in the union.[65] The Auto Workers and other Michigan unions endorsed Murphy, who, as governor in 1937, had refused to order the National Guard to force sit-down strikers out of the General Motors plants they were occupying.[66] The Michigan Communist party, then in a battle with Socialists and other radicals for control of the United Automobile Workers, endorsed Murphy and called for the defeat of "Ford, General Motors and their candidate Fitzgerald and to block the road to fascism and war."[67] Murphy, it may be noted, "refused to repudiate the Communist endorsement until he spoke out on the subject during the last week of his campaign."[68]

The Murphy issue, as Daniel Bell notes, "symbolized the full dilemma of the Socialist Party in relation to the unions and the New Deal." George Edwards, then head of the party caucus in the UAW, summed up the problem in a letter to Norman Thomas:

We are now faced with a very difficult situation on the political field. Our party here is growing in the unions in membership and influence. But our progress is jeopardized by the complex situation in the current political campaign. Some of the leading unionists cannot refrain from giving some support to Murphy without sacrificing their own positions. This handicaps the party's campaign and even endangers the party organization at a time when there is a splendid chance to build the party and draw in many new elements from the entire labor movement here.[69]

The Michigan Socialists tried to compromise by not disciplining Walter Reuther and other party members for supporting Murphy. Socialist unionists, however, were put in an impossible position and gradually drifted out of the party. As former Socialist and UAW leader Brendan Sexton put it, they could not "oppose the union's political choices" even though they wanted to stay in the party.[70] Reuther, as Irving Howe and B. J. Widick noted, "felt that those socialists who wished to exert an immediate, substantial influence on American life would have to abandon their party and its doctrines and join the New Deal parade."[71]

In New York, the Socialists were faced with the problem of reacting to the American Labor party, which, though formed to provide a separate ballot line for Roosevelt, ran independent candidates of its own for various local posts, particularly in New York City elections. In 1937, the Socialists decided not to run a candidate for mayor against incumbent ALP member Fiorello La Guardia. This signaled that the Socialists were now prepared to support the ALP, provided it nominated its own candidates.

The Socialist party, however, found it difficult to coexist with the ALP. The latter refused to allow it to affiliate as a unit, a condition that the party had set ever since 1924 for supporting a labor or farmer-labor party. In any case, the then dominant faction of the SP, the Clarity group, opposed any kind of cooperation on the grounds that the Laborites were not a true third party. As a result, the 1937 Socialist convention refused to allow party members to join the ALP as individuals.[72]

The effort to affiliate the Socialists with the ALP broke down in 1938 when the latter nominated the Democratic candidate for governor, Herbert Lehman, a strong New Dealer who was popular among trade unionists. Annoyed because the ALP bargained with the old parties, Norman Thomas ran for governor on the Socialist ticket. The result was another disaster; he received only 24,890 votes and the party lost its place on the ballot. The ALP, however, secured 419,979 votes for Lehman.[73]

Following the 1938 election fiasco, the party finally decided that Socialists could join the ALP as individual members while remaining in the SP, stating, "We consider the American Labor Party as the electoral expression of the working class in New York." Socialist leader Harry Laidler was nominated and elected to the city council on the ALP ticket in 1939. But this cooperative effort with the labor movement was short-lived. In 1940, Thomas ran once more as the Socialist nominee against Roosevelt. The ALP, however, backed the president. Socialists in the ALP and the union movement who were called on by the party to support Thomas found it "very hard . . . to buck union sentiment" for Roosevelt. This development simply accented the drift away from the Socialist party.[74]

In Wisconsin, Socialist efforts to cooperate with other groups in a third party were also harmful to the party. In 1935, the Socialist party helped form the Farmer-Labor-Progressive Federation. The Socialists wanted the Federation to run as the Farmer-Labor party, but by a vote of 129 to 56 its founding conference chose to take part instead in the La Follette–led Progressive party.[75] The Socialists had to be content with the fact that the Federation, led by Thomas Amlie, adopted a "production for use" platform which called for "the social ownership of the means of production and distribution."[76] The

Socialists ran joint tickets with the Federation within the Wisconsin Progressive party, whose nominees, including a number of Socialists, they endorsed.[77] But here too, pro-Roosevelt sentiment created a problem. Philip La Follette, the Progressive candidate for reelection as governor in 1936, supported Roosevelt and refused to join the Federation.[78] The Wisconsin situation illustrated the basic problem facing Socialists when they participated in third parties which sought to establish themselves as independent forces in their states, while supporting Roosevelt nationally. In each of the states where they pursued this strategy—Wisconsin, Minnesota, and New York— Socialists maintained a separate organization for national elections, while individual Socialists were obliged to support nonsocialists in state contests. In Wisconsin, for example, this meant supporting Philip La Follette for governor, even though he was urging Roosevelt's reelection. Thus, outside the Federation, Wisconsin Socialists backed Thomas for president; inside, they indirectly supported Roosevelt. With such divided loyalties, Thomas feared the Wisconsin Socialists were "close to possible suicide."[79]

The Wisconsin Federation came apart in the next two years as a result of internecine conflict among the Socialists and Communists, and farm and labor groups. The defeat of Governor Philip La Follette and most Federation candidates for congressional and legislative office in 1938 not only meant the end of the Federation as an effective force in Wisconsin politics, it also undermined the SP.[80] Socialist mayor Daniel Hoan of Milwaukee was defeated for reelection in 1940 after twenty-four years in office.[81] Hoan himself accepted an appointment from Roosevelt in 1940 to the National Defense Council, and he left the Socialist party in 1941 when the national party withdrew the right of Socialists to belong to the Farmer-Labor Progressive Federation. He later ran as a nominee for various offices on the Democratic ticket, including for governor in 1944.[82] Andrew Biemiller, who had sat as a Socialist member of the Wisconsin legislature during the 1930s and had edited the party's newspaper, also went over to the Democrats and was elected in 1944 to the U.S. House of Representatives. As Frank Warren notes, Socialist participation in the Farmer-Labor Progressive Federation and the Progressive party did not result in progress "toward socialism and leading labor toward independent political action"; rather the Wisconsin Socialists were "swallowed up in the liberal reformist tide."[83] The same conclusion applies to participation in the other state third parties in Minnesota and New York.

The voting record during the 1930s of the strongest Socialist city in the country, Milwaukee, in a state where third-party sentiment was powerful, epitomizes the appeal of Roosevelt to the left. In 1932, Norman Thomas received almost 13 percent of the city's presidential vote, but four years later his support dropped to only 2 percent. Milwaukee gave Roosevelt enormous majorities; it "was the most pro–New Deal large city in the country outside of the [one-party] South; and several large Milwaukee [industrial] suburbs, notably West Allis with 87 percent Democratic, and Cudahy with 90 percent, compared favorably with most southern cities."[84] In discussing Roosevelt's victory in Wisconsin in 1940, Samuel Lubell, who carefully analyzed precinct voting, listed as "the decisive factor" the support which he received from traditionally strong Socialist districts. He quoted a Milwaukee Socialist alderman, Alex Ruffing, as explaining this "shift to Roosevelt . . . with a little shrug of inevitability: 'He enacted all the laws we Socialists had advocated for years.' "[85]

Norman Thomas recognized that the failure of the Socialists to build their party during the Depression, and particularly their inability to sway support away from the New Deal during and after the 1938 recession, challenged their fundamental beliefs about the relationship of capitalist crisis to Socialist support in America. As he noted then: "If we cannot win the workers now, there is no particular reason to think we can do it in some future emergency. Is not the present crisis bad enough to 'start them broad awake?' "[86] Discouraged by the continued decline of the Socialist party, Thomas proposed in 1938 that the party give up electoral activity, announce that it would no longer run presidential candidates, and turn itself into an "educational and leavening force." He argued that "there is no use forever batting one's head against a stone wall." Thomas was now ready to go along with Socialists who contended that "the progressive and labor forces are definitely tied to the Democratic party. We will have to go to them."[87]

Thomas was prevented from pressing this position by the prospect of world war and the impending conflict between Socialists, most of whom remained loyal to their traditional antiwar position, and Roosevelt and most liberals, who favored American intervention against Hitler. In 1940, Thomas once again ran against Roosevelt on a peace platform. This time he received the smallest vote in the party's history, less than 100,000 out of almost 50 million cast.[88] The result of Socialist opposition to the Allied cause, in contradiction to the support for it by most other non-Communist

American leftists, "was a steady and persistent decimation of the party," involving the resignation of most of the remaining prominent members and of the rank and file as well.[89] There is no better example of the party's sectarianism than its persistence in maintaining its historical opposition to capitalist wars in the face of the Nazi juggernaut, a position rejected by every other affiliate of the Socialist International.

An evaluation of the failures of the Socialist party, made after its dissolution in 1963 by its last national leader, Michael Harrington, concluded that in the 1930s, Socialists, by insisting "on the traditional model of the Socialist party as an electoral alternative . . . missed participating in the most important political development in the history of the American working class." Harrington emphasized that had the party ceased running candidates, "it might have been able to maintain some kind of serious base in the unions. But it did not, and Socialists like Walter Reuther, when confronted with the choice between the party's political tactic and that of the labor movement itself, unhesitatingly chose the latter. The tragedy for the party was that the two were counterposed."[90]

The failure of left-third-party efforts apart, the electoral story of the 1930s is the extent to which the electorate divided on class or socioeconomic lines between Roosevelt and Landon in 1936 and Roosevelt and Wilkie in 1940. If, as abundant public opinion data document, American workers became more class conscious, more pro-trade-union, more favorable to an increased role for the state in the economy, and more opposed to corporate capitalism during the 1930s, that consciousness was expressed politically by their enthusiasm for Roosevelt and the Democrats as the representatives of the "common man" and their identification of the Republicans as the party of "business."[91] The Socialist party was essentially irrelevant.

The Communists: Opportunism Pays Off

The history of the Communists during the 1930s reveals how leftist movements in America could gain support by dropping sectarian policies. The party adopted an "opportunistic" reformist strategy in the latter half of the decade and made considerable headway. The Communist party had entered the Depression with an ultraleftist sectarian line dictated to it by Joseph Stalin and the Communist International. Stalin declared in 1929 that capitalism had entered its "third period" of economic collapse that would result in the triumph of the Communist revolution in advanced industrial countries, including the United States. This required that all Communist parties, including the tiny American one, which then had 7,500 members, refrain from cooperating with any other left-wing groups, including all socialist parties, and seek to build revolutionary unions and the Communist party.

In the United States, the Communists mounted a barrage of vituperation against Norman Thomas, Socialists in general, liberals, and AFL unions, describing all of them as "Social Fascists," as objective allies of fascism because they did not follow revolutionary policies.[92] In the first half of the Depression decade, the Communists pursued "policies of organizing unemployment demonstrations, exacerbating strikes, promoting ex-servicemen's leagues, and even creating, in imitation of the German Communists, a military arm, replete with uniforms, called the 'Red Front.' "[93] In opposition to AFL unions, Communists set up a rival federation, the Trade Union Unity League (TUUL), with affiliated organizations in a number of industries. They also created Unemployed Councils to mobilize the jobless for militant protests.[94]

During the early years of the Depression, the Communists were much more hostile to Roosevelt and the New Deal than the Socialists were. They repeatedly denounced the New Deal as a "movement toward fascism." In 1934, they described it as "a government serving the interests of finance capital and moving toward the fascist suppression of the workers' movement." The Wagner Labor Relations Act, which legitimated trade unions, was labeled as an "antistrike" law, while the National Recovery Act (NRA) was seen as a "slave" program.[95]

These policies failed to gain mass support, although the party was able to recruit some members from the unemployed.[96] The party's presidential vote in 1932 was 103,000, up from 48,228 in 1928, while party membership increased by sixteen thousand between 1930 and 1934.[97] In effect, as Irving Howe and Lewis Coser observed, "the party had grown from a tiny sect to a somewhat larger and more influential sect."[98] The Communists had less support than their Socialist rivals.

The Third Period ultraleftist sectarian line was dropped in 1935 by the Communist International in reaction to the threat posed to the Soviet Union by Nazi Germany.[99] Instead of attacking and refusing to cooperate with socialists, liberals, and progressives, the Communists everywhere began to follow a "Popular Front" strategy, ordered by Moscow, which called for united action by all democratic progressive forces and nations against the fascists.[100] In the United States the leader of the Communist party, Earl Browder, could report that this policy resulted in an invitation from Farmer-Labor governor of Minnesota Floyd Olson to attend a conference of "left" leaders designed to endorse Roosevelt, and that it also led to improved relations with the unions. The Communists, though now strongly favoring Roosevelt in their public activities, abstained from officially backing him because, as Browder explains,

> if we really wished to assure Roosevelt's reelection we would not endorse him because that would cause him to be labeled "the Communist candidate." . . . This would lose him many times as many votes from the "Right" as it would bring him from the "Left." . . . On the other hand we could put up our own candidate but conduct such a campaign that would assure Roosevelt all votes under our influence except the diehard opponents of all "capitalist" candidates. . . . Thus I became the logical Communist presidential candidate and made my ambiguous campaign in favor of "my rival," Roosevelt.[101]

Communist ideology changed drastically. Mention of capitalist exploitation of the workers and of the class struggle disappeared. The formal, overt program of the national organization became indistinguishable from a kind of populism. The party now saw socialism as some sort of vague, distant utopia whose values and assumptions had no relevance to the politics of the day. Basically, it sought to portray itself as the more advanced left wing of the Democratic party.

In effect, for the American Communists, in the United States the Popular Front became the Democratic party.[102] Though they took part in conferences to discuss forming a new national farmer-labor or labor party, their role invariably was to oppose or to urge delay in creating a new third party. They favored continued support for the Democratic party and appeared to have lost sight of their separate identity.[103]

The Communist party was particularly successful in operating within various left groups in the Pacific Coast states and in the large-state third parties, as well as in Democratic ranks generally. If Communist leader

Peggy Dennis' testimony in her autobiography is to be accepted (her husband, Eugene, became national secretary of the party after the war), Communists played important roles in "left center" electoral coalitions in thirty-five of the forty-eight states and dominated the Democratic party in four others.[104] They were also powerful in the intellectual and literary worlds, in Hollywood, among student and youth groups, in religious organizations, and even within farm groups.

The Popular Front strategy also paid off in membership recruitment. By early 1939, the CP claimed 100,000 members, although Irving Howe and Louis Coser estimate that the actual figure was between 80,000 and 90,000, while a former party leader, Philip Jaffee, reports that "the total membership never went beyond 70,000 (plus about 30,000 Young Communist League members.)"[105] Since there was rapid turnover in party membership, perhaps reflecting the unwillingness of many recruits to adapt to the high level of politicization and activity demanded by the party, many more passed through its ranks than remained members. A formerly active Communist, Frank Meyer, reports that the "turnover" figure approached "as high as 30 percent in the American party over a five-year period, 1936 to 1941."[106]

Social Basis of Communist Support

Where did increased Communist support come from? The Communist party, as noted earlier, began as an organization primarily composed of foreign-born members. Official party data indicate that in 1933, as much as 70 percent of the membership was still foreign-born.[107] In 1929, the party was rebuked publicly by the Executive Committee of the Communist International for being "an organization of foreign workers not much connected with the political life of the country."[108] During the latter half of the thirties, however, the opportunistic strategy enabled it to recruit more heavily among the younger native-born.[109]

The party's original ideology dictated recruitment of manual workers, particularly in basic industries. But from 1936 on, the party became especially concerned to secure a base among "urban middle-class elements," that is, in the words of a party directive, "among the middle class generally, among intellectuals and professional people."[110] In tandem with the shift in the party line from left to right, from sectarianism to opportunism, the class composition of Communist party membership changed dramatically, with disproportionate growth among white-collar workers and professionals. This category accounted for at least 44 percent of the party in 1941.[111] A study of the party's membership makes clear that "the proportion of party members who have been to college is very high. Even more striking is the great number of graduate degrees among them. . . . In fact, the Communist Party in America seems to be such a highly educated, non-manual laboring [sic] group that at times there would be more rejoicing in its headquarters over the recruiting of one common laborer than over ten Ph.D.s."[112] The party's greatest success in terms of support, though probably not in membership, was among intellectuals. During the Popular Front period, the party was especially strong among writers, academics, and the Hollywood elite.[113]

The contrast in the results achieved by Communists and Socialists in the late 1930s and early 1940s seemingly confirms the hypothesis that sectarianism was a source of political failure. Earl Browder, the head of the Communist party during the 1930s and early 1940s, argued this when he compared the strategy of his party with that of the Socialists, and his judgment was shared by Socialist leader Michael Harrington, writing in the early 1970s.[114] According to Browder:

> The Communist party . . . rapidly moved out of its extreme leftist sectarianism of 1930. . . . It relegated its revolutionary socialist goals to the ritual of chapel and Sundays on the pattern long followed by the Christian Church. On weekdays it became the most single-minded practical reformist party that America ever produced. Thus the Socialist party, despite its initial advantages over the Communists, lost ground steadily to them.
> . . . [The Socialists] learned nothing . . . from the spectacular capture of the Democratic party primary in California by Upton Sinclair's EPIC movement. . . .They repeated all their failures but none of their success. It was left to the Communists to learn from their successes, e.g., they copied Sinclair's EPIC movement and largely absorbed its remains. . . .[115]

Unlike their rivals on the left, the Communists offered an image of radicalism without requiring that supporters oppose liberal trends within unions and in the larger society generally. Communists were the most activist part of the Roosevelt coalition. They were able to voice their rejection of a system that produced mass distress without being forced to isolate themselves from the mainstream of politics. But, additionally, they possessed what has been described as an "organizational weapon." In contrast to the frequently divided sectarian Socialists, Communists operated during the Popular Front decade (1936–45) as a coherent force in struggles for power within the Democratic party, trade unions, and the intellectual community. Former party leader Joseph Starobin described the success of the Popular Front approach:

> The Communists . . . discovered that they could exert political power through local Democratic (and sometimes Republican) parties better than they could in their own name. The American political system's amorphous character, its direct primaries, and the absence of a really cohesive national party made this possible. Well known left-wingers [covert Communists] were soon being elected as congressmen. . . . It was not unusual for Communist Party legislative directors or state secretaries to be given cordial attention in the offices of senators, congressmen, mayors, governors, and intermediaries of the White House.[116]

Communists attempted to undermine all left-third-party efforts, not just the Socialist party. The Popular Front strategy dictated opposition to all independent third parties, i.e., opponents of Roosevelt and the Democrats. Following the Soviet lead, they enthusiastically supported Roosevelt's "quarantine the aggressor" foreign policy, which was opposed by most Republicans, Socialists, and Wisconsin Progressives.[117] After the 1936 election in which the Communists had vigorously campaigned for Roosevelt, the national committee of the party opposed proposals to channel the various left-of-center "coalitions" into a farmer-labor party. It declared emphatically that "the Party will resist any attempt" to form a farmer-labor party.[118]

The Communist "experiment" was temporarily halted by the Stalin-Hitler pact in 1939. It was no longer possible for the Communist party to seek to expand its influence by coalition tactics. The party was obliged by its ties to Moscow to turn isolationist, antiwar, and anti-Roosevelt, and to run an independent presidential campaign in 1940.[119] It received a pathetically small vote. Party membership declined for the next two years.[120]

The Popular Front tactic was revived after the Soviet Union was brought into the war by the German invasion of June 1941. The CP renewed its support of Roosevelt and the Democrats and became ardently interventionist and prowar. To facilitate this policy, it even formally dissolved as a party in 1944 to become the Communist Political Association, describing itself as "a nonparty association of Americans" which "adheres to the principles of scientific socialism."[121] The revived Popular Front strategy seemingly brought it renewed strength in the unions, among intellectuals, and in popular appeal. In 1943, two candidates, running openly as Communists, were elected to the New York city council. The party also won control of the American Labor party, which elected two other pro-Communists to the city council. Party membership more than doubled between 1941 and 1944.[122]

This phase of American Communism was again ended by political change in the Soviet Union. At the end of World War II, under orders from abroad, the Communists expelled their leader, Earl Browder, for excessive opportunism and reestablished the movement as a political party. The outbreak of the Cold War between the West and the Soviet Union, Soviet expansionism, the Berlin Blockade, and the Czech coup in 1948 led American Communists to reassert their opposition to the Democratic party. They played a major role in establishing an antiwar Progressive party, which nominated former vice-president Henry Wallace in 1948. This third-party strategy marginalized the Communists, much as the Socialists had been isolated when they opposed Roosevelt in the 1930s. Many Communist union officials and others quit the party, while non-Communists in the labor and political worlds campaigned actively to remove Communists from leadership positions. Thus, the "left turn" of the Communists led to a considerable decline in strength and influence.[123] Whatever support remained was largely eliminated by the repressive anticommunism which emerged during the Cold War with the Soviet Union and the hot war in Korea.

Does the success of the Communists within the New Deal Democratic coalition demonstrate that the most effective strategy for American radicals is to operate within—rather than against—the Democratic party? It is difficult to come to such conclusion, because the Communists never campaigned publicly as a faction along the lines of the Nonpartisan League or the EPIC movement, nor did they openly advocate even mild socialist policies. Rather, the Communists' public face was that of welfare state, New Deal, pro-union reformers. As Earl Browder acknowledged, their "activities were essentially *reformist*. As a *revolutionary* party it had not advanced an inch."[124] Radical historian Eric Foner noted that "the Communist Party was the most successful [during this period] precisely when it was most American."[125] Its policies, in fact, were much more moderate than those advanced by EPIC, the Commonwealth Federations, the Nonpartisan League, the Wisconsin Progressives, or the Minnesota Farmer-Laborites.

Sociologist Barrington Moore noted that the party was "perfectly willing to support reactionaries under certain conditions, as was the case in its endorsement of [anti-trade-union] Mayor Hague of Jersey City. This endorsement was given [in 1943] on the ground that the Hague machine supported Roosevelt, and also in order to head off a labor revolt that was threatening to develop into a third party movement and split Roosevelt's support in the state."[126]

While Communist influence during the Popular Front periods probably reached greater heights than the influence of any other American radical party, the achievement was covert. Communists usually concealed their political affiliation. John Gates, who served as a leader of the Young Communist League in the 1930s, described how Communists who had a majority of the delegates to the 1939 American Youth Congress voted for a resolution opposing all forms of totalitarianism, Nazism, fascism, and communism.[127] Joseph Starobin, party editor, revealed that "thousands of leaders of public, civil, political, and trade union organizations who privately adhered to Communism [did not] . . . make this adherence publicly known. . . . To avow their private faith openly would jeopardize their leadership in exactly those organizations and areas of public life on which the Communist Party had concentrated for a decade. . . . In the Party's own argot they were known as 'submarines.' "[128] The tactic was particularly effective within the trade union movement, which had grown greatly during the thirties.

The Communists controlled over a dozen CIO national unions and won posts in some AFL unions as well.[129] William Z. Foster, the national chairman of the party, described the role of Communists within the labor movement at the close of the thirties in exuberant terms: "We were no longer an opposition force . . . [but] now hold many official posts in both the AFL and CIO and we now share the official responsibility of carrying on the movement."[130] Another party leader, George Charney, writing of this period when "the 'left-wing' bloc sat high in the councils of the CIO," noted that the Communists "believed it would only be a matter of time before the CIO would resemble the [Communist-controlled] CGT of France, with the left as the dominant intellectual force in American labor."[131] Earl Browder stated years later: "By the end of the decade the Communists and their closest allies had predominant influence in unions representing approximately one-third of the membership [of the CIO] and various degrees of minority influence in another third. Added to this was their understanding with the centrist [official union] leadership to complete the isolation of the open anti-Communists."[132]

How were Communists able to gain such extensive influence in the labor movement in a relatively short time despite their electoral weakness? The answer is simple. The Socialist and Communist parties and the Communist and Socialist Youth Leagues, together with organizations of unemployed and youth groups largely controlled by Communists, constituted the major reservoir of dedicated organizers. These were the individuals who were willing to work for low pay and take physical risks in organizing unions. As Daniel Bell notes: "The CIO needed experienced organizers by the hundreds, and the communist and socialist movements were the most likely sources. In addition, the communists and socialists assigned men by the score to go into factories, establish a political base, and organize caucuses within the growing unions in order to gain control."[133] Given the surge in the number of leadership positions, radicals did not have to replace existing leaders to rise in the labor movement. In many CIO national unions, and in a large number of locals in both the CIO and AFL, they were the first leaders of new unions or took office in rapidly growing ones.[134]

John L. Lewis and other CIO leaders consciously tried to use the Communists and other radicals.[135] In steel, the most important industry organized by the CIO, Communist party leader William Z. Foster reported that sixty of two hundred full-time organizers in the CIO's Steelworkers Organizing Committee were Communists, as were many other Steelworkers officials at the state and local levels.[136] Harvey Klehr, historian of American communism, writes that by 1938 no fewer than forty CIO unions were dominated or significantly influenced by Communists. With the exception of the United Electrical, Radio and Machine Workers Union, which had a membership of 137,000 in 1937, these were mostly the smaller unions. Communist influence was limited in the leadership of the United Mine Workers, the Clothing Workers, the Textile Workers, and the Steelworkers. In

1937, the party claimed to dominate unions encompassing 650,000 members and to have influence among unions with an additional 600,000 members out of a total CIO membership of 3.25 million.[137] Although Lewis and other CIO leaders, such as Philip Murray in steel and James Carey in the electrical industry, primarily relied on Communist organizers, they were not pro-Communist. They were willing to make use of their radical rivals in the Socialist party as well, although fewer were available.[138]

When the Soviet Union signed a non-aggression pact with Nazi Germany in September 1939, American Communists came under sharp attack from their erstwhile union allies. To protect their position, the Communists went so far as to support anti-Communist resolutions at the 1940 CIO convention. A member of the national staff of the CIO, Leo Pressman, whose "Communist affiliation was an open secret," moved a resolution which declared:

> We neither accept nor desire and we firmly reject consideration of any policies emanating from totalitarianism, dictatorships and foreign ideologies such as Nazism, communism and fascism. They have no place in this great labor movement. The Congress of Industrial Organizations condemns the dictatorships and totalitarianism of Nazism, communism and fascism as inimical to the welfare of labor, and destructive of our form of government.[139]

By introducing this resolution, as Leon DeCaux, pro-Communist editor in the national CIO office, later explained, Pressman was following party policy, the same policy which had been pursued earlier in the American Youth Congress and other front groups. Communists and their close allies voted for the statement, as a " 'smart' move to save the necks of the left."[140] Six years later in 1946, with the Communist position within the unions again under strain, and with the Cold War under way, the CIO convention was to "unanimously" adopt a resolution saying: "We resent and reject efforts of the Communist party or other political parties and their adherents to interfere in the affairs of the CIO."[141] To gain influence, as Joseph Starobin notes, "the Communists had taken the line of least resistance"— they had encouraged members who were in a position to become union leaders to blur their party affiliation and "not participate in the Party's structure except on a semi-clandestine level." During the late thirties, the party dissolved its "fractions" or caucuses in the union movement, thus relieving Communist union leaders from "the obligation to 'build the Party' within these organizations."[142] Their separation from any public commitment to or involvement in radical political activity, as well as their attainment of privileged and powerful positions with labor and the general society, undoubtedly weakened their ties to the party. Thus, many Communist labor leaders were to leave the party when shifts in policy after 1948, determined largely by the international position of the Soviet Union, led it into opposition with the union leadership.[143]

Conclusions

The Great Depression politicized American labor. From the mid-thirties, the days of official neutrality and self-reliance on union power were over. All CIO leaders and the majority in the AFL saw political activity as a major tool for achieving labor goals. Business unionism, which had predominated among closed, craft unions, had to make room for the realization that market activity and political activity were intimately connected. Socialists and, particularly, Communists made significant headway within the labor movement in the 1930s. They had always been disproportionately strong among industrial unions in the AFL, but now such unions, organized in their own federation, had grown in membership and stature. Socialists and Communists welcomed the reorganization and renewed militancy of the labor movement in the thirties, but they were not the parties which gained the most. The most important development in unionism in the thirties was not the growth of leftist influence, but the depth and durability of union links to the Democratic party. George Meany, John L. Lewis, George Berry, and Sidney Hillman were among the key figures in the Democratic campaign in 1936. In that year, labor became the chief source of finance, not only for the Democratic party but for other liberal-left organizations directly involved in the campaign.[144] In 1940, when Roosevelt lost his majority among nonlabor voters, the critical factor in his reelection, as Arthur Schlesinger, Jr., emphasized, was the fact that he captured the labor vote: "Without it he could not have won."[145]

Union political involvement and support for statist reforms constituted a turning point in the history of American labor and of American political life more generally. As Michael Harrington stressed, during the thirties for the first time, "labor had entered into politics with a distinctive program and had organized on a class basis."[146] The two-party system continued, and trade unions had now become a constituent part of one of the major parties. From that point on, the Democratic party was concerned with retaining union support. Unions had decisively rejected Gompers' demand for political independence to "reward our friends, and punish our enemies," but by this time the creation of an independent third labor party was out of the question. By the 1930s the radical wing of the labor movement was far too weak and divided to serve as a core for a labor party, and neither Socialists nor Communists could counter the appeal of the Democratic party as the electoral avenue for union demands.

Economic conditions of the 1930s precipitated a second wave of working-class radicalism in America. Leftist influence during the thirties rivaled that of the first two decades of the century. However, the later period did not see the emergence of a national party with electoral appeal. By the end of the decade, the Socialist and Communist parties received far fewer votes than in 1932, despite the growth in Communist party membership. Even at its height in 1939 and 1944–45, the Communist party had fewer members than the Socialists had had in 1912 or 1918, although the population of the country was much greater. Still, it is worth noting that in terms of the proportion of the population expressing left-wing views in opinion polls and the number of leadership positions held by radicals in trade unions and other mass organizations, the 1930s were the period in which the American left reached its zenith.[147] In this period, the mainstream of the labor movement supported social democratic policies for the first time.

The Communist Popular Front experience seemingly demonstrates that leftists can gain strength in America if they do not take positions that separate them from the majority of reformists or trade union members. Yet it may also be argued that during the late 1930s the Communists helped to keep the potentially alienated within the mainstream of American politics. The party, following the international line of the Comintern, supported Franklin Roosevelt, the New Deal, the Democratic party, and nonradical leaders of the CIO. The reformist maneuvers of the "far left" actually discouraged radical political innovation and undermined the Socialist party and other third-party endeavors. Communists blocked movements that rejected the premises of American society at a time when the economy was at its nadir. Operating in mass electoral movements such as the Washington Commonwealth Federation and the Minnesota Farmer-Labor Party, Communists successfully opposed proposals for "production for use" or nationalization of various industries in favor of New Deal policies. As Communists gained power within left-progressive groups, they effectively moved them ideologically to the right. Similarly, as Richard Pells notes, "the insistence on cooperation among all good antifascists resulted in the decline of the intellectual as a critic of American culture and society. . . . In the process, the social and cultural ferment of the decade's early years was dissipated. . . ."[148] Ironically, Communists deflated the pressure among intellectuals for the renunciation of American culture and polity.

The record of Communist successes and failures from 1935 clearly does not provide evidence that American radicals can build a large movement by "opportunistic" tactics within established parties and reform groups, because, as we have seen, the CP concealed its objectives and operated by subterfuge. As Earl Browder himself commented, the Communist party "postponed revolutionary prospects indefinitely."[149] And when the party line shifted to reflect the new Soviet foreign policy line, the party was suddenly isolated. As former party leader George Charney noted: "It was the acid test of 'proletarian internationalism' to give instant and unquestioned support to all the policies enunciated by the Soviet Union, down to every *Pravda* editorial or casual utterance by Stalin, though it would be blasphemy to treat any utterance by Stalin as casual. . . . We slavishly adhered to this pernicious doctrine, as though every policy by some dialectical magic could serve the interests of all nations as well as the national interest of the Soviet Union. To question was itself an act of betrayal."[150]

The Socialist party, as Daniel Bell, Earl Browder, Michael Harrington, and Bernard Johnpoll have argued, failed to take advantage of opportunities for growth and influence during the Depression decade because it opted for sectarian policies that isolated it from mainstream liberal, radical, and working-class constituencies linked with the Roosevelt New Deal coalition. Those radicals who chose to work with the New Deal gained considerable influence in American institutions and politics. They helped to give the Democratic party and the labor movement "a social democratic tinge," to quote Richard Hofstadter.[151] Yet they failed to build a durable socialist movement. Socialist and socialist-leaning groups, such as EPIC, the Commonwealth Federations, and third parties at the state level, that backed Roosevelt did not outlive his presidency. The many Socialist union leaders who resigned from the party to back FDR were able to do little, if anything, to foster socialist objectives, other than to press the labor movement to support welfare reforms. As Frank Warren has emphasized, "The more reformist the section of the Socialist Party in the American Labor Party became, or the more reformist the Communist Party became, the more they served not their purposes, but the purposes of the New Deal— the more, in short, radicalism became indistinguishable from liberalism."[152]

Underlying these events is the Bolshevik Revolution, which in the United States, as in Germany, France, Italy, and Spain, split the labor movement into mutually hostile Socialist and Communist wings. In this respect, the United States followed the continental European pattern rather than that of other English-speaking and Scandinavian democracies where Communist parties remained weak in comparison to established labor parties. In the English-speaking and Northern European democracies, strong, unitary union movements provided the glue that kept contending political factions within a single party. The Communist/socialist division in Southern and Central Europe set back the labor movement by a generation or more and contributed in no small way to the victories of fascism and Nazism. In the United States, the division devastated a political movement that was already foundering during and after World War I.

Daniel Bell has argued that the dilemma of American radicals during the 1930s as in other periods has been to choose between isolation and absorption. Since participation in a small radical party is often based on a chiliastic belief that drastic changes are necessary to create a better world, it is doubtful that a consciously opportunistic movement can win and hold a following. What made the Communist success possible was the link to the Soviet Union, to the belief that socialism, the good society, was being built there, and that anything which helped the Soviet Union contributed to the ultimate triumph of socialism. For the core members of the party, covert tactics and concealment of Communist objectives were legitimated by the expectation of persecution should they operate openly. But additionally, as Philip Selznick notes, their revolutionary objectives dictated a "continuous and systematic search for 'pieces of power,' regardless of whether this search ultimately leads to the overthrow of a government. . . . Such a pattern of power-seeking leads to the use of conspiratorial methods in attempting to seize control of target groups. . . ."[153]

The Communist party could appear to be radical while following opportunistic policies because it was the party of the Russian Revolution. As Frank Meyer emphasized: "The whole of Communist training . . . drives towards the acceptance of the revolution as the end to which all things and all persons must be strictly subordinated as means."[154] Those American Socialists who believed in democratic methods that required winning majority support and who, like David Dubinsky, Sydney Hillman, and the "right-wingers" in the Social Democratic Federation, tried to work within the New Deal coalition turned away from radicalism. But as we have seen, those who rejected the New Deal chose isolation. For the Communists, the ends, the defense of the Soviet Union and the advancement of the revolution, justified opportunistic means. For democratic radicals who left the Socialist party, these means became their ends.

If the Socialist party had moved to the right, had worked within the Democratic party as the Communists did, is it possible that the Democratic party might have been changed into a social democratic labor party? The evidence is strongly against it. Like those who tried to build radical factions within a major party—EPIC, the Commonwealth movements, and the Nonpartisan League—socialists probably could have helped to elect left-oriented candidates. But, as in the statewide movements, such officeholders almost invariably moved to the center to enlarge their support and their organizations eventually dissolved into the broader coalition.

The statewide third parties—the Progressive party in Wisconsin, the Farmer-Labor party in Minnesota, the American Labor party in New York—also backed Roosevelt and Democrats in the national elections. And they eventually merged with the Democrats as economic conditions improved. They, and the left-organized factions in the western states, vanished almost without a trace. Trade union leaders who belonged to or supported the Socialists and Communists became liberal Democrats and gave up the effort to build a radical movement. As noted, the record indicates that the "entry" or alliance strategy failed to create a labor or social democratic faction or party. The sectarian alternative pursued by those who remained with the Socialist party also failed. It undermined the party's base of support in the unions and the electorate as a whole. Had the Socialist party taken Earl Browder's contemporary and Michael Harrington's retrospective advice to endorse Roosevelt and the New Deal, it would probably have retained many leaders and increased its membership. But it, like the Social Democratic Federation, formed by right-wing Socialists in 1936, would have disappeared.

While the 1930s appeared to offer leftists chances for gaining a foothold in American politics, by this time the basic institutional features of the labor movement had been set against socialism. Socialist parties in other English-speaking societies had developed from labor parties as unions came to advocate state welfare, planning, and ownership of the means of production. Broad-based support for socialism came about only after unions and working-class parties were connected in a single overarching movement. Unions in Britain, Australia, Canada, and New Zealand did not link with working-class parties to achieve socialism, but did so for more prosaic reasons mostly having to do with improving the legal standing of unions and using legislation to improve working conditions. But once unified labor movements were established, socialists and unionists operated together.

The Great Depression created economic circumstances that were propitious for radical movements. In the United States there was a tide of support for various forms of state intervention, but by the thirties the labor movement was hopelessly divided. The political wing of the labor movement was split between Socialists of diverse stripes and Communists. From 1935, industrial unions broke away from the closed craft unions that dominated the American Federation of Labor, and thus began a self-defeating and sometimes bloody conflict within the ranks of labor unions.

The immediate consequence was the failure of the left to mount a challenge to Roosevelt's New Deal. Labor leaders were particularly vulnerable to the lure of the Democratic party given the faint hopes of political success of a leftist alternative. The New Deal was effectively the only game in town, and most unionists realized that whatever their socialist sympathies, they were better off defending it than campaigning for a third-party alternative. The only third-party efforts that had some success were those that allowed or encouraged supporters to vote for Roosevelt in presidential elections.

Viewed from a longer time perspective, the disunity in the ranks of labor disabled the working class culturally as well as politically. In other English-speaking democracies and on the continent of Europe, working-class consciousness was built gradually over decades as labor-based parties mobilized their memberships and fought election after election on class issues. Class consciousness, which was initially weaker in the United States than in other western democracies, was further weakened by the failure to create a unified labor movement. American workers were not able to shape American culture as a class. They were not able to build class consciousness into American culture as a counterweight to individualism and antistatism.

Whatever form the socialist movement took, it could not escape the general political and cultural factors discussed here. It would still have operated in a society which was individualistic and antistatist, orientations which were strengthened again once the Depression and the war ended. Perhaps the best evidence of the enduring influence of libertarian values is what happened to organized labor and the Democratic party. The Depression, the great impact of class in politics, and the New Deal's "social democratic tinge" had helped produce a steady expansion in union membership, to 35 percent of the employed labor force by 1955. But union density then began to decline steadily in tandem with economic prosperity and the revival of the country's individualistic and meritocratic values. By 2000, union membership had fallen to 13.9 percent of the total employed labor force and 10 percent of those working in private employment. The latter level was last seen in 1929. A myriad of public opinion data revealed a steady erosion of support for statist welfare planning and regulatory policies. And in that context, the Republican party has become more antistatist on economic issues, while the Democratic party has reduced or rejected its New Deal and Great Society orientation. And what remains of the socialists are minuscule sects.

Chapter 7

POLITICAL

REPRESSION AND

SOCIALISM

T o what extent are the distinctive features of the American political system, American culture, and American society responsible for the failure of the Socialists to create a durable political party? Some radicals have challenged systemic explanations for the failure of socialism on the grounds that they ignore political repression, particularly during and following World War I and during the Korean War. In the words of James Green, war provided an opportunity for "opponents of socialism to use patriotism as a pretext for destroying a domestic enemy with tactics that would . . . [be] difficult to employ in peacetime."[1] Along these lines, political historian Gabriel Kolko notes that immediately after World War I, "at the very moment American socialism appeared on the verge of significant organizational and political success, it was attacked by the combined resources of the Federal and various state governments."[2] Socialists were denied positions to which they were elected, foreign-born leaders were deported, others were jailed, and party newspapers were suppressed. And during the Korean War, McCarthyite repression attempted to eliminate Communist influence in American labor unions and political life.

. . . .

Repression and Radical Movements

There can be little doubt that the police and judicial powers of the American state have been used at various times in this century to intimidate, harass, and jail members and leaders of left-wing movements in America. Anarchists, the IWW, the Socialist party, the Communist party, the Socialist Workers Party (Trotskyists), the Black Panthers, and some New Left groups have each suffered at the hands of political authorities.[3] Perhaps more important than overt repression has been what Tocqueville labeled "tyranny of the majority." Individuals who have identified with radical political groups have frequently been subjected to social and economic sanctions.[4] Socialist radicalism has never been a popular cause in America. Labeled as extremist, undemocratic, and un-American, many adherents have suffered for their views. Their punishment has included ridicule and ostracism, loss of or failure to attain employment, physical abuse by vigilante groups and enraged mobs, and indictment and conviction on an assortment of criminal charges. Experience or awareness of such harassment must have discouraged some members and supporters, or perhaps more important, potential supporters, from acting on their beliefs.

Repression has been most intense in time of war. During both world wars, radicals were subjected to numerous indictments and widespread economic discrimination. Communists who opposed American entry into World War II, prior to the Nazi attack on the Soviet Union in June 1941, were harassed by state and federal authorities, as were various profascist groups. Repression was also directed at the Trotskyists, who remained steadfastly opposed to the war even after the entrance of the Soviet Union and the Japanese attack on Pearl Harbor. With the intensification of the Cold War from 1948 onward, and particularly during the Korean War, anti-Communist attacks reached new heights. These were the years in which Senator Joseph McCarthy dominated the headlines. Public agencies would again take the offensive against radical and antiwar groups during the Vietnam War, though to a considerably lesser degree.

The conjunction of government repression with war and postwar periods does not mean that radical groups have escaped persecution in times of peace. The Industrial Workers of the World (IWW) faced indictments and mob hysteria before 1917.[5] Communists were subject to congressional and state legislative investigations and other forms of government persecution in the 1930s. Harassment of radicals was relatively mild during the pre–World War I peak of Socialist party popularity, in the latter half of the 1920s, during most of the 1930s, in the decade prior to American military involvement in Vietnam, and in the years following the end of that war.

At various times radicals have willingly subjected themselves to repression, sometimes to provoke authorities and thus galvanize broader support from all those wishing to defend civil rights and free speech. The tactic was first developed by followers of the French revolutionist August Blanqui in the nineteenth century.[6] In pre–World War I America, the Wobblies would bring hundreds of supporters to openly resist authority in communities which denied their right to organize. The idea would be to wear down the willingness of towns to enforce anti-IWW ordinances by congregating in such numbers that it would be too costly to arrest them, feed them while in prison, and then try them in court.[7]

Roger Baldwin, a lifelong defender of free speech and head of the American Civil Liberties Union, concluded that although these fights were won in principle, they hurt the IWW, for "the net effect on the public mind was that the violence was chiefly on the part of the IWW or directly incited by them."[8] William Preston, a historian of antiradical repression, comments that through these fights, "the IWW inoculated otherwise peaceful communities with the virus of repression."[9]

Although the movement rarely engaged in violence, the Wobblies' aggressive rhetoric implied support for revolutionary violence.[10] IWW leader William Haywood wrote in the *International Socialist Review* in February 1912 that *"no Socialist can be a law-abiding citizen. . . . I again want to justify direct action and sabotage. . . ."*[11] Such statements frightened the established classes and authorities.[12] The widespread belief that the IWW was a revolutionary organization disposed to violence played into the hands of those who wished to crush the movement during and after World War I.[13] Some Wobblies, arrested during the war and accused of criminal conspiracy, were given twenty-year sentences. In comparison, British socialist leaders, such as Arthur Cook, received very short periods of incarceration for their antiwar stands.[14] British courts were generally less punitive of antipatriotic political activism, but the difference in treatment also reflects that, unlike their American counterparts, British antiwar leaders eschewed revolutionary language.

While repression as a whole undoubtedly hurt the American Socialist party, there were times when some Socialist party leaders actively sought to be arrested to bring attention to their cause. The most famous instance was that of Eugene Debs' opposition to American intervention in World War I. In his biography of Debs, Ray Ginger described Debs' motivation and tactics: "He deliberately framed his indictment of the war in extreme terms; such an approach jibed with both of his objectives. He wanted to arouse resentment and opposition to the war; he also wanted to taunt the Federal authorities into placing him on trial."[15] Debs finally induced the government to respond to his militant antiwar stand in a speech at Canton, Ohio, on June 16, 1918.[16] He was arrested and indicted for sedition, an action that he welcomed. He had told friends that he had "a hunch that speech was likely to settle the matter."[17] Debs used his trial as a platform to eloquently set out his views of capitalism, the Russian Revolution, and the war. His subsequent imprisonment became a *cause célèbre*, one that many nonradicals rallied around as a civil liberties issue. Running for president from his prison cell in 1920, Debs secured close to a million votes.

Martin Luther King, Jr., also was effective in using the willingness of authorities to violently attack civil rights demonstrators to bring attention to the justice of their cause.[18] King was well aware that the police in Birmingham and Selma might react violently to civil rights demonstrations, but he reasoned that, if so, "a confrontation with injustice would take place, in full view of the millions looking on throughout this nation." He outlined the tactics as follows: "1) Nonviolent demonstrators go into the streets to exercise their constitutional rights. 2) Racists resist by unleashing violence against them. 3) Americans of conscience in the name of decency demand federal intervention and legislation. 4) The Administration, under mass pressure, initiates measures of immediate intervention and remedial legislation."[19] Various New Left student leaders, such as Stokely Carmichael, Carl Oglesby, and Steve Weisman, also openly discussed their strategy of provoking authority to be repressive. As Oglesby, once president of Students for a Democratic Society, emphasized: "Once your enemy hits back then your revolution starts. If your enemy does not hit back then you do not have a revolution."[20]

These cases suggest that repression is double-edged. On the one hand, repression may impose prohibitively high costs on activists and potential movement participants. It may stifle a radical movement by harming or threatening to harm its supporters. By denying freedom of expression or freedom of association, repression may choke off sources of new adherents for a movement. But the examples above reveal that repression may be ineffective or even self-defeating. It may heighten a sense of injustice within a group that was previously quiescent. It is almost certain to reinforce solidarity within a movement that is targeted. And repression may bring home to the society at large the merits of a particular cause or, at least, the demerits of coercion as a response to it.

Effects of Repression in Other Countries

To assess the effects of repression in the United States, it is useful to gain some comparative perspective by examining the effects of repression in other countries. The evidence reveals very clearly that repression does not necessarily weaken radical movements and may even strengthen them, as Blanqui and King believed. As noted earlier, Lenin, among others, believed that the relative prevalence of democratic rights in America inhibited the formation of a revolutionary party. This claim is supported by the fact that the lack of political rights for workers in most European countries in the half century before World War I helped to solidify the working class and provide Marxists with a means to elicit support from those not otherwise committed to socialism.

The attempt of the German government to eliminate socialism by outlawing Social Democratic organizations from 1878 to 1890 failed miserably. Despite a concerted policy of suppression directed against the major union movement (the Free Trade Unions) as well as the Social Democrats, involving bans on socialist newpapers and the imprisonment and deportation of socialist agitators, the Social Democratic party (SPD) increased its share of the vote in Reichstag elections from 7.6 percent in 1878 to 19.7 percent in 1890.[21]

Initially these Anti-Socialist laws appeared to work, as socialist organizations were disrupted or eliminated. In the Reichstag elections of 1881, the Social Democratic vote decreased to 6.1 percent—a drop of one-fifth from the previous election in 1878. The decline was particularly steep in the larger cities, where the authorities enforced a "state of emergency" involving draconian measures of arrest, deportation, and house searches. In Berlin, where police repression was especially intense, the Social Democratic vote fell by half. But from then on, until the laws were repealed in 1890, the SPD had repeated success. The 1880s witnessed the sharpest increase in the Social Democratic vote—in both proportional and absolute terms—of any decade before World War I. In Berlin, support grew more than sixfold in this period.

The Anti-Socialist laws strengthened the roots of the party by fostering a network of informal ties and an alternative culture. As Wilhelm Hasenclever, a Social Democratic deputy in the Reichstag, pointed out to the Reich's minister of the interior, "The organization has been thoroughly destroyed . . . but this destruction has not done any real damage. Your Anti-Socialist law has created another bond for us. . . . [Y]ou have made us into a real party."[22] In another speech to the Reichstag, the Social Democratic leader August Bebel claimed that the Anti-Socialist laws made "more propaganda for us than anything that has taken place previously, despite your intent."[23] These judgments of the ineffectiveness of state repression in Germany are confirmed in Vernon Lidtke's observation that the "external wall of oppression, emanating from the various levels of government, did as much as any other element to hold together the cultural milieu of the labor movement. . . .[T]he constant threat of persecution or minor harassment intensified the sense of solidarity, of the need to moderate internal conflicts in order to confront the common enemy with the greatest possible strength."[24] In retrospect, socialists described the period 1878 to 1890 as the "heroic years." In contrast to the ensuing period in which Marxian socialists had to come to terms with growing revisionism and a large and increasingly cautious union wing, repression enforced unity and an overriding sense of injustice within the movement.

Czarist repression in Russia, which was even more severe than repression in Germany, did not prevent the growth of powerful radical parties. In the wake of the Revolution of 1905, the army brutally crushed strongholds of insurgency, killing hundreds and wounding several thousand persons.[25] Thereafter, the czarist police force continued to infiltrate and disrupt opposition movements. As in Germany, the socialists initially withered under the attack, only to reemerge more strongly than ever. At its Fifth Congress in 1907, the Bolshevik and Menshevik wings of the Social Democratic party claimed a combined membership of 148,000. Their formal membership then declined to around 10,000 in 1910.[26] But from 1912 on, both parties revived strongly despite continued persecution, and by 1915 they were in position to mobilize the massive discontent generated by Russian casualties in World War I. As in Germany, czarist repression was effective only in the short term.

The socialist experience in Russia illustrates that repression may lead one to underestimate the strength of opposition forces because potential sympathizers initially stand on the sidelines. But repression can immensely deepen the reservoir of oppositional support. As Lenin claimed soon after the 1905 defeat: "There are ever increasing numbers of people to whom all plans and even revolutionary ideas of any sort are quite alien, but who nevertheless *see* and *feel* the necessity for an armed struggle when they witness the atrocities perpetrated by the police, the Cossacks, and the Black Hundreds against unarmed citizens."[27]

In Argentina, socialist movements faced much more overt repression in the first decade of the twentieth century than did their ideological counterparts in the United States. Between 1902 and 1910, authoritarian governments imposed a state of siege no less than five times for a total of eighteen months. Public demonstrations were prohibited, socialists imprisoned, party headquarters closed down, and newspapers banned.[28] Strikes were frequently broken by police violence in which workers were killed or wounded. The Anarchists and Socialists responded with mass demonstrations and occasional general strikes. This period has been described as one of "repression and growth."[29] The Socialist party grew in the face of what has been described as a state of siege. The party's percentage of the vote in the country's major urban and industrial center, Buenos Aires, rose from 1 percent in 1902, to 6 percent in 1904, to 25 percent in 1910.

State repression is not always self-defeating. A government willing to pay the costs of total repression can wipe out opposition movements. As Gaetano Mosca, writing in *The Ruling Class*, noted: "A pitiless and energetic persecution, which strikes at the opposing doctrine the moment it shows its head, is the very best tool for combatting it."[30] But repression becomes a double-edged weapon if a movement has a strong social base and if a government is unwilling to raise the stakes no matter what, and engage in the most brutal tactics. And even when total repression has been used, as in Nazi Germany, Fascist Italy, and, to a lesser degree, during the Franco regime in Spain and Pinochet's rule in Chile, it does not appear to be a stable outcome, either in sustaining the regime or in eliminating the sources of radical opposition.

.   .   .

Repression in the United States During World War I

The national comparisons we have drawn may be contested on the grounds that we have not controlled for relevant social, cultural, and political factors that vary across countries. The task of probing further into the consequences of repression for the failure of socialism in America is complicated because the number of variables one needs to control for is greater than the number of countries available for comparison. This is why we have also examined variations within the United States. Such comparison complements that across countries because it allows us to control for some important common influences, particularly the national political context. The effects of repression in the United States during World War I varied widely across regions: in some areas the Socialist party collapsed, while in others, the party actually increased its support. Our conclusion is that the causal weight of repression in explaining the failure of socialism is low compared to that of factors discussed earlier.

World War I and its aftermath produced the greatest wave of repression ever experienced by American leftists. Socialist historians Irving Howe and Lewis Coser have summarized these events: "Attacks upon radical, pacifist, and at times even liberal groups, some government-inspired and others the result of mob outbursts, began directly after the declaration of war. But with the passage of the Espionage Act of June 15, 1917—a legislative net wide enough to catch almost any fish, from Wobbly sharks to pacifist minnows—the repression of dissident movements became an explicit policy of the Wilson administration." [31] In addition to taking numerous legal actions against Socialists, the administration banned Socialist publications, including the official magazine, *The American Socialist*, from the mails.

With the passage in 1918 of the Espionage and Sedition Acts, repression of the Socialist party intensified. The government, with the endorsement of business leaders, attacked the Socialists' antiwar stance as un-American.[32] Hundreds of Socialist leaders and other radicals were convicted for sedition and antiwar activities, and party newspapers across the country were suppressed and barred from the mails. Public party meetings often took place in an atmosphere of intimidation and violence.

Repressive vigilante activities were most effective in smaller communities where party members could not hide their identity. Socialist support in Texas and Oklahoma, prewar centers of native radicalism, was reduced to nothing by the end of the war. During the last year of the war almost one-third of the five thousand Socialist party locals were suppressed, with locals in small communities being the hardest-hit.[33] Despite federal and state government repression, popular vigilante-like attacks, and widespread social ostracism—all of which were far more intense than in the McCarthy period—the Socialists gained in membership and electoral support during the war. Party membership increased to 109,000 in 1919, a total that was exceeded only by the all-time peak of 120,000 in 1912.

There was considerable regional variation in the effect of the war on the party. Socialists actually gained support in areas where antiwar sentiment was strong among the populace. The party did well electorally in communities where the ethnic background of the population discouraged support for the war, such as Milwaukee, Minneapolis, New York City, and Reading. Conversely, the Socialists collapsed where they found themselves surrounded by wartime patriotism, particularly if the party membership was also predominantly of Anglo-Saxon descent.

Milwaukee

The Socialist party made its biggest gains during the war in its strongest urban center, Milwaukee. As we have seen, the party had been able to win some electoral offices in the city from 1904. It retained and expanded its hold on municipal government and increased its representation in the state legislature from thirteen in 1916 to twenty-two in 1918. Daniel Hoan recaptured the mayor's office in 1916 and held it for the next twenty-four years.[34]

The party's strength was largely based on its appeal to the predominant ethnic group in the city—the Germans.[35] Victor Berger, who followed the national party's policy of opposing both sides in the European war as imperialist, lost his races for Congress in 1914 and 1916 to an opponent who outflanked him by appealing to the extreme pro-German vote. Following the American declaration of war in 1917, the Milwaukee party endorsed the decision of the Socialist national convention, which voiced "unalterable opposition to the war."[36]

During the election of 1918, Berger and the Milwaukee party faced particularly ugly pressures. As Berger recounted in a letter to Eugene Debs, "About six months ago, they took away the *Milwaukee Leader*'s second class mailing rights. A little later they tried to forbid our holding meetings, and they did forbid the [antiwar] People's council meetings. Socialist speakers have been tarred and feathered. Others have been imprisoned, some for as long as 30 years, practically a lifetime. They have indicted yours truly."[37] Four other Socialist candidates were also indicted for obstructing the draft. But Berger noted that the war and wartime repression created a golden opportunity for the Socialist party, which, he observed, had "never grown so fast as it has since the persecutions have started."[38] For its part, the *Milwaukee Leader* was convinced that "persecution and atrocities" would "give the cause of Socialism a boost by turning the hearts of the people away from the autocrats and towards us."[39]

Not only did the local party's opposition to the war strengthen its position in Milwaukee, but, for the first time, the party received significant support in outstate Wisconsin, from predominantly ethnic German towns in central and lakeshore Wisconsin. Daniel Hoan was reelected mayor of Milwaukee in the spring of 1918 with a slightly larger margin than two years earlier, while Socialists topped the list in contests for aldermen-at-large. Despite his indictment under the Espionage Act, Victor Berger, who was much more outspoken against the war than Mayor Hoan, received 41.7 percent of Milwaukee County's vote for the U.S. Senate in a special election in April 1918. He won 26 percent of the statewide vote, a fourfold increase over his previous attempt. Voting results for northern Wisconsin in the senatorial election of 1918 yield a correlation of 0.88 between the proportion of German ethnics at the precinct level and support for Berger.[40]

In November 1918, Berger was elected to Congress from the Fifth District, but the House of Representatives refused to seat him, by a vote of 311 to 1. He was reelected in 1920 and was again refused his seat. He finally took his place as the representative of the Fifth District in 1923, and continued to hold the position until 1929. The Socialists were also able to retain their control of the Milwaukee mayoralty in succeeding elections. When Frank P. Zeidler retired as mayor of Milwaukee in 1960, Socialist party members had occupied the position for all but twelve years of the previous half century.[41]

Minneapolis

In Minneapolis, Socialists were also able to maintain considerable support throughout the war. The Socialist mayor Thomas Van Lear, first elected in

1916, came very close to reelection in 1918, receiving 27,652 votes to his opponent's 28,967. Four Socialist party members were elected as aldermen, increasing the party's representation to seven, while another four were victorious in contests for the state legislature.[42]

Van Lear conducted his election campaign jointly with Charles A. Lindbergh, who as a Republican had voted in Congress against the declaration of war, and who ran as the Nonpartisan League candidate for governor in the Republican primaries. Although both Van Lear and Lindbergh proclaimed their support for the war effort in 1918, they clearly lacked enthusiasm for it. The ultra-jingoistic forces in the state, centered in the Minnesota Commission of Public Safety, launched an effort to repress the Socialist party, the IWW, and the Nonpartisan League. Van Lear was involved in a number of confrontations with the commission when he sought to reverse its rulings suppressing radical and antiwar meetings.[43] Lindbergh also was denounced as a preacher of "sedition and treason," and his and various Socialist meetings were often broken up or prevented by the authorities.[44]

As in Milwaukee, in Minneapolis the Socialists operated within a sympathetic ethnic environment composed of Germans and Scandinavian Lutherans, many of whom had either been pro-German or neutral in their reaction to the European war. The city's radicals also retained close relations with the organized labor movement.

The coalition of radicals and socialists in the Working People's Nonpartisan Political League remained an important force in Minneapolis politics after the war, and it gained control of the city council in 1923. The emergence of the Nonpartisan League and the Farmer-Labor party eliminated the Socialist party as a major force in the city.

New York City

New York City, another major urban center of Socialist party strength prior to World War I, increased its Socialist vote in the 1917 municipal and legislative elections. From 1912 on, Socialist electoral strength in New York City was significant, particularly in working-class Jewish districts. In alliance with the city's garment workers' unions, the party succeeded in electing and reelecting Meyer London as congressman in 1914 and 1916 and in gaining two seats in the state assembly in the latter year.[45]

In 1917, a half year after the United States entered the war, Morris Hillquit, running as a strong antiwar candidate, secured the highest vote the party had ever achieved up to that time, 22 percent, despite being attacked for his "disloyalty." Ten Socialists were elected to the legislature, and five became aldermen.[46] A year later, the party increased its vote, but lost some legislative offices because of electoral coalitions between the Democrats and Republicans.

These gains took place in spite of the fact that the New York radicals faced the same sort of reactive mass hysteria that occurred in the rest of the country. The most extensive raids by federal agents to locate draft evaders took place in New York, with more than ten thousand persons arrested in September 1918.[47] In early 1919, New York City police pressured hall owners to refuse to rent to radical meetings, a number of Socialist schoolteachers were fired, and a state legislative committee, the Lusk Committee, began investigating "seditious activities" and conducted a raid on the Socialist-run Rand School of Social Science.[48]

As we have seen, the New York party's following was primarily among Jewish immigrant workers who, hailing largely from areas ruled by the anti-Semitic Russian czar, did not support the Allies. Other groups with similar reservations concerning the Allied war effort, particularly the Germans and Irish, provided disproportionate support for the Socialists. In Jewish districts, the party was nourished by a steady flow of information and propaganda from the Yiddish-language *Forward*, which reported a daily circulation of 200,000.[49] An examination of election results from 1917 illustrates the widespread appeal of socialism in the Jewish population (see Table 7.1).

In spite of the fact that Socialist speakers and meetings were harassed by the government, party strength did not dissipate in New York during the war. The party's reliance on electoral tactics was challenged when the five Socialist assemblymen elected in 1918 were expelled from the state assembly in 1919 by an overwhelming majority, an action which was met with widespread national criticism. The *Literary Digest*'s survey of press opinions found "emphatic protest and almost universal condemnation . . . by Republican, Democratic, and Socialist newspapers alike at the unprecedented action of the New York State Assembly. . . ."[50]

The Socialists saw this violation of civil liberties as an opportunity to garner support.[51] At a special election to fill these seats, held on September 20,

Table 7.1 Election Returns in Selected Jewish Assembly Districts, 1917 (percentage)

	Manhattan			The Bronx		Brooklyn	
	4th	*6th*	*8th*	*3rd*	*4th*	*5th*	*23rd*
				Mayoralty Vote			
Democratic	38.3	30.3	32.5	32.6	30.4	28.7	27.4
Republican	1.2	5.3	3.5	4.0	3.9	3.5	6.9
Socialist	55.8	54.0	52.1	47.7	50.1	49.2	54.5
Fusion	4.7	11.5	11.9	15.6	15.3	18.4	11.1
				Votes for Assemblymen			
Democratic	40.4	23.5	32.4	32.5	35.9	34.7	36.9
Republican	3.8	24.5	15.2	24.9	16.1	22.1	
Socialist	55.8	52.1	52.4	42.6	48.0	43.2	63.1

Source: Melvyn Dubofsky, "Success and Failure of Socialism in New York City, 1900-1918: A Case Study," *Labor History*, 9 (Fall 1968), p. 371.

1920, the five Socialists were reelected by overwhelming majorities against Fusion bipartisan candidates. In the subsequent November elections, three Socialists were elected to the assembly, as well as the party's first state senator.[52] The Republicans, who had won the congressional elections by a small majority that year, decided not to try to oust the Socialists, because they concluded that their previous efforts had been self-defeating.[53] Socialist Meyer London was elected once more to Congress, but it would be his last term. As the repression associated with the Red Scare decreased, so did the strength of the Socialists in New York. One Socialist was elected to the assembly in 1922, but he proved to be the last such success the party had. Still, the New York party continued to retain a base among the Jewish garment unionists, readers of the *Forward*, and members of the Workmen's Circle, a large pro-Socialist Jewish fraternal order.

The New York Socialists were able to flourish under repression because large numbers of Jews were also opposed to the war and later welcomed the Russian Revolution, reactions that stemmed from their experiences with the anti-Semitism of the czarist regime. Important also was the continued loyalty of the various garment unions with their preponderantly Jewish membership. Throughout the 1920s, when the national party had little strength, New York provided a substantial part of its remaining membership and vote, even though the Socialist party there was badly affected by the Communist split. In 1924, Progressive and Socialist presidential nominee Robert La Follette secured close to one-fifth of the vote in New York City, largely on the Socialist line. Fiorello La Guardia, who left the Republican party to back the Wisconsin senator, was reelected to Congress running solely on the Socialist ticket, although he did not join the party. When Norman Thomas secured only 264,608 votes nationally in the election of 1928, New York state contributed l07,332 of them, most of which came from the city.

Reading

The Socialist party also sustained itself as a major force through the war and afterward in Reading, Pennsylvania. This Pennsylvania Dutch city, whose inhabitants were largely native-born (with ancestors from Germany), sent a Socialist, James Maurer, to the legislature in 1910. Maurer, as noted, had been president of the state AFL from 1912 to 1928, serving three terms in the legislature. In 1911, the Socialist party elected five members of the city council and secured 31 percent of the vote for mayor.[54]

The Reading party's strong antiwar position faced enormous hostility during the war. In 1917, the two major parties united under the name of the American party to try to defeat the Socialists. Socialists were vilified in the press and from the pulpit as pro-German traitors.[55] Efforts to discredit Maurer and other Socialist leaders continued during the 1919 Red Scare. The invective launched against the state party, after it had proclaimed its support for the Bolsheviks, threatened to erupt into violence. In November 1919, the Socialists were forced to cancel a meeting at the Labor Lyceum calling for amnesty for convicted radicals because they were confronted with a potentially violent patriotic rally.[56] With one-third of the vote in 1918, Maurer was defeated for a third term as mayor by a bipartisan Fusion candidate. But during the 1920s the party was again able to win control of the municipal administration.

Common Factors in the Cities

The ability of Socialists in Milwaukee, Minneapolis, New York City, and Reading to withstand the repressive conditions of 1917–19 rested on some common conditions. Crucially, support for the war was weak in each of these cities. Germans in Milwaukee, Scandinavians in Minneapolis, and Jews, Germans, and Irish in New York were antagonistic to American involvement on the side of the Allies. Although the ethnic composition of Reading was predominantly native-born American, the origins of the population were largely German rather than British and helped to produce a tilt toward Germany.[57] In addition, in all of these communities the Socialist Party had close relationships with many ethnic-linked unions.

Thus, where the surrounding environment was sympathetic, or at least not hostile, to an antiwar position, the Socialist movement survived or grew. Where the party faced populations supportive of the Allied cause, repression seemingly contributed to its collapse. Community size was also an important secondary factor. Not surprisingly, support fell greatly in smaller and rural communities where social pressure could be more coercive.

Oklahoma

In contrast to the Socialist party's resilience and growth in Milwaukee, Minneapolis, New York City, and Reading during wartime persecution and the postwar Red Scare, the Oklahoma Socialist party, which in 1914 was the party's strongest statewide organization, was totally destroyed.[58] The Oklahoma Socialists reached their zenith with 21 percent of the vote for governor in 1914, an increase of 5 percent from 1912. Electoral support declined to 15 percent in 1916 and plummeted to 4 percent in 1918.[59]

The Socialist party gained widespread support in Oklahoma before World War I for two main reasons. First, it was predominantly a wheat-growing area, and the economically and climatically unstable Wheat Belt in North America has been the center of agrarian radicalism, e.g., the Nonpartisan League in North Dakota and the Cooperative Commonwealth Federation in Saskatchewan.[60] Second, many farmers associated socialism with populism, and supported both in an effort to sustain their independent homesteads and counter the "plutocrats."[61] Prior to the war, the Oklahoma party had been more radical than most state organizations elsewhere.[62] The moderate "right-wing" electorally oriented elements were expelled by the left-wing "Red" group in 1912–13.[63] The ouster of the moderates opened the way to the most militant majority antiwar declaration issued by any state Socialist party. The Oklahoma statement was much more aggressively antiwar than that of the national party, stating that "if

war is declared . . . if forced to enter military service to murder fellow
workers, we shall choose to die fighting the enemies of humanity within
our own ranks rather than to perish fighting our fellow workers. We further
pledge ourselves to use our influence to the end that all toilers shall refuse
to work for the master class during such war."[64]

The position of the party and related radical movements in Oklahoma
was complicated by the formation in 1914 of the Working Class Union
(WCU), led by Dr. Wells LeFevre, an old Arkansas Socialist. The WCU was
an organization of tenant farmers against landlord exploitation. The illegal
and violent tactics of this movement, which gained a following in eastern
and southern Oklahoma, precipitated severe repressive measures. Between
1915 and 1917, members of the WCU engaged in a series of direct actions
ranging from strikes and boycotts to barn burning, bank robbing, and night
riding. Such tactics had more in common with the violent reaction of
southwestern vigilantes than industrial union bargaining.[65] The WCU was
not affiliated with the Socialist party, although it supported the party and
its programs. For its part, the Socialist party did not officially endorse the
WCU, on the grounds that it was a secret organization.[66] No matter how
the Socialists perceived their relationship with the WCU, it is clear that
the two organizations were linked in the press and the public mind.[67]
Some card-carrying Socialists rode with the "regulators." A presidential
straw vote taken in prison revealed that many convicts were imprisoned
for what they considered offenses against their class enemies, and a disproportionate percentage of convicts were Socialists.[68]

The wave of bank robberies and violent activities by the WCU evoked
severe repression against Oklahoma Socialists. As historian James Green
observes: "The opponents of socialism had always identified the party with
crime, and when Working Class Union violence erupted in areas of
Socialist influence, vigilante reactionaries argued for the destruction of all
opposition movements in order to preserve law and order. The seeds of war
time persecution were planted long before the United States actually
entered the European war."[69]

If the violence and illegal tactics of the prewar WCU helped legitimate
effective countertactics by the politically dominant groups, the reaction of
the WCU to the actual declaration of war stimulated an even greater wave
of repression that destroyed Oklahoma socialism as an organized force.
WCU members and leaders, including many members of the Socialist

party, decided to resist the draft and, ultimately, to rebel against the federal government. In the summer of 1917, they proclaimed: "Now is the time to rebel against this war with Germany boys. Boys, get together and don't go. Rich man's war. Poor man's fight. The war is over with Germany if you don't go. . . ."[70] Believing somehow that secret revolutionary antiwar groups had formed all over the country, the WCU organized thousands of farmers to begin a revolutionary march on Washington on the night of August 3, 1917, an event that has come to be known as the Green Corn Rebellion.[71] The rebellion was a fiasco. Sheriff's posses were speedily organized, and they hunted down the rebels in a few days. Plans to blow up bridges and pipelines came to naught.[72]

One result was a "veritable white terror" which swept through Oklahoma.[73] Thousands of Socialists and Wobblies were seized in post-rebellion roundups, although neither organization had been involved. An emergency convention of the state Socialist party voted to dissolve the organization. This extreme measure was taken to prevent the government from citing the rebellion as evidence in the ongoing trial of Victor Berger and the National Executive Committee of the Socialist party, accused of "conspiracy to obstruct the prosecution of the war."[74] By 1919, suppression of Socialist newspapers and local meetings and the imprisonment of many of the party's leaders left the Oklahoma Socialist party and the Socialist movement throughout the southwest in tatters.[75]

Although the state Socialist party regrouped and attempted a comeback in the following year, the struggle was hopeless. Oklahoma and southwestern socialism had come to an end; its branches, members, and voters disappeared. Severe repression and the delegitimation of radicalism, in a region where the foreign-born were few, destroyed socialism where it had thrived previously. Finally, ethnicity probably played a causal role in the disintegration of the party in Oklahoma and other southwestern states. The population of Oklahoma was largely of native-born British origin. The intensity of vigilante attacks on opponents of the war undoubtedly reflected the strong prowar and jingoistic sentiment among the dominant majority in communities where the Socialist party had support.[76]

Socialist opposition to American intervention in World War I drastically weakened the party among native-born of Anglo-Saxon background, alienated the mainstream union movement, and intensified the division between native-born and foreign-born supporters of the party.[77] The shift in the

base of socialist support to Eastern European immigrants and the decline
of links with the unions were to have disastrous consequences for the party
as it responded to the Russian Revolution and the Bolshevik demand that
parties everywhere should imitate its revolutionary strategy and tactics.
This essentially meant disavowing electoral participation and setting up
underground organizations. A majority of members either quit or were
expelled in the ensuing internal struggle within the party. In January 1919
the party reported 109,000 members; by July, the official figure was less
than 40,000.[78] In late 1919 the Eastern European foreign-language federations together with some native American radicals founded American
Communism.[79]

It is significant that the ethnically homogenous and politically moderate
locals of Milwaukee and Reading, which were unaffected by the Eastern
European influx into the party during the World War I era, alongside the
New York garment workers, continued to provide the Socialist party's
firmest bases of electoral support in the 1920s. In Milwaukee, Victor
Berger's German-origin followers remained loyal to the party. In Reading,
"the disintegrative influence of the Communist defection in 1919 . . . left
the local organization virtually unscathed. . . ."[80] But in areas where they
were numerous, Eastern European party members, most of whom had only
recently joined, provided a powerful base for Communism.

The Nonpartisan League

The decline of the Socialist party in most of the country after the war
stands in stark contrast with the successes of the radical Nonpartisan
League (NPL) in rural areas and small towns in the midwest, a contrast
that sheds light on the causal role of repression in the failure of the
Socialist party. The Nonpartisan League, a semisocialist, largely farm-based
organization, managed to survive and grow under repressive conditions
similar to those encountered by Socialists in Oklahoma. The electoral victories of the NPL in North Dakota and of the Farmer-Labor party it engendered in Minnesota also should dispel the notion that the repressive
measures and atmosphere generated by the war prevented radicals from
gaining support among the American public. Although repression in North
Dakota and Minnesota was probably not as severe as in many other areas,
it did occur. The National Civil Liberties Bureau (predecessor of the

American Civil Liberties Union) viewed the NPL as a major target of wartime violence, although unlike the Socialists, the NPL and its candidates attempted to shield themselves from attack by proclaiming support for the war, despite their previous opposition to it.[81]

In North Dakota, the Nonpartisan League faced charges of disloyalty, and efforts were made to prevent its meetings. But largely because the league had control of the state administration, there was little repression or violence.[82] Still, it was subject to a stream of propaganda that sought to arouse patriotic and antirevolutionary passions. One example of this is the expensively printed and illustrated monthly publication *The Red Flame*, whose distribution blanketed the state. The magazine proclaimed in November 1919, at the height of the national Red Scare, that the NPL was dominated by "a small coterie of red-tide fanatics who are not farmers, not workers, not property-holders, not tax payers, not home-owners, not producers in any sense,—in a number of instances not even American citizens . . . [and that] the National Nonpartisan League has degenerated into pure Bolshevism . . . dominated wholly by Mr. A. C. Townley and a group of radical international socialists. . . ." Issues of the magazine sought to link "free love," "anarchism," "IWWism," and "bolshevism" with the league.[83] *The Red Flame* and the opposition press exploited Governor Lynn Frazier's comment in a speech in September 1919 that if we cannot "change things here by use of the ballot . . . it may be necessary to have another just revolution."[84]

In Minnesota and other states where the NPL did not hold office before the twenties, it faced the full force of repressive pressures and mob violence. Three league leaders, including A. C. Townley, were convicted of sedition or disloyalty in Minnesota.[85] Throughout 1918 and 1919, NPL meetings in Minnesota and other states were banned by public authorities or broken up by crowds or police. The league suffered mob brutalities in hundreds of small towns, and by March 1918, nineteen counties in Minnesota had banned all league meetings.[86]

Repression directed against the league intensified in the fall and winter of 1918. League meetings were frequently disrupted by mobs led by local officials, and league leaders were regularly beaten and tarred and feathered. Those who openly sympathized with the league were targeted. Storefronts of friendly merchants were painted yellow. Professors at the University of Minnesota who were suspected of pro-NPL sympathies were harassed. Local law enforcement officials and home guards did little or nothing to

Table 7.2 Nonpartisan League
Elected Representatives by State

	Senate	House
North Dakota	23	54
Minnesota	11	33
Wisconsin	6	31
Nebraska	2	16
Montana	5	5
Idaho	4	2
South Dakota	2	5
Colorado	3	3
Washington	1	2

Source: Theodore Saloutos, "The Expansion and Decline
of the Non-Partisan League in the Western Middle West,"
Agricultural History 20 (October 1946).

protect the league and, in fact, threatened violence against its supporters.
At one point the Commission of Public Safety advocated public mob
action. This policy, later described by George Creel as "brutal intolerance,"
had the tacit support of state officials.[87]

The NPL suffered the same kind of governmental repression and popular vigilante activity as Socialists and Wobblies elsewhere. While the
Nonpartisan League was organizationally quite separate from the Socialist
and Communist lefts, its opponents tried to place it in the same revolutionary camp.[88] In the words of a historian of the league, it faced a "reign of
terror."[89] Yet under these harsh conditions, the NPL prospered in
Minnesota and spread to many other predominantly agricultural and small
community states where it was electorally viable and occasionally successful. In 1920, the league elected representatives in nine state legislatures,
mainly in the north-central states close to North Dakota.[90]

Why was the Nonpartisan League able to flourish under conditions that
curtailed the efforts of more ideologically committed Socialists elsewhere?
The answer may be found in the same phenomena that help to explain the
survival of the Socialist party in New York, Reading, and Milwaukee.

Support for the Allied cause was weak in North Dakota, Minnesota, and several other midwestern states. Concentrated in the region were German ethnics, alongside Scandinavian Lutherans, who were unsympathetic to the Allied cause and overwhelmingly opposed to American participation in the war. Accordingly they were not as easily aroused by charges of pro-German or antiwar sympathies as were populations in states composed largely of British or old American stock. In addition, many Wheat Belt farmers in the NPL regions (and Oklahoma) had long been sympathetic to anti-imperialist, antibanker doctrines, and these led them to believe that the European war would solely benefit eastern financial interests.

The Nonpartisan League was led by electorally opportunistic socialists. Although opposed to the war, they, like some Socialist officeholders and trade union officials, recognized that once the United States was at war, continued open opposition meant organizational suicide. Unlike many Socialists without the responsibilities of office, the NPL leaders refrained from engaging in provocative acts or speeches that might set off patriotic violence or governmental repression. While such behavior did not prevent their conservative opponents from organizing vigilante and official persecution against them, it did help to generate support from many who would never have defended manifestly antiwar groups.

The contrasting experiences of the Nonpartisan League and the Socialist party raise the question of what might have happened had the American Socialist party escaped repression by following the same policies as socialist parties in Europe, i.e., pursuing a less dogmatic attitude toward the war.[91] The force of this hypothetical argument is blunted, however, because repression is most successful precisely where actual and potential support for a cause is weak. John Laslett has argued, along similar lines, that repressive measures and an oppressive public opinion were more effective in eliminating radicalism in America than in various European societies, because class loyalty was weaker in the United States than in Europe:

Where you have a highly stratified society in which crucial elements of either the peasantry or the proletariat are already predisposed against constituted authority and at a time of crisis are willing to follow class leaders or otherwise to act in a class way, then repression simply drives the movement underground, from where it will reemerge, strengthened, at a suitable moment. On the other hand, if you have a society in which either the agrarian element or the urban working class lacks any coherent sense of class loyalty and is predisposed toward acculturation or assimilation, as in the United States, then repression will have the opposite effect. Instead of nourishing rebellion, in other words, it will induce its followers to draw back from any fundamental challenge to the society, and to accept their place instead in what may continue to be an unjust social system.[92]

There can be no doubt that persecution seriously weakened the Socialists in many communities during and immediately following World War I. It may be noted, though, that perennial Socialist presidential nominee Norman Thomas denied that repression was a major source of Socialist weakness, at least from 1920 to the World War II years:

> The difficulty faced by a Socialist candidate even in tense years like 1920 and 1932, is not overt hostility. . . . [Some assume] I usually faced at least hostile hecklers. This is not the case. . . . [I]n literally thousands of meetings in all parts of the United States (many of them street corner or other outdoor meetings) which I have addressed as candidate for the Presidency or lesser offices, I remember amazingly little actual or potential disorder. . . . Sometimes I have thought that more open hostility to what I said would be a better omen for democracy than indifference or a kind of fatalistic attitude summed up in the sentiment "You are right, but what can we do about it?" . . . No, the difficulty of Socialist campaigning as I have found in five races for the Presidency, is not overt hostility or threatened violence.[93]

Persecution or repression cannot explain the weakness of the Socialist party after World War I. The party was too small to be an effective actor nationally and secured relatively few votes, except briefly in 1932 when it managed to get 2 percent in the depths of the Depression. From the mid-thirties on, the Communists took over as the major force on the radical left. The Communists did suffer from popular and government repression, but their organizing strategy was basically to "bore from within," to conceal their Communist, even radical, identity, while seeking to place their people in key posts in the labor and liberal movements, including at times the Democratic party.

An aggressive anti-Communist effort, led by Senator Joseph McCarthy, emerged in the 1950s, as a hot war developed between the United States and the Asian Communist states of North Korea and China. The Korean War, like earlier conflicts, gave rise to severe repression against antiwar groups, particularly pro-Communist ones. But while McCarthyism did intimidate support for Communism, it should be noted that the Communists had lost most of their influence and membership *before* his crusade. To the extent that McCarthyite anticommunism was successful during the Korean War, it was for the same reasons that earlier repression undermined the Socialist party in predominantly Anglo-Saxon, old-American-stock areas in 1918–19. Repression is effective where the cause under attack has little actual or potential support. Prior to the Korean War, liberals and unionists turned against communism. They rejected Communist tactics and came to view communism as an external threat in the light of the overthrow of a democratic government in Czechoslovakia, overt anti-Semitism in the Soviet Union and Czechoslovakia, and the blockade of Berlin. By the early 1950s, few American Communists were prepared to openly voice their opinions or defend their rights.

Communists themselves played into the hands of McCarthy and his allies by rarely defending their constitutional rights to free speech, to agitate or organize as Communists. When attacked by government or congressional investigators, they would insist they were liberals and say that the investigations were designed to intimidate the Progressive movement. Socialists and Wobblies defended their civil rights as radicals when arrested during World War I (as did Trotskyists in 1941 and New Leftists during the Vietnam War). But Communists never stood up to McCarthy or other post–World War II investigators to proclaim their right to be revolutionaries. For the most part, they took the Fifth Amendment, either refusing to answer political questions or denying, even when under oath, that they were members of the Party. Hence, the issue was frequently whether a person targeted by McCarthy was in fact a Communist, not whether he or she had a right to be one. The unwillingness of the Communists to openly defend their right to oppose the system meant that a Blanquist response to repression, seeking to secure the sympathy of a wider public for basic political rights, could not succeed. Under such conditions, anti-Stalinist leftists and defenders of civil liberties generally found it difficult to speak up for people whom they regarded as committed supporters of an extremely repressive and anti-Semitic system.[94]

The evidence suggests that repression of leftists was never as extensive in America as it was in several European countries before World War I, and not nearly as severe as during the interwar years in fascist states, and subsequently in Franco's Spain, and in the 1980s in Pinochet's Chile. As John Laslett notes, "In America repression of radical movements has not taken the form of deliberate murder or destruction as often as it has in a number of European countries."[95] We conclude that the long history of repression of American socialists cannot explain their failure to establish a viable political party.

Chapter 8

THE END OF

POLITICAL

EXCEPTIONALISM?

he effort to build socialism in America was clearly unsuccessful. The hundreds of thousands of dedicated American radicals who sought to create a socialist movement from the late nineteenth century on repeatedly failed. The United States is the only Western democracy to have a party system dominated by two parties, both of which are sympathetic to liberal capitalism and neither of which has inherited a socialist or social democratic vision of society. At its peak, in the decade before 1920, the Socialist party never really challenged the supremacy of the major parties, nor did it manage to survive as a third party.

The obstacles they faced did not prevent socialists from being elected as mayors and council members in a number of cities, winning state legislative seats, and even, on occasion, a seat in Congress. Among the third parties that have competed at the national level, none has been as persistent as the Socialist party. With the exception of 1924, when the Socialists supported Robert La Follette, the party put forward a candidate in every presidential election from 1904 to 1952.[1] While Theodore Roosevelt (in 1912), La Follette (in 1924), George Wallace (in 1948), John Anderson (in 1980), and Ross Perot (in 1992 and 1996) received a much greater share of the presidential vote in challenging Democratic and Republican nominees than any single Socialist candidate, no minor party in American politics has received as much support as the Socialists over the twentieth century as a whole. In addition, Socialists have led many AFL and CIO unions. The Communists also were able to gain high public office and to control unions and other organizations, although, for the most part, they triumphed by concealing the fact that they were Communists. It is therefore accurate to say that socialism has been capable of winning the support of millions, though always a small minority, of Americans. But if one looks at American politics from a comparative perspective, there can be no question that one of its distinctive features has been the absence of a significant socialist or labor party, and it is for this reason that many historians and others have spoken of American exceptionalism.[2]

In this chapter we ask whether America remains exceptional. The absence of a socialist party no longer differentiates the United States from Western European and other English-speaking democracies. Over the past two decades, socialist and labor parties have dropped statist economic policies that they inherited from their socialist past. The policies of most of these parties are not very different from those of the Democratic party in the United States. They wish to regulate capitalism, not transform it. They are in favor of greater economic equality (along with social, racial, and gender equality), but they no longer envisage a large measure of state control in order to achieve these goals.

Yet the United States remains as different from other western democracies as it ever was. Taxation, social spending, and public spending in general are exceptionally low in the United States, as is the level of union organization. Economic growth has been comparatively strong over the past decade, and median income and wealth are extremely high, especially when measured in terms of purchasing power parity. At the same time, economic inequality, however it is measured, is much greater in the United States than in any other western or English-speaking democracy.

These features of public policy are intimately linked to the historical events described in this book. Comparative studies of public policy reveal that the organized strength of a society's lower class is immensely influential for its public policy. The institutions created in a society—perhaps above all, the institutions that reflect the relative power or impotence of those at the bottom of a society in relation to those at the top—shape a society's response to economic change. The inability of American socialists to create a durable labor or socialist party is not a historical quirk of a bygone era. On the contrary, it is a powerful influence on the present.

But let us proceed in stages. We begin by summarizing the basic thrust of our historical explanation.

Why Socialists Failed

Socialists failed in three respects. They were unable to sustain a strong and durable socialist party; they were unable to create an independent labor party in alliance with mainstream unions as in other English-speaking societies; and they were unable to capture one of the major parties. If one of these possibilities had taken place—if socialists had created a viable socialist or labor party, or if they had captured or exerted real influence in one of the two major parties—the left in the United States would have followed the pattern of that in other western democracies and American society today would, we conjecture, be different as a result.

The factors we evaluate in this book purport to explain these failures. We have engaged in diverse comparative analyses—of the United States with other societies, within the United States at the individual level, city level, and state level, and across time—in an effort to separate wheat from chaff. We have not tried to investigate every explanation that has been put forward—an almost impossible task. Instead we have taken up what we regard as the most plausible lines of explanation in order to see how they weather comparative evaluation. As we summarize below, several conventional explanations either fail completely or must be given minor roles. At the same time, we have sought to build a plausible explanation of our own. There is much to build on, and there are no unambiguous litmus tests that can tell us where we have erred. What we do claim is that the factors we weave together are plausible from a "process" standpoint and plausible from a comparative standpoint. That is to say, we claim our explanation makes sense historically as a story, a story in which human beings have intelligible goals and make choices under discernible constraints. And we claim that the causal logics of the building blocks we use are generalizable across societies with which the United States can be meaningfully compared.

While we wish to understand a nonevent—the fact that socialism never took hold in the United States—the only method open to us is to examine and attempt to explain what actually happened. One must come to grips with basic political, social, and cultural factors in American political development, and one must come to grips with the decisions that key political actors made in responding to them. American values—political structure—heterogeneous working class—party/union split: the interaction of these four factors holds the key to why socialists failed in America. The weight of our explanation is on the interactive effects of values and political structure, but we also stress the causal role of human agency, in particular the mistakes made by Socialists in refusing to compromise with mainstream unionists. When we put together particular elements of the American polity and culture that confronted socialists with the internal fragmentation of the labor movement, we have, we believe, a sufficient explanation for the failures of the socialist enterprise.

Key aspects of the American political system, including particularly the plurality electoral system, the winner-take-all presidency, and ideologically flexible major parties, created high hurdles for any third political party—socialist, labor, or otherwise. Many unionists who supported a labor party on pragmatic grounds in other English-speaking societies believed that it was impractical to do so in the United States. As Kenneth McNaught observes, many left-of-center Americans say that if they lived in Canada they would vote for the New Democratic party. Because the major parties are so permeable in the United States, the opportunity costs for labor of supporting a third party have been much higher than in other societies. At the same time, the electoral system for selecting a president, which effectively aggregates votes throughout the country, has magnified the penalty of voting for third-party candidates. As a result, third-party support is a less practical proposition than in other societies, including those which share the principle of a plurality electoral system. The fact that the two major parties have sustained a duopoly of 95 percent of the congressional and presidential vote since the Civil War in a society that has spawned literally thousands of political parties indicates just how stifling the American political system has been for challenging new parties.

Could the Socialist party have surmounted this political barrier? The experience of other English-speaking and European countries suggests that socialist or labor parties were able to succeed in political systems that were almost as inauspicious for minor parties. Moreover, some state and city socialist parties and factions in the United States had considerable success over extended periods of time. The American polity has not, in our view, been uniformly harmful for third parties. By carving up the polity into smaller units, federalism created political openings for Socialist and left parties at the regional level that were denied to minor parties in more centralized polities. It is also important to recognize that the American political system contributed only to the first two failures of American socialism, but not to the inability—or unwillingness—of Socialists to make headway in one of the major two parties. In fact, one of the key features of modern American politics that makes life so difficult for minor parties, the primary system, made a strategy of "boring from within," that is, contesting primaries within the major parties, more feasible.

Our comparative analyses lead us to the conclusion that the American social system is a starting point for explaining the failures of socialism. But beyond the inauspicious cultural context that confronted Socialists and the character of the working class they tried to organize, we must also take account of the strategic choices that they made in dealing with the American political system, American culture, and the American working class.

The values that motivate decision-making in a society are enormously stable over time, not just at the individual level, but across generations. A culture, as Max Weber suggested, can be viewed as a series of loaded dice in which the past constrains, but does not determine, the present. One reason for continuity is that the interaction of culture and institutions is to some extent self-reinforcing. This is so because cultural values constrain the kinds of social institutions that are created in a society, and these institutions—schools, government bureaucracies, churches, etc.—help shape beliefs. Another source of continuity lies in the rigidity of cultural norms. Individuals and communities often hold tenaciously to cultural values even when these are functionally irrational. But it is rarely clear whether a belief is irrational. Unless the consequences are severe, individuals are rarely willing to reassess the cultural norms they share with other members of their society.

It is impressive that American radicals have turned time and time again to the antistatist Declaration of Independence in voicing their opposition to capitalism. In an essay on workers' culture, Leon Fink quotes Seth Luther, the Massachusetts shoeworkers' leader, who in 1832 proclaimed he was "no longer to be deceived by cry of those who produce *nothing* and who enjoy *all*, and who insultingly term us—the farmers, the mechanics and labourers, the Lower Orders—and exultingly claim our homage for themselves as the Higher Orders—while the Declaration of Independence asserts that 'All Men Are Created Equal.' "[3]

Distinctive elements of American culture—antistatism and individualism—negated the appeal of socialism for the mass of American workers for much of the twentieth century. Socialism, with its emphasis on statism, socialization of the means of production, and equality through taxation, was at odds with the dominant values of American culture. The effects of antistatism and individualism can be seen positively in the character of American working-class republicanism, the strength of syndicalism in the AFL, and, later, in the student New Left of the 1960s and 1970s.[4]

Why did socialists not respond by being less ideologically rigid? Instead of trying to swim against the tide of American culture, why did they not establish a labor party that would be less purely socialist, but would aim, instead, to encompass the mass of American workers? After all, this is what mainstream socialists did in countries like Britain, Australia, Canada, and New Zealand. Once they had entrenched themselves in the party system, such labor parties served as incubators for socialism within the union movement as a whole. Socialists in these countries found that their initial ideological compromises paid off handsomely because labor parties gave them real influence in the labor movement as a whole.

In several countries in central and northern Europe, and to a lesser degree in English-speaking societies, socialists tried to insulate themselves from the dominant cultures of their societies by forming inclusive subcultures that encompassed socialist parties, labor unions, newspapers, pubs, party schools, and an ensemble of associational activities, from choral societies to chess clubs. This was also the case in cities in the United States, such as Milwaukee, Minneapolis, and Reading, where local Socialist parties were markedly more successful than the national party. In these towns and cities, Socialists escaped the national pattern and formed close ties to local unions in the American Federation of Labor. Such links between the party and the unions led one student of Milwaukee socialism to describe the leadership of both as an "interlocking directorate."[5]

At the national level, however, relations between Socialists and mainstream unions in the AFL were generally hostile from the mid-1890s to the 1930s and beyond. Efforts to create a labor party came to nothing. One consequence of this was that American socialists could not create a cultural milieu that reinforced class consciousness among workers while cushioning them against wider social pressures. It is noteworthy that early public opinion polls revealed widespread support for measures associated with socialism during the 1930s, such as nationalization of the coal mines and railways, but that by that time the Socialist party was in no condition to take advantage of this. The period of support for statist solutions to economic problems was short-lived. Once prosperity returned during and after World War II, the traditional emphases of American culture on anti-statism and individualism reemerged. These not only eliminated any possibility that the left in the Democratic party would turn toward socialism but galvanized libertarian ideological streams in the Republican party and eventually pressured the Democratic party to drop the more statist elements of its New Deal image.

From its inception, in the post–Civil War decades, the American working class was exceptionally diverse ethnically, racially, and religiously even when compared to the working classes of other English-speaking settler societies. What was even more important, however, was that ethnic, religious, and racial cleavages were more powerful sources of political identity for most American workers than was their commonality as workers. This made the project of creating a labor party both more critical for the success of the American left and less feasible. The Democratic and Republican parties exploited and reinforced the lack of political class consciousness among American workers. They appealed to workers through the lenses of their contending identities, and they had already built loyalty among many workers and union leaders in the closing decades of the nineteenth century, before the American Socialist party came on the scene. Manhood suffrage for white males from the late 1820s created a working-class electorate long before socialists commanded effective political organizations. Paradoxically, as Marxists themselves were well aware, the denial of basic citizenship rights to workers in most continental European societies until late in the nineteenth century or even later allowed socialists to take the lead in mobilizing workers for the suffrage. In countries where citizenship rights for workers preceded socialist mobilization—Switzerland, France, Australia, and Canada—socialists had to contend with major parties that had already sunk roots into the working class.[6]

The split between unions and socialists in the United States at the national level eliminated the possibility of a labor party, which, in turn, effectively reduced the possibility that the American working class would constitute itself as a strong and inclusive subculture. Given the severity of the political and cultural hurdles the party faced, it was disastrous for Socialists not to combine their forces with unionists. It is one thing for a movement to face an inhospitable polity and culture; it is quite another if that movement is itself split into antagonistic factions.

However, it would be simplistic to say that Socialists failed in America because they were overly divisive.[7] The split in the labor movement had its sources in embedded structural and cultural factors. The leaders of the American Federation of Labor were not only opposed to full-blooded socialism but committed to "pure and simple" unionism that made them wary of independent labor representation. Their syndicalist strategy reflected the antistatism and individualism characteristic of American culture and the domination of exclusive craft unionism in the American labor movement from the late 1880s to the mid-1930s. Socialists failed in the vital task of creating a coherent working-class movement, but the challenge they faced was awesome.

Finally, we find that claims in the literatures concerning the causal role of alternative factors do not withstand comparative scrutiny:

- Early manhood suffrage for white males did not necessarily diminish socialist mobilization. The case of Australia (and the contrast within Australia between Victoria and New South Wales), alongside that of France and Switzerland, suggests that strong labor or socialist parties were able to develop even when male suffrage was granted early. Early suffrage is important insofar as nonlabor political parties were able to build loyalties among workers before socialism came on the scene.
- Federalism is double-edged for socialism. Federalism fragments political authority and thereby makes the national state a less useful instrument for enacting labor or socialist reforms. But it also divides executive authority into smaller political units that can be targeted by minor parties, including Socialists, as is evident in Canada and Australia as well as the United States. If a minor party at the national level is able to establish itself as the leading or second party at the regional level, it can break out of the wasted-vote dilemma confronting third parties.
- The influence of the courts on the willingness of the American Federation

of Labor and its constituent unions to pursue a political rather than an economic strategy has been overblown. Court rejection of labor legislation cannot account for the wide disparity in union strategy from the 1890s to the 1930s or the contrasts among individual unions. Our analysis suggests that the courts were, at most, a relatively minor influence in reducing the benefits of a labor party or an alliance with the Socialists for American unions.

- State repression, even during its most intense period during and after World War I, cannot explain the failure of Socialists in America. This is revealed both by comparison within the United States and contrast of the United States with other countries. Internal comparison reveals that repression could not stop the Socialists from gaining strength in towns and cities where intervention in the war was unpopular. The main reason for the crisis experienced by the Socialist party from 1916 was that the party first alienated the bulk of its native-born supporters and then split when Communists broke away in 1919. International comparison shows that repression could not break socialism even in countries, such as Germany under the Anti-Socialist Laws (1878–1890), where it was more severe. Even when suppression is brutal, as in Franco's Spain or in Pinochet's Chile in the 1980s, it tends to be self-defeating in the long run.

Criticisms of American Exceptionalism

In recent years, the notion of American exceptionalism and the way it has structured our understanding of the United States in relation to other societies has come under sustained criticism. Exceptionalist analyses, it is has been argued, valorize national differences by offering ahistorical explanations that cannot explain variation within countries and across time. Rather than develop explanations of exceptionalism that seem to hover over history, without ever engaging historical processes directly, critics suggest that it is necessary to operate at the middle range. In his influential critique of the exceptionalism thesis, Sean Wilentz suggested a comparative historical cure: "One important departure might be to undertake a truly comprehensive comparative history of American labor, one that is as open to analogies between events and movements in this country and those abroad as it is to the differences."[8]

In this book we have responded to these suggestions by subjecting one important facet of the American experience to comparative analysis—over time, within the United States, and across (and within) other societies. On the basis of that research we believe that a strong case can be made that, indeed, the political development of American labor has been exceptional. The United States has been the only western democracy without a labor, social democratic, or socialist party. The consequences have been massive and long-lasting.

This is not to deny that, as many scholars have pointed out, every society may be regarded as exceptional.[9] The labor movements of Britain, Canada, France, and Germany are different from each other and different from the labor movements of any country one might compare them to. However, one may ask whether American exceptionalism is exceptional. Is there something special about the experience of the political left in the United States that fundamentally distinguishes it from the lefts of other western democracies?

Two lines of criticism challenge such reasoning. The first argues that the exceptionalism thesis assumes an ideal working-class consciousness and socialist commitment for comparison with the United States that has never actually existed.[10] If American workers failed to support a Marxist political movement, the same can be said of most workers in Europe as well. A revolutionary or radical proletarian social movement in the Marxian mold failed to materialize in most European countries as well as in the United States.

This is a valid point, but it does not refute the exceptionalism thesis. It is true that the mass revolutionary proletarian movement was more a fiction in the mind of committed activists than a historical reality. Edward Thompson has been followed by most social historians in emphasizing the artisanal roots of early labor protest. The archetypal radical in France, Germany, and England in the years up to and including the Paris Commune of 1870 was the skilled worker beaten down by economic change rather than the proletarian unskilled factory worker. When socialist parties were established from the last quarter of the nineteenth century in Germany, Sweden, France, and elsewhere in Europe their revolutionary programs were not representative of the views of their working-class supporters. On the basis of diverse evidence, including responses to a survey of workers' opinions carried out by Adolf Levenstein before World War I,

Barrington Moore, Jr., observes that most workers who supported the German Social Democratic party did so mainly because they wanted to be treated decently. Radical or revolutionary class-conscious proletarians were a small minority among the working classes of European countries as in America.[11]

One of the ironies of American political development is that the American Socialist party was more, not less, radical than most mainstream European working-class parties, and was far more radical than the labor parties established in other English-speaking societies.[12] If the ideology of working-class parties were the object of study one might argue that by comparison with other English-speaking societies, the exceptionalism of the United States is to be found in the *strength* of radical Marxism in the political party representing the working class. In the years before World War I, the labor parties of Britain, Australia, Canada, and New Zealand were coalitions dominated by unions that wished to defend their position under the law, legislate improvements in working conditions, and, in the case of Australia, prohibit nonwhite immigration. The late British labor historian Henry Pelling noted that the reforms demanded by the Labour party in 1906 were essentially the same as those pursued by the Liberal party.[13] This provides an important line of sight into the fate of socialism in the United States. The American Socialist party was a six-hundred-pound gorilla in its ideological pretensions, yet in terms of power and its roots in the working class it was a weakling.

It should be plain that our view of American exceptionalism does not deny that the Marxist model was rarely present in Europe and elsewhere. Nor do we dispute the obvious point that every society is unique in some respects. Every labor movement that has existed, or will exist, is "exceptional" in one way or another. However, we do maintain that the historical experience of the United States was fundamentally different from that of other western societies because it was the only society in which the working class did not create a strong and durable political party.

A second line of criticism of the exceptionalism thesis begins with the claim that American workers were not all that exceptional in their response to capitalism and industrialization. Several labor historians have emphasized the vitality of a tradition of collective resistance to capitalism that was expressed in a variety of social and political movements, from the plebeian radicalism of the Workingmen's parties of the 1820s and 1830s to the working-class republicanism of the second half of the nineteenth century and the sit-down strikes of industrial workers in the 1930s.[14] Summarizing the findings of recent studies of "new" labor historians, Sean Wilentz has argued that they "have not yet removed the exceptionalism problem from the agenda, but they have undermined some of the faulty assumptions in the exceptionalism literature. The rediscovery of recurring intense militancy in the strike situations has made it impossible to suppose that American workers simply accepted American capitalism or came to accept it."[15]

However, the exceptionalism thesis as we articulate it does not imply that American workers accepted the conditions that confronted them. The question that we pose is why the response of American workers to capitalism and economic exploitation took the form that it did. How can one explain the paradox of working-class militancy in the workplace and lack of organized class consciousness in politics? This theme is an old one. Selig Perlman and Philip Taft, deans of traditional, nonsocialist, labor studies, described the experience of American labor as "principally a fighting history" and went on in their coauthored book to observe that "on issues which affected the material welfare and the human dignity of the wage earner, American unionism battled against the claims of private property to the bitter end and often with a reckless daring. It battled not as a 'class conscious proletariat' but as a body of American citizens with an ideal of liberty of their own."[16]

More recently, Eric Foner has posed the question "Why was militancy in the factory so rarely translated into the politics of class?" Foner goes on to say: "Labor and socialist parties have emerged in the United States (indeed, Americans, in the late 1820s, created the first 'Workingmen's parties' in the world) but they have tended to be locally oriented and short-lived. As Montgomery observes, the American form of socialism has centered on control of the workplace, rather than creating a working-class presence in politics. 'Why there is no socialism' thus becomes a problem of explaining the *disjuncture* of industrial relations and political practice in the United States."[17]

These questions motivate the explanation we put forward. American workers were often the most militant in the labor market. The unions they formed, including those in the American Federation of Labor, represented the interests of their members as aggressively as unions in any Western European or English-speaking society. Until recently, American strike levels have been generally higher than those in Europe. The violence of industrial disputes has also been greater than in Europe. What is exceptional in the United States is that the intensity of conflict in the workplace was not expressed in politics by a working-class or socialist party.

American workers, like those elsewhere, adapted to, and sometimes resisted, capitalism. But the organizations they created in the process were different—decisively different—from those in other western societies. The failure to create a working-class political party meant that American workers could not act as a class in shaping the society in which they lived. They could fight employers in the workplace. Their unions could give or withhold support from one of the major parties prior to elections. But American workers had almost no collective capacity for participating in government. Government, which endows some human beings with the authority to legislate what members of a society can or cannot do, was beyond the reach of American workers as a class.

The End of Political Exceptionalism?

To what extent is the American left still exceptional? Over the past two decades, socialist and social democratic parties across western democracies have been influenced by a general swing away from state control of the economy toward a more market-oriented approach. Parties that were established as socialist, social democratic, or labor have gradually dropped the statist elements of their programs.[18] Some have distanced themselves from labor unions. None of the major socialist parties advocates more public ownership; most accept market principles even in areas of the economy that were formerly nationalized, such as transport, telecommunications, and utilities. The great breach between progressive socialization of the economy versus laissez-faire has narrowed into a debate between regulated capitalism versus neoliberalism. At issue is the character and degree of regulation of the economy, not the future of capitalism. In short, the absence of a socialist party in the United States now distinguishes it less sharply from other developed nations.[19]

In the immediate postwar decades, the right moved left as it accepted state economic planning, welfare reforms, Keynesian fiscal policy, statutory or consensual incomes policy, and, in several societies, neocorporatist bargaining. Since the 1980s, the left has moved right. Just how general this shift has been is evident from Table 8.1, which summarizes expert judgments of the position of socialist/social democratic parties along a conventional left-right scale from support for state intervention in the economy (1) to support for market liberalism (10).

Nowhere has the turn away from pro-state policies been more marked than in Britain, Australia, and New Zealand. In these countries, the working class was represented by labor parties, which were unionist rather than socialist. Only during and after World War I did labor parties in these countries adopt socialist programs. These countries pose the most difficult test for political exceptionalism. They suggest, indeed, that the United States is no longer exceptional in the way that we have described above.

The rightward distance covered by the British Labour party between 1984 and 1995 is greater than that for any other party surveyed in Table 8.1. The most direct way of summarizing the shift is to say, simply, that the Labour party is no longer socialist. This lies behind the reformulation of the party's image to "New Labour" and the disavowal of "socialism" in leadership speeches and party literature. Tony Blair, who led the Labour party to a landslide victory in the British general election of May 1997, has tenaciously eliminated those remnants of traditional socialism that remained in the party's constitution and program after the more timid reforms in the same direction by his predecessor, John Smith. Blair's often-quoted catchphrases are "The era of big government is over," which he proclaimed in 1995, a few months before Bill Clinton made the same statement, and "We shall govern from the centre."[20] Peter Mandelson, the ideologist of the Blairites, asserts that Labour is now "a market capitalist party." Samuel Beer, doyen of American scholars of British politics, describes Blair's policies as the "final purge of socialism from the Labour party."[21] In Beer's view, Blair is far closer to the social liberal tradition of Lloyd George than the socialist tradition of Clement Attlee, Labour's leader and prime minister following World War II.

The Labour government has built on, rather than reversed, previous Conservative government policies on markets, unions, and welfare. It has continued to privatize the economy by, among other things, undertaking to shift the national postal service to the private sector. Soon after the new government was in place, Gordon Brown, chancellor of the exchequer, shifted the power to control monetary policy and interest rates from the Treasury to the Bank of England. During the 1997 campaign, the Labour

Table 8.1: Social Democratic Parties in the EU

| Country | Party | Left-Right Position[1] | |
		1984	1995
Austria	SPÖ	3.00	4.80
Belgium	PS	2.50	4.20
Belgium	SP	2.90	4.00
Denmark	S	3.80	4.20
Finland	SDEM	3.00	4.40
France	PS	2.60	4.10
Germany	SPD	3.30	3.80
Greece	PASOK	4.66	4.60
Ireland	LAB	3.60	4.10
Italy	PSI/PDS	3.10	3.50
Netherlands	PVDA	2.60	4.20
Spain	PSOE	3.60	4.00
Sweden	SD	2.90	4.10
UK	LAB	2.30	4.40

[1] Party positions are indicated on a ten-point scale from one (support for state control of the economy) to ten (support for market liberalism). *Sources*: The scores are derived from expert judgments summarized by Francis Castles and Peter Mair, "Left-Right Political Scales: Some Expert Judgements," *European Journal of Political Research* 12 (1984), pp. 73–88; and John Huber and Ronald Inglehart, "Expert Judgements of Party Space and Party Locations in 42 Societies," *Party Politics* 1 (1995), pp. 73–111.

party released a special manifesto for business which promised that a Blair government would retain the "main elements" of Margaret Thatcher's union reforms and resist unreasonable demands. Blair noted in an interview that his administration would "leave British law the most restrictive on trade unionism in the Western world."[22] The unions, he now emphasizes, must cooperate "with management to make sure British industry is competitive."

Welfare policy under the Labour government has shifted away from traditional income support to preparing economically marginal groups to participate in the labor market. While New Labour remains committed to economic equality and reducing poverty, it has ditched the notion that

benefits are unconditional. Over the past several years the party has sought ways to use welfare as part of a tougher, market-oriented, "welfare to work" approach.[23] Soon after becoming prime minister, Blair warned he would "be tough on the long-term unemployed who refuse jobs."[24] Speaking in Parliament, he declared that "for millions, the welfare state denies rather than provides opportunity."[25]

Labour's radical welfare policy has been influenced by the electoral success of such policies for Clinton Democrats in the United States. At his first meeting with President Clinton after taking office, on May 31, 1997, Blair noted that both leaders prefer "reason to doctrine" and are "indifferent to ideology." Clinton and Blair agreed that the "progressive parties of today are the parties of fiscal responsibility and prudence."[26] The two leaders called for partnership with business to create jobs, replacing the "old battles between state and market."[27] Adair Turner, the director-general of the Confederation of British Industry, has noted that while most businessmen still vote Tory, "nobody now would think it odd for a leading businessman to support the Labour party."[28]

This reorientation in doctrine has been accompanied by a fundamental change in the organization of the party. Historically, the defining characteristic of the Labour party was its basis in the union movement. In recent years, union influence in the party has been watered down. Blair has reiterated on several occasions that he wishes to go further and cut the umbilical cord between the party and the unions. In a 1994 article in *The New Statesman*, Blair stressed that "it is in the unions' best interest not to be associated merely with one political party." Unions, he argued, "should be able to thrive with any change of government or no change in government."[29] Blair has made a case against unions affiliating with a labor party not essentially different from that of Samuel Gompers, the founding president of the American Federation of Labor, before World War I.

The labor parties of Australia and New Zealand engaged in "a great experiment" when they held national office during the 1980s, the core elements of which were abandoning protectionist policies, deregulating the economy, privatizing state enterprises, and moving from centralized wage fixing through arbitration to a market system at the enterprise level.[30] Paradoxically, in both Australia and New Zealand the shift to neoliberal market principles and the dismantling of state controls took place under

labor, rather than conservative, governments. As noted above, labor parties in these countries, as in Britain, were never wedded to traditional socialist recipes of wholesale nationalization of the means of production or fundamental opposition to market capitalism.[31] Also, rightist parties in both Australia and New Zealand were in power for almost the entire period from the 1960s to the early 1980s, when the relative decline of these economies became apparent. Conservatives were implicated in the failure of orthodox economic recipes, and their electoral success denied them an extended period of opposition in which they could rethink their positions.

In Australia, successive Labor governments pursued neoliberalism incrementally. Under the prime ministership of Robert Hawke, a former union leader, the Labor government negotiated a consensual policy with interest groups and entered into a formal "accord" with the unions that reduced real wages to encourage exports. In New Zealand, the Labour government was more confrontational, following what has been described as the most Thatcherite policy among western governments, including Britain's. Prime Minister David Lange believed that economic equality conflicted with economic growth, and that the latter should have priority: "Social democrats must accept the existence of economic inequality because it is the engine which drives the economy."[32] In both countries, labor parties tried to retain support among public-sector professionals and the left intelligentsia by giving more weight to environmental protection and women's issues in policy formulation, by making a conscious effort to confront the legacy of past oppression of indigenous minorities, and, particularly in New Zealand, by opposing nuclear power and weaponry.

The Canadian New Democratic party has also shifted away from traditional socialist policies, but with less fanfare. The impetus has come mainly from the provincial level, particularly in provinces where the NDP is the first or second party. The Saskatchewan New Democrats, who in September 1999 won their third consecutive election, campaigned on their success in balancing the provincial budget, improving the provincial health system, and the promise of a tax cut. At the federal level, NDP leader Alexa McDonough nudged the party to the right in favor of policies that accommodate business interests, balanced budgets, and some tax cuts.

Like other social democratic parties that are hamstrung by fiscal pressures in weakly growing economies, labor parties in English-speaking countries tend to be most radical on nonfinancial issues. The British Labour party has created legislatures with some important powers in Scotland and Wales and is reforming the House of Lords. The NDP proposes a new electoral system based on proportional representation and reform of the prime minister's office. The Australian Labor party favors cutting ties to the British monarchy. These constitutional policies place these parties in a tradition of liberal radicalism or populism that owes little to traditional socialism.

One cannot predict the future of a political ideology such as socialism. Those who tried to predict the future of market liberalism in the 1960s believed that it was all but finished with the rise of the mixed-economy welfare state. If western economies suffer a deep recession, or if the pendulum swings much farther to the right, we may see a revival of socialist—or, more likely, neosocialist—demands for a larger economic role for government. However, it is no longer possible to say that the United States is the only western society without a socialist party, because such parties no longer exist in most western societies. American political exceptionalism, as we describe it here, has run its course.

Still Different

Traditional socialism has faded away, but the unique failure to create a viable socialist or labor party in the United States still casts its shadow on American society. The paths that lead from a critical fork in the political development of a society may never join again. The creation or absence of a viable labor/socialist party is arguably such a critical juncture.[33] What, then, are the consequences of the outcome we have sought to explain?

Viewed in the short term, a political party is an expression of some social or ideological division that becomes politically salient. In a democracy, political parties respond to issues that citizens think are important and, in some fashion (depending on the rules of the game), the electoral success of a party reflects its responsiveness to citizens' concerns. But over the longer term, it makes sense to think that political parties shape preferences. Political parties reinforce particular world views, or ideologies. Parties tie together diverse issues in coherent packages that can be more easily understood and acted upon. Parties structure political contestation in a society. There are several ways in which voters could conceive their territorial, ethnic, class, status, and gender identities. Political parties bring some sources of identity to the foreground and leave others politically dormant. Finally, political parties influence legislation, and by doing so they may leave a durable imprint on a society.

Table 8.2 provides an overview of the relative economic and political strength of the lower class in seventeen Western European and English-speaking democracies. There are sharp contrasts in the extent to which social democratic parties have controlled national government, and equally wide differences in the coverage of labor unions. The United States is at the low extreme for lower-class political power, together with Canada. In the United States, social democracy is simply absent. In Canada, the social democratic NDP has held power in several provinces, but not at the national level.[34] In terms of union organization the United States is again at the low extreme, this time alongside France. In neither France nor the United States were unions united behind a labor or socialist party. In France, unions have been divided into syndicalist (after World War I, Communist), social-ist, and Catholic camps, and in the United States, as we have seen, unions never sustained a working-class political party. However, the vast majority of workers in France are covered by collectively bargained wage contracts because agreements for unionized workers are extended to unorganized workers by law. No country in Table 8.2 has less than *twice* the American level of union coverage. Union coverage is a more accurate measure than level of union membership of the degree to which unions influence the wage levels of an economy.[35] When one compares the United States with other western democracies, the picture that emerges from these and other data is one of continued lower-class weakness—in politics and in the labor market. No other western democracy remotely approximates America in this regard. When one considers the organized power of the lower classes, American political exceptionalism is still very much alive.

Alive, yes. But is it kicking? Analysis of the programs of social democrat-ic parties reveals convergence to a market orientation and a complete dis-avowal of traditional socialist recipes for nationalization of the economy. Has the absence of a durable socialist or social democratic party in the United States made any difference for American society? Does it still? The data in Table 8.3 are suggestive in this regard. They underpin the conven-tional wisdom that the United States is remarkable for its low level of taxa-tion and government spending. In 1996 it was the only western country in

Table 8.2: Lower-Class Power

	Social democratic participation in national government, 1945–94[1]	Trade union membership, 1990[2] (percent)	Union contract coverage (percent)
Australia	18.8		80
Austria	30.5	46	71
Belgium	15.9	55	90
Canada	0	32	38
Denmark	26.9	74	
Finland	19.3	72	95
France	12.6	10	92
Germany	12.3	31	76
Ireland	4.9		
Italy	5.6	34	
Netherlands	11.1	23	60
New Zealand	16.3		67
Norway	36.9	54	75
Sweden	38.9	83	83
Switzerland	12.5		43
United Kingdom	16.2	38	47
United States	0	15	18

[1]John Stephens provided these data. Social democratic participation in coalition governments is measured as the proportion of social democratic cabinet positions in relation to total cabinet positions prorated over the fifty-year period 1945–1994.

[2]Jelle Visser, "Trends in Trade Union Membership," in OECD, *Employment Outlook* (July 1991), pp. 97–134.

which government extracted less than 30 percent of gross domestic product. One has to go outside the western world to find societies with a smaller state. In 1996, the total tax take in Japan was 0.1 percent below that of the United States, but among the remaining OECD member states only Turkey (25.4 percent), Korea (23.2 percent), and Mexico (16.3 percent) were lower. That governments in some countries with entirely different

Table 8.3: State Spending

	Total tax receipts as % of GDP[1]	Social security transfer expenditure (% GDP, 1994)[2]
Australia	31.1	12
Austria	44.0	22
Belgium	46.0	24
Canada	36.8	15
Denmark	52.2	22
Finland	48.2	25
France	45.7	23
Germany	38.1	16
Ireland	33.7	15 (1993)
Italy	43.2	20
Netherlands	43.3	26
New Zealand	35.8	15 (1991)
Norway	41.1	22 (1993)
Sweden	52.0	25
Switzerland	34.7	18
United Kingdom	36.0	15
United States	28.5	13 (1993)

[1]Data are for 1996. OECD, *Revenue Statistics, 1965–1997* (Paris: OECD, 1998). All levels of government are included.
[2]Evelyne Huber and John D. Stephens, *Political Choice in Global Markets: Development and Crisis of Advanced Welfare States* (forthcoming).

institutions, cultures, and, in most cases, levels of economic development proportionally underspend the United States reinforces, rather than blunts, the notion that America is an extreme case.

Spending on social welfare as a proportion of gross domestic product is low in the United States. This is indicated in the figures for social security transfer payments, which place the United States toward the low end with 13 percent. The major European and English-speaking countries provided

important social services long before the United States, which did not
enact pension, unemployment, or industrial accident insurance until the
1930s.[36] It is the only developed nation that does not have a government-
supported, comprehensive medical system and it is the only western
democracy that does not provide child support to all families.[37]

Table 8.4 presents data on inequality and poverty. Once again the United
States stands out. No western democracy has as unequal a distribution of
income as the United States once tax and transfer payments are included
into the calculation. The standard scale for measuring inequality, the Gini
coefficient, is almost 10 percent higher in the United States than in the next
most inegalitarian country, the United Kingdom. Economic inequality was
high in the United States relative to other western democracies in the mid-
1970s, which is the first period for which we have reliable comparative
data. From 1974 to 1979, economic inequality declined from 32.3 to 30.9,
before a sustained rise in the 1980s and 1990s to 37.5 in 1997. The time
series for the United Kingdom has a similar pattern, going from 27.0 in
1979 to 34.0 in 1991 (an unparalleled increase for a single decade in both
absolute and relative terms) to 34.6 in 1995. Data on relative poverty tell a
similar story. The United States stands out as the society with the greatest
income differentials: 11.7 percent of the population has an income less than
40 percent of the median income, a figure that is almost double that of the
next most unequal country, Australia, and almost three times the average
(4.0) for the remaining countries in Table 8.4 for which we have data. One
obvious limitation of data on relative inequality is that they do not make
allowance for the fact that some countries are richer, or even much richer,
than others. If a person has an income of less than 40 percent of the median
income in the United States, he or she may still be better off than someone
elsewhere who receives more than 40 percent of the median income of his
or her country. The last column of Table 8.4 uses median income in the
United States as a baseline for all countries. On this measure, Ireland, with a
per capita income that in 1991 was less than half that of the United States,
has a significantly larger proportion of its population (15.6 percent) under
this baseline. Given its enormous wealth, it is noteworthy that the United
States ranks second among the countries surveyed here in the proportion of
its population living in poverty.

The United States remains well ahead of other large developed countries in per capita income terms, retaining the lead over Western Europe

Table 8.4: Inequality

	Gini coefficient (after tax and transfer payments)[1]	Relative poverty (% of pop. lower than 40% median income within each country, c.1991)[2]	Absolute poverty (% of pop. lower than 30% median income in the United States)[3]
Australia	31.7 (1994)	6.4	5.6 (1989)
Belgium	23.0 (1992)	2.2	2.2 (1992)
Canada	28.6 (1994)	5.6	3.1 (1991)
Denmark	24.0 (1992)	3.5	3.4 (1992)
Finland	22.6 (1995)	2.3	1.4 (1991)
France	32.4 (1989)	4.8	4.8 (1989)
Germany	30.0 (1994)	2.4	2.1 (1989)
Ireland	33.0 (1987)	4.7	15.6 (1987)
Italy	34.6 (1985)	5.0	5.6 (1991)
Netherlands	31.0 (1994)	4.3	4.2 (1991)
Norway	24.2 (1995)	1.7	0.7 (1991)
Sweden	22.2 (1995)	3.8	3.1 (1992)
Switzerland	32.3 (1982)	4.3	2.7 (1982)
United Kingdom	34.6 (1995)	5.3	6.1 (1991)
United States	37.5 (1997)	11.7	6.6 (1991)

[1] OECD, *Income Distribution in OECD Countries*, Social Policy Studies No. 18 (Paris: OECD, 1995) Table 4.8, p. 49. Luxembourg Income Study, Web site.

[2] After tax and transfer payments. Luxembourg Income Study data base. Data presented in Lane Kenworthy, "Do Social-Welfare Policies Reduce Poverty? A Cross-National Assessment," *Social Forces* 77:3 (March 1999), 1119–1139.

[3] After tax and transfer payments. Luxembourg Income Study data base. Data presented in Kenworthy, "Do Social-Welfare Policies Reduce Poverty?"

that it has had since the second half of the nineteenth century. Incomes in the United States tend to be higher relative to other countries when the metric of comparison is purchasing power parities rather than monetary income at given exchange rates. In 1998, GDP per capita based on purchasing power parities was $30,514, which was exceeded within the OECD only by the city-state of Luxembourg ($34,538). Norway ($27,497) and Switzerland ($26,576) are the only developed countries to come close to this, with Iceland, Denmark, and Canada following.[38] As of 2000, America had the lowest rate of unemployment in the developed world, less than 5 percent, while Europe had 20 million out of work, or more than 10 percent of the labor force. In recent years there are indications that poverty rates, in relative and absolute terms, are dropping.[39] The U.S. Census Bureau reports that the poverty rate has fallen from 15.1 percent in 1993 to 13.3 in 1997.[40]

Data on poverty in the United States, as in most other societies, are tricky because they are used as a political football. Observers with different political agendas pluck very different messages even when they are looking at the same data, and often the available data sources conflict with each other. Time series for poverty are sensitive to the selection of basis year, the metric used for comparison (e.g., absolute or relative poverty), and the group that one selects (e.g., type of family, age/racial group). Observations that poverty is decreasing tend to focus either on the very recent past, i.e., beginning with the poverty peak of 1993/94, or on the comparison of real income levels over much longer periods of time. The past two decades tell a different story for most groups toward the bottom of society, particularly those under eighteen. International comparisons, however, are unambiguous. In comparative terms, the United States combines an extremely high standard of living with exceptionally low levels of taxation and social spending, and exceptionally high levels of income inequality and poverty.

The Legacy of "No Socialism in the United States"

Is there a causal link between these distinctive characteristics of American society and the inability of socialists to establish a viable social democratic party in the United States? This question, like that of the sources of American political exceptionalism, demands that one compare the United States with other countries in order to gauge the relative influence of contending causal factors.

There exists a methodologically sophisticated literature concerned with public policy outcomes in Western Europe and English-speaking democracies that does precisely this.[41] A basic finding of this literature is that variations in state effort, social policy, and economic inequality correlate with the extent to which the lower classes of a society wield political power through social democratic parties that participate in government. Closely associated with social democratic participation in government is lower-class economic power exercised through trade unions.[42] The combination of the two—social democratic participation in government and union organization—is a powerful causal cocktail. Societies in which social democratic parties have consistently played a role in national government and in which unions are strongly organized tend to have extensive welfare systems and greater economic equality.[43] While social democratic governance over the period 1945–94 bears little relation to comparative rates of economic growth, it is strongly associated with indicators of total taxes (the Pearson correlation is 0.58), social security transfer expenditure (0.51), Gini coefficients after taxes (-0.72), and relative poverty (-0.56).[44] When we examine the *combined* effect of social democratic governance and trade union membership on these variables the associations are yet stronger. The correlation between our summary indicator of "working-class power" and total taxes is 0.71; with social security transfer expenditure it is 0.56; with Gini coefficients after taxes it is -0.83; with relative poverty it is -0.61; and with absolute poverty it is -0.59.[45]

These associations do not clinch the case that lower-class power has a causal influence on political economic outcomes because additional variables, having to do, say, with a country's political institutions, its overall income level, its vulnerability to international economic pressures, or its economic structure, may help to explain both working-class power and the policy features described in Tables 8.2 to 8.4. Statistical models that control for such variables confirm the implications we have drawn from these data. This finding is robust across the many smaller disagreements among scholars concerning the exact causal weights to assign to variables, differences in statistical method, and discrepancies in how lower-class power is operationalized. Based on exhaustive statistical and case study analysis, Evelyne Huber and John Stephens summarize the basic picture: "Social democratic incumbency leads to the construction of large welfare states, with generous entitlements, a heavy emphasis on public provision of social services, on labor mobilization, and on redistribution through the tax and transfer system."[46]

Alexander Hicks begins his forthcoming book examining the effects of social democracy across western and English-speaking democracies by posing the question "Why is there so much poverty in the United States?" "The United States," observes Hicks, "has one of the highest poverty rates of the twenty or so most affluent democracies. This is true even if poverty lines are drawn to a single standard of consumption provided by the prosperous United States."[47] Hicks writes:

> The book's broadest conclusion is that political organizations and organizational politics of employees—of workers into parties and unions, or parties into governing coalitions, and of unions into participation in those centralized national labor markets often dubbed "neocorporatist"—are the most persistently powerful force operating to advance income security policy. A more refined conclusion is that labor organizations and their politics build the welfare state by exploiting—sometimes quite fortuitously, sometimes most deliberately—the political opportunities offered to them. Militant social democrats pressed anxious autocrats such as Otto von Bismarck into bidding for employee loyalties with social insurance programs. Moderate labor parties turned votes into similar concessions from Herbert Asquith to Clement Atlee. Strong labor unions have helped set the stage for centrist as well as leftist reforms throughout post–World War II Europe. The most reformist centrist governments have often seemed to advance, when their parade was noteworthy, to a social democratic drummer.[48]

The decades following World War II were an era of social democracy in Western Europe that had no parallel in the United States. Prior to the war, social spending was no weaker in the United States than in the most advanced European countries. The proportion of gross domestic product spent by the Roosevelt administration on its social policy programs (employment assurance and public employment)—6.3 percent in 1938—was greater than that in Sweden (3.2 percent), France (3.5 percent), the United Kingdom (5.0 percent), and Germany (5.6 percent).[49] But American commitment to social policy evaporated during and after World War II, at the very time that social democratic parties pushed ahead with ambitious state and welfare policies in Europe.

The absence of social democracy in the United States has not only reduced state spending as a whole, but has tilted public policy toward strongly represented groups, in particular, the upper and middle classes, business and unions, farmers, and the elderly, and away from weakly represented groups, including nonunionists, single mothers, young people, and the poor.[50] Government spending in the United States on education (5.3 percent of GDP) and on pensions for the elderly (7.2 percent of GDP) is not much below the means for all OECD countries, whereas spending on other social programs (1.2 percent of GDP), most of which goes toward less privileged groups, is less than one-quarter of the OECD mean.[51]

When one examines annual changes rather than gross levels, the effect of social democratic incumbency in government on welfare policy markedly declined from the 1980s. Over the past two decades, the only broad budgetary component for which social democratic parties have made a palpable difference is civilian nontransfer expenditure, which includes day care and parental leave spending.[52] The difference is particularly significant in Scandinavia, where social democrats have taken the lead on a variety of women's issues and have actively sought to bring women into the labor force. But in other areas of social policy, including transfer payments, health, and public pensions, all governments, irrespective of their ideological stripe, have tried to cut back to balance their budgets. The extent to which they have been able to do so depends less on which kind of party is in control than on the degree to which the constituencies that benefit from particular kinds of welfare spending are able to resist.[53] Intense fiscal pressures arising from international financial markets, unusually high levels of unemployment, and, in Europe, the efforts of governments to meet the Maastricht criteria for monetary union have constrained government spending no matter what the goals of the party in power. And, as we have detailed above, the economic goals of social democrats have converged with parties to their right.

In recent years, the causal bite of social democracy as a distinctive approach to welfare policy has diminished because governments are constrained in new and formidable ways. But this does not mean that the history of social democracy makes little difference for current policy. Studies that find that social democratic participation in government has made little difference during the 1980s and 1990s also stress that *prior* experience of social democracy remains a powerful factor explaining contemporary variations.[54] This is because institutions, once created, can shape future change.

Once a government policy is in place it is likely to be defended by those who benefit from it. A policy legacy may also shape expectations about what government is able to do. Even if a new administration wishes to abolish a policy and has the support of a large majority of the public, its efforts may be torpedoed by those who mobilize to defend the status quo. Despite talk on the part of social democrats, echoing conservatives, that taxation is too high and that government spending should be reined back, government spending has steadily increased throughout the twentieth century, and while the rate of increase slackened during the 1990s, it was not reversed. In 1913, government spending in western capitalist societies (and Japan) averaged just 8.3 percent of GDP. By 1920 it was 15.4 percent, rising to 28.5 percent in 1960. Then came two decades of massive growth in absolute and proportional terms, to 43.3 percent in 1980. In 1990, after a decade of intense effort to cut government budget deficits, government spending had increased to 46.1 percent, and by 1996 it had inched up to 47.1 percent.[55] Countries in which social democratic parties have regularly participated in national government tend to have the highest government spending, but even conservative governments such as Thatcher's and Reagan's have found it extremely difficult to reduce spending.

In this book we argue that socialists failed in the United States for cultural and institutional reasons. To what extent do factors that help explain the absence of social democracy in the United States also explain distinctive policy outcomes?

Individualism and antistatism are commensurate with low levels of state spending on social programs and greater tolerance for economic inequality. Americans are generally more opposed to government involvement in economic affairs, whether through wage and price controls, public job creation, or the length of the work week, as well as government regulation in other realms, e.g., restrictions on smoking in public places and the required use of seat belts. Only 23 percent believe it is the government's responsibility "to take care of very poor people who can't take care of themselves."[56] Americans are also much less disposed than Europeans and Canadians to believe that it should be the government's responsibility to supply a job for everyone who wants one, to provide a decent standard of living for the unemployed, and to guarantee a basic income. Table 8.5 illustrates these discrepancies, controlling for income.

As noted above, state spending is not always lower in the United States.

Table 8.5 Government's Responsibility in Different Areas

	"The government should provide a job for everyone."		"The government should provide a decent standard of living for the unemployed."		"Government should provide everyone with a guaranteed basic income."	
	Income Level		*Income Level*		*Income Level*	
	High	*Low*	*High*	*Low*	*High*	*Low*
	Level of Agreement (%)					
USA	32	61	23	52	12	33
Great Britain	44	73	57	74	47	71
West Germany	77	84	61	72	45	66
Netherlands	60	82	57	68	39	58
Italy	70	93	55	76	53	80

Source: Adapted from Karlyn H. Keene and Everett Carll Ladd, "America: A Unique Outlook?"
American Enterprise 1 (March/April 1990), p.118.

Government programs for the elderly, including above all social security, are relatively generous. The elderly are perceived to be a large and cohesive voting block that can punish elected officials who threaten their entitlements. U.S. citizens are also more disposed than Europeans to favor increased expenditures for education.[57] Spending on education is consistent with the emphasis in American culture on achievement and equality of opportunity. But when asked what form government financial assistance to college students should take, more Americans than Europeans respond through loans (by 57 to 31 percent), while Europeans are more likely to favor government grants (by 51 to 31 percent).[58] Most Americans want students to repay the government, whereas Europeans are prepared to subsidize students.

Europeans find the idea that those with higher incomes should pay larger proportions of taxes more acceptable than do Americans. Interviewed in the late 1980s, overwhelming majorities—90 percent of West Germans, 86 percent of Italians, and 76 percent of Britons—believed in levying higher taxes on the rich to produce greater income equality, whereas 58 percent of Americans supported such a policy.[59] Only 28 percent of Americans support government action reducing income discrepancies. In Europe, by contrast, favorable response to such action ranges from 42 percent in Austria to 82 percent in Italy.[60] The British fall in the middle at 63 percent.

Americans are more likely than Europeans to agree that "large income differences are needed for the country's prosperity." Nearly one-third of Americans surveyed justify inequality this way as compared to an average of 23 percent for seven European countries (Great Britain, Austria, West Germany, Italy, Hungary, Switzerland, and the Netherlands).[61] A review of American public opinion data over fifty years reports: "Surveys since the 1930s have shown that the explicit idea of income redistribution elicits very limited enthusiasm among the American public. . . . Redistributive fervor was not much apparent even in [the] depression era. Most Americans appear content with the distributional effects of private markets."[62]

The 1930s led to a kind of Europeanization of American politics.[63] Conservatives, increasingly concentrated in the Republican party, remained antistatist and pro-laissez-faire, although many of them became willing to accommodate a more activist role for the state. Those on the left and center of the Democratic party more and more resembled Europe's social democrats.[64] These patterns, however, gradually declined after World War II as a result of long-term prosperity, which helped to produce a return to earlier values. A consequence of these developments has been a refurbishing of American libertarian conservatism. The class tensions produced by the Great Depression lessened, reflected in a great decline in union membership after the mid-1950s and lower correlations between class position and vote choices. Even before Ronald Reagan entered the White House, the United States had a lower rate of taxation, a less developed welfare state, and less government ownership of industry than other western democracies.

Alongside class power and cultural explanations, a third line of explanation for U.S. public policy is that distinctive features of the American polity, in particular the separation of powers and the fragmentation of authority under federalism, have limited the role of the state in the economy.[65] The general argument here is that the greater the number of veto points (e.g., in the courts, in the legislative process, and in relations between the federal executive and individual regions or states) the greater the opportunity for those opposed to block a particular legislative initiative.[66] The more fragmented authority is in a polity, the more difficult it is to enact reform in any direction. This logic suggests that parliamentary systems, in which disciplined political parties insulate the government from interest group pressures, are more amenable to social welfare or free market reform than presidential systems like that of the United States, which have weak parties and strong independent legislatures.

Two comparative historical studies of health insurance politics confirm this line of argument. Ellen Immergut relates the sharp contrast between policy stasis in Switzerland and extensive reform in Sweden to how different political institutions insulate or weaken governments in the face of societal pressures. In Switzerland, referenda and the diffusion of authority in the executive and the legislature render government prone to societal pressures. In Sweden, by contrast, disciplined parties assure the executive of majority legislative support for its proposals and limit the influence of interest groups over proposals once they enter the legislative process. In her comparison of health insurance politics in the United States and Canada, Antonia Maioni finds that the Canadian Medical Association has far less influence than the American Medical Association because it cannot target individual legislators.[67] If it is to exert leverage, an interest group in Canada must target the federal party as a whole. This is a much more difficult proposition than lobbying individual legislators in Congress, who are themselves responsible for raising the large sums of money necessary to fight election campaigns. The institutional hypothesis that dispersion of authority is a serious obstacle in constructing a generous welfare state is confirmed by Stephens and Huber in their quantitative analysis of the determinants of welfare.[68]

Clearly, many factors are responsible for the low level of state spending, weak commitment to social policy, and high economic inequality in the United States. These distinctive characteristics of public policy are commensurate both with American culture and with American political institutions, in particular, the diffusion of authority (checks and balances) in the U.S. polity. Moreover, as we have argued at length in previous chapters, American culture and political institutions are important sources of the failure to create a socialist or labor party. However, in seeking to untangle the causal connections between culture, political institutions, and political power, we find ample evidence that the organizational strength of the lower class of a society is decisive in determining the relative life chances of poorer people. This stands to reason in a liberal democracy. Lacking financial resources or economic power, those toward the bottom of a society must rely on political power if they are to influence the laws of their society. Liberal democracy opens the prospect that every individual, no matter how rich, has equal influence in electing rulers. But organization is decisive in framing alternatives. Democratic politics is like a tug-of-war determined by party representation and interest group power. The strategy of political struggle varies, of course, in response to differences in the rules of the game. The respective roles of interest groups, political parties, and government bureaucracies differ systematically from country to country. But every democracy allocates scarce resources in favor of those who have economic or political power, and those who have little of either are unheard or, if they are heard, ignored.

Conclusion

The legacy of the failure of socialism in the United States still shapes the present. But as social democratic parties the world over shift away from their traditional moorings toward the free market, one may expect the political gap between the United States and other western democracies to gradually narrow. An alternative view is that institutional legacies and values continue to shape a country's response to external events, which raises the possibility that different legacies may give rise to a continuing, systematic, or even widening, process of differentiation.

There are signs, however, that the influence of social democracy as a distinct approach to policy is not exhausted. The seemingly universal shift to support for capitalism and the free market may be of short duration. Strong advocates of such systems, including Joseph Schumpeter from the 1930s and Irving Kristol from the 1970s, have noted that they do not advance the same pretensions to solve major human problems that socialism and communism once did. Capitalism, the free market, is not a utopia even when limited to economic considerations. At best it holds out the promise of a lottery, but like all such awards, the jackpots go to a relatively small minority of players. Hence there must be many losers, some of whom will be receptive to reformist or antisystem movements. The distribution of rewards under capitalism is necessarily greatly unequal, and as Tocqueville pointed out a century and a half ago, the idea of equality presses the underprivileged to support redistributionist policies.

At the center of free market ideology is an emphasis on self-interest—in invidious terms, on greed. The argument has been put forth from Adam Smith to Milton Friedman that the uninhibited pursuit of personal or institutional gain results in a growing economy which benefits all, regardless of status or wealth. But, as we know, not only do some individuals fail to benefit, but countries differ enormously in economic performance. And the business cycle, which seems inherent in market economies, not only fosters growth, it leads to downswings—periods of economic recession and increased unemployment.

Moreover, capitalism, which, unlike socialism, does not promise to eliminate poverty, racism, sexism, pollution, or war, appeals only weakly to the idealism inherent in the position of young people and intellectuals. As Aristotle emphasized 2,500 years ago, the young look for inspiring solutions. Hence, new movements, new ideologies, and even old ones that hold out reformist and utopian promises will appear and reappear. Economic downswings may reinforce communitarian efforts to relegitimate the state's role in reducing, if not eliminating, social, sexual, and racial—even more than economic—inequalities. To these may be added environmental concerns. Not surprisingly, such issues have begun to take priority among left-wing parties, both old (i.e., social democratic) and new (i.e., Green) parties. Classic free market liberals resist such policies because they require state interference with the market.

It is noteworthy, in this regard, that the United States once more stands out politically among western democracies in that it lacks even a minimally effective Green party. Green parties are represented in national parliaments and/or the European parliament in every one of the thirteen richer countries that are members of the European Union.[69] In 1999, they participated in ruling government coalitions in Belgium, Finland, France, Germany, and Italy (in Sweden the Greens support but do not participate in the government).

The struggle between the left, the advocates of change, and the right, the defenders of the status quo, is not over. In the once Communist-dominated countries, the terms *left* and *liberal* have been used to describe free market and democratic tendencies that seek to reduce the power of state bureaucracies; the terms *right* and *conservative* usually refer to groups that defend state controls. Ironically, this is the way these concepts were first used during the nineteenth century. In the West, following the rise of socialist movements, left came to mean greater emphasis on communitarianism and equality, on the state as an instrument of reform. The right, linked to defensive establishments, has, particularly since World War II, been identified with opposition to government intervention. The rise of Green parties in Western Europe is merely one indication that the contest between these two orientations has not ended. The United States, without a viable Green party, appears as different from Western Europe as ever.

NOTES

1. An Exceptional Nation

1. Alexis de Tocqueville, *Democracy in America*, vol. 2 (New York: Alfred A. Knopf, 1948), pp. 36–37; Engels to Weydemeyer, August 7, 1851, in Karl Marx and Friedrich Engels, *Letters to Americans, 1848–1895* (New York: International Publishers, 1953), pp. 25–26. For evidence of the continued validity and applicability of the concept see Seymour Martin Lipset, *American Exceptionalism: A Double-Edged Sword* (New York: W. W. Norton, 1996), esp., pp. 32–35, 77–109. On American cultural exceptionalism, see Deborah L. Madsen, *American Exceptionalism* (Jackson: University Press of Mississippi, 1998).

2. See Seymour Martin Lipset, "Why No Socialism in the United States?" in S. Bailer and S. Sluzar, eds., *Sources of Contemporary Radicalism*, I (Boulder, Colo.: Westview Press, 1977), pp. 64–66, 105–108. See also Theodore Draper, *The Roots of American Communism* (Chicago: Ivan R. Dee, 1989), pp. 247–248, 256–266; Draper, *American Communism and Soviet Russia: The Formative Period* (New York: Viking Press, 1960), pp. 269–272, 284.

3. Richard Flacks, *Making History: The Radical Tradition in American Life* (New York: Columbia University Press, 1988), pp. 104–105. See also Kim Voss, *The Making of American Exceptionalism: The Knights of Labor and Class Formation in the Nineteenth Century* (Ithaca, N.Y.: Cornell University Press, 1993). For other efforts

to deal with "socialist exceptionalism," see also Robert J. Fitrakis, *The Idea of Democratic Socialism in America and the Decline of the Socialist Party* (New York: Garland Publishers, 1993); Mike Davis, *Prisoners of the American Dream: Politics and Economy in the History of the U.S. Working Class* (New York: Verso, 1988), pp. 3–51; Rick Halpern and Johnathan Morris, eds. *American Exceptionalism: U. S. Working-Class Formation in an International Context* (New York: St. Martin's Press, 1997; and Brian Lloyd, *Left Out: Pragmatism, Exceptionalism, and the Poverty of American Marxism, 1890–1922* (Baltimore: Johns Hopkins University Press, 1997).

4. See "Unpublished Letters of Karl Marx and Friedrich Engels to Americans," ed. and trans. Leonard E. Mins, *Science and Society* 2 (1938), pp. 368, 375; Engels to Sorge, January 6, 1892, *Letters to Americans*, p. 239; Engels to Sorge, November 29, 1886, Karl Marx and Fredrich Engels, *Selected Correspondence, 1846–1895* (New York: International Publishers, 1942), p. 449.

5. Werner Sombart, *Why Is There No Socialism in the United States?* (White Plains, N.Y.: International Arts & Sciences Press, 1976) first published in German in 1906; H. G. Wells, *The Future in America* (New York: Harper & Bros., 1906); Karl Marx, *Capital* I (Moscow: Foreign Languages Publishing House, 1958), pp. 8–9.

6. Alexis de Tocqueville, *Democracy in America*, vol. 2 (New York: Alfred A. Knopf, 1948), pp. 36–37.

7. For elaboration of these points, see Seymour Martin Lipset, *The First New Nation: The United States in Historical and Comparative Perspective* (New York: Basic Books, 1963; expanded ed., New York: W. W. Norton, 1979); and Lipset, *American Exceptionalism*. Also relevant is Michael Harrington, *Socialism* (New York: Saturday Review Press, 1970), pp. 111–118.

8. Howard H. Quint, *The Forging of American Socialism: Origins of the Modern Movement* (Indianapolis: Bobbs-Merrill, 1953), p. 380.

9. Sombart, *Why Is There No Socialism*, p. 15. See also Daniel Bell, *Marxian Socialism in the United States* (Ithaca, N.Y.: Cornell University Press, 1996).

10. Cited in R. Laurence Moore, *European Socialists and the American Promised Land* (New York: Oxford University Press, 1970), p. 70.

11. *Ibid.*, pp. 58, 102.

12. *Ibid.*, p. 77.

13. *Ibid.*, pp. 78–79.

14. *Ibid.*, p. 91.

15. Daniel De Leon, *Flashlights of the Amsterdam Congress* (New York: New York Labor News Co., 1904), p. 133.

16. Quoted in James D. Young, "Daniel De Leon and Anglo-American Socialism," *Labor History* 17 (Summer 1976), p. 344.

17. Quint, *Forging*, p. 380.

18. Max Beer, *Fifty Years of International Socialism* (London: George Allen & Unwin, 1935), pp. 109–110.

19. Leon Trotsky, *The Living Thoughts of Karl Marx* (New York: Longmans, Green, 1939), pp. 38–39.

20. Howard Kimeldorf, *Reds or Rackets? The Making of Radical and Conservative Unions on the Waterfront* (Berkeley: University of California Press, 1988), p. 1.

21. Harvey Klehr, "The Theory of American Exceptionalism" (Ph.D. thesis, Department of History, University of North Carolina, Chapel Hill, 1971). The full discussion of Fraina-Corey is on pp. 126–130.

22. Seymour Martin Lipset, "North American Labor Movements: A Comparative Perspective," in Seymour Martin Lipset, ed., *Unions in Transition: Entering the Second Century* (San Francisco: Institute for Contemporary Studies Press, 1986), pp. 421–471; Thomas S. Axworthy, "Left Turn in Canada?" *Public Opinion* 10 (September/October 1987), pp. 52–54; Seymour Martin Lipset, "American Values and the Market System," in Thomas R. Dye, ed., *The Political Legitimacy of Markets and Governments* (Greenwich, Conn.: JAI Press, 1990), pp. 107–121; Lipset, *American Exceptionalism*, pp. 77–109.

23. For a detailed analysis of the differences and similarities between the United States and Canada, see Seymour Martin Lipset, *Continental Divide: The Values and Institutions of the United States and Canada* (New York: Routledge, 1990).

24. On Marx's views, see Lewis S. Feuer, *Marx and the Intellectuals* (Garden City, N.Y.: Doubleday/Anchor Books, 1969), pp. 198–209. On the Workingmen's parties, see Helen Sumner, "Citizenship (1827–1833)," in John R. Commons et al., *History of Labor in the United States*, vol. 1 (New York: Macmillan, 1926), pp. 169–332; Nathan Fine, *Labor and Farmer Parties in the United States, 1828–1928* (New York: Rand School of Social Sciences, 1928), pp. 13–14; Edward Pessen, *Most Uncommon Jacksonians* (Albany: State University of New York Press, 1967), pp. 183–189; and Walter Hugins, *Jacksonian Democracy and the Working Class* (Stanford, Calif.: Stanford University Press, 1960), pp. 13, 18–20, 132–134.

25. Thomas Hamilton, *Men and Manners in America* (Edinburgh and London: William Blackwood & T. Cadell, 1833). See Feuer, *Marx and the Intellectuals*, pp. 198–209; Maximilian Rubel, "Notes on Marx's Conception of Democracy," *New Politics* 1 (Winter 1962), pp. 83–85.

26. "Republican Education," in Walter Hugins, ed., *The Reform Impulse, 1828–1850* (Columbia: University of South Carolina Press, 1972), pp. 135–139.

27. William Appleman Williams, *The Contours of American History* (Cleveland: World Publishing Co., 1961), p. 238; Edward Pessen, "The Workingmen's Movement of the Jackson Era," *Mississippi Valley Historical Review* 43 (December 1956), p. 434.

28. Pessen, "The Workingmen's Party Revisited," *Labor History* 4 (1963), p. 225.

29. "Republican Education," p. 135.

30. Karl Marx and Friedrich Engels, *The German Ideology* (New York: International Publishers, 1960), p. 123.

31. Engels to Sorge, February 8, 1890, in *Selected Correspondance*, p. 467.

32. Engels to Sorge, December 31, 1892, in *Ibid.*, p. 501.

33. Max Weber, *The Protestant Ethic and the Spirit of Capitalism* (New York: Scribner's, 1935; first published in German), pp. 55–56.

34. Antonio Gramsci, *Selections from the Prison Notebooks* (New York: International Publishers, 1971), pp. 21–22, 272, 318.

35. Weber, *Protestant Ethic*, pp. 155–183; and Weber, "The Protestant Sects and the Spirit of Capitalism," in *Essays in Sociology*, trans. Hans Gerth and C. W. Mills (New York: Oxford University Press, 1946), pp. 309, 313.

36. Gramsci, "Americanism and Fordism," in *Selections from the Prison Notebooks*, p. 305. See also pp. 281, 285.

37. David DeLeon, *The American as Anarchist: Reflections on Indigenous Radicalism* (Baltimore: John Hopkins University Press, 1978), p. 4. See also pp. 32–34.

38. William M. Dick, *Labor and Socialism in America: The Gompers Era* (Port Washington, N.Y.: Kennikat Press, 1972), pp. 183–184, 116; Melvyn Dubofsky, *We Shall Be All: A History of the Industrial Workers of the World* (Chicago: Quadrangle Books, 1969).

39. Bell, *Marxian Socialism*, pp. 118–120, 160–162; Davis, *Prisoners of the American Dream*, p. 15.

40. Richard Flacks, "Reflections on Strategy in a Dark Time," *Boston Review* 20 (December–January 1995–1996), p. 25.

41. Charles Derber, *What's Left? Radical Politics in the Post-Communist Era* (Amherst: University of Massachusetts Press, 1995), pp. 140–161.

42. William Appleman Williams, *The Great Evasion* (Chicago: Quadrangle Books, 1964), p. 155.

43. C. Wright Mills, *White Collar* (New York: Oxford University Press, 1951), p. 10.

44. Irving Howe, *Socialism and America* (San Diego: Harcourt Brace Jovanovich, 1985), p. 136.

45. "Engels to Weydemeyer," August 7, 1851, in *Letters to Americans*, p. 26.

46. Marx, *Capital* I, pp. 769–770.

47. *Ibid.*, p. 777. Harvey Klehr has pointed out that elsewhere in *Capital*, "Marx maintained that needs were culturally determined, so that the wages paid to workers would vary from area to area, depending on historical factors. Unlike the price of other commodities, the price of labor-power had a historical component." Klehr also notes that Marx's discussion of the relevance of such factors "suggests that American wages might always remain higher and satisfy more needs than those paid in Europe." Harvey Klehr, "Marxist Theory in Search of America," *Journal of Politics* 35 (May 1973), p. 319.

48. Engels to Sorge, October 24, 1891, in *Letters to Americans*, p. 237.

49. Engels to Sorge, December 2, 1893, "Unpublished Letters," p. 375.

50. Karl Marx, "The Eighteenth Brumaire of Louis Bonaparte," in *Selected Works*, vol. 2 (Moscow: Cooperative Publishing Society of Foreign Workers in the USSR, 1936), p. 324. See also Bell, *Marxian Socialism*, pp. 3–16.

51. Engels to Florence Kelley Wischnewetsky, June 3, 1886, in *Selected Correspondance*, p. 449.

52. Translated by Michael Harrington in *Socialism*, p. 115.

53. Quoted in Gerald Friedberg, "Comment," in John H. M. Laslett and Seymour Martin Lipset, eds., *Failure of a Dream? Essays in the History of American Socialism* (Garden City, N.Y.: Doubleday/Anchor Books, 1974), p. 351.

54. Sombart, *Why Is There No Socialism*.

55. *Ibid.*, pp. 97, 109–117.

56. David Hecht, "Plekhanov and American Socialism," *Russian Review* 9 (April 1950), pp. 114, 118–121.

57. Wells, *Future in America*, pp. 105–106.

58. Leon Trotsky, *My Life* (New York: Pathfinder Press, 1970), p. 271.

59. Peter R. Shergold, "Reefs of Roast Beef: The American Worker's Standard of Living in a Comparative Perspective," in Dirk Hoerder, ed., *American Labor and Immigration History, 1877–1920s* (Chicago: University of Illinois, 1983), pp. 95–101. Indeed, Shergold concludes that unskilled workers were better off in Birmingham than in Pittsburgh.

60. Harrington, *Socialism*, pp. 130–131.

61. Flacks, *Making History*, p. 216. See also Lee M. Wolfle, "Socialist Voting Among Coal Miners, 1900–1940," *Sociological Focus* 16 (January 1983), pp. 37–47.

62. Robert W. Smuts, *European Impressions of the American Worker* (New York: King's Crown Press, 1953), pp. 26–27.

63. Wells, *Future in America*, pp. 72–76.

64. See Davis, *Prisoners of the American Dream*, pp. 21–29, for an analysis of their effect on class organizations.

65. Marx to Siegfrid Meyer and August Vogt, April 9, 1870, in Karl Marx, *On the First International*, ed. and trans. Saul K. Padover, *The Karl Marx Library*, vol. 3 (New York: McGraw-Hill, 1973), pp. 499–500 (emphasis in original).

66. Engels to Schlüter, March 30, 1892 in *Selected Correspondence*, pp. 496–497.

67. Quoted in Michael Kazin, "The Right's Unsung Prophet," *Nation* 248 (February 20, 1989), p. 242.

68. Michael Ignatieff, *Blood and Belonging* (London: BBC Books, 1993), p. 7.

69. Flacks, *Making History*, p. 99. Flacks describes Americanism as a "new vision," but goes on to stress the importance of the ideological components of that vision.

70. Lipset, *American Exceptionalism*, p. 18–19, 288–292.

71. Hermann Keyserling, *America Set Free* (New York: Harper & Bros., 1929), pp. 237–240, 251–252; Leon Samson, *Toward a United Front* (New York: Farrar and

Rinehart, 1935), pp. 16–17. For an earlier discussion of Samson, see Lipset, "Why No Socialism in the United States?" pp. 75–77; and Seymour Martin Lipset, *The First New Nation: The United States in Historical and Comparative Perspective* (New York: W. W. Norton, 1979), pp. 393–394.

72. Samson, *Toward a United Front*, pp. 16–17 (emphasis in original).

73. Gramsci, "State and Civil Society" and "Americanism and Fordism," in *Selections from the Prison Notebooks*, pp. 272, 318.

74. *Ibid.*

75. Louis Hartz, *The Liberal Tradition in America* (New York: Harcourt, Brace & World, 1955), p. 28.

76. Morris Hillquit, *Socialism in Theory and Practice* (New York: Macmillan, 1909), pp. 162–165.

77. V. I. Lenin, "Preface to the Russian Translation of 'Letters by J. Ph. Becker, J. Dietzgen, F. Engels, K. Marx and Others to F. A. Sorge and Others,' " in V. I. Lenin, *On Britain* (Moscow: Foreign Languages Publishing House, n.d.), p. 51.

78. Engels to Sorge, November 29, 1886, in *Letters to Americans*, p. 163.

79. Engels to Florence Kelley Wischnewetsky, December 28, 1886, *Selected Correspondence*, pp. 453–454.

80. *Socialist Review* 2 (1908), p. 566.

81. J. Keir Hardie, "Socialism in America," *Socialist Review* 3 (1909), p. 94.

82. Bell, *Marxian Socialism in the United States*, pp. 9–10.

83. Harrington, *Socialism*, p. 122. See also Bell, *Marxian Socialism*. Bell argues that the American Socialist party's continual refusal to compromise its principles destroyed its chances of influence.

84. Engels to Sorge, June 29, 1883, "Unpublished Letters," p. 231.

85. Quoted in Sidney Hook, *Marx and the Marxists* (New York: D. Van Nostrand, 1955), p. 64.

86. Engels to Sorge, November 29, 1886, *Selected Correspondance*, pp. 449–450.

87. Engels to Sorge, May 12, 1894, in *Letters to Americans*, p. 263.

88. V. I. Lenin, "Preface to the Russian Translation," p. 51.

89. Moore, *European Socialists*, pp. 205–206. See also Howard Kimeldorf and Judith Stepan Norris, "Historical Studies of Labor Movements in the United States," *Annual Review of Sociology* 18 (1992), pp. 495–517.

90. Engels to Sorge, September 16, 1886, "Unpublished Letters," p. 358.

91. Karl Marx, "On the Jewish Question," in Karl Marx and Friedrich Engels, *Collected Works*, vol. 3 (London: Lawrence & Wishart, 1975), p. 151 (emphasis in original).

92. Moore, *European Socialists*, p. 110.

93. V. I. Lenin, *Capitalism and Agriculture in the United States of America* (New York: International Publishers, 1934), p. 1.

94. Lenin, "Preface to the Russian Translation," p. 61.

95. Morris Hillquit, *History of Socialism in the United States* (New York: Funk & Wagnalls, 1910), p. 358.

96. *Ibid.*, pp. 139–140.

97. Beer, *Fifty Years*, p. 113.

98. Sombart, *Why Is There No Socialism*, pp. 50–51.

99. Hillquit, *History of Socialism*, p. 349.

100. Yehoshua Arieli, *Individualism and Nationalism in American Ideology* (Cambridge, Mass.: Harvard University Press, 1946), pp. 238–239.

101. Hillquit, *History of Socialism*, pp. 359–360.

102. Engels to Sorge, December 2, 1893, "Unpublished Letters," p. 374 (emphasis in original).

103. Friedrich Engels, "The Conditions of England," in *Collected Works*, vol. 3, p. 446.

104. Engels to Sorge, January 6, 1892, *Letters to Americans*, p. 239 (emphasis in original).

105. Sombart, *Why Is There No Socialism*, pp. 12–13.

106. John R. Commons, "American Labor History, Introduction," in John R. Commons et al., *History of Labor in the United States*, vol. I (Newark: Macmillan, 1926), p. 3.

107. *Ibid.*, p. 5.

108. Selig Perlman, *A Theory of the Labor Movement* (New York: Macmillan, 1928), pp. 167–168. For a more recent statement by a labor historian see David Montgomery, *Beyond Equality: Labor and the Radical Republicans, 1862–1872* (Urbana: University of Illinois Press, 1981).

109. Perlman, *A Theory of the Labor Movement*, pp. 171–173.

110. *Ibid.*, p. 202.

111. *Ibid.*, p. 113.

112. *Ibid.*, p. 164.

113. Commons, "Class Conflict," pp. 761–762.

114. Perlman, *A Theory*, pp. 165–166.

115. *Ibid.*, pp. 168–169.

116. Richard Hofstadter, *The Age of Reform: From Bryan to F.D.R.* (New York: Alfred A. Knopf, 1972), p. 308.

117. Samuel Lubell, *The Future of American Politics*, 3rd ed. (New York: Harper & Row, 1965), pp. 55–68.

118. Richard Rose, "How Exceptional Is American Government?" *Studies in Public Policy* 150 (Glasgow: Centre for the Study of Public Policy, University of Strathclyde, 1985).

119. Nathan Glazer, "Welfare and 'Welfare' in America," in Richard Rose and Rei Shiratori, eds., *The Welfare State East and West* (New York: Oxford University Press, 1986), p. 62.

120. Flacks, *Making History*, p. 115 (emphasis in original).

121. Quoted in Moore, *European Socialists*, p. 114.

122. Sombart, *Why Is There No Socialism*, p. 16.

123. Quoted in Moore, *European Socialists*, p. 106.

2. The American Party System

1. See Walter Dean Burnham, "The United States: The Politics of Heterogeneity," in Richard Rose, ed., *Electoral Behavior: A Comparative Handbook* (New York: Free Press, 1974), Table 3, pp. 718–719. Under national elections we include both presidential elections and off-year congressional elections aggregated to the national level.

2. The one exception to this, the replacement of the Whigs by the Republican party, resulted because the Whigs split over the slavery issue, and their northern cohorts, together with third-party abolitionists and Free-Soilers, reassembled under a new label.

3. Theodore Roosevelt secured 27 percent in 1912, but this resulted from a split in the Republican party.

4. Maurice Duverger, *Political Parties: Their Organization and Activity in the Modern State*, trans. Barbara North and Robert North (London: Methuen, 1954), p. 217. See also Douglas W. Rae, *The Political Consequences of Electoral Laws* (New Haven: Yale University Press, 1967), ch. 5; and Gary W. Cox, *Making Votes Count: Strategic Coordination in the World's Electoral Systems* (Cambridge: Cambridge University Press, 1997). Arendt Lijphart, "The Political Consequences of Electoral Laws, 1945–85," *American Political Science Review* 84 (June 1990), pp. 481–496, confirms the association between the plurality electoral system and the two-party system. Over the period 1945–1985 the plurality systems of the United States, Canada, New Zealand, and Great Britain had an average of 2.5 parties competing in elections (the number represented in legislatures would be even closer to two), contrasted to a little over four for proportional representation (PR) systems.

5. The implications of the existing plurality electoral system can be gauged by imagining what might happen under a proportional system if a party's legislative representation mirrors its share of the vote. Under a proportional system the two major parties might easily be replaced by a variety of smaller, more clearly defined parties representing farmers, trade unionists, southern racists, conservatives, liberals, and socialists. Democratic House Speaker Tip O'Neill once commented that under proportional representation, his party would probably split five ways.

6. La Guardia was elected to Congress in 1924 on the Socialist ticket, though he sat as a Republican.

7. In Australia, a simple plurality electoral system was replaced by the alternative vote system in 1918.

8. In the seven interwar elections the Labour party received an average 33.5 percent of the vote and 23.8 percent of the seats, or the equivalent of over 70 percent of the seats it would have received under a perfectly proportional system of representation.

9. Paul Moller, *Politisk handbog; en samling konkrete oplysninger,* data reproduced in Thomas T. Mackie and Richard Rose, *The International Almanac of Electoral History* (New York: Free Press, 1974), p. 88.

10. In the four elections it fought, the Canadian Labor party received an average of 0.9 percent of the seats on the basis of 1.6 percent of the vote.

11. The electoral system was majoritarian within single member constituencies. If no party gained an absolute majority in the first ballot, the two leading parties would compete in a second ballot. To take two pre–World War I elections: in 1871, the Social Democratic party received 3.2 percent of the vote and 0.5 percent of Reichstag seats and in 1907 the party received 29.0 percent of the vote and 10.8 percent of Reichstag seats.

12. The French presidential electoral system, in place since 1962, allows small parties to gather votes in the first round and trade support to the larger parties or candidates for the final round.

13. While, logically, two parties could agree to share the presidency and vice-presidency, this has never happened—probably because the positions are highly unequal.

14. Of course, these were constituencies, mainly in Milwaukee, where the Socialists were strongest. But if the party were to receive just 1 to 2 percent of the vote in the remaining constituencies, it would have exceeded Debs' total Wisconsin vote. As the state in which the Socialists were strongest in the period as a whole, Wisconsin is an interesting case, but in the absence of corroborating data from other states it must be considered an illustrative one.

15. Absolute levels of Socialist voting in each of these elections were, of course, influenced by numerous factors that cannot be dealt with here. By comparing consecutive elections, we control for differences across presidential and midterm elections.

16. Socialist performance in the years 1900 and 1902 was much poorer than in subsequent years. When we exclude the first case, namely 1900, 1902, and 1904, for each district, the average difference increases to 6.4 percentage points.

17. Cited in Ray Ginger, *Eugene V. Debs: A Biography* (New York: Collier Books, 1962), p. 294.

18. Norman Thomas, *Socialism Re-examined* (New York: W. W. Norton, 1963), p. 118.

19. Jews tended to be anti–czarist Russia and Germans pro-Germany.

20. Daniel Bell, *Marxian Socialism in the United States* (Ithaca, N.Y.: Cornell University Press, 1996), p. 120.

21. See, for example, Adolph Strasser's contribution to the debate over the formation of a labor party in *A Verbatim Report of the Discussion on the Political Program at the Denver Convention of the American Federation of Labor*, December 14–15, 1894, pp. 19–20.

22. Selig Perlman, *A Theory of the Labor Movement* (New York: Macmillan, 1928), pp. 169–171.

23. Sidney Webb and Beatrice Webb, *Industrial Democracy*, vol. 1 (London: Longmans, Green, 1897), p. 255.

24. *Report of Proceedings of the Thirty-second Trades Union Congress*, 1899, p. 63.

25. Victoria C. Hattam, *Labor Visions and State Power: The Origins of Business Unionism in the United States* (Princeton, N.J.: Princeton University Press, 1993), p. ix.

26. Melvyn Dubofsky, *Industrialism and the American Worker 1865–1920* (Arlington Heights, Ill.: AHM Publishing Corp., 1975), ch. 3.

27. Hattam's evidence for the hypothesis that the American Federation of Labor turned away from its legislative agenda because of resistance from the courts is based on an exhaustive compilation of statements to this effect by labor leaders. However, leaders of the AFL in their speeches and writings referred to a variety of reasons for their support of business unionism, including fear of political divisions among workers, their belief that legislation of working conditions would weaken unions as organizations, and their generalized antistatist orientations.

The most striking reference to the courts in Hattam's account is the chapter in Samuel Gompers' autobiography in which he describes his early years in the New York Cigar Makers' Local 144 and the lessons he learned about the difficulty of legislating working conditions (and the relative advantage of collective bargaining) when hard-won legislation prohibiting tenement cigar production was blocked by the New York Court of Appeals in 1884. But Gompers related several reasons for his voluntarist convictions, one of which was his perception of perfidy among socialists, a lesson which was also drawn from the tenement legislation episode (see Samuel Gompers, *Seventy Years of Life and Labor: An Autobiography* [New York: Dutton, 1925], vol. 1, p. 191), and another of which was his growing disbelief in the value of party-political activity, revealed tellingly in his disappointment with Henry George's 1888 campaign for mayor of New York; see Gerald N. Grob, *Workers and Utopia: A Study of the Ideological Conflict in the American Labor Movement, 1865–1900* (Chicago: Quadrangle Books, 1969), p. 164–165. In his toughest battles with those who wished to pursue a partisan political strategy, Gompers focused far more on its divisive effects than on the role of courts in making such a strategy impractical. For example, in 1894, addressing the only convention of the American Federation of Labor in which he was turned out of the office of president of the organization, Gompers related a series of legislative initiatives taken by the AFL on immigration, government ownership, seamen's working conditions, a presidential commission on industry, and an eight-hour day for women and children, but criticized heavily the political program for independent labor representation on the grounds that "if our organization is committed to it, [this] will unquestionably prevent many sterling national trade unions from joining our ranks to do battle with us to attain first things first. . . . During the past year the trade unions in many localities plunged into the political arena by nominating their candidates for public office, and sad as it may be to record, it is nevertheless true that in each one of these localities politically they were defeated and the trade union movement more or less divided and disrupted." *Report of Proceedings of the Fourteenth Annual Convention of the American Federation of Labor,* 1894, p. 14. In explaining the general orientation of the American labor movement before the U.S. Commission on Industrial Relations in 1914 (published as two articles in the *American Federationist* 7 [July 1914], pp. 537–548; 8 [August 1914], pp. 621–635), Gompers made a brief plea for restricting the power of judges to nullify laws, but returned time and time again to the theme of union and worker autonomy from the state in defending business unionism.

28. Theodore J. Lowi, "Why Is There No Socialism in the United States? A Federal Analysis," in Jean Heffer and Jeanine Rovet, eds., *Why Is There No Socialism in the United States?* (Paris: L'École des Hautes Études en Sciences Sociales, 1987), pp. 39, 40, 82.

29. The Australian Labor party was more reformist, more closely tied to labor unions, and in its early years more racist than the American Socialist party, while the Canadian Cooperative Commonwealth Federation was more agrarian in orientation. However, it is difficult to see how such differences can save the federalism thesis. The argument that the American Socialist party failed because it was too radical (a hypothesis taken up in Chapter 5) raises a different set of issues. We do not need an explanation couched in American exceptionalism to explain the failure of Marxian socialism across western society.

30. For example, Dennis J. Murphy, ed., *Labor in Politics: The State Labor Parties in Australia 1880–1920* (St. Lucia: University of Queensland Press, 1975); and P. Loveday, A.W. Martin, and R. S. Parker, eds., *The Emergence of the Australian Party System* (Sydney: Hale & Iremonger, 1977).

31. Seymour Martin Lipset, *Political Man: The Social Basis of Politics,* 2nd ed. (Baltimore: Johns Hopkins University Press, 1982), pp. 76, 199–200, 214–215, 265–266.

32. In the United States, left third parties backed by socialists won office in Minnesota and Wisconsin, but then had to make a presidential choice in national elections, as Canadian parties did not.

33. Frank Farrell, "Socialism, Internationalism, and the Australian Labour Movement," *Labour/Le Travail* 15 (Spring 1985), p. 126.

34. *Ibid.,* p. 127.

35. Jürg Steiner, *Gewaltlose Politik und kulturelle Vielfalt* (Bern: Verlag Paul Haupt, 1970), p. 38.

36. Erwin Bucher, "Historische Grundlegung: Die Entwicklung der Schweiz zu einem politischen System," in Jürg Steiner et al, eds., *Das politische System der Schweiz* (Munich: R. Piper & Co. Verlag, 1971), p. 48.

37. Amy Bridges, "Becoming American: The Working Classes in the United States Before the Civil War," in Ira Katznelson and Aristide R. Zolberg, eds., *Working-Class Formation: Nineteenth-Century Patterns in Western Europe and the United States* (Princeton, N.J.: Princeton University Press, 1986), p. 192. See also Erik Olssen, "The Case of the Socialist Party That Failed, or Further Reflections on an American Dream," *Labor History*, Fall 1988, pp. 416–449, especially pp. 442f.

38. Martin Shefter, "Party, Bureaucracy, and Political Change in the United States," in Louis Maisel and Joseph Cooper, eds., *Political Parties: Development and Decay* (Beverly Hills, Calif.: Sage, 1978), pp. 221–223.

39. Ira Katznelson, *City Trenches: Urban Politics and the Patterning of Class in the United States* (New York: Pantheon Books, 1981), p. 65.

40. Martin Shefter, "Trade Unions and Political Machines: The Organization and Disorganization of the American Working Class in the Late Nineteenth Century," in Katznelson and Zolberg, eds., *Working-Class Formation*; Richard Oestreicher, "Urban Working-Class Political Behavior and Theories of American Electoral Politics, 1870–1940," *Journal of American History* 74 (March 1988), pp. 1257–1286. Oestreicher summarizes the outcome: "By providing potential access to power, political machines undercut some of the reasons for alternative forms of working-class political mobilization at the same time they dramatically raised the costs of effective alternative mobilization." See also Alan DiGaetano, "The Origins of Urban Political Machines in the United States: A Comparative Perspective," *Urban Affairs Quarterly* 26 (1991), pp. 324–353. DiGaetano makes the point that the extraordinary strength of city machines in the United States reflected a combination of early manhood suffrage and political decentralization.

41. P. Dolan, an AFL delegate from the United Mine Workers of America, in a speech to the 1902 British Trades Union Congress. *Report of Proceedings of the Thirty-fifth Annual Trades Union Congress*, 1902, p. 61.

42. Gary Marks, *Unions in Politics: Britain, Germany, and the United States in the Nineteenth and Early Twentieth Centuries* (Princeton, N.J.: Princeton University Press, 1989).

43. Gabriel Almond and Sidney Verba, *The Civic Culture: Political Attitudes and Democracy in Five Nations* (Boston: Little, Brown, 1965), p. 205.

44. Steven J. Rosenstone, Roy L. Behr, and Edward H. Lazarus, *Third Parties in America: Citizen Response to Major Party Failure* (Princeton, N.J.: Princeton University Press, 1984), pp. 19–25.

45. Norman Thomas, *A Socialist's Faith* (New York: W. W. Norton, 1951), p. 94.

46. *Ibid.*, pp. 93–94.

47. This factor was recognized by John Commons and Selig Perlman as a criti-

cal one for the failure of the American Socialist party. Commons argued that while early suffrage led to efforts to form labor parties, these invariably failed because one of the major parties would adopt the planks proposed by the third party. John R. Commons, *Labor and Administration* (New York: Macmillan, 1913), p. 149. Perlman made the point: "It is to this uncanny adaptability of the established American political parties . . . that the uniform failure of American independent labor parties has been due." Perlman, *Theory*, pp. 171–173.

48. This was understood by Friedrich Engels. In 1892, when the People's party appeared well entrenched, Engels concluded that "there is no place yet in America for a *third* party" because of the size, complexity, and heterogeneity of the country. "The divergence of interests even in *the same* class group is so great in that tremendous area that wholly different groups and interests are represented in each of the two big parties, depending on the locality." Engels to Sorge, January 6, 1892, in Karl Marx and Friedrich Engels, *Letters to Americans, 1848–1895* (New York: International Publishers, 1953), p. 239 (emphases in original).

49. James MacGregor Burns, *The Deadlock of Democracy* (London: Calder and Boyar, 1965), pp. 40-41.

50. Duverger, *Political Parties*, pp. 418–419; Leon D. Epstein, *Political Parties in Western Democracies* (New Brunswick, N.J.: Transaction, 1980), pp. 264–265.

51. Nelson W. Polsby, *Congress and the Presidency* (Englewood Cliffs, N.J.: Prentice-Hall, 1976), p. 74.

52. This argument is elaborated in Epstein, *Political Parties*, pp. 131–132.

53. Rosenstone, Behr, and Lazarus, in *Third Parties in America*, discuss this perspective.

54. Richard Hofstadter, *The Age of Reform: From Bryan to FDR* (New York: Alfred A. Knopf, 1972), p. 97.

55. Sean Wilentz, *Chants Democratic: New York City and the Rise of the American Working Class, 1788–1850* (New York: Oxford University Press, 1984), p. 213. See also Bridges, "Becoming American," pp. 166–168. Helen Sumner argues that the failure of the Workingmen's parties was the result of two processes: first, the growth of prosperity that shifted workers' interests from "politics to trade unionism," and second, the ability "of the old parties [to take up] some of its most popular demands." See Helen Sumner, "Citizenship (1827–1833)," in John R. Commons et al., *History of Labor in the United States*, vol. 1 (New York: Macmillan, 1926), p. 326. Similarly, Edward Pessen observes that the Jacksonian Democrats responded to the electoral successes of the Workingmen's parties by showing "greater concern than ever before for the various reform provisions of the Working Men's program." Edward Pessen, *Most Uncommon Jacksonians* (Albany: State University of New York Press, 1967), p. 225. The Workingmen's parties also suffered from the perception that votes for them were wasted, or even counterproductive. Like many subsequent radical third parties, these parties were unable

to surmount the fear that their own successes would contribute to the electoral success of the more conservative major party nominees. An article in the *New York Working Man's Advocate* of November 3, 1832, observed that by nominating their own candidate they would "risk the election of Jackson by dividing the vote." Quoted in Sumner, "Citizenship," pp. 269–270. The newspaper went on to endorse Jackson and Van Buren.

56. Selig Perlman argued along these lines that American unionists rejected an independent labor party because they "grasped the definite limitations of the political instrument under the American Constitution and under American conditions of political life." Perlman, *Theory*, pp. 201–202.

57. Cited in Kenneth C. MacKay, *The Progressive Movement of 1924* (New York: Columbia University Press, 1974), pp. 152–153; Murray B. Seidler, *Norman Thomas: Respectable Rebel* (Syracuse, N.Y.: Syracuse University Press, 1961), pp. 64–65.

58. In MacKay, *Progressive Movement*, p. 155.

59. Quoted in Philip Taft, *The AF of L in the Time of Gompers* (New York: Harper & Bros., 1957), p. 484; George G. Higgins, *Voluntarism in Organized Labor in the United States, 1930–1940* (Washington, D.C.: Catholic University of America Press, 1944), p. 52; Juanita Morris Kreps, "Developments in the Political and Legislative Policies of Organized Labor, 1920–1947" (Ph.D. thesis, Department of Economics, Duke University, 1947), pp. 31–36. For the story of the 1924 Progressive campaign, see MacKay, *Progressive Movement*.

60. Mackay, *Progressive Movement*, p. 250.

61. George Soule, *Sidney Hillman: Labor Statesman* (New York: Macmillan, 1939), pp. 151–152.

62. Daniel A. Mazmanian, *Third Parties in Presidential Elections* (Washington, D.C.: Brookings Institution, 1974), p. 63.

63. *Ibid.*, p. 38.

64. *Ibid.*, p. 137; pp. 185–188; p. 257; pp. 191–192.

65. The Farmer-Labor party arose in Minnesota, the Progressive party in Wisconsin, and the American Labor party in New York. For a good overview of economic protest movements, see Bernard Karsh and Phillips L. Garman, "The Impact of the Political Left," in Milton Derber and Edwin Young, eds., *Labor and the New Deal* (Madison, Wis.: University of Wisconsin Press, 1957), p. 77.

66. Robert Burke, *Olson's New Deal for California* (Berkeley: University of California Press, 1953), pp. 32–33; William Edward Leuchtenburg, *Franklin D. Roosevelt and the New Deal* (New York: Harper & Row, 1963), pp. 114–115.

67. Albert Anthony Acena, "The Washington Commonwealth Federation: Reform Politics and the Popular Front" (Ph.D. thesis, Department of History, University of Washington, 1975); Jill Hopkins Herzig, "The Oregon Commonwealth Federation: The Rise and Decline of a Reform Organization" (M.A. thesis, Department of History, University of Oregon, 1963).

68. Edward Blackorby, *Prairie Rebel: The Public Life of William Lemke* (Lincoln: University of Nebraska Press, 1963), p. 190; Robert L. Morlan, *Political Prairie Fire: The Nonpartisan League, 1815–1922* (Minneapolis: University of Minnesota Press, 1955), p. 360.

69. Bernard K. Johnpoll, *Pacifist's Progress: Norman Thomas and the Decline of American Socialism* (Westport, Conn.: Greenwood Press, 1987), pp. 57, 96; Svend Petersen, *A Statistical History of the American Presidential Elections* (New York: Ungar, 1981), pp. 89, 91. See also Lawrence Goodwyn, *Democratic Promise: The Populist Movement in America* (New York: Oxford University Press, 1976).

70. By 1940 the Socialist vote had fallen to 116,514. See Petersen, *Statistical History*, p. 97.

71. Peggy Dennis, *The Autobiography of an American Communist: A Personal View of a Political Life, 1925–1975* (Westport, Conn.: L. Hill, 1977), p. 122.

72. Harvey Klehr, *The Heyday of American Communism: The Depression Decade* (New York: Basic Books, 1984), ch. 14.

73. Percentages were calculated from polls reported in Hadley Cantril, ed., *Public Opinion, 1935–1946* (Princeton, N.J.: Princeton University Press, 1951), pp. 576–577.

74. T. Harry Williams, *Huey Long* (New York: Alfred A. Knopf, 1969), p. 693; Alan Brinkley, *Voices of Protest: Huey Long, Father Coughlin, and the Great Depression* (New York: Alfred A. Knopf, 1982), pp. 71–74; Seymour Martin Lipset and Earl Raab, *The Politics of Unreason: Right-Wing Extremism in America, 1790–1970*, rev. ed. (New York: Harper & Row, 1977), pp. 191–194.

75. James Aloysius Farley, *Jim Farley's Story: The Roosevelt Years* (New York: Whittlesey House, 1948), p. 51; Harold Ickes, *The Secret Diary of Harold L. Ickes: The First Thousand Days, 1933–1936* (New York: Simon & Schuster, 1953), p. 462; James Farley, *Behind the Ballots* (New York: Harcourt, Brace, 1938), p. 250.

76. Letter from Franklin Roosevelt to Edward House (February 16, 1935) in Elliott Roosevelt, ed., *FDR, His Personal Letters, 1928–1945*, 1 (New York: Duell, Sloan & Pearce, 1950), pp. 452–453; Patrick Maney, *"Young Bob" La Follette* (Columbia: University of Missouri Press, 1978), p. 162.

77. Early in 1935, President Roosevelt "actually used the phrase 'steal Long's thunder'" in a conversation with Raymond Moley and others: Moley, *After Seven Years* (New York: Harper & Bros., 1939), p. 351.

78. Arthur M. Schlesinger, Jr., *The Age of Roosevelt: The Politics of Upheaval*, vol. 3 (Boston: Houghton Mifflin, 1969), pp. 325–326, 328–329.

79. *Ibid.*, p 328.

80. *Ibid.*

81. *Ibid.*, p. 329.

82. Leuchtenburg, *Franklin D. Roosevelt and the New Deal*, p. 151.

83. On interpretations of the passage of the Wagner Act see the work of Theda

Skocpol and Kenneth Finegold, particularly "Why Not Repression? Why Not Company Unionism? State Capacities, Party Alignments, and Industrial Labor Policy in the New Deal," (Paper presented at the Social Science History Association Meeting, Washington, D.C., 1989), and the debate between them and Michael Goldfield: "Explaining New Deal Labor Policy," *American Political Science Review* 84 (December 1990), pp. 1297–1316.

84. Moley, *After Seven Years*, p. 351.

85. See, for example, George H. Mayer, *The Political Career of Floyd B. Olson* (Minneapolis: University of Minnesota Press, 1951), pp. 240–241.

86. Lester F. Schmidt, "The Farmer-Labor Progressive Federation: The Study of a United Front Movement Among Wisconsin Liberals, 1934–1941" (Ph.D. thesis, Department of History, University of Wisconsin, 1954), p. 375.

87. Rexford G. Tugwell, *The Democratic Roosevelt: A Biography of Franklin D. Roosevelt* (Garden City, N.Y.: Doubleday, 1957), pp. 409-415; Maney, *"Young Bob" La Follette*, p. 190.

88. Schlesinger, *Age of Roosevelt*, p. 592.

89. Prior to 1935, the Communists had engaged in a policy of independent political action. From 1935 on, however, under the slogan of the Popular Front, Communist policy underwent a transformation. The Communists made efforts to work "under the New Deal umbrella in both the Democratic party and the Washington bureaucracy." Derber and Young, *Labor and the New Deal*, p. 128.

90. Harold L. Ickes, *The Secret Diary of Harold L. Ickes: The Inside Struggle, 1936–1939* (New York: Simon & Schuster, 1953), p. 395.

91. *Ibid.*

92. Leuchtenburg, *Franklin D. Roosevelt and the New Deal*, p. 271.

93. Letter from Franklin Roosevelt to Josephus Daniels, November 14, 1938, in Elliott Roosevelt, ed., *FDR: His Personal Letters 1928–1945*, vol. 2 (New York: Duell, Sloan & Pearce, 1950), p. 827.

94. Ickes, *Secret Diary*, p. 654.

95. J. Haynes, "Liberals, Communists, and the Popular Front in Minnesota: The Struggle to Control the Political Director of the Labor Movement and Organized Liberalism, 1936-1950" (Ph.D. thesis, Department of History, University of Minnesota, 1978), pp. 107, 109–111, 177–179.

96. Walter White, former president of the NAACP, reported that President Roosevelt expressly admitted this policy to him in a private discussion at the White House. Roosevelt told White, "I did not choose the tools with which I must work." Frank Freidel, *Franklin D. Roosevelt* (Boston: Little, Brown, 1952), pp. 86, 71–103; Walter White, *A Man Called White: The Autobiography of Walter White* (New York: Viking Press, 1948), pp. 168–169. Nevertheless, Mr. White, according to his own account, remained committed to the president for years to come, primarily because of Eleanor Roosevelt's involvement in the cause.

97. Leuchtenburg, *Franklin D. Roosevelt and the New Deal*, p. 224.

98. In addition to works cited above, see Eric Leif Davin and Staughton Lynd, "Picket Line and Ballot Box: The Forgotten Legacy of the Local Labor Party Movement," *Radical History Review* 22 (Winter 1979–80), pp. 42–63; and Klehr, *Heyday of American Communism*.

99. Martin Robin, *Radical Politics and Canadian Labour, 1880–1930* (Kingston, Ont.: Queens University Press, 1968), p. 43.

100. Kenneth McNaught, *A Prophet in Politics: A Biography of J. S. Woodsworth* (Toronto: University of Toronto Press, 1959), pp. 165–192.

101. Robin, *Radical Politics*, p. 43.

102. *Ibid.*, p. 273.

103. Gad Horowitz, *Canadian Labour in Politics* (Toronto: University of Toronto Press, 1968), pp. 48–49.

104. *Ibid.*, p. 39.

105. *Ibid.*, pp. 32–33.

106. *Ibid.*, pp 54–55.

3. The Split Between Unions and the Socialist Party

1. The best pre-World War I result for an explicitly socialist party before World War I in Britain was 1 percent of the national vote—less than fifty thousand votes—for the Independent Labour party in 1895. The Social Democratic Federation, the leading Marxist party in Britain, never received more than 1 percent of the vote in any individual constituency.

2. The Australian Socialist party had some strength in Sydney, but it received a tiny share in national elections. After 1907 the party gave up the electoral ghost and decided on a syndicalist strategy focusing on the trade unions. In New Zealand, the socialists realized that they were not strong enough to fight elections on their own and turned to working within the Labour party.

3. Nathan Fine, *Labor and Farmer Parties in the United States 1828–1928* (New York: Rand School of Social Science, 1928). Other noteworthy treatments of the topic are Richard W. Judd, *Socialist Cities: Municipal Politics and the Grass Roots of American Socialism* (Albany: State University of New York Press, 1989), p. 16; Nick Salvatore, *Eugene V. Debs: Citizen and Socialist* (Urbana: University of Illinois Press, 1982); and James Weinstein, *The Decline of Socialism in America 1912–1925* (New York: Monthly Review Press, 1967).

4. Fine, *Labor and Farmer Parties*, p. 249.

5. The comparative history of union organization in western societies has yet to be written. Clearly, the story is characterized by path dependence, for once a particular form of unionism has been established it constrains future development. Partial analyses are Gary Marks, *Unions in Politics: Britain, Germany, and the United*

States in the Nineteenth and Early Twentieth Centuries (Princeton, N.J.: Princeton University Press, 1989); Lloyd Ulman, *The Rise of the National Trade Union* (Cambridge, Mass.: Harvard University Press, 1955); and H. A. Turner, *Trade Union Growth, Structure and Policy* (London: George Allen & Unwin, 1962).

6. Kim Voss, *The Making of American Exceptionalism: The Knights of Labor and Class Formation in the Nineteenth Century* (Ithaca, N.Y.: Cornell University Press, 1993), p. 227. See also Leon Fink, *Workingmen's Democracy: The Knights of Labor and American Politics* (Urbana: University of Illinois Press, 1983).

7. Marks, *Unions in Politics*, pp. 88–89.

8. Calculated from Leo Wolman, *The Growth of American Trade Unions 1880–1923* (New York: National Bureau of Economic Research, 1924); and Walter Galenson, *The CIO Challenge to the AFL: A History of the American Labor Movement 1935–1941* (Cambridge, Mass.: Harvard University Press, 1960).

9. The adjectives "exclusive" and "inclusive" appear more precise than those used previously by Gary Marks in *Unions in Politics* in setting out the distinction between "closed" and "open" unions.

10. Philip Taft, *The AF of L in the Time of Gompers* (New York: Harper & Bros, 1957), p. 294; Tomlins, *The State and the Unions*, ch. 3; Victoria C. Hattam, *Labor Visions and State Power: The Origins of Business Unionism in the United States* (Princeton, N.J.: Princeton University Press, 1993), p. 164.

11. This line of argument owes much to H. A. Turner's ideas, in particular his classic analysis: *Trade Union Growth*, part 5, ch. 1.

12. Robin Archer, "Why Is There No Labor Party? Class and Race in the United States and Australia," in Rick Halpern and Jonathan Morris, eds., *American Exceptionalism? U.S. Working Class Formation in an International Context* (New York: St. Martin's Press, 1997).

13. *Report of Proceedings of the Thirteenth Annual Convention of the American Federation of Labor*, Chicago, 1893, p. 36; *Report of Proceedings of the Twenty-second Annual Convention of the American Federation of Labor*, New Orleans, 1902, p. 179; *Report of Proceedings of the Thirty-first Annual Convention of the American Federation of Labor*, Atlanta, 1911, p. 217; *Report of Proceedings of the Thirty-fifth Annual Convention of the American Federation of Labor*, San Francisco, 1915, pp. 503–504. See Marks, *Unions in Politics*, Appendix A, for details of the delegate votes for 1893 to 1915.

14. *Report of Proceedings of the Fortieth Annual Convention of the American Federation of Labor*, Toronto, 1920, p. 419.

15. Ira Kipnis, *American Socialist Movement* (New York: Columbia University Press, 1952), p. 238.

16. Weinstein, *Decline of Socialism*, p. 41.

17. William C. Pratt, "The Reading Socialist Experience: A Study of Working Class Politics" (Ph.D. thesis, Department of History, Emory University, 1969), p. 40.

18. A question that arises directly from our analysis is why exclusive unionism was stronger relative to inclusive unionism in the United States than elsewhere. To answer this would demand detailed comparative study that would take us beyond scope of this book. The following hypotheses appear to us plausible enough to warrant empirical investigation:

- The greater the dislocation in the relevant features of the political, economic, and social environment facing unions (e.g., as measured by political and constitutional continuity, rate of industrialization, geographical mobility of labor), the greater the role of inclusive unions in a country's labor movement. Conversely, the greater the political, economic, and social continuity, the greater the predominance of older exclusive unions.
- The greater the heterogeneity of a country's labor force and economy, the greater the predominance of exclusive unions.
- The earlier industrialization, the greater the predominance of exclusive unions.
- The earlier the establishment of the labor movement relative to the establishment of a socialist party, the greater the predominance of exclusive unions.
- The greater the legal constraints on mass industrial action and the weaker the legal constraints on rules that constrict the supply of labor into an occupation, the greater the predominance of exclusive unions. This argument is made by William E. Forbath, *Law and the Shaping of the American Labor Movement* (Cambridge: Harvard University Press, 1991).
- The greater the organizational cohesion of employers in the society, the greater the predominance of inclusive unions.

19. The percentages are based on data provided in *Report of Proceedings of the Thirty-second Annual Trades Union Congress*, 1899, and *Report of Proceedings at the Forty-sixth Annual Trades Union Congress*, 1913. For 1899, the following are included as inclusive unions (membership rounded to the nearest hundred): Dock Labourers (12,000); Dock, Wharf, Riverside, and General Labourers (10,000); Gas Workers and General Labourers (45,000); National Amalgamated Union (21,600); Miners' Federation (213,000); Navvies, Bricklayers, Labourers (5,000); Railway Servants (54,000); Weavers (73,600). The following are included as inclusive unions in 1913: Dock Labourers (32,000); Dock, Wharf, Riverside, and General Workers (37,000); Sailors and Firemen (60,000); Gasworkers and General Labourers (82,100); Gasworkers, Brickmakers, and General Labourers (7,600); National Amalgamated Union (51,000); Miners' Federation (600,000); Railwaymen (132,000); Weavers (182,800); Postmen (42,600).

20. A list of affiliated unions is provided in the *Report of the First Annual Conference of the Labour Representation Committee*, Manchester, February 1901.

21. *Taff Vale*, which found unions liable for costs imposed on employers through strikes, convinced even the most politically cautious unions that they had to gain

working-class representation to change the law. See *Second Annual Conference of the Labour Representation Committee*, Birmingham, February 1902; *Third Annual Conference of the Labour Representation Committee*, Newcastle-on-Tyne, February 1903. The role of the Independent Labour party and the grounds for conversion to support for the LRC are discussed in David Howell, *British Workers and the Independent Labour Party 1888–1906* (Manchester: Manchester University Press, 1983), part 1; and Henry Pelling, *The Origins of the Labour Party 1880–1900* (Oxford: Oxford University Press, 1965), pp. 195–201.

22. John H. M. Laslett, "Labour Party, Labor Lobbying, or Direct Action? Coal Miners, Immigrants, and Radical Politics in Scotland and the American Midwest, 1880–1924," in Camille Gurein Gonzales and Carl Strikwerda, eds., *The Politics of Immigrant Workers: Labor Activism and Migration in the World Economy since 1830* (New York: Holmes & Meier, 1993), p. 90.

23. *Ibid.*, pp. 91–92.

24. *Ibid.*, p. 90. Sharon Reitman constrasts the political orientations of the UMWA and the Western Federation of Miners in the years around the turn of the twentieth century. Her assertion that "after the 1897 strike, the UMWA turned its attention away from political change and concentrated instead on working with employers to stabilize competition and increase wages" (p. 215) is at odds with the research of Laslett and others. However, her main contention, that the WFM was the more radical of the two unions, and that this reflected its experience of particularly intense political repression, is consistent with the argument being made here. Sharon Reitman, "The Politics of the Western Federation of Miners and the United Mine Workers of America: Uneven Development, Industry Structure, and Class Struggle," in Scott G. McNall, Rhonda F. Levine, and Rick Fantasia, eds., *Bringing Class Back In: Contemporary and Historical Perspectives* (Boulder, Colo.: Westview Press, 1991).

25. R. Markey, "The White Ghost of Jefferson," in Ann Curthoys and Andrew Markus, eds., *Who are Our Enemies?* (Sydney: Hale & Iremonger, 1978), p. 75, quoted in Jim Hagan, *The History of the ACTU* (Melbourne: Longman Cheshire, 1981), p. 14.

26. Robin Gollan, *Radical and Working Class Politics: A Study of Eastern Australia, 1850–1910* (Melbourne: Melbourne University Press, 1960), p. 141.

27. Archer, "Why Is There No Labor Party?"

28. David DeLeon, *The American as Anarchist: Reflections on Indigenous Radicalism* (Baltimore: Johns Hopkins University Press, 1978), p. 102.

29. *Ibid.*, p. 114.

30. Julie Greene, *Pure and Simple Politics: The American Federation of Labor and Political Activism, 1881–1917* (Cambridge: Cambridge University Press, 1998), pp. 255–256. The quotation of Samuel Gompers is from "Eight Hour Constitutional Amendment," *American Federationist* 5 (June 1989), p. 110.

31. Selig Perlman, *A Theory of the Labor Movement* (New York: Macmillan, 1928), p. 202.

32. *Ibid.*, p. 113.

33. This applies also to the AFL's attempt to limit immigration, for antipathy to immigration was founded on the belief that it would swell the labor supply and thereby threaten standards.

34. *Ibid.*, pp. 175–176.

35. William M. Dick, *Labor and Socialism in America: The Gompers Era* (Port Washington, N.Y.: Kennikat Press, 1972), p. 118.

36. Christopher L. Tomlins, *The State and the Unions: Labor Relations and the Organized Labor Movement in America, 1880–1960* (Cambridge: Cambridge University Press, 1985), pp. 56–57. Quotations from William H. Sewell, *Work and Revolution in France* (Cambridge: Cambridge University Press, 1980), p. 242; Samuel Gompers, "Trade Unions—Their Philosophy," *American Federationist* 17 (1910), p. 696.

37. Quoted in Tomlins, *The State and the Unions*, p. 118.

38. Samuel Lubell, "Post-Mortem: Who Elected Roosevelt?" *Saturday Evening Post*, January 25, 1941, p. 9. See also Lubell, *The Future of American Politics* (New York: Doubleday/Anchor Books, 1965), pp. 55–68.

39. Morris Hillquit, *History of Socialism in the United States* (New York: Funk & Wagnalls, 1910), pp. 247–248.

40. Henry Pelling, *America and the British Left* (London: Adam & Charles Black, 1956), p. 63. Leon Fink observes that "the momentum of the 1880s was great. Indeed, examined both at the level of working-class organization and industrial militancy, a European visitor might understandably expect the most to happen here first. At the political level, as well, American workers were in certain respects relatively advanced." Leon Fink, *Workingmen's Democracy*, p. 229.

41. Michael Rogin, "Radicalism and the Agrarian Tradition: Comment," in John Laslett and Seymour Martin Lipset, eds., *Failure of a Dream? Essays in the History of American Socialism* (Garden City, N.Y.: Doubleday/Anchor Books, 1974), p. 149. See also Theodore Saloutos, "Radicalism and the Agrarian Tradition," in Laslett and Lipset, *Failure of a Dream?*; Philip Foner, *History of the Labor Movement in the United States*, 2nd ed., vol. 2 (New York: International Publishers, 1975), ch. 21.

42. *Report of Proceedings of the Twelfth Annual Convention of the American Federation of Labor*, 1892, p. 43.

43. See Taft, *The AF of L in the Time of Gompers*, p. 72.

44. *A Verbatim Report of the Discussion on the Political Programme, 1984* (New York: Freytag Press, 1985), p. 63.

45. Foner, *History of the Labor Movement in the United States*, vol. 2, p. 293.

46. *Report of Proceedings of the Fifteenth Annual Convention of the American Federation of Labor*, 1895, p. 80.

47. *Report of Proceedings of the Twenty-second Annual Convention of the American Federation of Labor*, 1902, p. 183.

48. *American Federationist*, 1908, quoted in Dick, *Labor and Socialism in America*, p. 120.

49. Stanley Shapiro, "The Great War and Reform: Liberals and Labor 1917–1919," *Labor History* 11 (1971), p. 326; Chester W. Wright, *Economic History of the United States* (New York: McGraw-Hill, 1949), ch. 42.

50. Stanley Shapiro, "'Hand and Brain': The Farmer-Labor Party of 1920," *Labor History* 26 (Summer 1985); Dick, *Labor and Socialism in America*, pp. 163–170.

51. Quoted in Dick, *Labor and Socialism in America*, p. 176.

52. *Federationist*, September 1924, p. 710.

53. Theodore Roosevelt received 27.4 percent of the national vote in 1912.

54. Galenson, *CIO Challenge to the AFL*, pp. 606–607; Philip Taft, *Organized Labor in American History* (New York: Harper & Row, 1964), pp. 607–608. CIO unions were archetypal inclusive unions. See Howard Kimeldorf, *Reds or Rackets? The Making of Radical and Conservative Unions on the Waterfront* (Berkeley: University of California Press, 1988), on the strategy of the International Longshoremen's and Warehousemen's Union.

55. Congress of Industrial Organizations, *Proceedings of the Third Constitutional Convention*, November 1940, p. 50.

56. The bases of occupational community are detailed in Marks, *Unions in Politics*, ch. 1; and S. M. Lipset, M. Trow, and J. S. Coleman, *Union Democracy* (Glenroe: The Free Press, 1956), pp. 68–140, 227–229, 367–371.

57. Leon D. Epstein, *Political Parties in Western Democracies* (New York: Frederick Praeger, 1967), p. 140.

58. Pelling, *The Origins of the Labour Party*, p. 227.

59. According to an 1898 editorial in the labor journal *Tocsin*, the party "never meets as a party to decide on measures to be introduced. . . . It is leaderless, functionless, out-classed . . . [lacking] the cohesion of a party." Quoted in Humphrey McQueen, "Victoria," in D. J. Murphy, ed., *Labor in Politics: The State Labor Parties in Australia 1880–1920* (St. Lucia, Queensland: University of Queensland Press, 1975), p. 303. The first full-time secretary of the Victorian Labor party was appointed in 1907, seventeen years after the party was established.

60. Maurice Duverger, *Political Parties: Their Organization and Activity in the Modern State*, trans. Barbara and Robert North (New York: John Wiley, 1954), p. 76. Duverger emphasizes that the strength of the bond between indirect members, such as those provided by unions, and the party is an empirical issue. The British Labour party managed to maintain about two-thirds of its union membership after the law was changed in 1927, making party membership a matter of explicit choice.

61. Adam Przeworski and John Sprague, *Paper Stones: A History of Electoral Socialism* (Chicago: Chicago University Press, 1986).

62. Adam Przeworski, *Capitalism and Social Democracy* (Chicago: Chicago University Press, 1985), pp. 100–101.

63. Ira Katznelson, *City Trenches: Urban Politics and the Patterning of Class in the United States* (New York: Pantheon Books, 1981), pp. 71–72. For a firsthand interpretation of a case where work and community coincided, see Robert Bruno, "Everyday Constructions of Culture and Class: The Case of Youngstown Steelworkers," *Labor History* 40 (1999), pp. 143–176. As Stephan Thernstrom has argued, less skilled workers generally formed less stable communities than in Europe because they were relatively geographically mobile. See Stephan Thernstrom, "Urbanization, Migration, and Social Mobility in Late Nineteenth-Century America," in Barton J. Bernstein, ed., *Towards a New Past: Dissenting Essays in American History* (New York: Pantheon Books, 1967).

64. Herbert Gutman has stressed this.

65. Fine, *Labor and Farmer Parties in the United States*, pp. 302 and 307.

66. See, for example, Horst Üeberhorst, "Turners and Social Democrats in Milwaukee: Five Decades of Cooperation (1910–1960)" (Lecture to the discussion group "Politics and Science" at the research institute of the Friedrich Ebert Endowment, Bonn, March 1980), trans. Joseph Hahn.

67. Sally M. Miller, "Casting a Wide Net: The Milwaukee Movement to 1920," in Donald T. Critchlow, ed., *Socialism in the Heartland: The Midwestern Experience, 1900–1925* (Notre Dame, Ind.: University of Notre Dame Press, 1986), pp. 24–25.

68. Quoted in Dick, *Labor and Socialism in America*, p. 66.

69. David Shannon, *The Socialist Party of America: A History* (New York: Macmillan, 1955), p. 21.

70. Frederick I. Olson, "The Milwaukee Socialists, 1897–1941" (Ph.D. thesis, Department of Government, Harvard University, 1952), pp. 175–176.

71. *Ibid.*, p. 204.

72. *Ibid.*, pp. 213–214.

73. *Ibid.*, p. 225.

74. Miller, "Casting a Wide Net," pp. 28–29.

75. Douglas E. Booth, "Municipal Socialism and City Government Reform: The Milwaukee Experience, 1910–1940," *Journal of Urban History* 12 (November 1985). Property taxes declined while indirect taxes increased.

76. Miller, "Casting a Wide Net," pp. 36–37; Miller, "Milwaukee," p. 57.

77. The formal link between the Milwaukee Socialist party and the FTC continued until the early 1930s.

78. Henry G. Stetler, *The Socialist Movement in Reading, Pennsylvania, 1896–1936* (Storrs, Conn.: privately printed, 1943), pp. 36–38.

79. Shannon, *Socialist Party of America*, p. 15.

80. *Ibid.*, p. 15.

81. *Ibid.*, pp. 39–40.

82. William C. Pratt, "'Jimmie Higgins' and the Reading Socialist Community: An Exploration of the Socialist Rank and File," in Stave, ed., *Socialism and the Cities*, p. 144.

83. Charles Leinenweber, "The Class and Ethnic Bases of New York City Socialism, 1904–1915," *Labor History* 22 (1981), p. 56.

84. Sari Bennett, "The Geography of American Socialism: Continuity and Change, 1900–1912," *Social Science History* 7 (Summer 1983), p. 284.

85. David Paul Nord, "Hothouse Socialism: Minneapolis, 1910–1925," in Critchlow, ed., *Socialism in the Heartland*, p. 135.

86. *Ibid.*, pp. 152-156.

87. *Ibid.*, p. 143.

88. Richard M. Valelly, *Radicalism in the States: The Minnesota Farmer-Labor Party and the American Political Economy* (Chicago: University of Chicago Press, 1989), p. 48.

89. Judd, *Socialist Cities*, p. 16.

4. Immigrants and Socialism: Double-Edged Effects

1. The view that working-class ethnic and racial diversity undermined class consciousness and weakened socialism in America was put forward in 1870 by Marx, who emphasized that American socialists should press for a coalition among workers of different ethnic backgrounds. See Marx to Siegfrid Meyer and August Vogt, April 9, 1870, Karl Marx, *On the First International*, ed. and trans. Saul K. Padover (New York: McGraw-Hill, 1973), pp. 499–500.

2. Charles Leinenweber, "The American Socialist Party and 'New' Immigrants," *Science & Society* 32 (Winter 1968), p. 1; Herbert Gutman, *Work, Culture, and Society in Industrializing America* (New York: Random House, 1977), p. 40.

3. John R. Commons et al., *History of Labor in the United States, 1896–1932*, vol. 3 (New York: Macmillan, 1935), p. 41.

4. Simon Kuznets, *Economic Growth and Structure* (New York: W. W. Norton, 1965), p. 312. See also Martin A. Schain, "The Development of the American State and the Construction of Immigration Policy (1880–1924)" (Paper delivered at the American Political Science Association Conference, 1994), pp. 2–5.

5. Bureau of the Census, *Immigrants and Their Children, 1920, Census Monographs VII* (Washington, D.C.: U.S. Government Printing Office, 1927), p. 62.

6. Joseph S. Roucek, "The Image of the Slav in U.S. History and in Immigration Policy," *The American Journal of Economics and Sociology* 28 (January 1969), pp. 29–48.

7. Peter J. Hill, "Relative Skill and Income Levels of Native and Foreign Born Workers in the United States," *Explorations in Economic History* 12 (1975), p. 25; Paul McGouldrick and Michael Tannen, "Did American Manufacturers Discriminate

Against Immigrants Before 1914?" *Journal of Economic History* (September 1977), pp. 723–746.

8. Engels to Schlüter, March 30, 1892, in Karl Marx and Friedrich Engels, *Selected Correspondence: 1846–1895* (New York: International Publishers, 1936), pp. 496–497.

9. Engels to Sorge, December 2, 1893, in Karl Marx and Friedrich Engels, *Letters to Americans, 1848–1895* (New York: International Publishers, 1953), p. 258. Max Beer, an Austrian socialist who spent three years around the turn of the century in the United States, made a similar point: "Even when the time is ripe for a Socialist movement, it can only produce one when the working people form a certain cultural unity, that is, when they have a common language, a common history, a common mode of life. This is the case in Europe, but not in the United States. Its factories, mines, farms, and the organizations based on them are composite bodies, containing the most heterogeneous elements, and lacking stability and the sentiment of solidarity." Max Beer, *Fifty Years of International Socialism* (London: George Allen & Unwin, 1935), pp. 112–115.

10. Mike Davis, *Prisoners of the American Dream: Politics and Economy in the History of the U.S. Working Class* (New York: Verso, 1988), pp. 24–25.

11. Benjamin C. Bacon, *Statistics of the Colored People of Philadelphia* (Philadelphia, 1856), p. 15; quoted in Noel Ignatiev, *How the Irish Became White* (New York: Routledge, 1995), p. 101.

12. Ignatiev, *How the Irish Became White*, ch. 4.

13. The consequences of the internal stratification of the American working class for socialist support are discussed in Davis, *Prisoners*, pp. 16–40. Also see K. Gerald Marsden, "Patriotic Societies and American Labor: The American Protective Association in Wisconsin," *Wisconsin Magazine of History* 41 (Summer 1958), for a discussion of the intermixture of nativism and anti-Catholicism in the last decades of the nineteenth century.

14. Walter MacArthur, a leading West Coast unionist, stated in the 1894 AFL convention debate on the political program: "I am in favor of political action. What bothers me is how to do it. I am satisfied that we cannot do it as trade unionists and preserve the efficiency of the trades union. It is all very well to cite our British brethren on the subject, but the illustrations are irrelevant, immaterial. . . . In San Francisco we have all nationalities in our unions, men who will stand together to a unit on wages and conditions generally in every craft, but if you mix politics, even a suspicion of them, the specter of disintegration arises right there and stays there." *A Verbatim of the Discussion on the Political Program at the Denver Convention of the American Federation of Labor,* December 14–15, 1894 (New York: Freytag Press, 1895), p. 6. Speeches by AFL delegates at TUC congresses and by TUC delegates at AFL conventions provide an interesting commentary on differences of perception in the two countries. In a speech before the 1902 TUC congress, P. Dolan, an AFL dele-

gate from the miners, pointed out: "There was one thing, however, in which America had to give Great Britain best—that was with regard to the Parliamentary representative of Labour. So far, they had totally failed in that direction. They possessed the franchise fully enough, but did not use it in the right way. The Democrats and Republicans adhered to their parties as closely as to their religion. . . . Many of us think it just as easy to get the most bigoted Roman Catholic and Protestant to kneel down at the same altar to pray as to get the workers to vote together." See *Report of Proceedings of the Thirty-fifth Annual Trade Unions Congress*, 1902, p. 61.

15. Seymour Martin Lipset, *The First New Nation: The United States in Historical and Comparative Perspective* (New York: Basic Books, 1963), ch. 5.

16. Ira Katznelson, *City Trenches: Urban Politics and the Patterning of Class in the United States* (New York: Pantheon Books, 1981), p. 19.

17. Catherine Collomp, "Immigrants, Labor Markets, and the State. A Comparative Approach: France and the United States, 1880–1930," *Journal of American History* 86 (June 1999), p. 46.

18. John Commons argued that even if the resistance of native workers was overcome, the potential for class solidarity would continue to be undermined by cultural divisions. John R. Commons, "Is Class Conflict in America Growing and Is It Inevitable?" *American Journal of Sociology* 8 (May 1908), p. 762.

19. Irwin Yellowitz, *Industrialization and the American Labor Movement: 1850–1900* (Port Washington, N.Y.: Kennikat Press, 1977), pp. 128–129. See Gwendolyn Mink, *Old Labor and New Immigrants in American Political Development: Union, Party, and State, 1875–1920* (Ithaca, N.Y.: Cornell University Press, 1986), pp. 165–167, 46–49. Where unions, such as the UMWA, were successful in mobilizing individuals from diverse ethnic groups, this had the effect of breaking down ethnic barriers by focusing on common grievances and socializing workers as Americans. See James R. Barrett, "Americanization from the Bottom Up: Immigration and the Remaking of the Working Class in the United States, 1880–1930," *Journal of American History* 79 (1992), pp. 996–1020.

20. Samuel Gompers and Herman Gutstadt, *Meat vs. Rice: American Manhood vs. Asiatic Coolieism: Which Shall Survive?* (San Francisco: American Federation of Labor, 1902). Ann Archer makes the interesting point that while racial hostility was divisive in the United States, it was inclusive in Australia: "In Australia, hostility towards Chinese and Melanesian immigrants helped to consolidate the new unions by providing them with a popular rallying cry which enabled them to mobilise cross-class support. Racial hostility also helped to consolidate the fledgling Labor party by enabling it to reinforce its credentials as a national party and to appeal beyond the working class to small farmers and the urban middle class. In the United States, by contrast, hostility towards Chinese immigrants and blacks melded with an earlier tradition of ethno-religious nativism to produce a new racial

nativism which set the old immigrants from northern and western Europe against the new immigrants from southern and eastern Europe." Ann Archer, "Why Is There No Labor Party? Class and Race in the United States and Australia," in Rick Halpern and Jonathan Morris, eds., *American Exceptionalism? U.S. Working Class Formation in an International Context* (New York: St. Martin's Press, 1997). On the issue of race and American socialism, see also Eric Foner, "Why Is There No Socialism in The United States?" *History Workshop Journal* 17 (1984); Roger M. Smith, "Beyond Tocqueville, Myrdal and Hartz: The Multiple Traditions in America," *American Political Science Review* 87 (September 1993); Mink, *Old Labor and New Immigrants*, pp. 71–121; Ralph Mann, "Community, Change and Caucasian Attitudes Towards the Chinese," in Milton Cantor, ed., *American Working Class Culture* (Westport, Conn.: Greenwood Press, 1979), pp. 397–419; Susan Olzak, "Labor Unrest, Immigration, and Ethnic Conflict in Urban America, 1880–1914," *American Journal of Sociology* 94 (May 1989), pp. 1303–1333 (Olzak's research suggests that the growth of unionism coincided with anti-black activity, pp. 1328–1329); and Michael Goldfield, "Class, Race, and Politics in the United States: White Supremacy as the Main Explanation for the Peculiarities of American Politics from Colonial Times to the Present," *Research in Political Economy* 12 (1990), pp. 83–127. Goldfield goes further than any of the other commentators on race and identifies white supremacy as the principal factor that ensured there would be no socialist success in the United States.

21. *Abstracts of Reports of the Immigration Commission*, 61st Congress, 3rd Session, Senate Document No. 747, 1911, p. 780; Michael Harrington, *Socialism* (New York: Saturday Review Press, 1970), p. 132; E. P. Hutchison, *Immigrants and Their Children* (New York: John Wiley, 1965), pp. 114, 138–139, 171. See also Seymour Martin Lipset and Reinhard Bendix, *Social Mobility in Industrial Society* (Berkeley: University of California Press, 1959).

22. Isaac Hourwich, *Immigration and Labor* (New York: G. P. Putnam's Sons, 1912), pp. 9–12, 19, 165; see also Jeremiah Jencks and W. Jett Lauck, *The Immigration Problem: A Study of American Immigration Conditions and Needs* (New York: Funk & Wagnalls, 1922), pp. 165–196.

23. John T. Cumbler, *Working-Class Community in Industrial America: Work, Leisure, and Struggle in Two Industrial Cities, 1880–1930* (Westport, Conn.: Greenwood Press, 1979).

24. Richard Flacks, *Making History: Radical Tradition in American Life* (New York: Columbia University Press, 1988), p. 110.

25. John Bodnar, *Immigration and Industrialization: Ethnicity in an American Mill Town, 1870–1940* (Pittsburgh: University of Pittsburgh Press, 1977), pp. 150–151. Thomas Göbel, "Becoming American: Ethnic Workers and the Rise of the CIO," *Labor History* 29 (Spring 1988), pp. 173–198.

26. William C. Pratt, "The Reading Socialist Experience: A Study of Working Class Politics" (Ph.D. thesis, Department of Modern History, Emory University, 1969), p. 506.

27. Errol Wayne Stevens, "Heartland Socialism: The Socialist Party of America in Four Midwestern Communities" (Ph.D. thesis, Department of History, Indiana University, 1978), p. 63. Also see Errol Wayne Stevens, "Main-Street Socialism: The Socialist Party of America in Marion, Indiana, 1900–1921," in Donald T. Critchlow, ed., *Socialism in the Heartland: The Midwestern Experience, 1900–1925* (Notre Dame, Ind.: University of Notre Dame Press, 1986), pp. 68–89.

28. Garin Burbank, "Agrarian Radicals and their Opponents: Political Conflict in Southern Oklahoma, 1910–1924," *Journal of American History* 58 (June 1971), p. 7. See also H. L. Meredith, "Agrarian Socialism and the Negro in Oklahoma, 1900–1918," *Labor History* 11 (Summer 1970), p. 278.

29. Melvyn Dubofsky, *We Shall Be All: A History of the Industrial Workers of the World* (Chicago: Quadrangle Books, 1969), pp. 23–24.

30. Nathan Fine, *Labor and Farmer Parties in the United States, 1828–1928* (New York: Rand School of Social Sciences, 1928), p. 230.

31. *Ibid.*, p. 231.

32. Sally Miller, "Milwaukee: Of Ethnicity and Labor," in Bruce M. Stave, ed., *Socialism and the Cities* (Port Washington, N.Y.: Kennikat Press, 1975), pp. 50, 61.

33. Marlene P. Terwilinger, "Jews and Italians and the Socialist Party, New York City, 1901–1917." (Ph.D. thesis, Department of Sociology, Union Graduate School, 1977), p. 91. Italian immigrants to the United States came largely from southern Italy, while those in Argentina came largely from northern Italy, a difference we explore below.

34. Fine, *Labor and Farmer Parties*, p. 324.

35. Computed from data presented in Bureau of the Census, *Immigrants and Their Children, 1920*, p. 286.

36. Sally M. Miller, "Different Accents of Labor," *Labor's Heritage* 2 (1990), pp. 62–75.

37. Joseph R. Conlin, *The American Radical Press, 1880–1960*, vol. 1 (Westport, Conn.: Greenwood Press, 1974), p. 22.

38. Stan Nadel notes: "There have been times when German-American radicalism seemed to be the only class-conscious radicalism in the U.S. . . . the Socialist Labor Party, the left wing of the American Federation of Labor, or the Chicago anarchists—all predominantly German." Stan Nadel, "The German Immigrant Left in the United States," in Paul Buhle and Dan Georgakas, eds., *The Immigrant Left in the United States* (Albany: State University of New York Press, 1996), p. 45. See also John H. M. Laslett, *Labor and the Left: A Study of Socialist and Radical Influences in the American Labor Movement, 1881–1927* (New York: Basic Books, 1970), p. 9; Paul Buhle, *Marxism in the United States:*

Remapping the History of the American Left, rev. ed. (New York: Verso, 1991).

39. Cited in Fine, *Labor and Farmer Parties,* p. 48.

40. Morris Hillquit, *History of Socialism in the United States* (New York: Funk & Wagnalls, 1910), pp. 193–194.

41. Buhle, *Marxism in the United States,* pp. 51–56.

42. Report by Daniel De Leon to the Zurich Congress in *The People,* June 8, 1893, p. 1.

43. This ecological analysis uses county data, which is the only comparative source of data available. Conclusions drawn from these data for individual voting must be tentative, for they assume the absence of countervailing community effects. The proportion of immigrants from a particular country in a county may be a proxy for economic/social variables that we cannot measure separately, yet which help explain the associations we find. For more details, see Gary Marks and Matthew Burbank, "Immigrant Support for the American Socialist Party, 1912 and 1920," *Social Science History* 14 (Summer 1990), pp. 175–202.

44. Klaus Ensslen and Heinz Ickstadt, "German Working-Class Culture in Chicago: Continuity and Change in the Decade from 1900 to 1910," in Hartmut Keil and John B. Jentz, eds., *German Workers in Industrial Chicago, 1850–1910: A Comparative Perspective* (DeKalb: Northern Illinois University Press, 1983); Charles Leinenweber, "The Class and Ethnic Bases of New York City Socialism, 1904–1915," *Labor History* 22 (1981), pp. 31–56; Miller, "Milwaukee"; Miller, "Different Accents of Labor"; Lee Wolfe, *The Seamy Side of Democracy: Repression in America* (New York: Longman, 1978); Klause J. Bade, "German Emigration to the United States and Continental Immigration to Germany in the Late Nineteenth and Early Twentieth Centuries," in Dirk Hoerder, ed., *Labor Migration in the Atlantic Economies: The European and North American Working Classes During the Period of Industrialization* (Westport, Conn.: Greenwood Press, 1985), pp. 117–142; Hubert Perrier, "The Socialists and the Working Class in New York, 1890–96," in Dirk Hoerder, ed., *American Labor and Immigration History, 1877–1920s: Recent European Research* (Urbana: University of Illinois Press, 1983); James L. Lorence, "Socialism in Northern Wisconsin, 1910–1920s: An Ethno-Cultural Analysis," *Mid-America* 69 (April–July 1982), pp. 25–51.

45. John Bodnar, *The Transplanted: A History of Immigrants in Urban America* (Bloomington: Indiana University Press, 1985), p. 86.

46. Gerald Rosenblum, *Immigrant Workers: Their Impact on American Labor Radicalism* (New York: Basic Books, 1973), p. 152.

47. For details on the decline of German dominance in socialism, see Buhle, *Marxism in the United States,* pp. 44–45.

48. Fine, *Labor and Farmer Parties,* p. 234.

49. James Weinstein, *The Decline of Socialism in America, 1912–1925* (New Brunswick, N.J.: Rutgers University Press, 1984), pp. 23–24.

50. Ensslen and Ickstadt, "German Working-Class Culture in Chicago," pp. 236–252.

51. *Ibid.*, pp. 236–252.

52. James L. Lorence, "Dynamite for the Brain: The Growth and Decline of Socialism in Central and Lakeshore Wisconsin, 1910–1920," *Wisconsin Magazine of History* 66 (Summer 1983), p. 271. Also see Lorence, "Socialism in Northern Wisconsin."

53. Paul Buhle, "Themes in American Jewish Radicalism," in Buhle and Georgakas, eds., *Immigrant Left*, pp. 46–49, 78; Irwin Yellowitz, "Jewish Immigrants and the American Labor Movement, 1900–1920," *American Jewish History* (1981), pp. 188–217. In his study of Jewish radicalism, Arthur Liebman concludes that "in terms of proportion, the Jewish balloting on behalf of socialism was perhaps exceeded only by that of the German-Americans and the Finnish-Americans." Arthur Liebman, *Jews and the Left* (New York: John Wiley, 1979), p. 48. Also see Peter Kivisto, *Immigrant Socialists in the United States: The Case of Finns and the Left* (Rutherford, N.J.: Fairleigh Dickinson University Press, 1984), pp. 29–31.

54. Arthur Gorenstein, "A Portrait of Ethnic Politics: The Socialists and the 1908 and 1910 Congressional Elections on the East Side," *American Jewish Historical Society* 1 (1961), pp. 202–227; Leinenweber, "Class and Ethnic Bases," pp. 31–56.

55. Buhle, "Themes in American Jewish Radicalism," p. 80.

56. Census data do not categorize immigrants by religion. Of over 1.6 million immigrants classified as "Russian" in 1910, 52.3 percent reported Yiddish or Hebrew as their mother tongue while only 2.5 percent reported Russian as their native language (in addition, 26.1 percent reported Polish, 8.6 percent Lithuanian or Lettish, and 7.6 percent German).

57. Neither New York nor the Bronx is an "influential" case in this analysis using the DFITS measure discussed by Kenneth A. Bollen and Robert W. Jackman, "Regression Diagnostics: An Expository Treatment of Outliers and Influential Cases," *Sociological Methods and Research* 13 (May 1985), pp. 510–542. When we exclude New York (1912) and New York and the Bronx (1920) from the analysis, the coefficients for the proportion of Russian immigrants change only slightly.

58. Nathan Glazer observes that "the circumstances of their lives [in America] had less to do with *making* them Socialists than with *keeping* them Socialists." Nathan Glazer, *The Social Basis of American Communism* (Westport, Conn.: Greenwood Press, 1974), p. 21 (emphases in original). The same conclusion is suggested by Paul Buhle, "Italian-American Radicals and Labor in Rhode Island, 1905–30," in Herbert G. Gutman and Donald H. Bell, eds., *The New England Working Class and the New Labor History* (Chicago: University of Illinois Press, 1987).

59. Rosenblum, *Immigrant Workers*, pp. 151–153.

60. Gutman, *Work, Culture, and Society*, pp. 577, 571.

61. Arthur Liebman, "The Ties that Bind: The Jewish Support for the Left in the

United States," *American Jewish Quarterly* 66 (1976), p. 301.

62. "In the process of immigration to America, many of the Russian Jews brought with them the political skills, organizational forms, and memories that emerged from their experience or association with the Jewish Left. These were the people who proved to be the major base and architects of a Jewish Left in America." Liebman, *Jews and the Left*, p. 134.

63. United States Senate Documents, 61st Congress, 3rd Session, *Immigrants Commission Report*, vol. 7 (Washington, D.C.: U.S. Government Printing Office, 1910), pp. 417–419, 530–531. See Samuel L. Baily, "The Italian and Organized Labor in the United States and Argentina: 1880–1910," *International Migration Review* 1 (Summer 1967), pp. 56–66; Edward Fenton, *Immigrants and Unions* (New York: Arno Press, 1975), pp. 574–575.

64. Joseph Barton, *Peasants and Strangers* (Cambridge, Mass.: Harvard University Press, 1975), pp. 27–36; Fenton, *Immigrants and Unions*, pp. 1–30. See also Irving Howe, *Socialism and America* (San Diego: Harcourt Brace Jovanovich, 1985), pp. 124–129. Howe notes that after the Italians, Eastern Europeans had the highest rate of return to their homelands, although there were few Jews among them.

65. See Michael Miller Topp, "The Italian-American Left: Transnationalism and the Quest for Unity," in Buhle and Georgakas, eds., *Immigrant Left*, pp. 119–126. Paul Buhle, writing about Italians, notes: "Hunger riots, landowners' leagues, rural fasci and other forms of 'primitive rebellion' flared up repeatedly and were repressed with great bloodshed. The main activists in these riots, the *contadini* (agricultural workers), combined an unabashed hatred for the rich with elements of fatalism. Confined by the hundreds of thousands to poverty within the 'rural cities,' by and large illiterate, they remained loyal to the traditions of family unity, village provincialism, and superstition (as opposed to institutionalized religion). As a result, the socialists made few inroads into the south. And it was this region which provided the bulk of immigrants to the United States." Buhle, "Italian-American Radicals and Labor," p. 272.

66. Auvo Kostiainen, *The Forging of Finnish-American Communism, 1917–1924* (Turku, Finland: Migration Institute, 1978), p. 32. See Al Gedicks, "The Social Origins of Radicalism Among Finnish Immigrants in Midwest Mining Communities," *Review of Radical Political Economics* 8 (Fall 1976), p. 28. See also Paul George Hummasti, "Finnish Radicals in Astoria, Oregon, 1904–1940: A Study in Immigrant Socialism" (Ph.D. thesis, University of Oregon, 1975); Kivisto, *Immigrant Socialists in the United States*.

67. Reino Kero found that the right-wing papers' supporters were from the two northern provinces, Vaasa and Oulu, in which the Finnish socialists were relatively weak. Conversely, the population which came from the more radicalized sections of southern and eastern Finland "contributed relatively more material to

the Finnish-American left than it did to the Finnish immigration as a whole."
Reino Kero, *The Roots of Finnish-American Left-Wing Radicalism* (Turku, Finland:
Publications of the Institute of General History, 1973), pp. 52–53; as cited in
Gedicks, "Social Origins of Radicalism," p. 26. Various additional factors have
been hypothesized to explain the strength of socialism among rural Finnish
immigrants. In the first place, Finns brought with them traditions of resistance to
Russian imperialism that reinforced their much-noted lack of respect for authority. See Gedicks, "Social Origins of Radicalism," pp. 1–31; Kivisto, *Immigrant
Socialists in the United States*. Rebellious activity was justified in terms of the
basic demand for national autonomy. Finnish socialists had the benefit of an
experienced set of radical leaders who were driven from Finland by Russophile
despots. Barely half of the Finns conscripted to serve in the czar's army in the
early 1900s actually served. Second, their ability to organize was facilitated by
the strong common traditions symbolized in the communal buildings where they
came together to eat, talk, and share their leisure time. In recognition of the communal basis of Finnish radicalism, the resulting socialist movement is aptly
termed "hall socialism." The organizational capacity engendered by hall socialism
was strengthened by the close-knit, often geographically isolated occupational
communities formed by Finns in the copper-mining and lumber industries, industries in which Finns were numerous. See Al Gedicks, "Ethnicity, Class Solidarity,
and Labor Radicalism Among Finnish Immigrants in Michigan Copper Country,"
Politics and Society 7 (1977), pp. 127–156.

68. Gedicks, "The Social Origins of Radicalism Among Finnish Immigrants," p.
28. See also Paul George Hummasti, "Finnish Radicals in Astoria, Oregon"; Kivisto,
Immigrant Socialists in the United States.

69. *Abstract of Thirteenth Census of the United States*, 1910, p. 204.

70. The Census does not provide the number of Finnish immigrants at the
county level, but only Scandinavians. The coefficient reported in the appendix to
this chapter includes Danes, Norwegians, and Swedish, all of whom where less
ardent supporters of socialism than were the Finns.

71. Fine, *Labor and Farmer Parties*, p. 326.

72. *Ibid.*, p. 326.

73. David Shannon, *The Socialist Party of America* (Chicago: Quadrangle Books,
1967), p. 47.

74. Charles Leinenweber, "Immigration and the Decline and Internationalism in
the American Working Class Movement, 1864–1919" (Ph.D. thesis, University of
California, Berkeley, 1968), p. 210.

75. Fine, *Labor and Farmer Parties*, p. 328; Kivisto, *Immigrant Socialists in the
United States*, pp. 185–186.

76. Glazer, *Social Basis of American Communism*, p. 25.

77. Marcus Lee Hansen, *The Immigrant in American History* (New York: Harper

Torchbooks, 1964), pp. 82, 85–96. See also Oscar Handlin, *The Uprooted* (Boston: Little, Brown, 1973), pp. 81, 109–110.

78. *Ibid.*, pp. 78–79.

79. *Ibid.*, p. 95.

80. Oscar Handlin, "The Immigrant and American Politics," in David F. Bowers, ed., *Foreign Influence in American Life* (Princeton, N.J.: Princeton University Press, 1944), pp. 90–91. See also Handlin, *Uprooted*, pp. 194–195.

81. Richard Hofstadter, *The Age of Reform: From Bryan to FDR* (New York: Alfred A. Knopf, 1972), pp. 183–184.

82. Handlin, *Uprooted*; Hofstadter, *Age of Reform*; Martin Shefter, "Trade Unions and Political Machines: The Organization and Disorganization of the American Working Class in the Late Nineteenth Century," in Ira Katznelson and Aristide R. Zolberg, eds., *Working Class Formation: Nineteenth-Century Patterns in Western Europe and the United States* (Princeton, N.J.: Princeton University Press, 1986), pp. 267–268.

83. Rosenblum, *Immigrant Workers*, p. 143.

84. *Ibid.*, p. 159.

85. Rudolph Vecoli, "Contadini in Chicago: A Critique of *The Uprooted*," *Journal of American History* 51 (1964), p. 407; David Brody, *Steelworkers in America: The Nonunion Era* (New York: Russell & Russell, 1970).

86. Rosenblum, *Immigrant Workers*, p. 125; Jerome Karabel, "The Reason Why?" *New York Review of Books* 26 (February 8, 1979), p. 24; Thomas Kessner, *The Golden Door: Italian and Jewish Mobility in New York City, 1880–1915* (New York: Oxford University Press, 1977), p. 28; Brody, *Steelworkers*, pp. 45–53.

87. Rosenblum, *Immigrant Workers*, p. 79.

88. Report by Daniel De Leon to the Zurich Congress in *The People*, June 8, 1893, p. 1.

89. R. Laurence Moore, *European Socialists and the American Promised Land* (New York: Oxford University Press, 1970), p. 148–150.

90. Hillquit, *History of Socialism*, pp. 139–140.

91. Harrington, *Socialism*, p. 132.

92. Thomas Mayer, "Some Characteristics of Union Members in the 1880s and the 1890s," *Labor History* 5 (Winter 1964), p. 65.

93. David J. Saposs stressed the "significant and predominant role of the Catholic Church in shaping the thought and aspiration of labor. . . . Its influence explains, in part at least, why the labor movement in the United States differs from others. . . ." In David J. Saposs, "The Catholic Church and the Labor Movement," *Modern Monthly* 7 (May 1933), p. 225. See also Marc Karson, *American Labor Unions and Politics, 1900–1918* (Carbondale: South Illinois University Press, 1958), pp. 284–287.

94. G. D. H. Cole, *The Second International 1889–1914* (London: Macmillan,

{

1956), p. 777. Patricia Cayo Sexton, *The War on Labor and the Left: Understanding America's Unique Conservatism* (Boulder, Colo.: Westview Press, 1991), pp. 41–42.

95. Marc Karson, "The Catholic Church and the Political Development of American Trade Unions, 1900–1918," *Industrial and Labor Relations Review* 4 (July 1951), p. 528.

96. Saposs, "Catholic Church and the Labor Movement," p. 297.

97. Selig Perlman, *A Theory of the Labor Movement* (New York: Macmillan, 1928), p. 168.

98. Karson, "Catholic Church and the Political Development of American Trade Unions," p. 528.

99. Eric Foner, *History of the Labor Movement*, vol. 3 (New York: International Publishers, 1964), p. 3; Laslett, *Labor and the Left*, p. 76. See also Robert E. Doherty, "Thomas J. Haggerty, the Church and Socialism," *Labor History* 3 (Winter 1962), p. 46.

100. Doherty, "Thomas J. Hagerty," p. 46.

101. Perlman, *Theory*, p. 169.

102. Karson, "Catholic Church and the Political Development of American Trade Unions," p. 531.

103. Saposs, "Catholic Church and the Labor Movement," pp. 294–298.

104. *Ibid.*, p. 298.

105. Laslett, *Labor and the Left*, p. 76.

106. Karson, "Catholic Church and the Political Development of American Trade Unions," p. 535.

107. Melvyn Dubofsky, "Success and Failure of Socialism in New York City, 1900–1918: A Case Study," *Labor History* 9 (Fall 1968), p. 372.

108. Aaron L. Abell, *American Catholicism and Social Action: A Search for Social Justice 1865–1950* (Garden City, N.Y.: Hanover House/Doubleday, 1960), p. 147.

109. Cited in Abell, *American Catholicism*, p. 148.

110. *Ibid.*, p. 172.

111. Shannon, *Socialist Party of America*, pp. 58–59.

112. David Paul Nord, "*The Appeal to Reason* and American Socialism, 1901–1920," *Kansas History* 1 (Summer 1978), p. 84.

113. Abell, *American Catholicism*, p. 171.

114. John Higham, *Strangers in the Land* (New Brunswick, N.J.: Rutgers University Press, 1955), p. 180; Abell, *American Catholicism*, p. 172.

115. Abell, *American Catholicism*, p. 171.

116. *Ibid.*, p. 171.

117. Beatrice Golden Schultz, "The Socialist Party Conventions, 1904–1912, and the International Rhetoric" (Ph.D. thesis, Department of Speech, University of Michigan, 1969), pp. 167–170.

118. Handlin, *Uprooted*, p. 199.

119. Dubofsky, "Success and Failure," p. 372.

120. Saposs, "Catholic Church and the Labor Movement," p. 297.

121. Philip Taft, *The AF of L in the Time of Gompers* (New York: Harper & Bros., 1957), p. 336; and Gerald N. Grob, *Workers and Utopia: A Study of the Ideological Conflict in the American Labor Movement, 1865–1900* (Chicago: Quadrangle Books, 1969), pp. 165–166.

122. Grob, *Workers and Utopia*, p. 166.

123. Foner, *History of the Labor Movement*, pp. 383–384.

124. Weinstein, *Decline of Socialism*, p. 36.

125. Laslett, *Labor and the Left*, p. 5.

126. *Ibid.*, p. 230.

127. As Marc Karson stresses: "Catholics engaged in this [antisocialist] task during a period when American trade unionism, still in its infancy, was developing its institutional traditions. Like all traditions, these would prevail during future generations and tend to become almost conditioned responses. Furthermore, this period also began as one in which the socialist movement seemed on the threshold of becoming a major American political force. . . . Catholicism could take partial credit for the political philosophy and policies of the federation, for socialism's weakness in the trade union movement, and the absence of a labor party in the United States." Karson, "Catholic Church and the Political Development of American Trade Unions," pp. 528–535. In so commenting, Karson reiterated the conclusion of the first labor historian to deal extensively with the issue, David Saposs, who stated unequivocally that "Catholic domination has more than any other factor made the American Federation of Labor safe for capitalism and a violent opponent of socialism." Saposs, "Catholic Church and the Labor Movement," p. 298. See also Cole, *Second International*, p. 77.

128. Leinenweber, "American Socialist Party," pp. 1–2.

129. Sally Miller, "Americans and the Second International," *Proceedings of the American Philosophical Society* 120 (October 1976), pp. 383–385. See also Andrew Neather, "Labor Republicanism, Race, and Popular Patriotism in the Era of Empire, 1890–1914," in John Bodnar, ed., *Bonds of Affection: Americans Define Their Patriotism* (Princeton, N.J.: Princeton University Press, 1996).

130. Cited in Shannon, *Socialist Party of America*, pp. 49–50; Ira Kipnis, *The American Socialist Movement, 1897–1912* (New York: Columbia University Press, 1952), pp. 282–287.

131. As Gerald Friedberg reports: "The convention thus took a position permitting whatever degree of restriction or exclusion Socialists might want, while preserving the spirit of righteousness with a phrase rejecting exclusion because of race alone." Friedberg concludes that opposition to the Hillquit motion "came mainly from those who wanted still greater restriction without what members of all factions viewed as an evasion." Gerald Friedberg, "Marxism in the United States: John

Spargo and the Socialist Party of America" (Ph.D. thesis, Department of Government, Harvard University, 1952), pp. 282–287.

132. For circulation figures, see Weinstein, *Decline of Socialism*, p. 90.

133. David Shannon, *The Great Depression* (Englewood Cliffs, N.J.: Prentice-Hall, 1960), p. 48.

134. Edward J. Muzik, "Victor L. Berger: A Biography" (Ph.D. thesis, Department of History, Northwestern University, 1960), p. 184.

135. Quoted in Leinenweber, "Immigration and the Decline," p. 172. In 1912, the year the party received its highest presidential vote, the official Socialist Campaign Book contained material written by party leader Robert Russell, which discussed the "dangers" flowing from immigration, including what "seem the most important, the likelihood of race annihilation and the possible degeneration of even the succeeding American type." *Ibid.*, p. 128.

136. Kipnis, *American Socialist Movement*, p. 278.

137. Robert Alexander, "Splinter Groups in American Radical Politics," *Social Research* 20 (Autumn 1953), pp. 308–309. See his detailed discussion of the Socialist party's attention to foreign events, p. 309. The alienation and isolation of the earliest socialist movements from mainstream politics has frequently been attributed to the predominance of foreign immigrants among their membership. Samuel Bernstein, in his analysis of the First International in America, explains the failure of the International Workingman's Association to establish itself as part of the labor movement as resulting from the isolation of its foreign immigrant supporters from other workers. He does so in terms which could also be applied to its successor, the Socialist Labor party: "The foreign elements in the organization. . . lived apart from the American workers, spoke their native tongues and claimed the superiority of their imported cultures. The most culpable were the Germans who at times behaved towards Americans like Prussian schoolmasters." Samuel Bernstein, *The First International in America* (New York: Augustus M. Kelley, 1962), p. 193.

138. Laslett, *Labor and the Left*, p. 4.

139. Rosenblum, *Immigrant Workers*, p. 167.

140. Miller, "Americans and the Second International," p. 383.

141. Glazer, *Social Basis of American Communism*, p. 28; Shannon, *Socialist Party of America*, pp. 77–78.

142. Bernard Johnpoll, "The Demise of the American Socialist Party" (Unpublished paper, Department of Political Science, State University of New York at Albany, September 1976), pp. 11–12.

143. Peter Roberts, *The New Immigration* (New York: Macmillan, 1912), p. 104.

144. Bertram Benedict, "The New Socialism in Great Britain and the United States," *American Political Science Review* 18 (May 1924), pp. 279–280.

145. Leinenweber, "American Socialist Party," p. 14.

146. Dubofsky, *We Shall Be All*, p. 242.

147. *Final Report and Testimony of the United States Commission on Industrial Relations* (Washington, D.C.: 1915), vol. 5, p. 4947; quoted in *ibid.*, p. 151.

148. Alexander, "Splinter Groups," pp. 308–309. See Paul Buhle's discussion of the IWW's involvement in immigrant strikes, "Italian-American Radicals and Labor," pp. 281–283.

149. Thomas M. LoFaro, "The Legitimization and Assimilation of the American Labor Movement, 1900–1940," *Industrial and Labor Relations Forum* 8 (December 1972), p. 11; Rosenblum, *Immigrant Workers*, pp. 164–166.

150. Marks and Burbank, "Immigrant Support for the American Socialist Party 1912 and 1920."

151. Firebaugh, "The Ratio Variable Hoax in Political Science," *American Journal of Political Science* 32 (1988), pp. 523–535.

152. Damodar N. Gujarati, *Basic Econometrics*, 2nd ed. (New York: McGraw-Hill, 1988).

153. Firebaugh, "Ratio Variable Hoax," pp. 525–535; W. P. Shively, "'Ecological' Inference: The Uses of Aggregate Data to Study Individuals," *American Political Science Review* 63 (1969), pp. 1183–1196.

5. Sectarians vs. Reformists: Were Socialists Undermined by Their Own Strategy?

1. Daniel Bell, *Marxian Socialism in the United States* (Ithaca, N.Y.: Cornell University Press, 1996), pp. 9–10. See also J. David Gillespie, *Politics at the Periphery: Third Parties in Two–Party America* (Columbia: University of South Carolina Press, 1993), pp. 179–189.

2. Engels referred to "that sectarian land, America," where purists could always count on support. Engels to Sorge, June 29, 1883, in "Unpublished Letters of Karl Marx and Friedrich Engels to Americans," ed. and trans. Leonard E. Mins, *Science and Society* 2 (1938), p. 231. Engels repeatedly criticized the first major American socialist party, the Socialist Labor party (SLP), for treating Marxist theory in a "doctrinaire and dogmatic way, as something which has got to be learnt off by heart but which will then supply all needs without more ado. To them it is a *credo* and not a guide to action." Engels to Sorge, November 29, 1886, in Karl Marx and Friedrich Engels, *Selected Correspondence, 1846–1895* (New York: International Publishers, 1942), pp. 449–450. In 1894 he criticized the American SLP and the British Social Democratic Federation for being "the only parties that have managed to reduce the Marxian theory of development to a rigid orthodoxy, which the workers are not to reach themselves by their own class feeling, but which they have to gulp down as an article of faith at once and without development. That is why both of them remain sects and come, as Hegel says, from nothing through nothing to nothing." Engels to Sorge, May 12, 1894, in Karl Marx and Friedrich Engels, *Letters to*

Americans, 1848–1895 (New York: International Publishers, 1953), p. 263. Marx, as well, "confessed to a certain suspicion of 'Yankee socialists' as 'crotchety and sectarian.'" Quoted in Sidney Hook, *Marx and the Marxists* (New York: D. Van Nostrand, 1955), p. 64. Lenin also emphasized socialist sectarianism, which he attributed to the high relative degree of political freedom in America. See V. I. Lenin, "Preface to the Russian Translation of 'Letters by J. Ph. Becker, J. Dietzgen, F. Engels, K. Marx and Others to F. A. Sorge and Others,'" in V. I. Lenin, *On Britain* (Moscow: Foreign Languages Publishing House, n.d.), p. 51. Like Marx, Engels, and Lenin, Trotsky also found it necessary to add to his "materialistic" explanation of the continued strength of bourgeois democracy, the sectarian character of Marxists in America. Leon Trotsky, *The Living Thoughts of Karl Marx* (New York: Longmans, Green, 1939), p. 36. See also Sally M. Miller, "Different Accents of Labor," *Labor's Heritage* 2 (1990), pp. 62–75.

3. Mark A. Lause, "The American Radicals and Organized Marxism: The Initial Experience, 1869–1874," *Labor History*, Winter 1992, p. 79; See also Miller, "Different Accents of Labor."

4. Robert F. Hoxie, " 'The Rising Tide of Socialism': A Study," *Journal of Political Economy* 19 (October 1911), pp. 609–631.

5. Samuel Gompers, *Seventy Years of Life and Labor* (New York: E. P. Dutton, 1925), pp. 50–53, 57, 104; William M. Dick, *Labor and Socialism in America: The Gompers Era* (Port Washington, N.Y.: Kennikat Press, 1972), p. 20; Richard W. Judd, *Socialist Cities: Municipal Politics and the Grass Roots of American Socialism* (Albany: State University of New York Press, 1989), pp. 3–7; Bernard K. Johnpoll, *Pacifist's Progress: Norman Thomas and the Decline of American Socialism* (Westport, Conn.: Greenwood Press, 1987), pp. 108–111; Bruce M. Stave, *Socialism and the Cities* (Port Washington, N.Y.: Kennikat Press, 1975), pp. 188–189; Aileen Kraditor, *The Radical Persuasion, 1890–1917* (Baton Rouge: Louisiana State University Press, 1981), pp. 284–285; Stan Nadel, "The German Immigrant Left in the United States," in Paul Buhle and George Georgakas, eds., *The Immigrant Left in the United States* (Albany: State University of New York Press, 1996), pp. 62–63.

6. Gompers, *Seventy Years*, p. 101; Norman J. Ware, *The Labor Movement in the United States 1860–1895* (New York: D. Appleton, 1929), p. 262.

7. Gompers, *Seventy Years*, p. 202; Miller, "Different Accents of Labor," p. 382.

8. Dick, *Labor and Socialism*, p. 21. See also Henry Pelling, *American Labor* (Chicago: University of Chicago Press, 1960), pp. 88–89; Stuart B. Kaufman, *Samuel Gompers and the Origins of the American Federation of Labor 1848–1896* (Westport, Conn.: Greenwood Press, 1973), pp. 190–213; Gompers, *Seventy Years*, pp. 384–389.

9. *Ibid.*, pp. 311–326.

10. Louis S. Reed, *The Labor Philosophy of Samuel Gompers* (New York: Columbia University Press, 1930), p. 102.

11. Dick, *Labor and Socialism*, p. 31.

12. *Ibid.*, p. 31.

13. Quoted in Reed, *Labor Philosophy*, p. 102.

14. D. H. Leon, "Whatever Happened to the Socialist Party? A Critical Survey of Spectrum of Interpretations," *American Quarterly* 23 (May 1971), pp. 250-251; Morris Hillquit, *Loose Leaves from a Busy Life* (New York: Macmillan, 1934), p. 96; Patricia Cayo Sexton, *The War on Labor and the Left: Understanding America's Unique Conservatism* (Boulder: Westview Press, 1991), pp. 42-44.

15. Gompers, *Seventy Years*, p. 388.

16. Engels to Sorge, January 6, 1892, in *Letters to Americans*, p. 240.

17. Engels to Schlüter, January 29, 1891, in *Letters to Americans*, p. 233.

18. Howard H. Quint, *The Forging of American Socialism: Origins of the Modern Movement* (Indianapolis: Bobbs-Merrill, 1953), p. 331.

19. Michael Harrington, *Socialism* (New York: Saturday Review Press, 1970), p. 253.

20. John H. M. Laslett, *Labor and the Left: A Study of Socialist and Radical Influences in the American Labor Movement, 1881-1924* (New York: Basic Books, 1970), pp. 271, 217.

21. Quoted in Marc Karson, *American Labor Unions in Politics: 1900-1918* (Carbondale: Southern Illinois University Press, 1958), p. 190.

22. Morris Hillquit, Samuel Gompers, and Max J. Hayes, *The Double Edge of Labor's Sword: Discussion and Testimony on Socialism and Trade Unionism before the Commission on Industrial Relations* (Chicago: Socialist Party National Office, 1914), pp. 44-57.

23. Laslett, *Labor and the Left*.

24. Lewis Lorwin, *American Federation of Labor* (Washington, D.C.: Brookings Institution, 1933), p. 115.

25. William C. Seyler, "The Rise and Decline of the Socialist Party in the United States." (Ph.D. thesis, Department of History, Duke University, 1952), p. 195.

26. Quoted in Dick, *Labor and Socialism in America*, p. 65.

27. Irving Howe, *Socialism and America* (San Diego: Harcourt Brace Jovanovich, 1985), p. 25.

28. Dick, *Labor and Socialism in America*, pp. 62-64, 67, 166, 170; Ira Kipnis, *American Socialist Movement, 1897-1912* (New York: Columbia University, 1952), pp. 124-126, 230.

29. Kipnis, *American Socialist Movement*, p. 125.

30. *Ibid.*, p. 126.

31. Nathan Fine, *Labor and Farmer Parties in the United States, 1828-1928* (New York: Rand School of Social Science, 1928), pp. 291-294; Dick, *Labor and Socialism in America*, p. 64.

32. Kipnis, *American Socialist Movement*, p. 126.

33. Laslett, *Labor and the Left*, pp. 212–213.

34. *Ibid.*, p. 213.

35. Gerald Friedberg, "Marxism in the United States: John Spargo and the Socialist Party of America" (Ph.D. thesis, Department of Government, Harvard University, 1952), p. 110; Seyler, "Rise and Decline," p. 200.

36. *Ibid.*, p. 203.

37. Quoted in Fine, *Labor and Farmer Parties*, p. 296.

38. Quoted in David A. Shannon, *The Socialist Party of America* (Chicago: Quadrangle Books, 1967), p. 67; Seyler, "Rise and Decline," p. 199.

39. *Ibid.*, p. 231.

40. Kipnis, *American Socialist Movement*, p. 126.

41. *Ibid.*, p. 126.

42. Fine, *Labor and Farmer Parties*, p. 295.

43. Shannon, *Socialist Party*, pp. 16–17; Kipnis, *American Socialist Movement*, pp. 427–428.

44. Cited in David Paul Nord, "Hothouse Socialism: Minneapolis, 1910–1925," in Donald T. Critchlow, ed., *Socialism in the Heartland: The Midwestern Experience, 1900–1925* (Notre Dame, Ind.: University of Notre Dame Press, 1986), p. 117.

45. Michael Bassett, "Municipal Reform and the Socialist Party, 1910–1914," *Australian Journal of Politics and History* 19 (August 1973), pp. 179–187.

46. Quoted in Shannon, *Socialist Party*, p. 259.

47. Floyd J. Stachowski, "The Political Career of Daniel Webster Hoan" (Ph.D. thesis, Department of History, Northwestern University, 1966), p. 46.

48. Albert J. Nock, "Socialism in Milwaukee," *Outlook*, July 11, 1914, as cited in Frederick I. Olson, "The Milwaukee Socialists, 1897–1941" (Ph.D thesis, Department of History, Harvard University, 1952), p. 246.

49. Stachowski, "Political Career," p. 46.

50. Marvin Wachman, *History of the Social-Democratic Party of Milwaukee, 1897–1910* (Urbana: University of Illinois Press, 1945), p. 75.

51. Olson, "Milwaukee Socialists," p. 246.

52. *Ibid.*, p. 319.

53. Chad Gaffield, "Big Business, The Working-Class, and Socialism in Schenectady, 1911–1916," *Labor History* 19 (Summer 1978), pp. 356–357.

54. *Ibid.*, pp. 356–357.

55. Seyler, "Rise and Decline," p. 233.

56. Shannon, *Socialist Party*, p. 39.

57. Weinstein, *Decline of Socialism*, p. 112.

58. Laslett, *Labor and the Left*, pp. 220–221.

59. These cases are drawn from Judd, *Socialist Cities*, pp. 134–136.

60. *Ibid.*, p. 135.

61. *Ibid.*, p. 139.

62. Weinstein, *Decline of Socialism*, p. 110.

63. Quoted in *ibid.*, p. 112.

64. Edward S. Kerstein, *Milwaukee's All-American Mayor: Portrait of Daniel Webster Hoan* (Englewood Cliffs, N.J.: Prentice-Hall, 1966), p. 200; W. A. Swanberg, *Norman Thomas: The Last Idealist* (New York: Charles Scribner's Sons, 1976), p. 133. Historian David Shannon points out that "most Socialists never saw the value of political organization. They regarded the building of local machines as 'ward heeling,' sordid truckling for votes beneath the ideals of Socialism." "This lack of interest in local matters," Shannon notes, "was a disregard of one of the basic features of American politics." Shannon, *Socialist Party*, pp. 259–260.

65. Quoted in Fine, *Labor and Farmer Parties*, p. 371.

66. Jackson K. Putnam, "The Socialist Party of North Dakota, 1902–1918" (M.A. thesis, Department of History, University of North Dakota, 1956), p. 73.

67. *Ibid.*, pp. 138–142.

68. *Ibid.*, p. 164.

69. Robert H. Bahmer, "The Economic and Political Background of the Nonpartisan League" (Ph.D. thesis, Department of History, University of Minnesota, 1941), p. 434; Paul John Doure, "A Study of the Nonpartisan League Persuasion, 1915–1920" (Ph.D. thesis, Department of Speech, Northwestern University, 1963), pp. 27–30.

70. Robert L. Morlan, *Political Prairie Fire: The Nonpartisan League, 1915–1922* (Minneapolis: University of Minnesota Press, 1955), p. 358.

71. Bahmer, "Economic and Political Background," p. 442.

72. Morlan, *Political Prairie Fire*, pp. 237–238.

73. *Ibid.*, p. 224.

74. Putnam, "Socialist Party," pp. 31, 174, 354; Doure, "Nonpartisan League Persuasion," pp. 29–30.

75. Morlan, *Political Prairie Fire*, p. 277.

76. *Ibid.*, pp. 200–202.

77. *Ibid.*, pp. 301–302. See Millard L. Gieske, *Minnesota Farmer-Laborism: The Third-Party Alternative* (Minneapolis: University of Minnesota Press, 1979).

78. Arthur Naftalin, "A History of the Farmer-Labor Party of Minnesota" (Ph.D. thesis, Department of Political Science, University of Minnesota, 1948), pp. 53–63.

79. *Ibid.*, p. 345.

80. *Ibid.*, p. 346.

81. Friedberg, "Marxism in the United States," p. 212.

82. Quoted in *ibid.*, p. 212; Seyler, "Rise and Decline," p. 425.

83. Friedberg, "Marxism in the United States," pp. 212–213.

84. Doure, "Nonpartisan League Persuasion," p. 30.

85. Jackson Putnam concludes: "The demise of the North Dakota Socialist party was to a considerable extent, an eventuality of its own making." Putnam, "Socialist Party," p. 190.

86. David Paul Nord, "Minneapolis and the Pragmatic Socialism of Thomas Van Lear," *Minnesota History* 45 (Spring 1976), p. 10.

87. Nord, "Hothouse Socialism," pp. 150–152.

88. *Ibid.*, pp. 155–157.

89. Morris Hillquit, *Socialism in Theory and Practice* (New York: Macmillan, 1912), p. 181.

90. Fine, *Labor and Farmer Parties*, p. 303.

91. *Ibid.*, p. 304.

92. Shannon, *Socialist Party*, p. 98; also see Bell, *Marxian Socialism*, pp. 101–104; Friedberg, "Marxism in the United States," pp. 209–210.

93. Friedberg, "Marxism in the United States," p. 193.

94. Bell, *Marxian Socialism*, p. 102. David Shannon has pointed out that "the strong European socialist parties had as the basis of their strength the trade unions, which were generally pro-war, and these parties had to compromise their principles to retain their labor support. If the American Socialists . . . had possessed a comparable labor strength . . . they too might have not been so militantly antiwar." Shannon, *Socialist Party*, p. 98. See also Fine, *Labor and Farmer Parties*, p. 307.

95. Weinstein, *The Decline of Socialism*, pp. 47–49.

96. Olson, "Milwaukee Socialists," p. 393.

97. Howe, *Socialism and America*, p. 44.

98. Milton Cantor, "The Radical Confrontation with Foreign Policy: War and Revolution, 1914–1920," in Alfred F. Young, ed., *Dissent: Explorations in the History of American Radicalism* (DeKalb: Northern Illinois University Press, 1968), p. 230–231.

99. Quoted in Stanley Shapiro, "The Great War and Reform: Liberals and Labor, 1917–1919," *Labor History* 2 (Summer 1971), pp. 332–333.

100. Nord, "Hothouse Socialism," pp. 137–139.

101. *Ibid.*, pp. 149–152.

102. Thomas W. Gavett, *Development of the Labor Movement in Milwaukee* (Madison: University of Wisconsin Press, 1965), pp. 126–131.

103. Gavett, *Development of the Labor Movement*, pp. 130, 128.

104. Quoted in Olson, "Milwaukee Socialists," p. 342. Hoan regretted and privately opposed the party's militant antiwar program and avoided endorsing it publicly. As mayor, he cooperated with the draft registration program, and he served as cochairman of the local defense council. In the latter role, he pressed for "laws against profiteering and aid in raising wages of substandard income groups." *Ibid.*, pp. 345–346.

105. Melvyn Dubofsky, "Success and Failure of Socialism in New York City,

1900–1918: A Case Study," *Labor History* 9 (Fall 1968), p. 370; Arthur Liebman, "The Ties that Bind: The Jewish Support for the Left in the United States," *American Jewish Quarterly* 66 (1976), p. 301.

106. Dubofsky, "Success and Failure," p. 169.

107. Franklin L. Jonas, "The Early Life and Career of B. Charney Vladeck, 1886–1921: The Emergence of an Immigrant Spokesman" (Ph.D. thesis, Department of History, New York University, 1972), pp. 167–168.

108. *Ibid.*, p. 171.

109. Kenneth E. Hendrickson, Jr., "The Pro-War Socialists, the Social Democratic League and the Ill-Fated Drive for Industrial Democracy in America, 1917–1920," *Labor History* 11 (Summer 1970), p. 315.

110. Weinstein, *Decline of Socialism*, pp. 154–157.

111. *Ibid.*, p. 159.

112. *Ibid.*, p. 115.

113. Fine, *Labor and Farmer Parties*, p. 326.

114. *Ibid.*, p. 326.

115. Hillquit, *Loose Leaves from a Busy Life*, p. 300.

116. See Nathan Glazer, *The Social Basis of American Communism* (Westport, Conn.: Greenwood Press, 1974), p. 32.

117. James Weinstein, *The Decline of Socialism in America, 1912–1915* (New York: Vintage Books, 1969), pp. 222–225; Bell, *Marxian Socialism*, pp. 118–119.

118. Stanley Shapiro, "Hand and Brain: The Farmer-Labor Party of 1920" (Ph.D. thesis, Department of History, University of California, Berkeley, 1967), pp. 177–181.

119. Scott D. Johnston, "The Socialist Party in the Conference for Progressive Political Action" (Ph.D. thesis, Department of Political Science, University of Minnesota, 1952), p. 14.

120. Johnston, "Socialist Party," pp. 14–15; Fine, *Labor and Farmer Parties*, pp. 417–419.

121. Fine, *Labor and Farmer Parties*, p. 424; Weinstein, *Decline of Socialism*, pp. 224–226.

122. Shapiro, "Hand and Brain," p. 165.

123. Dixon, "Issue of Race," pp. 99, 101.

124. Kipnis, *American Socialist Movement*, pp. 403–406; Nick Salvatore, *Eugene V. Debs: Citizen and Socialist* (Urbana: University of Illinois Press, 1982), p. 255.

125. Robert W. Iverson, "Morris Hillquit: American Social Democrat" (Ph.D. thesis, Department of History, University of Iowa, 1951), p. 134.

126. Weinstein, *Decline of Socialism*, p. 27.

127. R. Laurence Moore, *European Socialists and the American Promised Land* (New York: Oxford University Press, 1970), p. 207.

128. Salvatore, *Eugene V. Debs*, p. 258.

129. *Ibid.*, pp. 258–259.

130. Mike Davis, *Prisoners of the American Dream: Politics and Economy in the History of the U.S. Working Class* (New York: Verso, 1988), pp. 46–47. See also Sidney Lens, *Radicalism in America* (Cambridge, Mass.: Schenkman Publishing Co., 1981), pp. 241–242.

131. Kipnis, *American Socialist Movement*, p. 418.

132. Quoted in Moore, *European Socialists*, p. 206.

133. Iverson, "Morris Hillquit," p. 135.

134. Friedberg, "Marxism in the United States," p. 193.

135. Shannon, *Socialist Party*, pp. 16–17, 39–40, 70–71.

136. *Ibid.*, p. 80.

137. Moore, *European Socialists*, pp. 205–206.

138. Hillquit, *Socialism*, pp. 179–181.

139. Moore, *European Socialists*, pp. 204–205.

140. H. G. Wells, *Social Forces in England and America* (New York: Harper & Bros., 1914), pp. 345–346.

141. Henry Pelling, "The Rise and Decline of Socialism in Milwaukee," *Bulletin of the International Institute of Social History* 10 (1955), pp. 91–92.

142. Henry Pelling, *America and the British Left* (London: A. & C. Black, 1956), p. 90.

143. *Ibid.*, pp. 91–92.

144. Moore, *European Socialists*, p. 205.

145. *Ibid.*, p. 204.

146. The statements made by Berger were reported in the *Social-Democratic Herald*, April 15, 1905, quoted in Wachman, *History of the Social-Democratic Party*, p. 75.

147. Quoted in Wachman, *History of the Social-Democratic Party*, p. 74.

148. Quoted in Gavett, *Development of the Labor Movement*, p. 129.

149. Moore, *European Socialists*, p. 205.

150. Richard W. Fox, "The Paradox of 'Progressive' Socialism: The Case of Morris Hillquit, 1901–1914," *American Quarterly* 26 (1974), pp. 127–128.

151. *Ibid.*, p. 128.

152. *Ibid.*, p. 128.

153. J. Dennis McGreen, "Norman Thomas and the Search for an All-Inclusive Socialist Party" (Ph.D. thesis, Department of History, Rutgers University, 1976), p. 18.

154. *Ibid.*, p. 20.

155. Morris Hillquit, *From Marx to Lenin* (New York: Hanford Press, 1921), p. 53.

156. *Ibid.*, pp. 59, 106–107.

157. Quoted in Fox, "Paradox of 'Progressive' Socialism," p. 131; Hillquit, *Socialism*, p. 103.

158. Fox, "Paradox of 'Progressive' Socialism," p. 132 (emphasis in original).

159. *Ibid.*, p. 133.

160. Harvey Klehr, "Lenin on American Socialist Leaders and on Samuel Gompers," *Labor History* 17 (Spring 1976), pp. 267, 269. See also Klehr, "Leninist Theory in Search of America," *Polity* 9 (Fall 1976), pp. 81–96.

161. Seymour Martin Lipset, *Rebellion in the University* (Chicago: University of Chicago Press, 1976), pp. 12–14.

162. Robert J. Alexander, "Splinter Groups in American Radical Parties," *Social Research* 20 (Autumn 1953), pp. 282–283.

6. Socialist Sectarianism and Communist Opportunism in the Thirties

1. Bernard K. Johnpoll, *Pacifist's Progress: Norman Thomas and the Decline of American Socialism* (Westport, Conn.: Greenwood Press, 1987), p. 88. For an extensive look at the history behind socialist newspapers, refer to Elliott Shore, *Talkin' Socialism: J. A. Wayland and the Role of the Press in American Radicalism, 1890–1912* (Lawrence: University Press of Kansas, 1988).

2. Frederick I. Olson, "The Milwaukee Socialists, 1897–1941" (Ph.D. thesis, Department of History, Harvard University, 1952), pp. 485–486, 490–491; Bayard Still, *Milwaukee: The History of a City* (Madison: State Historical Society of Wisconsin, 1948), p. 529.

3. Bruce M. Stave, "The Great Depression and Urban Political Continuity: Bridgeport Chooses Socialism," in Bruce M. Stave, ed., *Socialism and the Cities* (Port Washington, N.Y.: Kennikat Press, 1975), pp. 157–158.

4. Johnpoll, *Pacifist's Progress*, pp. 96–98, 106–108.

5. William C. Seyler, "The Rise and Decline of the Socialist Party in the United States" (Ph.D. thesis, Department of History, Duke University, 1952), p. 471; David A. Shannon, *The Socialist Party of America* (Chicago: Quadrangle Books, 1967), p. 223.

6. Seyler, "Rise and Decline," p. 471; see also Norman Thomas, *A Socialist's Faith* (New York: W. W. Norton, 1951), p. 98. For a review of Norman Thomas' philosophy, see Robert Hyfler, *Prophets of the Left: American Socialist Thought in the Twentieth Century* (Westport, Conn: Greenwood Press, 1984), pp. 121–141.

7. Olson, "Milwaukee Socialists," p. 507; Thomas, *Socialist's Faith*, pp. 250–251.

8. Seyler, "Rise and Decline," p. 540.

9. Aileen Kraditor, *The Radical Persuasion, 1890–1917* (Baton Rouge: Louisiana State University Press, 1981), p. 286. See also Michael Kazin, "The Agony and Romance of the American Left," *American Historical Review* 100 (December 1995), pp. 1510–1511; Robert J. Fitrakis, *The Idea of Democratic Socialism in America and the Decline of the Socialist Party* (New York: Garland Publishing, 1993), pp. 160–161.

10. Daniel Bell, *Marxian Socialism in the United States* (Ithaca, N.Y.: Cornell University Press, 1996), p. 158.

11. Johnpoll, *Pacifist's Progress*, p. 118; Bell, *Marxian Socialism*, pp. 158–163.

12. Fitrakis, *Idea of Democratic Socialism*, pp. 178–179. Also see Dennis McGreen, "Norman Thomas and the Search for the All–Inclusive Socialist Party" (Ph.D. thesis, Department of History, Rutgers University, 1976), pp. 18–27.

13. McGreen, "Norman Thomas," pp. 109–118; see also Fitrakis, *Idea of Democratic Socialism*.

14. Kenneth A. Waltzer, "American Labor Party: Third Party Politics in New Deal–Cold War New York, 1936–1954" (Ph.D. thesis, Department of History, Harvard University, 1977), pp. 44–45.

15. Nickolai Bakunin, "The Role of Socialists in the Formation of the American Labor Party" (M.A. thesis, Department of History, City College of New York, 1965), p. 10.

16. Nathan Fine, "Socialism," in Albert B. Hart, ed., *The American Yearbook: A Record of Events and Progress, Year 1934* (New York: American Year Book Corp., 1935), pp. 575–576; Johnpoll, *Pacifist's Progress*, pp. 122–126; McGreen, "Norman Thomas," p. 125. The declaration is contained in full in Frank A. Warren, *An Alternative Vision: The Socialist Party in the 1930s* (Bloomington: Indiana University Press, 1974), pp. 191–194.

17. Warren, *Alternative Vision*, p. 193; Johnpoll, *Pacifist's Progress*, p. 123; McGreen, "Norman Thomas," p. 123.

18. Johnpoll, *Pacifist's Progress*, p. 125; McGreen, "Norman Thomas," p. 130.

19. Fine, "Socialism," p. 576.

20. On attitudes toward Roosevelt and the New Deal, see works by Norman Thomas, *A Socialist Looks at the New Deal* (New York: League for Industrial Democracy, 1933); *The New Deal: A Socialist Analysis* (Chicago: Committee on Education and Research of the Socialist Party of America, 1934); *The Choice Before Us* (New York: Macmillan, 1934); and Warren, *Alternative Vision*, pp. 123–133.

21. Waltzer, "American Labor Party," p. 54.

22. Thomas, *Choice Before Us*, pp. 230–231.

23. Waltzer, "American Labor Party," p. 55; Bakunin, "Role of Socialists," pp. 44–46, 48–53.

24. Fitrakis, *Idea of Democratic Socialism*, pp. 184–186; Johnpoll, *Pacifist's Progress*, pp. 174–177; Murray Seidler, "The Socialist Party and American Unionism," *Midwest Journal of Political Science* 5 (August 1961), pp. 218–219.

25. Bell, *Marxian Socialism*, p. 169; Louis Waldman, *Labor Lawyer* (New York: E. P. Dutton, 1944), pp. 258–274.

26. Johnpoll, *Pacifist's Progress*, p. 157; Waltzer, "American Labor Party," p. 52; McGreen, "Norman Thomas," pp. 173–234; J. David Gillespie, *Politics at the*

Periphery: Third Parties in Two-Party America (Columbia: University of South Carolina Press, 1993), p. 189.

27. Bell, *Marxian Socialism*, pp. 175–176.

28. Quoted in Shannon, *Socialist Party*, p. 248.

29. Richard Oestreicher, "Urban Working Class Political Behavior and the Theories of American Politics, 1870–1940," *Journal of American History* 74 (March 1988), pp. 1257–1286.

30. Bruce Nelson, "Give Us Roosevelt: Workers and the New Deal Coalition," *History Today* 40 (January 1990), pp. 40–48. Among trade unionists, for example, the 1940 election saw 79 percent of CIO members and 71 percent of AFL members voting for Roosevelt. Gillespie, *Politics at the Periphery*, p. 189.

31. Kazin, "Agony and Romance," p. 1510.

32. Robert S. McElvaine, "Thunder Without Lightning: Working-Class Discontent in the United States" (Ph.D. thesis, Department of History, State University of New York at Birmingham, 1974), p. 179.

33. Clarence Frederick McIntosh, "Upton Sinclair and the EPIC Movement, 1933–1936" (Ph.D. thesis, Department of History, Stanford University, 1955), pp. 19–20, 37–38.

34. *Ibid.*, p. 39.

35. McElvaine, "Thunder Without Lightning," p. 209.

36. Warren, *Alternative Vision*, p. 75.

37. McElvaine, "Thunder Without Lightning," pp. 209–210.

38. Johnpoll, *Pacifist's Progress*, pp. 136–137; Bell, *Marxian Socialism*, pp. 161–163.

39. In Johnpoll, *Pacifist's Progress*, pp. 101–105; McElvaine, "Thunder Without Lightning," pp. 183–185.

40. McElvaine, "Thunder Without Lightning," pp. 183–184.

41. Johnpoll, *Pacifist's Progress*, pp. 130–134.

42. *Ibid.*, pp. 171–172.

43. McGreen, "Norman Thomas," p. 290.

44. James MacGregor Burns, *Roosevelt: The Lion and the Fox* (Norwalk, Conn.: Easton Press, 1989), p. 242. For an elaboration of Thomas' critique of Roosevelt and the New Deal, see Norman Thomas, *After the New Deal: Then What?* (New York: Macmillan, 1936), pp. 16–55; and Warren, *Alternative Vision*, pp. 123–133.

45. Thomas, *After the New Deal*, p. 7.

46. McGreen, "Norman Thomas," p. 292; Bell, *Marxian Socialism*, pp. 165–166.

47. Shannon, *Socialist Party*, pp. 247–248; Bell, *Marxian Socialism*, pp. 169–171.

48. Johnpoll, *Pacifist's Progress*, p. 171; Shannon, *Socialist Party*, pp. 249–250.

49. Fitrakis, *Idea of Democratic Socialism*, pp. 185–186; Johnpoll, *Pacifist's Progress*, pp. 101–105.

50. Johnpoll, *Pacifist's Progress*, pp. 170–174; Bell, *Marxian Socialism*, pp. 177–178; Bakunin, "Role of Socialists," pp. 111–113.

51. William Riker, "The CIO in Politics, 1936–1946" (Ph.D. thesis, Department of Government, Harvard University, 1948), pp. 16–17.

52. Matthew Josephson, *Sidney Hillman: Statesman of American Labor* (Garden City, N.Y.: Doubleday, 1952), pp. 453–454. See also Nelson, "Give Us Roosevelt," pp. 40–48. Just a few years earlier the ACW was actively supporting the creation of a third party rather than backing the Democrats.

53. Saul Alinsky, *John L. Lewis* (New York: Vintage Books, 1970), pp. 182–184.

54. Nelson Lichtenstein, "The Making of the Post-War Working Class: Cultural Pluralism and Social Structure in World War II," *Historian* 51 (November 1988), pp. 42–63.

55. Irving Bernstein, *Turbulent Years: A History of the American Worker, 1933–1941* (Boston: Houghton Mifflin, 1970), p. 449. See also Bakunin, "Role of Socialists"; Richard Carter, "Pressure from the Left: The American Labor Party, 1936–1954" (Ph.D. thesis, Department of History, Syracuse University, 1965), pp. 16–17; William Stewart, "A Political History of the American Labor Party" (M.A. thesis, Department of Political Science, American University, 1959), pp. 3–5.

56. See David Saposs, *Communism in American Politics* (Washington, D.C.: Public Affairs Press, 1960); Carter, "Pressure from the Left," pp. 11–14. Edward Flynn has described the origin of the American Labor party as follows: "President Roosevelt with Jim Farley and myself, brought the American Labor Party into being. It was entirely Roosevelt's suggestion. Farley and I never believed in it very much, but he felt at the time—and it is true today—that there were many people who believed in what Roosevelt stood for but who, for some reason or another . . . would not join the Democratic party. If another party were created, you could bring these people into it actively. That was really why it was created. . . . Sidney Hillman and David Dubinsky played a great part in it and we couldn't have formed the party without them. They were the nucleus. These and other people were names but the voting strength was from the unions that were controlled by Dubinsky and Hillman. At that time both of those unions were rather leftist—more so than the Democratic party. There again it would attract a great many more who would . . . vote for Roosevelt who might not have voted at all." Edward Flynn, "The Reminiscences of Edward J. Flynn" (Interview by Owen Bombard, March 1950, Oral History Project, Butler Library, Columbia University), quoted in Carter, "Pressure from the Left," pp. 13–14.

57. Josephson, *Sidney Hillman*, p. 397.

58. William Leuchtenburg notes that "the defection of Socialist union leaders, and the immense appeal of Franklin Roosevelt's New Deal, all but destroyed the Socialist party." William Leuchtenburg, *Franklin D. Roosevelt and the New Deal* (New York: Harper & Row, 1963), p. 188.

59. Max Danish, *The World of David Dubinsky* (Cleveland: World Publishing Co., 1957), p. 94.

60. Hugh T. Lovin, "The Persistence of Third Party Dreams in the American Labor Movement, 1930–1938," *Mid-America* 5 (October 1976), p. 142.

61. Norman Thomas, *Socialism on the Defensive* (New York: Harper & Bros., 1938), p. 286.

62. Will Herberg, "American Marxist Political Theory," in Donald Drew Egbert and Stow Persons, eds., *Socialism and American Life*, vol. 1 (Princeton, N.J.: Princeton University Press, 1952), p. 504.

63. Bell, *Marxian Socialism*, p. 177.

64. Jill Hopkins Herzig, "The Oregon Commonwealth Federation: The Rise and Decline of a Reform Organization" (M.A. thesis, Department of History, University of Oregon, 1963), pp. 108, 112.

65. Warren, *Alternative Vision*, p. 106.

66. Samuel T. McSeveney, "The Michigan Gubernatorial Campaign of 1938," *Michigan History* 45 (June 1961), pp. 109–111.

67. *Ibid.*, p. 112.

68. *Ibid.*

69. Quoted in Bell, *Marxian Socialism*, p. 179.

70. Brendan Sexton, "The Traditions of Reutherism," *Dissent* 19 (Winter 1972), p. 57; McSeveney, "Campaign of 1938," p. 117.

71. Irving Howe and B. J. Widick, *The UAW and Walter Reuther* (New York: Da Capo Press, 1973), p. 195.

72. Waltzer, "American Labor Party," p. 122.

73. Warren, *Alternative Vision*, pp. 94–101; Johnpoll, *Pacifist's Progress*, pp. 191–196; Bell, *Marxian Socialism*, pp. 179–180.

74. Johnpoll, *Pacifist's Progress*, pp. 195–196; Warren, *Alternative Vision*, pp. 104–105.

75. Floyd J. Stachowski, "The Political Career of Daniel Webster Hoan" (Ph.D. thesis, Department of History, Northwestern University, 1966), pp. 188–189; Lester F. Schmidt, "The Farmer-Labor-Progressive Federation: The Study of a 'United Front' Movement Among Wisconsin Liberals, 1934–1941" (Ph.D. thesis, Department of History, Northwestern University, 1954), pp. 59–62.

76. Schmidt, "Farmer-Labor-Progressive Federation," pp. 55–56.

77. Olson, "Milwaukee Socialists," pp. 524–529.

78. Stachowski, "Political Career," p. 199.

79. McGreen, "Norman Thomas," pp. 313–314.

80. Stachowski, "Political Career," pp. 199–203.

81. Warren, *Alternative Vision*, pp. 72–73.

82. Stachowski, "Political Career," pp. 212–214.

83. Warren, *Alternative Vision*, p. 73; Olson, "Milwaukee Socialists," p. 530.

84. Harold Gosnell, *Grass Roots Politics: National Voting Behavior of Typical States* (New York: Russell & Russell, 1970), p. 49.

85. Samuel Lubell, "Post-Mortem: Who Elected Roosevelt?" *Saturday Evening Post*, January 25, 1941, p. 92.

86. David Herreshoff, "The Socialist Review: An Introduction and Appraisal," *Labor History* 11 (Spring 1970), p. 224.

87. Johnpoll, *Pacifist's Progress*, pp. 203-204.

88. *Ibid.*, p. 217.

89. Warren, *Alternative Vision*, p. 159; Bell, *Marxian Socialism*, pp. 181-182.

90. Michael Harrington, *Socialism* (New York: Saturday Review Press, 1970), pp. 262-263.

91. Lichtenstein, "The Making of the Post-War Working Class," pp. 42-57.

92. Philip J. Jaffee, *The Rise and Fall of American Communism* (New York: Horizon Press, 1975), pp. 133-135; Irving Howe and Lewis Coser, *The American Communist Party: A Critical History, 1919-1957* (New York: Da Capo Press, 1974), pp. 177-191; Bell, *Marxian Socialism*, pp. 138-141.

93. Bell, *Marxian Socialism*, p. 140. See also Howard Kimeldorf and Judith Stepan-Norris, "Historical Studies of the Labor Movement in the United States," *Annual Review of Sociology* 18 (1992), pp. 495-517.

94. Howe and Coser, *American Communist Party*, pp. 191-197.

95. *Ibid.*, pp. 232-233; Jaffee, *Rise and Fall*, pp. 33-34; James Weinstein, *Ambiguous Legacy: The Left in American Politics* (New York: New Viewpoints, 1975), p. 58; Waltzer, "American Labor Party," pp. 59-60.

96. On the party's extensive activities among the unemployed, see Albert Prago, "The Organization of the Unemployed and the Role of the Radicals, 1929-1935" (Ph.D. thesis, Department of History, Union Graduate School, 1976).

97. Howe and Coser, *American Communist Party*, pp. 172, 225, 235.

98. *Ibid.*, p. 225.

99. Bell, *Marxian Socialism*, pp. 143-145; Jaffee, *Rise and Fall*, pp. 36-37.

100. Edward P. Johanningsmeier, *Forging American Communism* (Princeton, N.J.: Princeton University Press, 1994), pp. 280-284; John Patrick Diggins, *The Rise and Fall of the American Left* (New York: W. W. Norton, 1992), pp. 165-174.

101. Earl Browder, "The American Communist Party in the Thirties," in Rita James Simon, ed., *As We Saw the Thirties* (Urbana: University of Illinois Press, 1967), p. 234.

102. Howe and Coser, *American Communist Party*, p. 331.

103. Malcolm Sylvers, "American Communists in the Popular Front Period: Reorganization or Disorganization?" *Journal of American Studies* 23 (1989), pp. 375-393.

104. Peggy Dennis, *The Autobiography of an American Communist: A Personal View of a Political Life, 1925-1975* (Westport, Conn.: Lawrence Hill, 1977), p. 122.

105. Howe and Coser, *American Communist Party*, p. 386; Jaffee, *Rise and Fall*, p. 11. See also Sylvers, "American Communists in the Popular Front Period," p. 377; Eric Foner, "Why Is There No Socialism in the United States?" *History Workshop Journal* 17 (Spring 1984), p. 73.

106. Frank S. Meyer, *The Moulding of Communists* (New York: Harcourt, Brace, 1961), p. 105. The FBI has estimated that 700,000 different individuals actually have been party members. See Morris L. Ernst and David Loth, *Report on the American Communist* (New York: Henry Holt, 1952), p. 14; Howe and Coser, *American Communist Party*, p. 529. The sources of this rapid turnover in membership have been analyzed by former party leader George Charney: "We always suffered from severe fluctuation. . . . Most recruits were attracted to the party on the basis of a particular issue, . . . and there they found our ways beyond understanding. The individual was lost in the myriad of tasks imposed on the branch, the atmosphere was too unfamiliar and congested, and he gradually drifted away. It was difficult to relate the issues to the overall aim of the party, to socialism. This was achieved more effectively in middle-class areas than in the working-class sections of the movement." George Charney, *A Long Journey* (Chicago: Quadrangle Books, 1968), p. 116. See also Meyer, *Moulding of Communists*, p. 105.

107. Nathan Glazer, *The Social Basis of American Communism* (Westport, Conn.: Greenwood Press, 1974), p. 100.

108. Quoted in William M. Goldsmith, "The Theory and the Practice of the Communist Front" (Ph.D. thesis, Department of Political Science, Columbia University, 1971), p. 498.

109. Robert Jay Alperin, "Organization in the Communist Party, U.S.A., 1931–1938" (Ph.D. thesis, Department of Political Science, Northwestern University, 1959), pp. 63–65.

110. Glazer, *Social Basis*, p. 149.

111. *Ibid.*, p. 114.

112. Ernst and Loth, *Report on the American Communist*, pp. 3–4.

113. Howe and Coser, *American Communist Party*, pp. 314–315; Richard H. Pells, *Radical Visions and American Dreams: Culture and Social Thought in the Depression Years* (New York: Harper & Row, 1973), pp. 253–319.

114. Sylvers, "American Communists in the Popular Front Period," pp. 376–378.

115. Browder, "American Communist Party," pp. 237–238.

116. Joseph R. Starobin, *American Communism in Crisis, 1943–1957* (Berkeley: University of California Press, 1975), pp. 36–37. For further detail on the way Communists were welcomed by leaders of both major parties, also see Browder, "American Communist Party."

117. Richard Flacks, *Making History: The Radical Tradition in American Life* (New York: Columbia University Press, 1988), pp. 145–146.

118. Dennis, *Autobiography of an American Communist*, p. 123.

119. John Gates, *The Story of an American Communist* (New York: Thomas Nelson & Sons, 1958), pp. 74–79.

120. Bert Cochran, *Labor and Communism: The Conflict That Shaped American Unions* (Princeton, N.J.: Princeton University Press, 1977), pp. 146–155.

121. Howe and Coser, *American Communist Party*, p. 428. See also Jaffee, *Rise and Fall*, pp. 66–68.

122. Howe and Coser, *American Communist Party*, pp. 419–420; Cochran, *Labor and Communism*, p. 245.

123. Charney, *Long Journey*, pp. 165–198.

124. Browder, "American Communist Party," p. 246.

125. Foner, "Why Is There No Socialism," p. 73.

126. Barrington Moore, Jr., "The Communist Party of the USA: An Analysis of a Social Movement," *American Political Science Review* 39 (February 1945), p. 41.

127. Gates, *Story of an American Communist*, pp. 70–71.

128. Starobin, *American Communism*, pp. 38–39. See also Harvey Klehr and John E. Haynes, "Communists and the CIO: From the Soviet Archives," *Labor History*, Summer 1994, pp. 442–446.

129. Bell, *Marxian Socialism*, pp. 145–148; Howe and Coser, *American Communist Party*, pp. 319–386; Browder, "American Communist Party," pp. 222–232.

130. Dennis, *Autobiography of an American Communist*, p. 129.

131. Charney, *Long Journey*, pp. 79–80. See also Sylvers, "American Communists in the Popular Front Period," pp. 375–393.

132. Browder, "American Communist Party," p. 231.

133. Bell, *Marxian Socialism*, p. 145. See also Bernard Karsh and Phillip L. Garman, "The Impact of the Political Left," in Milton Derber and Edwin Young, eds., *Labor and the New Deal* (Madison: University of Wisconsin Press, 1957), pp. 112–113; and Moore, "Communist Party," p. 37.

134. For a view by a pro-Communist CIO leader, see Leon DeCaux, *Labor Radical* (Boston: Beacon Press, 1970), pp. 298–299.

135. Alinsky, *John L. Lewis*, pp. 152–153; Cochran, *Labor and Communism*, pp. 97–98.

136. William Z. Foster, *History of the Communist Party of the United States* (New York: Greenwood Press, 1968), pp. 349–350. See also Cochran, *Labor and Communism*, pp. 96–97.

137. Klehr, *Heyday of American Communism*, pp. 238–259.

138. Cochran, *Labor and Communism*, p. 99.

139. Quoted in DeCaux, *Labor Radical*, p. 380. See also Cochran, *Labor and Communism*, p. 145; Al Richmond, *A Long View from the Left: Memoirs of an American Revolutionary* (New York: Houghton Mifflin, 1972), p. 243.

140. DeCaux, *Labor Radical*, p. 381.

141. *Ibid.*, p. 475.

142. Starobin, *American Communism*, pp. 39–40.

143. *Ibid.*, pp. 40–41.

144. Arthur M. Schlesinger, Jr., *Politics of Upheaval* (Boston: Houghton Mifflin, 1988), p. 594.

145. *Ibid.*, p. 249.

146. Harrington, *Socialism*, p. 263.

147. In addition to works cited above, see Eric Leif Davin and Staughton Lynd, "Picket Line and Ballot Box: The Forgotten Legacy of the Local Labor Party Movement," *Radical History Review* 22 (Winter 1979–80), pp. 42–63; Michael Goldfield, "Worker Insurgency, Radical Organization, and New Deal Labor Legislation," *American Political Science Review* 83 (December 1989), pp. 1257–1284; and Klehr, *Heyday of American Communism*.

148. Pells, *Radical Visions*, p. 318.

149. Browder, "American Communist Party," p. 246.

150. Charney, *Long Journey*, p. 111.

151. Richard Hofstadter, *The Age of Reform* (New York: Alfred A. Knopf, 1972), p. 308.

152. Warren, *Alternative Vision*, pp. 118, 120.

153. Philip Selznick, *The Organizational Weapon* (New York: Arno Press, 1979), p. 54.

154. Meyer, *Moulding of Communists*, p. 130.

7. Political Repression and Socialism

1. James R. Green, *Grass-Roots Socialism: Radical Movements in the Southwest, 1895–1943* (Baton Rouge: Louisiana State University Press, 1978), p. 346.

2. Gabriel Kolko, *Main Currents in Modern American History* (New York: Harper & Row, 1976), pp. 206–207.

3. Alan Wolfe, *The Seamy Side of Democracy: Repression in America*, 2nd ed. (New York: Longman, 1978), p. 6. See also Robert K. Murray, *Red Scare: A Study in National Hysteria, 1919–1920* (Westport, Conn.: Greenwood Press, 1980); William Preston, Jr., *Aliens and Dissenters: Federal Suppression of Radicals, 1903–1933* (Urbana: University of Illinois Press, 1994); Horace C. Peterson and Gilbert C. Fite, *Opponents of War, 1917–1918* (Westport, Conn.: Greenwood Press, 1986); Earl Latham, *The Communist Controversy in Washington* (Cambridge, Mass.: Harvard University Press, 1966); Audrie Girdner and Anne Loftis, *The Great Betrayal: The Evacuation of the Japanese-Americans During World War II* (New York: Macmillan, 1969); Murray B. Levin, *Political Hysteria in America* (New York: Basic Books, 1971); Robert Justin Goldstein, *Political Repression in Modern America* (Cambridge,

Mass.: Schenkman Publishing Co., 1978); Bruce Nelson, "J. Vance Thompson: The Industrial Workers of the World and the Mood of Syndicalism, 1914–1921," *Labor's Heritage* 2 (October 1990), pp. 45–65; and Patricia Cayo Sexton, *The War on Labor and the Left: Understanding America's Unique Conservatism* (Boulder, Colo.: Westview Press, 1991), pp. 122–125.

4. Alexis de Tocqueville, *Democracy in America* (New York: Alfred A. Knopf, 1948), especially vol. 1, ch. 15. James Stuart Mill also makes this point with great force in *On Liberty* (New York: W. W. Norton, 1975), p. 6. See also Sexton, *War on Labor and the Left*, pp. 122–125.

5. Nelson, "J. Vance Thompson," pp. 45–65; Peter Kivisto, *Immigrant Socialists in the United States: The Case of Finns and the Left* (Rutherford, N.J.: Fairleigh Dickinson University Press, 1984) pp. 141–146.

6. Patrick H. Hutton, *The Cult of the Revolutionary Tradition: The Blanquists in French Politics, 1864–1893* (Berkeley: University of California Press, 1981), pp. 53–54, 60.

7. Patrick Renshaw, *The Wobblies* (Garden City, N.J.: Doubleday, 1967), p. 119.

8. Cited in Preston, *Aliens and Dissenters*, p. 44.

9. *Ibid.*, p. 44.

10. Terry Wayne Cole, "Labor's Radical Alternative: The Rhetoric of the Industrial Workers of the World" (Ph.D. thesis, Department of Speech, University of Oregon, 1974), p. 262; Preston, *Aliens and Dissenters*, p. 45. Joseph Robert Conlin, *Bread and Roses Too: Studies of the Wobblies* (Westport, Conn.: Greenwood Publishing Corporation, 1969), discusses the lack of actual violence by the IWW; see esp. pp. 96, 107, 113.

11. Quoted in Daniel Bell, *Marxian Socialism in the United States* (Ithaca, N.Y.: Cornell University Press, 1996), p.76.

12. Preston, *Aliens and Dissenters*, p. 39; Nelson, "J. Vance Thompson," pp. 45–65.

13. Cole, "Labor's Radical Alternative," p. 265; see also Joseph G. Rayback, *A History of American Labor* (New York: Free Press, 1966), p. 249.

14. Nelson, "J. Vance Thompson," p. 55. Nelson notes the particular hysteria in California against the IWW, particularly with *The Sacramento Bee* advocating the lynching of IWW members. See also John H. M. Laslett, "Three Anglo American Radicals and the Dilemmas of Syndicalism and Social Democracy," *Labor* 25 (Spring 1990), pp. 236–246.

15. Ray Ginger, *Eugene V. Debs: A Biography* (New York: Collier Books, 1962), p. 372.

16. Debs' speech can be found in Albert Fried, *Socialism in America: From the Shakers to the Third International* (New York: Columbia University Press, 1992), pp. 527–529.

17. Ginger, *Eugene V. Debs*, p. 379.

18. David J. Garrow, *Protest at Selma* (New Haven, Conn.: Yale University Press, 1978), p. 223.

19. Martin Luther King, Jr., "Behind the Selma March," *Saturday Review* 48 (April 3, 1965), pp. 16–17.

20. Quoted and referenced in Seymour Martin Lipset, *Rebellion in the University* (Chicago: University of Chicago Press, 1976), pp. xx–xxii.

21. Vernon L. Lidtke, *The Outlawed Party: Social Democracy in Germany, 1878–1890* (Princeton, N.J.: Princeton University Press, 1966); Güenther Roth, *The Social Democrats in Imperial Germany* (Totowa, N.Y.: Bedminster Press, 1963), pp. 73–84.

22. Quoted in W. L. Guttsman, *The German Social Democratic Party, 1875–1933* (London: George Allen & Unwin, 1981), p. 61.

23. Quoted in Reinhard Höhn, *Die vaterlandlosen Gesellen: Der Sozialismus im Licht der Geheimberichte der preussischen Polizei 1878–1914* (Köln: Westdeutscher Verlag, 1964), p. xxv.

24. Vernon L. Lidtke, *The Alternative Culture: Socialist Labor in Imperial Germany* (New York: Oxford University Press, 1985), pp. 200–201.

25. Laura Engelstein, *Moscow, 1905: Working-Class Organization and Political Conflict* (Stanford, Calif.: Stanford University Press, 1982), pp. 220–221.

26. Ralph Carter Elwood, *Russian Social Democracy in the Underground: A Study of the RSDRP in the Ukraine, 1907–1914* (Assen, The Netherlands: Van Gorcum, 1974), p. 36.

27. V. I. Lenin, "Black Hundreds and the Organization of an Uprising" (August 16, 1905), quoted in Engelstein, *Moscow, 1905*, p. 190.

28. Richard J. Walter, *The Socialist Party of Argentina 1890–1930* (Austin: Institute of Latin American Studies, University of Texas, 1977), p. 45.

29. *Ibid.*, pp. 43–66.

30. Gaetano Mosca, *The Ruling Class* (New York: McGraw-Hill, 1939), p. 191.

31. Irving Howe and Lewis Coser, *The American Communist Party: A Critical History, 1919–1957* (New York: Da Capo Press, 1974), pp. 22–23. A detailed account of the repressive efforts may be found in William C. Seyler, "The Rise and Decline of the Socialist Party in the United States" (Ph.D. thesis, Department of Political Science, Duke University, 1952), pp. 304–324.

32. Laslett, "Three Anglo-American Radicals," pp. 236–246; Andrew Neather, "Labor Republicanism, Race, and Popular Patriotism in the Era of Empire, 1890–1914," in John Bodnar, ed., *Bonds of Affection: Americans Define Their Patriotism* (Princeton, N.J.: Princeton University Press, 1996), pp. 89–91. Neather notes the aggresssive antisocialist and antiunion position taken by the National Association of Manufacturers and by certain papers, such as the *Los Angeles Times*, which faked photographs of Samuel Gompers stomping on the U.S. flag at a Labor Day rally.

33. James Weinstein, *The Decline of Socialism in America, 1912–1915* (New Brunswick, N.J.: Rutgers University Press, 1984), pp. 161, 172.

34. Frederick I. Olson, "The Milwaukee Socialists, 1897–1941" (Ph.D. thesis, Department of History, Harvard University, 1952), pp. 147–332; Sally M. Miller, "Milwaukee: Of Ethnicity and Labor," in Bruce M. Stave, ed., *Socialism and the Cities* (Port Washington, N.Y.: Kennikat Press, 1975); Richard W. Judd, *Socialist Cities: Municipal Politics and the Grass Roots of American Socialism* (Albany: State University of New York Press, 1989), pp. 22–25.

35. Olson, "Milwaukee Socialists," pp. 1–2. Also see Paul Buhle, "German Socialists and the Roots of American Working Class Radicalism," in Hartmut Keil and John B. Jentz, eds., *German Workers in Industrial Chicago, 1850–1910: A Comparative Perspective* (DeKalb: Northern Illinois University Press, 1983); Stan Nadel, "The German Immigrant Left in the United States," in Paul Buhle and Dan Georgakas, eds., *The Immigrant Left in the United States* (Albany: State University of New York Press, 1996), pp. 45–76; Karen Falk, "Public Opinion in Wisconsin During World War I," *Wisconsin Magazine of History* 25 (June 1942), pp. 389–407.

36. Olson, "Milwaukee Socialists," pp. 339–340, 343.

37. Edward Muzik, "Victor L. Berger, A Biography" (Ph.D. thesis, Department of History, Northwestern University, 1960), p. 290. See also Olson, "Milwaukee Socialists," pp. 358–360, 365–377; and Sally M. Miller, "Casting a Wide Net: The Milwaukee Movement to 1920," in Donald T. Critchlow, *Socialism in the Heartland: The Midwestern Experience, 1900–1925* (Notre Dame, Ind.: University of Notre Dame, 1986), pp. 18–45.

38. Quoted in James J. Lorence, "Dynamite for the Brain: The Growth and Decline of Socialism in Central and Lakeshore Wisconsin, 1910–1920," *Wisconsin Magazine of History* 66 (Summer 1983).

39. *Ibid.*

40. James J. Lorence, "Socialism in Northern Wisconsin, 1910–1920: An Ethnocultural Analysis," *Mid-America* 69 (April–July 1982). As Lorence observes, "Not until wartime repression unleashed the force of ethnicity did the radical gospel make serious inroads in the more remote districts of central Wisconsin." Lorence, "Dynamite for the Brain."

41. Muzik, "Victor L. Berger," pp. 313–318; Frederick I. Olson, "The Socialist Party and the Union in Milwaukee, 1900–1912," *Wisconsin Magazine of History* 44 (Winter 1960–61), p. 110.

42. David Paul Nord, "Hothouse Socialism: Minneapolis, 1910–1925," in Critchlow, ed., *Socialism in the Heartland*, pp. 151–152.

43. *Ibid.*, pp. 143–145.

44. Weinstein, *Decline of Socialism*, pp. 141–142, 169–170.

45. Melvyn Dubofsky, "Success and Failure of Socialism in New York City, 1900–1918: A Case Study," *Labor History* 9 (Fall 1968), pp. 363–369.

46. Morris Hillquit, *Loose Leaves from a Busy Life* (New York: Macmillan, 1934).

47. Goldstein, *Political Repression*, p. 112.

48. *Ibid.*, pp. 146–148.

49. See Nathan Fine, *Labor and Farmer Parties in the United States, 1828–1928* (New York: Rand School of Social Science, 1928), pp. 228–230, 234; Dubofsky, "Success and Failure," pp. 362–374.

50. Thomas E. Vadney, "The Politics of Repression: A Case Study of the Red Scare in New York," *New York History* 49 (1968), p. 61.

51. James B. Rhoads, "The Campaign of the Socialist Party in the Election of 1920" (Ph.D. thesis, Department of History, American University, 1965), pp. 79–80.

52. Vadney, "Politics of Repression," pp. 70–71.

53. David R. Colburn, "Governor Alfred E. Smith and the Red Scare, 1919–1920," *Political Science Quarterly* 88 (September 1973), p. 442.

54. William C. Pratt, "The Reading Socialist Experience: A Study of Working Class Politics" (Ph.D. thesis, Department of History, Emory University, 1969), pp. 36–51.

55. Kenneth E. Hendrickson, Jr., "The Socialists of Reading, Pennsylvania and World War I: A Question of Loyalty," *Pennsylvania History* 36 (October 1969), p. 442.

56. See Henry G. Stetler, *The Socialist Movement in Reading, Pennsylvania 1896–1936* (Storrs, Conn.: privately printed, 1943), p. 79; Pratt, "Reading Socialist Experience," pp. 58–59.

57. Stetler, *Socialist Movement*, pp. 8, 22; Pratt, "Reading Socialist Experience," p. 31.

58. For a full account of the story of Oklahoma socialism, see Howard Meredith, "A History of the Socialist Party in Oklahoma" (Ph.D. thesis, Department of History, University of Oklahoma, 1970); Garvin Burbank, *When Farmers Voted Red: The Gospel of Socialism in the Oklahoma Countryside, 1910–1924* (Westport, Conn.: Greenwood Press, 1976); Ellen I. Rosen, "Peasant Socialism in America: The Socialist Party in Oklahoma Before the First World War" (Ph.D. thesis, Department of Sociology, City University of New York, 1975); Green, *Grass-Roots Socialism*; Oscar Ameringer, *If You Don't Weaken: The Autobiography of Oscar Ameringer* (Norman: University of Oklahoma Press, 1983).

59. Burbank, *When Farmers Voted Red*, p. 205.

60. For documentation and interpretation, see Seymour Martin Lipset, *Agrarian Socialism: The Cooperative Commonwealth Federation in Saskatchewan* (Berkeley: University of California Press, 1950).

61. Fried, *Socialism in America*, p. 381.

62. Green, *Grass-Roots Socialism*, pp. 345–395.

63. Meredith, "Socialist Party in Oklahoma," p. 138.

64. Burbank, *When Farmers Voted Red*, p. 111. See also Meredith, "Socialist Party in Oklahoma," p. 165.

65. Green, *Grass-Roots Socialism*, p. 325; Meredith, "Socialist Party of Oklahoma," pp. 167–168; Burbank, *When Farmers Voted Red*, pp. 136–138.

66. Green, *Grass-Roots Socialism*, p. 324.

67. Meredith, "Socialist Party in Oklahoma," p. 192.

68. The Socialists were also linked with "the epidemic of bank robberies," which swept part of Oklahoma in 1914. The best-known outlaw actually announced via the Socialist *Appeal to Reason* that "many of the bankers he victimized were in the 'robbery business too.'" Green, *Grass-Roots Socialism*, pp. 339–342. See also Burbank, *When Farmers Voted Red*, pp. 137–144.

69. Green, *Grass-Roots Socialism*, p. 355. See also Meredith, "Socialist Party in Oklahoma," pp. 170–171; Burbank, *When Farmers Voted Red*, pp. 137–144.

70. Burbank, *When Farmers Voted Red*, p. 145.

71. Ameringer, *If We Don't Weaken*, pp. 347–355; Green, *Grass-Roots Socialism*, pp. 355–361; David A. Shannon, *The Socialist Party of America* (Chicago: Quadrangle Books, 1967), pp. 107–108.

72. Shannon, *Socialist Party*, p. 108; Meredith, "Socialist Party of Oklahoma," pp. 193–194.

73. Ameringer, *If We Don't Weaken*, p. 355; Green, *Grass-Roots Socialism*, p. 368; Burbank, *When Farmers Voted Red*, p. 152–153.

74. Ameringer, *If We Don't Weaken*, pp. 356–358; Meredith, "Socialist Party in Oklahoma," pp. 196–197.

75. Green, *Grass-Roots Socialism*, p. 346.

76. Weinstein, *Decline of Socialism*, p. 161.

77. David Montgomery, "Nationalism, American Patriotism, and Class Consciousness among Immigrant Workers in the United States in the Epoch of World War I," in Dirk Hoerder, ed., *"Struggle a Hard Battle": Essays on Working-Class Immigrants* (DeKalb: Northern Illinois University Press, 1986), p. 339.

78. Theodore Draper, *The Roots of American Communism* (Chicago: Ivan R. Dee, 1989), p. 158.

79. Nathan Glazer, *The Social Basis of American Communism* (Westport, Conn.: Greenwood Press, 1974), p. 37.

80. Stetler, *Socialist Movement*, p. 38. See also Pratt, "Reading Socialist Experience," pp. 56–57.

81. Carol Jenson, "Loyalty as a Political Weapon: The 1918 Campaign in Minnesota," *Minnesota History* 43 (Summer 1972), p. 57.

82. Robert L. Morlan, *Political Prairie Fire: The Nonpartisan League, 1915–1922* (Minneapolis: University of Minnesota Press, 1955), p. 173.

83. *Ibid.*, pp. 266–267.

84. *Ibid.*, p. 269.

85. Andrew A. Bruce, *Non–Partisan League* (New York: Macmillan, 1921), pp. 160–161.

86. Morlan, *Political Prairie Fire*, pp. 159, 180, 201.

87. *Ibid.*, pp. 157–158. See also Bruce L. Larson, *Lindbergh of Minnesota* (New York: Harcourt Brace Jovanovich, 1973), pp. 235–242; Jenson, "Loyalty as a Political Weapon," pp. 43–57.

88. Millard L. Gierske, *Minnesota Farmer-Laborism: The Third-Party Alternative* (Minneapolis: University of Minnesota Press, 1979), p. 31.

89. This is the title of ch. 8 of Morlan, *Political Prairie Fire*, pp. 152–182.

90. Theodore Saloutos, "The Expansion and Decline of the Non-Partisan League in the Western Middle West, 1917–1921," *Agricultural History* 20 (October 1946), pp. 235–252.

91. Bell, *Marxian Socialism*, p. 134.

92. John H. M. Laslett, "Social Scientists View the Problem," in John H. M. Laslett and Seymour Martin Lipset, eds., *Failure of a Dream? Essays in the History of American Socialism* (Garden City, N.Y.: Doubleday/Anchor Books, 1974), pp. 52–53. See also Bell, *Marxian Socialism*, pp. 48–49, 52–54.

93. Norman Thomas, "Reflections of an Old Campaigner," *Commonwealth* 41 (December 22, 1944), p. 247.

94. This material is taken from Seymour Martin Lipset, *American Exceptionalism: A Double-Edged Sword* (New York: W. W. Norton, 1995), p. 190.

95. Laslett, "Social Scientists," pp. 52–53.

8. The End of Political Exceptionalism?

1. In recent decades, the older and tiny Socialist Labor party has put forward a presidential ticket on the ballot in a few states.

2. For recent discussions of American radicalism that identify American exceptionalism with the absence of socialism, see Kim Voss, *The Making of American Exceptionalism: The Knights of Labor and Class Formation in the Nineteenth Century* (Ithaca, N.Y.: Cornell University Press, 1993); and Rick Halpern and Jonathan Morris, eds., *American Exceptionalism? U.S. Working-Class Formation in an International Context* (New York: St. Martin's Press, 1997).

3. "An Address to the Working-Men of New England . . . ," Boston, 1832; quoted in Leon Fink, *In Search of the Working Class: Essays in American Labor History and Political Culture* (Urbana: University of Illinois Press, 1994), p. 179.

4. On American working-class republicanism, see Sean Wilentz, *Chants Democratic: New York City and the Rise of the American Working Class, 1788–1850* (New York: Princeton University Press, 1984); B. H. Moss, "Republican Socialism and the Making of the Working Class in Britain, France, and the United States: A

Critique of Thompsonian Culturalism," *Comparative Studies in Society and History* 35 (1993), pp. 390–413. Bernard Moss makes the point that American republicanism was "federalist and property oriented" (p. 412); it was therefore no substitute for socialism. On the paradoxical consequences of individualism see Melvyn Dubofsky, *The State and Labor in Modern America* (Chapel Hill: University of North Carolina Press, 1994), pp. 235f.

5. Marvin Wachman, *History of the Social-Democratic Party of Milwaukee* (Urbana: University of Illinois Press, 1945), pp. 34–40.

6. Depending on where one draws the line, Britain and Norway might both fit into this category of societies. Both cases reinforce the conclusions we draw.

7. For a convincing argument along similar lines see Michael Kazin, "The Agony and Romance of the American Left," *American Historical Review* 100 (December 1995), pp. 1480–1512.

8. Sean Wilentz, "Against Exceptionalism: Class Consciousness and the American Labor Movement," *International Labor and Working Class History* 26 (Fall 1984), p. 5. See also Larry G. Gerber, "Shifting Perspectives on American Exceptionalism: Recent Literature on American Labor Relations and Labor Politics," *Journal of American Studies* 31 (August 1997), pp. 253–274; Ira Katznelson, "Working-Class Formation and American Exceptionalism, Yet Again," in Halpern and Morris, eds., *American Exceptionalism*, pp. 36–41; and Aristide R. Zolberg, "How Many Exceptionalisms?" in Ira Katznelson and Aristide R. Zolberg, eds., *Working-Class Formation: Nineteenth Century Patterns in Western Europe and the United States* (Princeton, N.J.: Princeton University Press, 1986), p. 397.

9. Zolberg, "How Many Exceptionalisms?" p. 455; James E. Cronin, "Neither Exceptional Nor Peculiar: Towards the Comparative Study of Labor in Advanced Society," *International Review of Social History* 38 (1993); George Fredrickson, "From Exceptionalism to Variability: Recent Developments in Cross-National Comparative History," *Journal of American History* 82 (September 1995); Rick Halpern and Jonathan Morris, "The Persistence of Exceptionalism: Class Formation and the Comparative Method," in Halpern and Morris, eds., *American Exceptionalism*, p. 4.

10. Mary Nolan, "Against Exceptionalisms," *American Historical Review* 102 (June 1997), p. 769–774. Nolan writes: "Arguments about American exceptionalism invariably culminate in the proud conclusion that America had no socialism. Such a sweeping and negative formulation hardly captures the complex nature of class politics and class consciousness in the United States. It ignores the high degree of state and employer violence and coercion and is silent on racial conflict. Of greater importance, such an assertion assumes that in the late nineteenth and early twentieth centuries there was a monolithically class-conscious Europe, with strong socialist trade unions and political parties in contrast to an America of business unionism and two-party machine politics" (p. 771). For a nuanced overview of crit-

icisms of American exceptionalism, see Michael Kammen, "The Problem of American Exceptionalism: A Reconsideration," *American Quarterly* 45 (March 1993), pp. 1–43.

11. Barrington Moore, Jr., *Injustice: The Social Bases of Obedience and Revolt* (White Plains, N.Y.: M. E. Sharpe, 1978), pp. 192ff.

12. See Chapter 5 for an extended discussion.

13. Henry Pelling, *A History of British Trade Unionism*, 3rd ed. (London: Penguin, 1976), pp. 127–128.

14. Michael Kazin argues that "the replacement of 'Why no socialism?' with 'Look at all the republicanism!' had its costs. The term itself was impossibly fuzzy; any concept that supposedly united James Madison, Terence Powderly, and millions of small farmers explained very little about political conflict; indeed it risked replicating, albeit under another name and for different purposes, the Hartzian concept of a dominant ideological tradition that New Left intellectuals had originally set out to demolish. . . . In the end, the intellectual vogue did little to clarify how and why socialism, as theory and tentative practice, had proved so unpopular on American soil." Michael Kazin, "Agony and Romance of the American Left," pp. 1500–1501.

15. Sean Wilentz, "Against Exceptionalism," p. 4.

16. Selig Perlman and Philip Taft, *History of Labor in the United States, 1896–1932* (New York: Macmillan, 1935), pp. 623, 625.

17. Eric Foner, "Why Is There No Socialism in the United States?" *History Workshop Journal* 17 (Spring 1984), pp. 57–80; Foner's emphasis. See also Ira Katznelson, *City Trenches*.

18. See Seymour Martin Lipset, "Still the Exceptional Nation?" *Wilson Quarterly* 24 (Winter 2000), pp. 31–45; and "No Third Way," in Daniel Chirot, ed., *The Crisis of Leninism and the Decline of the Left* (Seattle: University of Washington Press, 1991), pp. 183–232. Brad Rose and George Ross speak of "postworkerist" socialism. Brad Rose and George Ross, "Socialism's Past, New Social Democracy, and Socialism's Futures," *Social Science History* 18 (Fall 1994), pp. 439–469. See also Christiane Lemke and Gary Marks, "From Decline to Demise? The Fate of Socialism in Europe," in Lemke and Marks, eds., *The Crisis of Socialism in Europe* (Durham: Duke University Press, 1992), pp. 1–25.

19. The implications of the American example were appreciated by Louis Corey (see pp. 18–19).

20. Samuel Beer, "Liberalism Rediscovered," *Economist*, February 7–14, 1998, p. 23.

21. Samuel Beer, "Britain After Blair," *Political Quarterly* p. 68 (October–December 1997), p. 322.

22. Madaline Druhan, "Union Reforms Stay, Labour Leader Says," *Globe & Mail*, April 1, 1997.

23. Desmond King and Mark Wickham-Jones, "From Clinton to Blair: The Democratic (Party) Origins of Welfare to Work," *Political Quarterly* 70 (January–March 1999), pp. 62–74.

24. Michael Prescott, "Labour Assault on Single Mothers," *Sunday Times*, June 1, 1997.

25. Fred Barbach, "New British Budget Offers Aid to the Unemployed," *Washington Post*, July 3, 1997, p. A27.

26. Alison Mitchell, "2 Baby Boomers Who Share a Single View of Democracy," *New York Times*, May 30, 1997, pp. 1, 3; Harris and Barbash, "Blair Savours Colleague," pp. A27–A28.

27. David Wigton, "Job Creation: Clinton and Blair in Joint Initiative," *Financial Times*, May 30, 1997.

28. Quoted in *Economist*, August 14–20, 1999, p. 48.

29. Tony Blair, "No Favours," *New Statesman and Society*, November 28, 1994, p. 33.

30. Francis Castles, Rolf Gerritsen, and Jack Vowles, *The Great Experiment: Labour Parties and Public Policy Transformation in Australia and New Zealand* (St. Leonards: Allen & Unwin, 1996), pp. 212ff. There has been scant evidence of a corresponding decline in welfare commitment on the part of labor governments in these countries. Generally speaking, the shift away from social democracy is most evident in opposition to state ownership of industry and support for market competition and least evident in health care and social welfare.

31. We use the term "labor parties" to refer to the New Zealand Labour party and the Australian Labor party.

32. Quoted in John Warnock, "Lambs to the Slaughter," *Canadian Forum*, November 1989, p. 13.

33. This is to extend the idea elaborated in Katznelson, "Working-Class Formation and American Exceptionalism, Yet Again," that "working class formation has been shaped by the organization of state-society transactions," which has in turn "been affected by the agency of working-class people" (p. 53).

34. The NDP was in office in Saskatchewan from 1944 to 1964, from 1971 to 1982, and again from the late 1980s to the present, in British Columbia from 1972 to 1975 and during the 1980s and 1990s, in Manitoba from 1967 to 1977 and from 1981 to 1986, and in Ontario from 1990 to 1995.

35. Miriam A. Golden, Michael Wallerstein, and Peter Lange, "Postwar Trade-Union Organization and Industrial Relations in Twelve Countries," in Herbert Kitschelt, Peter Lange, Gary Marks, and John Stephens, eds., *Continuity and Change in Contemporary Capitalism* (Cambridge: Cambridge University Press, 1999), p. 202.

36. Source: Robert T. Kudrle and Theodore R. Marmor, "The Development of Welfare States in North America," in Peter Flora and Arnold J. Heidenheimer, eds.,

The Development of Welfare States in Europe and North America (New Brunswick, N.J.: Transaction Books, 1984), p. 83.

37. Japan is the only developed democracy, apart from the United States, not to provide child support.

38. "Purchasing Power Parity," *World Bank*, <*www.worldbank.org/data/databy topic/gnppc97.pdf*> (accessed September 17, 1999).

39. For a contrary view, see Lawrence Mishel, Jared Bernstein, and John Schmitt, *The State of Working America, 1996–97* (Armonk, N.Y.: M. E. Sharpe, 1997), ch. 1.

40. The figure for African-Americans is 26.5 percent, down from 29 percent in 1995, which was the first time in the nation's history that the poverty rate for African-Americans dropped below 30 percent. <www.census.gov/hhes/poverty/histpov/hstpov3> (accessed September 28, 1999). Other racial groups and other categories have not fared so well in relative terms. For example, the proportion of people under eighteen below the official poverty level in 1997 was 19.9 percent, less than the peak of the 1990s (22.7 percent in 1993), but well above the lowest point of the 1970s (15.1 percent in 1972). The definition of poverty used in the U.S. Census is based on annually updated thresholds that take into account family size. See U.S. Bureau of Census, "Current Population Reports," in *Money and Income in the United States: 1997 (with separate data on valuation of non cash benefits)* (Washington, D.C.: U.S. Government Printing Office, 1998), pp. 60–200.

41. In addition to the literature cited below, see Frank Castles, ed., *Families of Nations* (Dartmouth: Aldershot, 1993); and Gøsta Esping-Andersen, *Social Foundations of Postindustrial Economies* (Oxford: Oxford University Press, 1999), esp. pp. 74ff.

42. The causal connection between social democratic governance and level of union organization is substantiated in Bruce Western, *Between Class and Market: Postwar Unionization in the Capitalist Democracies* (Princeton, N.J.: Princeton University Press, 1997). His argument is parallel to that in this chapter: working-class parties in government can insulate labor movements from competitive market pressures.

43. This was the conclusion of several early studies of neocorporatism, including David R. Cameron, "Social Democracy, Corporatism, Labour Quiescence, and the Representation of Economic Interest in Advanced Capitalist Society," in John Goldthorpe, ed., *Order and Conflict in Contemporary Capitalism* (Oxford: Clarendon Press, 1984), pp. 157–174; Francis Castles, ed., *The Impact of Parties* (London: Sage, 1982), pp. 71–75; Douglas Hibbs, "Political Parties and Macroeconomic Policy," *American Political Science Review* 71 (1977), 1467–1482; Walter Korpi, *The Democratic Class Struggle* (London: Routledge & Kegan Paul, 1983), ch. 9; Gary Marks, "Neocorporatism and Incomes Policy in Western Europe and North America," *Comparative Politics* 17 (April 1986), pp. 253–277. A recent book that builds on and

extends this work is Geoffrey Garrett, *Partisan Politics in the Global Economy* (Cambridge: Cambridge University Press, 1998).

44. All correlations are significant at the 0.1 level except for that with Gini coefficients, which is significant at the 0.05 level.

45. All correlations are significant at the 0.1 level except for those with total taxes and Gini coefficients, which are significant at the 0.05 level.

46. Evelyne Huber and John D. Stephens, *Political Choice in Global Markets: Development and Crisis of Advanced Welfare States* (forthcoming), ch. 3. See Walter Korpi, *The Working Class in Welfare Capitalism: Work, Unions and Politics in Sweden* (London: Routledge & Kegan Paul, 1978). For a suggestive application of these ideas to American exceptionalism see Michael Shalev and Walter Korpi, "Working Class Mobilization and American Exceptionalism," *Economic and Industrial Democracy* 1 (1980), pp. 31–61.

47. Alexander Hicks, *Social Democracy and Welfare Capitalism: A Century of Income Security Politics* (Ithaca, N.Y.: Cornell University Press, 1999), p. ix. See also Ira Katznelson, "Considerations on Social Democracy in the United States," *Comparative Politics* 11 (October 1978), pp. 77–99.

48. Hicks, *Social Democracy and Welfare Capitalism*, p. x.

49. Data are from Edwin Amenta, *Bold Relief: Institutional Politics and the Origins of Modern American Social Policy* (Princeton, N.J.: Princeton University Press, 1998), p. 5.

50. See, for example, John Myles, "When Markets Fail: Social Welfare in Canada and the United States," in Gøsta Esping-Andersen, ed., *Welfare States in Transition: National Adaptions in Global Economies* (London: Sage, 1996).

51. Figures are for 1989. Richard Rose, "Is American Public Policy Exceptional?" in Byron E. Shafer, ed., *Is America Different: A New Look at American Exceptionalism* (Oxford: Clarendon Press, 1991), p. 198.

52. Huber and Stephens, *Political Choice in Global Markets*.

53. This in turn depends on the extent to which government is insulated from those constituencies, as discussed below. *Ibid.*

54. *Ibid.*

55. "A Survey of the World Economy: The Future of the State," *Economist*, September 20, 1997, p. 8. Countries included in these data are Austria (from 1920), Belgium (from 1960), Britain, Canada (from 1920), France, Germany, Italy, Japan, the Netherlands, Norway, Spain, Sweden, and Switzerland.

56. Everett Carll Ladd, *The American Ideology: An Exploration of the Origins, Meanings and Role of American Political Ideas* (Stowe, Conn.: Roper Center for Public Opinion Research, 1990), p. 79.

57. Page and Shapiro, *Rational Public*, p. 133.

58. Smith, "Social Inequalities in Cross-National Perspective," p. 24.

59. Karlyn H. Keene and Everett Carll Ladd, "America: A Unique Outlook?" *American Enterprise*, March/April 1990, p. 113.

60. "Taxes," *Economist*, September 28, 1996, p. 22.

61. Thomás Kolosi, "Beliefs About Inequality in Cross-National Perspective" (paper prepared for 1987 conference "The Welfare State in Transition"), p. 33.

62. Benjamin I. Page and Robert Y. Shapiro, *The Rational Public: Fifty Years of Trends in Americans' Policy Preferences* (Chicago: University of Chicago Press, 1992), p. 300.

63. Samuel Lubell, *The Future of American Politics*, 3rd ed. (New York: Harper & Row, 1965), pp. 55–68.

64. Richard Oestreicher argues that the 1930s "gave advocates of a more class-based politics the opportunity to partially—but only partially—overcome the structural and cultural biases which had shaped American politics up to that time." Richard Oestreicher, "The Rules of the Game: Class Politics in Twentieth-Century America," in Kevin Boyle, *Organized Labor and American Politics 1894–1994: The Labor-Liberal Alliance* (Albany: State University of New York Press, 1988), p. 35.

65. For a similar rubric and insightful discussion of the institutional perspective see Sven Steinmo, "Political Institutions and Tax Policy in the United States, Sweden, and Britain," *World Politics* 41 (July 1989), pp. 500–535.

66. Huber and Stephens, *Political Choice in Global Markets*, ch. 1; Amenta, *Bold Relief*, pp. 24–27.

67. Antonia Maioni, *Parting at the Cross-Roads: The Emergence of Health Insurance in the United States and Canada* (Princeton, N.J.: Princeton University Press, 1998).

68. Huber and Stephens, *Political Choice in Global Markets*.

69. The only member countries of the European Union in which Green parties have not gained representation are Greece and Portugal.

INDEX